A CONSTITUTIONAL HISTORY OF GERMANY

Also available from Longman:

A HISTORY OF PRUSSIA
H.W. Koch

A CONSTITUTIONAL HISTORY OF GERMANY

in the nineteenth and twentieth centuries

H. W. Koch

LONGMAN
London and New York

LONGMAN GROUP LIMITED
Longman House, Burnt Mill, Harlow
Essex CM20 2JE, England
Associated companies throughout the world

*Published in the United States of America
by Longman Inc., New York*

First published 1984

BRITISH LIBRARY CATALOGUING IN PUBLICATION DATA
Koch, H.W.
  A constitutional history of Germany in the
  nineteenth and twentieth centuries.
  1. Germany—History—1789–1900
  2. Germany—History—20th century
  I. Title
  943 .07   DD203
  ISBN 0-582-49182-7

LIBRARY OF CONGRESS CATALOGUING IN PUBLICATION DATA
Koch, H.W. (Hannsjoachim Wolfgang), 1933 –
  A constitutional history of Germany in the
  nineteenth and twentieth centuries.

  Bibliography: p.
  Includes index.
  1. Germany—Politics and government—19th century.
  2. Germany—Politics and government—20th century.
  3. Germany—Constitutional history.
  I. Title.
  JN3295.K63   320.943   83–26826
  ISBN 0-582-49182-7 (Pbk.)

Set in 10/11 pt Linoterm Times
Printed in Singapore by
Huntsmen Offset Printing (Pte) Ltd

CONTENTS

LIST OF MAPS

LIST OF TABLES

LIST OF ABBREVIATIONS

ADAV (Allgemeiner Deutscher Arbeiterverein) General German Workers' Association
ADF (Aktion Democratischer Fortschritt) Action for Democratic Progress
APO (Ausserparlamentarische Opposition) Extra-parliamentary Opposition
AUD (Aktionsgemeinschaft Unabhängiger Deutscher) Action Community of Independent Germans
BdD (Bund der Deutshen) League of Germans
BDO (Bund Deutscher Offiziere) League of German Officers
BHE (Block der Heimatvertriebenen und Entrechteten) Bloc of Refugees and those deprived by the Law
BP (Bayern Partei) Bavarian Party
BVP (Bayerische Volkspartei) Bavarian People's Party
CDU (Christlich-Demokratische Union) Christian Democratic Union
CSU (Christlich-Soziale Union) Christian Social Union
CVP (Christliche Volkspartei) Christian People's Party
DBP (Demokratische Bauern-Partei) Democratic Peasant Party
DDP (Deutsche Demokratische Partei) German Democratic Party
DFU (Deutsche Friedens-Union) German Peace Union
DG (Deutsche Gemeinschaft) German Community
DKP (Deutsche Kommunistische Partei) German Communist Party
DNS (Deutsche Nationale Voksparteisammlung) German National People's Party Rally
DNVP (Deutsche-Nationale Volkspartei) German National People's Party
DP (Deutsche Partei) German Party
DRP (Deutsche Reichspartei) German Reich Party

DVP	(Deutsche Volkspartei) German People's Party
EP	(Europäische Partei) European Party
EVD	(Europäische Volksbewegung Deutschland) European People's Movement of Germany
FDGB	(Freier Deutscher Gewerkschaftsbund) League of Free German Trade Unions
FDJ	(Freie Deutsche Jugend) Free German Youth
FDP	(Frei Demokratische Partei) Free Democratic Party
FU	(Föderalistische Union) Federalist Union
GB	(Gesamtdeutscher Block) United German Bloc
GDP	(Gesamtdeutsche Partei) German Unity Party
GVP	(Gesamtdeutsche Volkspartei) United German People's Party
KBW	(Kommunistischer Bund Westdeutschlands) West German Communist League
KPD	(Kommunistische Partei Deutschlands) Communist Party of Germany
LDP	(Liberal-Demokratische Partei) Liberal Democratic Party
LPD	(Liberale Partei Deutschlands) Liberal Party of Germany
NKFD	(Nationalkommittee Freies Deutschland) National Committee for a Free Germany
NPD	(Nationaldemokratische Partei Deutschlands) National Democratic Party of Germany
NS	(National sozialistisch) National Socialist
NSDAP	(National sozialistische Deutsche Arbeiterpartei) National Socialist Workers' Party
OHL	(Oberste Heeresleitung) Supreme Army Headquarters
RSF	(Radikal-Soziale Freiheitspartei) Radical Social Liberal Party
RWVP	(Rheinisch-Westfälische Volkspartei) Rhenish-Westphalian People's Party
SA	(Sturmabteilung) Storm-troopers
SAP	(Sozialistische Arbeiterpartei) Socialist Workers' Party
SED	(Sozialistische Einheitspartei) Socialist Unity Party
SKL	(Oberste Seekriegsleitung) Supreme Command of the Navy
SMAD	(Sowjetische Militäradministration Deutschlands) Soviet Military Administration in Germany
SPD	(Sozialdemokratische Partei Deutschlands) Social Democratic Party of Germany
SRP	(Sozialitische Reichspartei) Socialist Reich Party
SS	(Schutzstaffel) Protection Squad
SSW	(Südschelswiger Wählerverband) South Schleswig Electoral Association
UDM	(Union Deutscher Mittelstandspartein) Union of German Mittlestand Parties

USPD   (Unabhängige Sozialdemokratische Partei Deutschlands)
Independent Social Democratic Party of Germany
WAV   (Wirtschaftliche Aufbau-Vereinigung) Economic
Recovery Party

PREFACE

The primary intention of this volume, as in the case of my book *A History of Prussia*, is to fill a gap in the existing literature on German history, at least in English-speaking countries. It is addressed to the general reader, the student and specialist alike. The latter may well want to pursue some of the issues raised in this constitutional history further, and consequently the bibliography contains titles which will assist him in this task. This author is at one with the opinion expressed by P.M. Kennedy that the student of modern German history who ignores recent German historical scholarship does so at his own peril.

Although numerous general histories of Germany in the nineteenth and twentieth centuries are available, the constitutional development of the individual German states is a topic mostly ignored. What most of these histories have to say – like A.J.P. Taylor's *Course of German History* or G. Barraclough's *Origins of Modern Germany* – on the Bismarckian constitution, especially on the powers of the Reichstag, simply demonstrates that their authors have never read the text of the constitution. Even more recent treatments exhibit this shortcoming. If the Reichstag, to paraphrase Bebel, was no more than the figleaf covering up Hohenzollern absolutism, then one wonders why for instance Bismarck was forever busy trying to obtain the necessary majorities, and in the end when this became increasingly difficult he despaired at his own creation – a major factor contributing to his downfall. Consequently the Reichstag must have had some important powers after all – small of course when compared with those of Westminster or the US Congress, but important all the same. No German chancellor between 1871 and 1918 could afford to ignore the Reichstag. But German constitutional development did not begin with the Bismarckian constitution, nor for that matter at the beginning of the nineteenth century where this volume begins. A constitutional history of the Holy Roman Empire of the German Nation is still a major desideratum, and not only in English.

The constitutional life of any country embraces rather more than its political institutions; but to do justice to this fact within one volume would have been impossible – as the work of the German historian E.R. Huber, to which this book is heavily indebted, shows. So far Huber has produced six massive volumes, well over a 1000 pages each, and there are at least two further volumes to come. What are essentially economic factors have constrained this author to look in the main at the political development.

Immense gratitude must be expressed to my publishers whose patience, painstaking work and encouragement accompanied this volume from the moment of its inception. I am equally indebted to the assistance and criticism offered by Dr Derek McKay of the London School of Economics and my colleague William J.D. Trythall at York, though of course whatever shortcomings or possible mistakes this volume may contain are my own responsibility. My thanks are also due to the staff of the Goethe Institute in York for all their help, and to Joanne Trythall for typing the original manuscript.

Since this book, like most of my work, was written in Germany my thanks also go forth to those who ensured that my stay there was as comfortable as possible, notably Frau Karla Zapf in Munich, Frau Magdalena Sailer in Kirchdorf and all the members of the *Stammtisch beim Eib* of the *Unterwirt* in Kirchdorf. All of them combined to restore spirits when they appeared flagging, not least with the aid of a few halves of *Moy Bier*!

HANNSJOACHIM W. KOCH
York/Munich/Kirchdorf 1983

ACKNOWLEDGEMENT

We are indebted to Statistisches Bundesamt, Wiesbaden for permission to reproduce Tables 1, 2, 3a & b, 4, 5a & b, 6.

For Roger, Marcus and Freya

Chapter 1

THE DISSOLUTION OF THE HOLY ROMAN EMPIRE

THE END OF THE EMPIRE

German constitutional history in the nineteenth century begins with three clear cases of the violation of the constitution of the Holy Roman Empire of the German Nation, bringing the Empire itself to an end. It had been in its death agonies anyway since the Westphalian peace of 1648 that had concluded the Thirty Years War (1618–48).

The first breach of the old constitution took place on 11 August 1804, when Emperor Francis II assumed the title of Emperor of Austria in addition to that of Holy Roman Emperor in order to consolidate his position and that of the Hapsburg crown lands. According to the Imperial Constitution only one imperial title was to exist, namely the Roman-German one.

The second breach occurred a year later when Bavaria, Baden and Württemberg joined Napoleon against Austria when the latter, together with Great Britain and Russia, tried once more to stem this French bid for hegemony in Europe. The action of these three was a gross violation of the old constitution but, so it seemed, they stood to gain more from Napoleon's hands than from those of Francis. The defeat of the Austro-Russian armies at Austerlitz put an end for the time being to the opposition to Napoleon in Europe. Bavaria and Württemberg became kingdoms by Napoleon's grace; and the creation of the Confederation of the Rhine on 12 July 1806, to which ultmately sixteen German states adhered, broke up the old Empire since *de facto* the German members of the Confederation left the Reich and became Napoleon's protectorate.

The immediate consequence of this was the third breach of the old constitution, when on 6 August 1806 Emperor Francis laid down his imperial crown in response to Napoleon's demand. In strictly legal and constitutional terms the Emperor had no right to do so and thus nullify the Empire. His imperial office represented the tie that held the states of the Empire together and that tie, in strictly legal terms, could not be

1

severed by a unilateral action but only by the Reichstag as the representative organ of the estates of the Empire. According to the law, since the Imperial Crown was elective, all the Emperor could do was to abdicate. In simple terms, although corresponding with the political realities of the day, Francis acted in a way he had no right to do. This renunciation resulted in the dissolution of the Reichstag and the Imperial courts. It was the end of the Holy Roman Empire of the German Nation.

However, it was not seen in this light by contemporaries, who considered the Empire suspended. Whether the factual dissolution also meant the legal dissolution would depend on future developments. Indeed between 1813 and 1815 schemes were considered to restore the Empire and nullify Francis's renunciation of the Imperial Crown. Only when these schemes proved abortive was the action of 1806 legally sanctioned.

The German body politic was now divided into three parts: the Austrian Empire; the German middle states organized in the Confederation of the Rhine under Napoleon's explicit protection; and Prussia, along with the territories of Danish Holstein and Swedish Pomerania. In the Austrian Empire the law remained very much what it had been before; in some of the French vassal states of the Confederation the *Code Napoléon* was introduced, notably in Westphalia, Baden, Frankfurt and Berg, where it produced a beneficial legal uniformity in the area of civil and criminal law. But in the final analysis its objective was the consolidation of French hegemony in Central Europe. Napoleon was not prepared to built up a European and German federal system any more than the princes of the Confederation were willing to integrate themselves fully into a federal structure. Thus the elements of federalism inherent in the Confederation remained stillborn and instead what emerged were centrally governed and administered unitary states. Only those states which had adopted the *Code Napoléon* produced imitations of Napoleon pseudo-constitutionalism, behind which, however, the old social hierarchy maintained its positions.

Prussia retained its institutions, of which the most notable was the new Prussian legal code, the *Allgemeine Preussische Landrecht*, introduced as recently as 1794, in its scope so all-embracing that in Alexis de Tocqueville's judgement it really amounted to a constitution. Prussia's attempt to stem the tide of French encroachment in 1806 was disastrously defeated at Jena and Auerstädt in 1806, and by the Treaty of Tilsit of 1807 Prussia lost half of its territory. But it was precisely this defeat that opened the way for a group of reformers in the Prussian government and administration who had been waiting in the wings for some time. Within a matter of less than five years profound reforms had been carried in three sectors: administration, education and military affairs. Reforms in a fourth sector, the constitutional sector, were also aimed at. From the very outset the Prussian Reform Movement was determined to acquire a constitution which would serve as a model for Germany as a whole. The territories of the Prussian Kingdom were to have delegates in one representative assembly, freely elected. But on this issue King Friedrich Wilhelm III stalled. The new Prussian legal code which effectively had put the Crown under the law seemed to him to be quite sufficient. But, as he was seriously in need of funds, Friedrich Wilhelm on 27 October 1810 gave his first constitutional promise to establish a representative assembly, a promise repeated twice, for the third and last time on 22 May 1815 when he undertook to give Prussia a constitution which was to establish a parliament with advisory powers. The promise was not kept; when in 1821 Prussia raised a huge private loan from the Rothschilds in London, the state no longer needed to raise loans at home and the question of the constitution was readily forgotten until 1847 when new financial needs brought it to the fore again.

EARLY CONSTITUTIONAL MOVEMENTS

The constitutional movement, especially in the four greatest south German states, Bavaria, Württemberg, Baden and Hesse-Darmstadt (discussed individually below), received fresh impetus mainly as a result of the acquisition and consolidation of new territories. At first, in the process of consolidation they chose the way of strong bureaucratic centralization: Bavaria under Montgelas was a good example of this. His policy was draped with pseudo-constitutionalism of Napoleonic origin. As in Prussia the ruling element was really the bureaucracy, though it lacked the Prussian impulse for reform. What was achieved was to its credit. But after the collapse of the Napoleonic system it became clear that the monarchic-bureaucratic system needed popular support: subjects should become citizens with corresponding rights and duties. After 1815 the south German states decisively opted for the constitutional state modelled on the French charter of 1814 which combined monarchic sovereignty with participation by representative assemblies. Thus there emerged in Germany the first written constitution containing basic rights, the separation of powers, the two-chamber system and elected representatives. Similar developments took place in other smaller German states like Nassau which in fact was the first to issue a written constitution in 1814. Bavaria, Baden and Hanover followed in 1818, Württemberg in 1819. Between 1814 and 1830 fifteen German states had introduced constitutions. Some of these were imposed from above, like those of Nassau and Bavaria; others were agreed between monarch or prince and a representative assembly as in the case of Württemberg. But irrespective of whether agreed or imposed, once the population had accepted a representative assembly it had *de facto* and *de jure* accepted the constitution. They were now removed from unilateral interference by the monarch, and constitutional changes could only be carried out with the agreement of parliament. That is not to say that these constitutions were democratic. In the First Chamber the privileged classes – the landowning nobility – were represented, while in the Second Chamber the educated and propertied bourgeoisie had its place. The ruling prince participated in the legislative process and he possessed sole executive power. The monarchical principle remained untouched; sovereignty resided in the monarch, not in the people.

Bavaria under Montgelas between 1799 and 1817 had become a strongly centralized unitary state. His revolution from above did away with the relics of feudalism and patrimonialism throughout the kingdom. Montgelas used the constitution of 1 May 1808 simply to codify the law of the realm, and by building up an all-pervading bureaucracy to unify the kingdom. Crown Prince Ludwig became his most bitter opponent, especially as he was increasingly influenced by the widespread movement for German national unity. Mainly through his efforts King Max I Joseph abandoned the Confederation of the Rhine at the last minute and participated in the Wars of Liberation (1813–15). But in constitutional terms the way was blocked by Montgelas until his departure in 1817, a move which Crown Prince Ludwig had demanded for several years. As Bavaria was insistent on regaining the Palatinate on the right bank of the Rhine, which had been acquired by Baden, it was thought that pressure could best be exerted by popular support through a representative assembly. Baden came to the same conclusion in defence of the Palatinate, and one can speak of a virtual constitutional race between Baden and Bavaria, which the latter won. However, it failed to regain the Palatinate. On 26 May 1818 Bavaria had a representative constitution imposed upon her.

Baden was beset by a number of problems. In contrast to Bavaria, it was religiously heterogeneous, which made unity and integration a difficult task. Thus at first an absolutist policy imposed unity from the river Main to Lake Constance. Then there was the problem of succession to the Grandducal throne. Added to this were the differences with Bavaria over the Palatinate. Although Bavaria and Austria agreed on 23 April 1815 on a further enlargement of Bavaria at the expense of Baden, when Baden joined the allies on 12 May 1815 it was only on condition that it would not suffer any territorial losses. Grand Duke Charles, who had no immediate heirs to his throne, proclaimed as his successor the Margrave of Baden, Count von Hochberg. To consolidate these arrangements he introduced a representative assembly through a constitution which came into force on 22 August 1818. This was very much supported by the nobility, the clergy and the educated propertied bourgeoisie who had long clamoured for an end to the absolutist bureaucracy.

Württemberg, which between 1803 and 1805 had trebled in size and like Bavaria been elevated to the status of kingdom by Napoleon, originally maintained representation by the estates until King Friedrich, shortly after ascending the throne, unilaterally dissolved the assembly of the estates, a step widely welcomed since the representatives were anything but reform–orientated. Though preparatory work on a constitution was already in hand, King Friedrich did not make up his mind until the Congress of Vienna. As first he wanted to impose a constitution. But an opposition, part of the nascent movement for German unity combining nobility and bourgeoisie virulently opposed this imposition. Their spokesman, Count Waldeck, one of many members of the German nobility who had been mediatized, rejected the constitution submitted by the King. Württembergers demanded consultation and a right of participation in the constitution. For the first time in Germany the contractual theory of the constitution became the subject of public debate. The king was ready for a compromise: he agreed to the right of parliament to control the budget, its participation in the legislative process and the responsibility of all civil servants to parliament. For the opposition this was still not enough. King Friedrich died in 1816 and his successor King Wilhelm I pursued a hard line at first, returning to absolutist government. The Carlsbad Decrees (see below) rather alarmed the opposition in Württemberg and when King Wilhelm ordered new elections for the Diet on 10 June 1819, goverment supporters gained the majority and the German nationalists lost. Under these circumstances the Diet accepted the new constitution introducing a two-chamber system, which the King signed on 25 September 1819.

Hesse, the Grand Duchy of Hesse-Darmstadt, also managed to abandon Napoleon in time to change over to the allies. But this did not alter the fact that at the Congress of Vienna Grand Duke Ludwig lost some territory. As this Grand Duchy consisted of three provinces, Upper Hesse, Rhine-Hesse and Starkenburg, the Grand Duke saw as the best means to consolidate his territory the introduction of a constitution. Initially he tried to impose this, but the opposition in Hesse would not accept it, taking particular exception to the narrow franchise. Ludwig made further amendments, the First Chamber then accepted it, and part of the Second Chamber were also prepared to swear on oath on the constitution. Those who failed to do so lost their seats.

Every one of the four south German constitutions mentioned was based on the principle of hereditary monarchy. Monarchical legitimacy was never questioned. Sovereignty resided with the monarch. With the exception of Hesse none of the constitutions contained emergency provisions. In the case of Hesse the Grand Duke was allowed to do what was considered necessary for the security of the state without the participation of the chambers. This allowed him to use his army, suspend the constitutional rights of his subjects and institute special courts. Not until the early 1860s was emergency legislation submitted to the chambers, if it had lasted longer than one year.

All constitutions marked the transition from cabinet to ministerial government but this was also the case in states without a constitution like Prussia and Austria. Nothing was said in the constitutions about legislation requiring the counter-signature of the responsible ministers. But the parliaments had the right to raise complaints against legislation infringing the constitution and in fact indict the responsible minister. Both Hesse and Württemberg introduced ministerial counter-signature, and ministerial responsibility to parliament by 1824. To hold ministerial office and be a member of the chambers was not considered incompatible. The principle of the separation of powers played no role at that stage and most ministers were also members of the First Chamber, which naturally tended to support the government. Nor was ministerial office and membership in the Second Chamber incompatible. The Minister of the Interior for Baden, Ludwig Winter, was also a Liberal member of the Second Chamber. But in this and other instances it soon became evident that as soon as such persons had obtained office they were absorbed by the 'establishment'.

The First Chamber represented the nobility, the Second the bourgeois progressives, as well as the lower nobility, the clergy and civil servants.

It was the monarch who called the chambers but they had to meet at least once every three years (in Baden every two years). Even when they were prorogued the session formally continued. The legislative period, that is to say the duration of the mandate of each representative body, lasted six years (in Baden eight). The dissolution of parliament was followed by new elections in Württemberg and Hesse within six months, in Bavaria and Baden within three. The chambers had no right to assemble on their own initiative nor to dissolve themselves. Each deputy could lay down his mandate, but he could not be forced to do so by his fellow deputies or his electors.

Membership in the First Chamber was hereditary, or because of holding an important office, or by princely appointment. Only Baden had an elected First Chamber. Membership in the Second Chamber was by election only. There was no general and equal franchise. The Liberals especially considered those who were not independent because of their employment, or who lacked property, unqualified to judge political affairs. Thus a large part of the population was driven into the open arms of democratic radicalism. Initially the chambers' functions were limited to deliberation but within a relatively short time they gained well-defined competencies and participated in decision-making. Laws could only be passed with the agreement of both chambers, and changes in the constitution could only be carried out with their consent. The most important aspect of parliamentary power was its agreement to the levying of taxation. In Bavaria fiscal legislation could be passed for six years and was not subject to annual review. This also applied with some minor modification to the other south German constitutions. However, the state budget was not subject to parliamentary control. Members of the chambers could submit petitions as well as complaints if the constitution was violated. The ultimate weapon was the right to indict a minister of violating the constitution.

Like the American and French constitutions, the south German constitutions contained a list of basic rights: those of citizenship, equality before the law, personal liberty and freedom of opinion and property. Much of what had been achieved in Prussia by reform legislation was achieved in southern Germany by constitutionalism. Obviously these basic rights were still very narrowly defined and the nobility, propertied bourgeoisie and clergy enjoyed considerable privileges. Birth, property and religion formed narrow boundaries around the principle of equality. Freedom of opinion and freedom of the press were severely curtailed by the Carlsbad decrees (see below), and it was little wonder therefore that constitutions had hardly been introduced before constitutional struggles came to the fore.

In *Bavaria* it was the Liberals who demanded the legislative initiative, but more important was the question of the oath sworn by the army. Was it to swear its oath to 'King and Country' or to the constitution? In the former case the army would have to carry out unquestioningly any order from its supreme commander; in the latter case it had, theoretically at least, to examine the constitutionality of any order. This implied the intrusion of politics into the army. When Bavarian officers, NCOs and rank-and-file submitted a petition to retain the traditional form of the oath, the opposition in the Second Chamber was immense. Consequently the Bavarian King entertained the idea of doing away with the constitution altogether. When he sought Prussian support, the Prussians replied that as Bavaria had taken the road of constitutionalism, it should adhere to it or go it alone. This was followed by a conflict about the military budget which the Diet had cut. The King argued that the budget had to be increased so that Bavaria could fulfil its obligations towards the German Confederation. And in fact the constitution of the German Confederation stood above the constitutional law of its member countries. The King obtained his budget. When liberally-inclined civil servants were elected into the Second Chamber, the Bavarian bureaucracy refused them leave of absence. It could hardly afford to have any of its members speak on behalf of the opposition.

King Max I Joseph died in 1825 and King Ludwig I inherited the constitutional conflict. Rather more liberal than his father, he reduced military expenditure, relaxed press censorship and also reformed the Bavarian system of education on the Prussian model. On the whole, until the eve of the 1848 revolution, greater harmony existed between the King and his parliament than beforehand.

In *Baden* a reactionary course was pursued under Minister von Berstett which inevitably led to conflict with the Second Chamber. Liberal tendencies in it were even more pronounced than in Bavaria and the opposition were in the majority. The government had issued a decree which reduced the privileges of the nobility, who saw in this a violation of Article 14 of the Confederate Constitution and so the government had to revoke its decree. As in Bavaria, Grand Duke Ludwig considered a *coup d'état*, but Prussia and Austria opposed it. Instead government policy endeavoured to reduce drastically the influence of the chambers and the basic rights. One step in this direction was a revision of the constitution which prolonged the time allowed before elections became mandatory from two to six years. The budget was extended to run for three years, which meant that the Diet had to be assembled only every three years. The government thus gained increasing independence from its parliament.

In contrast to Bavaria and Baden, *Württemberg*'s parliament initially had no strong Liberal opposition. The majority of the members of the Second Chamber were civil servants. Thus harmony prevailed between 1820 and 1830 with the exception of the case of the economist Friedrich List, the untiring propagator of a German *Zollverein* and German unification. He was elected twice into the Second Chamber, and the government found far-fetched reasons for his exclusion. But after his third election in 1820 entry could no longer be blocked. However, the government soon found ways and means to proceed against this propagator of national and liberal ideas. His criticizing and in fact insulting the government gave the latter the lever to exclude him once again.

Some comment must now be made on the role of the *Churches*, since they represented not only an ecclesiastical but also a secular institution. The demand for separation of church and state was part of the earliest challenges by Liberalism, while the Conservatives replied with their emphasis upon the alliance between 'Crown and Altar'. Yet the Liberal position was paradoxical. While demanding the separation of church and state, they insisted at the same time on greater control by the state of the church, especially the Roman Catholic Church. Bavaria, predominantly Catholic, but under Montgelas pursuing an anti-clerical course, had made its peace with the church by the Concordat of 1817. In Protestant German lands the Protestant Church represented one of the main pillars of the state. The Catholic Church in Germany had suffered heavily under the policies of the Confederation of the Rhine. They had lost most of their territorial substance. Politically Catholics could be found who sympathized with the movement for German unity, epitomized by persons such as the publicist Joseph von Görres. At the same time there were political Catholics who were vociferous opponents of 'rational liberalism'. They opposed modernization, the omnipotence of the state, absolutism, democracy and bureaucracy. The Congress of Vienna failed to deal with the problem of church and state and left it to the member states of the German Confederation to make their own arrangements to conclude concordats. Points at issue were the question of education and the state's participation in the appointment of bishops. In Prussia, which for a long time had learnt to live with its Catholic Silesians, conflict arose in 1835 when the newly appointed Archbishop of Cologne prohibited mixed marriages and forbade Catholic students at Bonn to attend lectures given by professors known to be firm supporters of the Prussian state.

The state reacted vigorously, removing the Archbishop and imprisoning him in the fortress at Minden. The Curia reacted with equal vigour by appointing an Archbishop who supported the policies of his predecessors. He was imprisoned too and brought to Kolberg in Pomerania. Only after the death of Friedrich Wilhelm III was a proper relationship restored between the Catholic Church and Prussian state. Apart from Prussia only Hanover had an independent Catholic Church.

Like the Catholicism of the early nineteenth century, Protestantism experienced a wave of regeneration, but from the point of view of the Prussian state the main issue was to unite the Lutheran and Reformed (Calvinist) churches into one state church, an objective already attained in Prussia during the reign of Friedrich Wilhelm III.

However, with the Roman Catholic Church's attitude over the question of mixed marriages – an unavoidable problem in a state in which religious toleration was a fundamental structural princple – the seed had been sown that was ultimately to ripen in the *Kulturkampf*.

Chapter 2

THE GERMAN CONFEDERATION

As Napoleon's star was descending, there arose the awareness that the German problem, in the form of the reorganization of Germany, required a new solution. Many of the Prussian reformers and Germany's youth who had fought for the liberation of Germany from the Napoleonic yoke, and the urban and rural inhabitants of the states of the Confederation of the Rhine, desired a nationally unified German state based on unity and liberty, guaranteeing independence and security. Remembering what was thought to be the glory of the old Empire, they at the same time developed, or rather rediscovered, such a national consciousness as had not been witnessed in Germany since the Reformation and which had been buried since then under the sediments of foreign rule, intervention and particularism.

On the Prussian side it was particularly Karl Freiherr vom Stein and Wilhelm von Humboldt who represented the idea of national unity, a state with a strong central executive power and a national assembly for legislation. But the supporters of German unity and the German unity movement as a whole encountered the solid opposition of the German particularist states. Bavaria, for instance, having just become a kingdom, was not prepared to submerge its newly-found glory in German unity. Moreover, it was not Germany which had won the war against Napoleon, it was Prussia in alliance with Russia, Austria, and Great Britain. In the final analysis the solution of the German question in the sense of the German unity movement was prevented by the combination of Germany's two major powers, Austria and Prussia, the former states of the Confederation of the Rhine, Russia, Great Britain and France. It was the Quadruple Alliance which had won victory, not Germany.

GERMANY AND THE EUROPEAN POWERS

It was hardly in the interest of the Great Powers to have a strong

10

centralized power re-emerge in the heart of Europe. Neither, of course, did they wish a power vacuum and France in particular was determined to follow its traditional policy of keeping the heart of Europe as weak as possible, to allow nothing more than a loose confederation of German states, each strong enough to maintain internal security but weak enough not to tip the scales of international power. These were the premises from which the European powers, under the guidance of Prince Metternich, the Austrian Foreign Minister, proceeded to solve the German question at the Congress of Vienna.

Austria shared these sentiments though for different reasons. Having turned its eyes towards south and south-eastern Europe it was obvious that the implementation of the principle of national self-determination carried within it the seed of decay of the multi-national empire. The German national state in Metternich's eyes did not represent an adequate substitute for the supra-national position which the Hapsburg Empire occupied. The Imperial Crown of the Holy Roman Empire of the German Nation had been a burden, its authority had been withering away and had added nothing to the power of the House of Hapsburg. Metternich closed his eyes firmly to the fact that the dynasty he served had once had a specifically German mission, which allowed the Hapsburgs to attain greatness. Any idea that it could resume that mission he firmly rejected.

Prussia, too, followed its own narrow interests. A restoration of the Reich would inevitably have meant Prussia's subordination to Austria, which in spite of the sentiments of Stein, Humboldt and many others, the Prussian Crown, backed by the Prussian Conservatives was not willing to accept, unless, of course, its position was elevated to that of 'Field Marshal' of the Reich, implying the acceptance of its predominance in northern and central Germany. But the result would not have been German unity but two spheres in which Austria and Prussia exercised their respective hegemony. It would have been the perpetuation of the Austro-German dualism which had existed since 1740. The states of the Confederation of the Rhine put up an equally strong barrier against any attempt to deprive them of the spoils so recently gained at the expense of the German body politic.

The scheme for a unified Germany had not the least chance of success in Vienna. Fichte, the fanatical advocate of German unity, was already dead. Stein and Humboldt had their plans but were convinced that they were doomed to failure even before they were put on the conference table. The publicists and agitators who supported them, men like Ernst Moritz Arndt or Joseph von Görres, in the end also accepted the 'facts of life'. Germany's youth itself was at that time not yet politically organized, while the representatives of liberal-democratic ideas were in an insignificant minority and whenever they aired their sentiments they were suspected of French Jacobinism or

11

Napoleonism.

On the surface, as has been shown in the previous chapter, the restoration of the Holy Roman Empire of the German Nation would have been the easiest solution from a legal point of view. The seven years of Napoleon's rule would merely have been an interregnum. This was Stein's original idea. For a moment even Great Britain adopted this attitude. But it would have depended on how far the German rulers would have been prepared to subject themselves to Emperor and Empire. Such readiness by the German princes simply no longer existed. The restoration of the Empire lacked all the necessary preconditions whose fulfilment would have facilitated such a solution.

Another alternative was a federal state. The territorial states of Germany would have retained their territorial integrity, but Stein and Humboldt were insistent that those of the German princes who had adhered to Napoleon's cause to the last should be severely punished and lose large parts of their territory, particularly the King of Saxony (a loss that was to benefit Prussia). Constitutionally a federal state should also have had a strong central executive power, but who was to exercise this power, Prussia or Austria? A dual executive consisting of Austria *and* Prussia was envisaged. The federal solution would also have corresponded with the principles of federal constitutionalism and the establishment of a nationally representative organ. But the federal solution would also have transferred part of the sovereignty, if not all of it, from the princes of the federation and their states to the federal authority. This caused not only Austria's opposition but also that of other German kingdoms and principalities.

Thus there only remained the solution of a confederation, an aim which Metternich pursued with a singlemindedness hard to match. All the wishes of the German princes could be accommodated within it. It required no single recognized head of state, no unified judicial legislation, no economic unity, no customs union and no unified army. The German Confederation was founded on a collection of negatives. Confederation meant the negation of national unity, of protecting civil liberties throughout the German states, a negation of democratic participation in the making of the German constitution. But above all, confederation meant the maintenance of the balance of power in Europe, while national self-determination would only have had a destabilizing effect.

METTERNICH AND THE CONGRESS OF VIENNA

Nevertheless Metternich's concept was a grand scheme with the ultimate aim of combating the principle of national self-determination where and whenever it arose. It rested on the principle of 'legitimacy', its restoration wherever it was attacked, and a return to the *status quo ante bellum* of 1789, the securing of the order thus restored and its defence against aggression and revolutionary subversion. As in the case of Bismarck several decades later, Metternich's primary motive force was the fear of revolution, and therefore any constitutional innovations and greater liberalization met his explicit opposition. But he had also to make concessions to the political realities of his day. Thus he was prepared to underwrite and guarantee the territorial changes made in Germany under Napoleon's rule. He was not prepared to reverse the drastic changes which had occurred in the wake of the French Revolution. This would have put stability at risk and the principle of stability exercised a constraining effect on his interpretation of the principle of legitimacy. Monarchical legitimacy was the bulwark against the forces of liberalism and democracy. From it derived authority, the centre of gravity of a static order, directed against change and political upheaval.

For Europe as a whole Metternich aimed at a re-establishment of the balance of power which implied that France was to take its place again among the Great Powers. Austria, Prussia, Russia, France and Great Britain were to form a pentarchy exercising hegemony in Central Europe. But to him the German question was only one aspect of a whole series of European problems. The continued division of Italy was to ensure that the principle of nationalism was contained. In principle his concept was a return of Europe to the shape it possessed in the previous century, in which form it would represent a bulwark against the revolutionizing power of nationalism and democracy. Therefore he opposed the creation for the German Confederation of any form of institution upon which the movement for German unity could have built, such as a united German army, a German national assembly or the restoration of the Prusso-Austrian dualism. The principle of national self-determination had to be held down since it acted only as an agent of decomposition in the European order. He opposed the institution of a direct or indirect central power in Germany, opting for a loose confederation of thirty-six legally independent sovereign individual states.

At the Congress of Vienna the internal aspects of the German question were dealt with by the 'German Committee' which included Austria, Prussia, Bavaria, Württemberg, and Hanover, the powers of the German pentarchy. But as the negotiations proceeded all German states were included. By the middle of October 1814 Metternich and Prince Hardenberg had agreed on a draft for the formation of an 'Eternal Confederation, to preserve and defend German independence'. There was to be no head of the confederation but a 'Confederate Directory' in the hands of Austria. Added to it was the *Rat der Kreisobersten*, a council of the major states in which Prussia and

Austria had two votes each, Bavaria, Württemberg and Hanover one vote each. Finally there was to be a 'Council of the Princes and Cities'. The Confederation was to have its own legislature and executive, the former to be in the hands of the German pentarchy as well as in those of the Council of Princes and Cities.

It seemed an acceptable solution, but it was opposed by most German states, notably by Bavaria and Württemberg. Bavaria demanded that the German states should be able to conclude alliances with foreign powers and to participate in wars on their own initiative, demands supported by Württemberg. Metternich rejected these demands outright and Stein asked Czar Alexander I to intervene. Alexander soon declared his readiness to support the Austro-Prussian plan. At the same time, via the publicity of Görres, Stein mobilized the states not represented in the German Committee, and those states outside the German pentarchy were not prepared to accept the Austro-Prussian Hegemony in Germany. On 16 November 1814 twenty-nine German governments (including four free cities) addressed a note to the German Committee in which they rejected the pre-eminence of the five German powers represented in it and instead insisted on equal rights for all members within the German Confederation. When Württemberg withdrew from it, the German Committee came to an end. Stein and Humboldt created a crisis by trying to resurrect their old plans, which were disowned by the Prussian government. Divisions of opinion ran deeply, not only among the German powers but also among the great powers of Europe. Territorial questions had also played a role. The Kingdom of Saxony and the Duchy of Warsaw had since 1807 been under the personal union of the King of Saxony, who had supported Napoleon to the last. Prussia was intent on acquiring large parts of Saxony but in the end her gains were only marginal. In part it also depended on the solution of the Polish question where Russia demanded the annexation of the Duchy of Warsaw. The situation deteriorated to such an extent that Great Britain, France and Austria concluded a secret alliance against Prussia and Russia. Napoleon's return, however, defused the situation and under British mediation Saxony lost some territory to Prussia, and Poland was divided once again.

Hardenberg introduced a new draft, essentially devised by Humboldt, and so did Metternich. Seventeen articles emerged from both drafts which Metternich on 23 May 1815 submitted to the German governments. After due consultation the seventeen articles were expanded into twenty, in which form the 'German Conference' accepted the 'Act of German Confederation' on 8 June 1815. Nevertheless Bavaria, Württemberg and Saxony raised their opposition prior to acceptance but obtained only few changes. The institution of a Supreme Court of the Confederation was dropped, as were a number of points of lesser importance.

Metternich excepted, few were really happy about the Vienna

progeny. Stein commented that 'one will never be able to stop Germany becoming one state, one nation somehow'; Humboldt accepted the situation as the least of quite a number of evils.

According to the Constitution of the German Confederation, its members were the sovereign princes and the free cities of Germany. Each was representative of its own sovereign state, making a total of forty-one states. They included the Empire of Austria; the five kingdoms of Prussia, Bavaria, Saxony, Hanover and Württemberg, the Electoral Duchy of Hesse-Kassel; seven grand duchies (Baden, Hesse-Darmstadt, Luxemburg, Mecklenburg-Schwerin, Mecklenburg-Strelitz, Saxe-Weimar-Eisenach and Oldenburg); ten duchies: Holstein-Lauenburg, Brunswick, Nassau, Saxe-Gotha-Altenburg, Saxe-Coburg-Saalfeld, Saxe-Meiningen, Saxe-Hildburghausen, Anhalt-Dessau, Anhalt-Bernburg, Anhalt-Köthen; twelve principalities: Schwarzburg-Sondershausen, Schwarzburg-Rudolstadt, Hohenzollern-Hechingen, Hohenzollern-Sigmaringen, Liechtenstein, Waldeck, Reuss-Greiz, Reuss-Schleiz, Reuss-Ebersdorf and Reuss-Lobenstein, Lippe, Schaumburg-Lippe, the Landgrave Hesse-Homburg; and the four free cities of Hamburg, Bremen, Lübeck and Frankfurt.

Austrian and Prussian participation in the Confederation involved only those teritories which had been part of the Empire in 1805. For Austria this excluded Hungary, Transylvania, Galicia, Croatia, Slovenia, Dalmatia, Lombardy, Venetia and Istria. For Prussia it excluded East and West Prussia, the province of Posen and the Duchy of Neuenburg. The German Confederation had no rights in these excluded territories. There were also three foreign princes within the Confederation: the King of Great Britain as King of Hanover, the King of Denmark as Duke of Holstein and Lauenburg and the King of the Netherlands as the Grand Duke of Luxemburg. The membership of the British Crown ceased as early as 1837 after the death of William IV and the dissolution of the personal union between Great Britain and Hanover, since Queen Victoria as a woman could not inherit the Hanoverian Crown under Salic Law. The Dutch-Luxemburg union lasted until 1890 when with the death of King Wilhelm III the male line of the House of Nassau-Orange became extinct. Finally the personal union between Denmark and Holstein-Lauenburg ceased with the war of 1864.

INSTITUTIONS AND FUNCTIONS OF THE GERMAN CONFEDERATION

The German Confederation was to be a permanent institution which member states could neither be excluded from nor leave. The

Assembly of the German Confederation sat permanently in the old imperial city of Frankfurt, adopting as its official name the term 'Bundestag'. Represented in it were the envoys of the German states. It was chaired by Austria. The distribution of votes differed, depending on whether the assembly met in a Closed Council (*Engerer Rat*) which comprised seventeen votes, or as a full assembly when the larger states had more votes than the smaller ones. Deliberation was only carried out by the Closed Council, which also decided which issues should come before the full assembly, which could thus only vote on the issues already formulated by the Closed Council. Agreement in the full assembly required a two-thirds majority. On several important issues unanimity was required in the Closed Council and in the full assembly, especially over changes in existing or introduction of new laws, decisions concerning the institutions of the Confederation, in matters of religion, in the admission of a new member wishing to join the Confederation, and for issuing decrees affecting the whole of the Confederation. In practice every member possessed the power of veto.

The Confederation was to protect the internal and external security of Germany. It was to prevent or reconcile disagreements between member states, to secure the position of the princes *vis à vis* their respective subjects and to ward off attacks on the Confederation from within. The question of defence against attacks from without was not very satisfactorily solved, since no confederate army was created.

In the legislative sphere the Confederation was to introduce basic laws 'with regard to external, military and inner conditions'. It had a legislative competency for external affairs, military organization and internal executive measures. Laws passed by the Confederation did not require subsequent assent by the sovereigns but merely their publication. Thus the Carlsbad Decrees were even published by those who had declared their scepticism over their wisdom and necessity. As already indicated, the law of the Confederation took precedence over the laws of the individual member states. The German Confederation could exchange envoys with other countries, enter into alliances with foreign powers, conclude international treaties, conduct war and conclude peace. But it did not possess these rights exclusively. Each member state could exchange envoys with other states, conclude treaties and alliances with foreign powers, as well as conduct war and conclude peace. This meant Germany occupied a double position in terms of international law. It was a repetition of the concessions made to the German states by the Westphalian Peace Treaties of 1648. Thus there was no unified German foreign policy, no head of state of a common confederate executive, while the individual states guarded their separate rights with great zeal and suspicion.

The Confederation's right to make war was restricted to defensive war, a restriction extended also to all member states. In case of war the Closed Council had to decide upon the counter-measures. Member states were compelled to participate. Unilateral declarations of neutrality were inadmissible, as was the payment of subsidies in place of military contingents. Nor could a member state, in case of war, conclude a separate armistice or peace. In point of fact the German Confederation conducted only one war, that against Denmark in 1849–50. In the Crimean War Prussia and Austria concluded a defensive alliance which was sanctioned by the Confederation, while in the Austro-Italian War of 1850 the Confederation maintained strict neutrality.

But none of these provisions was matched by any to create a confederate army. The Act of Confederation does not mention one at all. Only a military commission was established at the Confederate Assembly which finally, by 1821, ruled that in case of war the individual states were to provide military contingents. Every member state in such a case had to provide one per cent of its male population as its military contingent, and they were also to make financial contributions of varying amounts to finance the conduct of war. On paper the army of the German Confederation amounted to ten army corps totalling about 300,000 men. Austria and Prussia each provided three army corps, Bavaria one and the remaining three came from all the other member states. There was no supreme commander; a Prussian commander was rejected for fear of Prussian hegemony, so instead this post was decided by elections by the Closed Council as each case arose. Once elected the commander had to name his own general staff and quartermaster. The Confederation contained five fortresses, Mainz, Luxemburg, Landau-Germersheim, Rastatt and Ulm, which were occupied by garrisons from the member states.

Nor did the German Confederation establish a Supreme Court. Judicial proceedings were only envisaged in the case of differences between various member states, or of constitutional conflicts with a member state, and amounted to no more than acts of arbitration. There was no legislation for the protection of the Confederate Constitution. Cases such as treason had to be dealt with in accordance with the laws of the member state concerned.

The 'constitution' of the German Confederation also contained provisions for its own protection by way of 'intervention' or of 'execution', the latter meaning executive action. The two are often confused, but they are in fact quite different from one another. 'Intervention' was intended in cases when a member state was threatened by upheaval from *within*, 'execution' (i.e. executive action) was to be directed *against* any member state which refused to comply with laws and demands of the Bundestag. Thus the Austro-Prussian war of 1866 was legally an executive action against Prussia.

The Confederate Assembly could decide to intervene militarily in a member state, especially when that state was unable to cope with subversive forces. Intervention could be requested but it could also be decided upon in spite of the fact that no such request had been made. The aim of any *intervention* was the restoration of the *status quo*. The first such occasion arose in 1830 when the revolution in Belgium spread to the Grand Duchy of Luxemburg. In 1831 by the decision of the Bundestag a 24,000-strong army of Hanoverians commanded by Duke Bernhard of Saxe-Weimar restored the position. Without being asked for aid the Confederation in 1833 intervened in Frankfurt where Austrian and Prussian troops suppressed a local uprising. The precondition for any confederate *execution* was to compel a member state to fulfil the duties imposed upon it by the constitution of the Confederation. The first such execution was carried out in 1827 against Duke Charles of Brunswick who had seriously violated the Brunswick Constitution; this was followed in 1864 in Holstein where Danish rule was destroyed and, as mentioned, formally against Prussia in 1866, which resulted in the Austro-Prussian War.

Articles 54 and 56 of the Vienna *Schlussakte*, the final part of the *Bundesakte* but not enacted until 15 May 1820, compelled the sovereigns of the member states to introduce constitutions where these did not exist already. Changes could be made only by the means described in the constitution. But each member state was constitutionally autonomous. Whatever the constitution, according to Article 57, its main aim had to be the preservation of the principle of monarchical legitimacy.

The *Bundesakte* of 8 June 1815 was a constitutional treaty between the individual German states. It was one part of the general settlement arrived at at the Congress of Vienna, signed by Austria, Prussia, Great Britain, Russia, France, Sweden, Portugal and Spain. This also meant the recognition in international law of the new order in Germany by the non-German signatory powers: indeed they guaranteed it which in turn gave them the right to intervene in German affairs. In 1850–51 Great Britain and France, as guarantor powers, opposed the planned inclusion of the entire Hapsburg Empire into the German Confederation. They had, or at least demanded, the right to intervene if a constitution had been violated anywhere in Germany. However, in the early years the German Confederation was only interested in receiving outside guarantees against any intervention by France, a country which had continually intervened over the previous two centuries.

The first attempt at foreign intervention was caused by the passing of the Carlsbad Decrees of 1819. Czar Alexander I was prompted by King Wilhelm of Württemberg to intervene against them but upon consultation with Great Britain, where Lord Castlereagh defended the principle of non-intervention in all German constitutional questions, he held back. In fact Castlereagh fully supported the Carlsbad Decrees. When revolutionary ferment began in Germany in the wake of the revolution in France in 1830, the Bundestag was determined to put it down by any means. This caused great excitement in Great Britain but

Palmerston at first rejected any idea of intervention. He still insisted, however, on Great Britain's right to do so derived from the agreements signed in Vienna in 1815. France and Great Britain intervened diplomatically in 1833 when Prussian and Austrian troops occupied Frankfurt (see above). They claimed this right on the basis of being guarantor powers of the German Confederation. Only at the end of 1834, when Palmerston resigned, did this affair end.

REACTION TO THE GERMAN CONFEDERATION

It cannot be said that the creation of the German Confederation provided an adequate and satisfactory solution to the German problem. Hardly had it come into existence when there were calls for its reform throughout Germany. The most vociferous critics came from the younger generation, many of whom had fought in the Wars of Liberation. They represented revolutionary nationalism, a force originally stimulated by the French Revolution. For them the *ancien régime* had been re-established, disguised by constitutionalism but lacking any authority and legitimacy emanating from the people. The more radical groups among them were determined to overthrow the state if it failed to create a unitary German national state. They were influenced by the liberal and democratic ideas of western Europe. They would have been satisfied with a federal state based on a constitutional monarchy and the extension of parliamentary government. Only the extreme radicals among them aimed at the transformation of Germany into a republic. Their organizational structure still derived from the time when Germany was under the Napoleonic yoke. They were secret societies and as such the nucleus of the later political parties which existed in the political underground between 1819 and 1840. But at that time they still lacked a durable organization, a specific programme and firm leadership and discipline. The *Tugendbund* was the most important among the early groupings. It enjoyed the support of Stein and Gerhard von Scharnhorst, though it was too revolutionary for Friedrich Wilhelm III and he had it dissolved in 1809. Its members founded other groups and after 1814 found their way into the *Deutschen Gesellschaften* which enjoyed the support of Ernst Moritz Arndt and spread throughout Germany. The advocate Karl Hoffmann founded the Hoffmann League which spread into southwestern Germany and aimed at German unification under Prussia's leadership. When Prussia renounced that aim at Vienna, democratic and republican aims took over. But the two most important movements were the *Turnerschaften*, the gymnastics societies founded by Friedrich Ludwig Jahn, and the *Burschenschaften*, the student corporations. The gymnastics societies were the first to demand publicly the right of German self-determination. In the universities students were originally divided according to their provinces of origin. The *Burschenschaften* endeavoured to overcome the regionalism and particularism of the *Landsmannschaften* and established themselves first at the University of Jena from where they spread to most north German universities and played an important part in the war against Napoleon. In 1816 they adopted as their motto 'Honour, Liberty, Fatherland' and chose black, red and gold as the colours for their banners, taken from the uniforms of the *Freikorps* Lützow in the ranks of which Germans from all states fought against Napoleon. After 1815 they spread to all German universities but soon aroused the suspicions of the police. They rejected the particularism which the German Confederation appeared to have cemented anew, and advocated a centralized German unitary state.

Their first large public demonstration was carried out at the *Wartburgfest* of 1817 which combined the tricentenary of Luther's Reformation and the fourth anniversary of the Battle of Leipzig. Documents of oppression, like the *Code Napoléon*, the collection of Prussian police laws, and other documents of German submission to alien rule were ritually burnt on the evening of the celebration. Added to these were Prussian military wigs, corporals' sticks and other remnants of the *ancien régime*. Instead of ignoring this incident, the governments took alarm. On Metternich's orders Prussia prohibited the *Burschenschaften* and other German princes acted likewise. The effect was a further radicalization of the student movement. Whereas their programme so far had been the political and economic unity of Germany, the creation of a German army, the development of a constitutional monarchy with representative institutions, ministerial responsibility to parliament, equality before the law, trial by jury, freedom of press and opinion, the radical elements within the *Burschenschaften* now shifted towards republicanism. The student unrest in Germany was a major topic at the Congress of Aachen in September – October 1818. Metternich personally put it on the agenda. In the course of the debate the Russian representative advocated nothing less than the abolition of German universities. Metternich did not go quite so far, while Prussia opposed it and rejected measures which would have inhibited the freedom of teaching and research. Prussia's police, though, were determined to keep a close eye on the students and their teachers.

Events reached a climax when a member of the radicals, Karl Ludwig Sand, murdered the writer August von Kotzebue, reputed to be a Russian spy. Sand was caught but refused to name any of his fellow conspirators. Before decapitating him the executioner asked Sand's pardon. He dismantled the wooden execution platform and from it built a garden hut where Heidelberg students gathered for their conspiratorial meetings.

THE CARLSBAD DECREES

Metternich's answer was the Carlsbad Decrees which had the force of law. Universities were to be investigated and supervised, all university teachers shown or suspected to have been engaged in subversive teachings were to be dismissed and each member state had to proceed against student societies which had not been registered and approved by the police authorities. The *Burschenschaft* was to be dissolved. Altogether the Carlsbad Decrees represented a substantial degree of intervention into the sovereignty of the member states: consequently their severity of application varied from Land to Land. Besides curbing students and universities, the freedom of the press was severely restrained and all papers, periodicals and books subjected to censorship. A journalist who violated the censorship was not allowed to exercise his profession for five years. Again the severity – or laxity – in applying censorship varied from Land to Land, although each member state had to introduce and pass laws which allowed the carrying out of the Carlsbad Decrees on its territory. Furthermore the authorities were to instigate investigations into 'revolutionary activities'. For this purpose a 'Central Commission of Investigation' was created at Mainz subject to the Bundestag. It acted for nine years and the results of its report submitted in 1827 were in inverse proportion to its efforts, and it became the object of public ridicule. It was claimed that Arndt, Friedrich Schleirmacher, Jahn and Fichte (who had been dead for several years) had been at the roots of the revolutionary movement.

In the meantime the completion of the work begun in Vienna in 1814 had taken place with the acceptance by the German Confederation of the *Wiener Schlussakte*, essentially the joint work of Prussia and Austria. The return to the *status quo ante bellum*, with some modifications, had been completed. However, the other German states were suspicious of the joint Austro-Prussian cooperation, and consequently the idea of a German Trialism was born, according to which the smaller German states would increase their cooperation to provide a counterweight to Austria and Prussia. Publications to that effect began to circulate in Germany. The major exponent of the idea at the Bundestag was the Württemberg envoy. Metternich in a countermove broke off relations with Württemberg and thus forced it to recall and replace him.

THE ZOLLVEREIN

Whatever the Congress of Vienna had achieved or failed to achieve for

Germany, one area had been almost completely ignored: the economic sphere. Economically the German states still remained divided, each state having its own tolls and tariffs. A customs union was not even mentioned. When the issue arose in the Bundestag representatives of free trade confronted those defending protectionism. Prussia was the first to suggest German economic unity and free trade but met the firm opposition of Austria, Bavaria and some smaller central and north German states. Of course Prussia stood to gain most, since it possessed in Silesia, the Ruhr and the Saar the vital mineral upon which Prussia's and Germany's industrial revolution was based: coal. Thus from about 1819 onwards Prussia pursued a dual policy: in the political sphere, close conformity within the German Confederation in support of Metternich's system; in the economic sphere, however, it aimed at *Zollverein* (customs union) outside the political confines and restraints of the Confederation. Nevertheless the first step had to be to transform Prussia itself into a consolidated economic unit from which she then could proceed to attract other German states to join her. In other words, Prussia abandoned protectionism within its kingdom while still maintaining tariffs against the other German states. This was not carried out without opposition, since within Prussia there were enclaves of no less than thirteen other German states which were thus shut off, the inevitable consequence being an intensive smuggling, tacitly and actively supported by the other states.

Friedrich List, the advocate of German economic unity, loudly opposed this step by Prussia since he hoped to realize his ideas within the German Confederation. But List was not attended to in Frankfurt. Prussia's policy bore early fruit: the president of Prussia's Erfurt province, Friedrich Christian von Motz succeeded through patient negotiations in having Schwarzburg-Sondershausen join the Prussian customs union. It was Motz's first step in this direction and he became the driving force behind the movement which culminated in the German *Zollverein*. The argument about Prussia's policy came into the open at the Vienna conference of 1820. Prussia rejected all complaints and maintained that the Confederation had no competence over customs and tariffs and that in fact the matter had been left open for negotiations between the individual member states. While shipping on the Rhine was unimpeded, the Elbe was another matter since it was the one river which many of the enclaves in Prussia could use to avoid Prussian customs. Prussia was agreeable, provided that it was protected against misuse by smuggling. A compromise solution was reached which in effect made shipping on the Elbe free of duties. Sustained resistance to Prussian economic policy by the Anhalt duchies was only possible if they were backed by Austria and the south German states. Since Austria was not prepared to abandon its own protectionist policy it could hardly object to the Prussian practice. The only alternative was the Trialism advocated by Württemberg's envoy. On 19 May 1820 Bavaria, Württemberg, Baden, Hesse-Darmstadt, Nassau and the states of Reuss in Thuringia agreed on a preliminary customs treaty which abolished tariffs among the member states. This treaty was to be the basis for the customs conference to be held in Darmstadt and Stuttgart. But at Darmstadt differences between free traders and protectionists arose and the conference failed, and that held in Stuttgart in 1825 suffered the same fate.

In this year Motz became the minister of finance in Prussia. Like most reformers he was not a native but came from Hesse. His long-term objective was to unite Germany under Prussian leadership, excluding Austria. His first step to reach this was his economic policy, which was the basis of his work. A customs union was the economic precondition for political union. In the five years of life left to him he secured all the essential conditions necessary for the success of his entire work. In 1826 Anhalt-Bernburg joined Prussia, followed in 1828 by Anhalt-Dessau and Anhalt-Köthen. Before that he even managed to penetrate into southern Germany. In 1828 Hesse-Darmstadt joined the customs union, and Bavaria and Württemberg reacted by concluding their own South German Customs Union. Hesse-Darmstadt was no immediate gain for Prussia since they had no joint frontier, but it was an important outpost for the further penetration of southern Germany. Apart from the South German Customs Union Saxony, Thuringia, Kur-Hesse and Nassau created the Central German Commercial Association which Brunswick and Bremen joined, while Hamburg remained aloof, not joining any customs union until 1888. It looked a formidable association but appearances were deceptive as no genuine customs union emerged from it. Bavaria and Württemberg faced greater disadvantages from this association than Prussia and this led them to the Prussian side in 1829. The South German Customs Union had not fulfilled its supporters' high expectation. There was no significant economic upswing. Joining Prussia opened great economic opportunities to both kingdoms. The Prussian–South German Treaty of 27 May 1829 really meant the economic containment of the Central German Commercial Association, though it still formed a formidable barrier between Bavaria and Württemberg on the one hand and the states of the Prussian *Zollverein* on the other. But as a result of secret negotiations with Saxe-Meiningen and Saxe-Coburg-Gotha the right to build two duty-free roads was obtained. This in fact made the treaties between southern and northern Germany operative. After Motz's death his successor Karl Georg von Maassen, the Prussian minister of finance, continued his policy. By 1830 the enclaves of Meisenheim, Birkenfeld and Waldeck had joined Prussia, followed on 25 August 1831 by Kur-Hesse which left the Central German Commerical Association. This was a vital breakthrough, leading on 22 March 1833 to the economic and commercial fusion of Bavaria and

Württemberg with the Prussian-Hessian *Zollverein*. During the same year Saxony became a member.

Metternich was far from pleased with this development, which he described as having created a state within a state with the aim of establishing the preponderance of Prussia. In addition, it promoted the 'highly dangerous teaching of German Unity'. Supporters of the *Zollverein* were alleged to be unwitting supporters of the principle of revolution. Metternich's opposition proved in vain: on 12 May 1835 Baden joined the union followed by Nassau, and on 2 January 1836 the city of Frankfurt. With that, except for Austria, all but the German coastal states had joined the *Zollverein*, i.e. Hanover, Brunswick, Oldenburg, Holstein-Lauenburg, both Mecklenburgs and both Lippes, as well as Hamburg, Bremen and Lübeck. The leadership of these states lay in the hands of Hanover which essentially pursued and promoted British interests. The *Zollverein* treaties concluded in 1833 were to run for eight years. In 1841 they were extended for a twelve-year period during which Lippe-Detmold, Brunswick and the County of Schaunburg which belonged to Kur-Hesse became members. Luxemburg joined on 1 April 1842. This association survived the end of the German Confederation and lasted until 1919. Membership in the German *Zollverein* consisted of three groups. The first consisted of enclaves and smaller states already associated with one of the larger member states of the German Confederation. Indeed they were members not in their own right but as part of the larger state with which they had associated. Secondly there was the group of states which had joined another customs union and had become members through the latter joining the *Zollverein*. Thirdly there were the immediate members of the *Zollverein* like Prussia, Bavaria and Württemberg, but also Nassau, Frankfurt and Luxemburg. Of the thirty-nine members of the German Confederation in 1842, twenty-eight joined the *Zollverein* while eleven, for the time being, chose to remain outside it.

The main institution of the *Zollverein* was the General Conference which met annually, each member having one vote. Like the Bundestag it contained envoys of the various member states. The General Conference deliberated and made decisions, but these had to be carried unanimously. It decided the entire range of tariff legislation, and its decisions had the force of law. It concluded commercial treaties with foreign powers – a total of twenty-eight treaties between 1839 and 1865. Most were concluded by Prussia on behalf of the other member states. The administrative measures enacted by the *Zollverein* were executed by the individual member states, each of which had identical institutions to deal with them. Customs duties and tariff receipts were distributed among the member states. The receipts went to those who collected them since the *Zollverein* did not possess its own treasury, but their distribution was the responsibility of the *Zollverein*. To settle any differences between member states courts of arbitration were usually referred to. The *Zollverein* existed formally from 1834 until 1871, and membership inevitably involved parting with one essential part of sovereignty by each state. In practice this meant subordination to Prussia. But since each member at the General Conference could veto any decision, this subordination was in effect neutralized. There were numerous occasions in which Prussian recommendations were overruled. Prussia's potential hegemony was contained as long as there were still hopes that Austria would join. The very existence of Austria within the German Confederation acted as a check to Prussian hegemony even within the *Zollverein*.

CONSTITUTIONAL DEVELOPMENTS

In the meantime political and constitutional development had continued apace. The era of reform had come to an end in *Prussia* in 1819–20 with the resignation of Humboldt, Hermann von Boyen and others. Representative assemblies only existed in the provinces. The pillars of the state were the monarchy, the state council, the ministries, the officer corps and the bureaucracy; its authoritarian hierarchic character had been maintained. Legislation lay exclusively within the hands of the King. But the judiciary was completely independent, the monarchy had retained only its power to confirm death and life sentence. Since 1814 the army was based on conscription and numbered 120,000 men. As this was also a period of rapid population growth the conscript potential was actually never exhausted and in 1833 the period of conscription was reduced from three to two years. Since Hardenberg's death in 1822 the state council continued to operate in a collegiate fashion. But no new State Chancellor or chief minister was appointed.

The reform impulse having exhausted itself, all that remained was proper and efficient administration. With the acquisition of the Rhenish territories Prussia had gained lands where the *Code Napoléon* was still in force. Drafts for reform with the aim of giving all Prussian territories the same legal system were drawn up but never fully enacted. This meant that in the 1840s the *Code Napoléon* was still in operation in Prussia's western territories.

The event that affected Prussia most was the onset of the industrial revolution between 1820 and 1840. Already in the early stages of the process it was realized that state intervention would be necessary if serious damage to the social fabric was to be avoided. What was needed was workers' protection. The harmful effects of child labour, for instance, were quickly recognized by the condition of health among those mustered for conscription. Therefore on 12 May 1828

King Friedrich Wilhelm III issued an order in cabinet asking his ministers to draw up legislation which would prevent the abuse of children in the factories. But it took until 1839 before a regulation concerning their employment was enacted. This prohibited the employment of children under the age of 9 and limited the working hours for those between 9 and 12 to ten hours a day. Breaks during working hours were made compulsory and work on Sundays and public holidays was prohibited. This was a very modest beginning to social legislation, but a beginning nevertheless which was received with misgivings not only by employers but also by parents who had become accustomed to the idea of additional breadwinners from the earliest age. But the fundamental importance of this measure lies in the fact that in an age dominated by the Liberalism of the Manchester school, the state intervened for the first time in the public sector and thus created a precedent for the future.

The French July Revolution of 1830 gave new encouragement to liberal and radical forces in the German states. In southern and south-western Germany representative institutions gained ground and effectiveness. In those states of central and northern Germany while as yet had no constitution the demand for it increased, while in others radicals endeavoured to transform monarchical into republican constitutions. Brunswick, Hanover, Kur-Hesse and Saxony experienced unrest while in Bavaria, Württemberg, Baden, Hesse-Darmstadt and Nassau calm was maintained on the whole. By handling the Carlsbad Decrees with considerable laxity tensions there were lower than elsewhere. In so far as public polemics occurred, they were addressed to Prussia and Austria which had remained totally unaffected by the aftermath of the July Revolution. But nevertheless even in the south German states demands for greater parliamentary power increased.

In *Bavaria* the elections of December 1830 produced large gains for the Liberals, causing student demonstrations which were devoid of any concrete aim. The Bavarian Minister of the Interior, Eduard von Schenck, tightened the reigns of press censorship, which led to his being formally indicted by the Diet for violating the constitution. While a resolution with this aim was defeated, the Diet considered the complaints about the restriction of the freedom of the press as justified. Ludwig I responded by dismissing his minister. A more moderate law concerning press censorship was introduced and passed. Schenck's dismissal was a precedent which could have had serious repercussions not only in Bavaria but throughout many parts of Germany. But its inherent significance and potential were completely overlooked by his contemporaries.

As has already been mentioned the bureaucracy, when one of its liberal members was elected, could prevent him from taking his seat by refusing leave of absence. This was the case with Freiherr von Closen who on his election laid down his office. The Bavarian bureaucracy endeavoured to prevent this, arguing that at the time of the election he had been a civil servant. The Bavarian Diet overruled the bureaucracy and Closen took his seat, thus establishing its right to supervise and check elections.

Ludwig I was renowned as a patron of the arts and it was due to him and his architecture that Munich became Germany's 'Athens of the North'. His contemporary parliamentarians did not see it in quite the same light since his buildings cost huge sums of money. Therefore the Diet cut the civil list of the King and refused funds for the *Pinakothek* which had just begun to be built. But it was the military budget which was most severely cut. This implied an inroad into the King's pre-rogative as supreme commander of the army, especially since the Diet wanted the army to swear loyalty to the constitution. Fortunately for the King, when it came to the actual vote, the Conservatives won and a constitutional conflict was avoided. But this led Ludwig to abandon the liberal course he had pursued so far. The Diet was dismissed and a new Conservative ministry appointed.

In *Württemberg* parliament was not in session when the tremors of the July Revolution reached Germany. Its members demanded that it be called but King Wilhelm I refused and the government increased its watchfulness on the press, political associations and public assemblies. Elections were not held until December 1831, and brought victory to the Liberals. But in spite of that Wilhelm insisted that the first legal assembly could not take place until 1833. When it did so on 15 January 1833, of the 93 members of the Second Chamber there were only 32 government supporters. One of the leaders of the opposition, Paul Pfizer, was also the advocate of German unity under Prussian leader-ship, though the time for the policies he advocated was ill-chosen and premature.

Baden was more affected by the July Revolution than most German states. In March 1830 Grand Duke Ludwig died and was succeeded by Grand Duke Leopold of the House of Hochberg. He instituted a basically liberal government and liberal policies were gaining ground throughout the land. Surprisingly enough, the Catholic clergy were especially the spokesmen of the liberal cause. When the Second Chamber met in March 1831 it was dominated by Liberals of various shades, among them a large number of civil servants. In contrast to Bavaria the Baden bureaucracy put no obstacles in their way. The Second Chamber achieved a number of significant victories, among them the revocation of the reactionary constitutional changes intro-duced in 1825 by Grand Duke Ludwig and the passing of liberal press censorship legislation. But one of the deputies went a step too far, demanding a constitutional guarantee of the freedom of the press. This implied legislative initiative by a Diet which no Diet as yet possessed. Moreover, the Carlsbad Decrees prohibited the freedom of the press. The government applied delaying tactics, which led the Diet to try to use the budget to put it under pressure. Constitutionally speaking, the Diet was misusing its powers. But the government was still willing to compromise and submitted a law lifting censorship except in matters concerning affairs of the German Confederation and those of other German states. The Diet accepted it, with the result that Baden was soon flooded by radical democratic publications. The Bundestag intervened, and on 5 July 1832 demanded that the law be suspended. As the law of the German Confederation superseded the law of the individual member states, the new law had to be revoked.

Hesse-Darmstadt, like Baden, was affected by a change of ruler. Grand Duke Ludwig II came to the throne in 1830. Both he and his father had contracted considerable debts and therefore Ludwig demanded either an increase in his civil list or that the state should assume his debts. The Diet rejected both suggestions which left Ludwig with the option of cutting his own expenditure, but he was clever enough to divert public attention by blaming the effects of the *Zollverein* for decreasing ducal support for the arts and architecture. Mobs destroyed Prussian customs houses and the popular movement thus called into being soon formed revolutionary centres which represented a potential danger to the state.

In *Nassau* Duke Wilhelm had created the first German Constitution in 1814. To secure a maximum income for himself, he maximized the output of the ducal domains including those which previously had not been his personal property. He further increased his income by the emancipation of the peasantry who had to pay horrendous sums in compensation for ending their feudal services. The Diet objected, but since the Duke was unwilling to come to an agreement, almost all members resigned their seats. Only five government supporters remained and these voted through the budget of 1833.

In *Brunswick* Duke Charles had succeeded to the throne in 1815 as a minor, the guardianship and regency being exercised by Duke Friedrich Wilhelm of Hanover, the Prince Regent who as George IV succeeded to the throne of Great Britain in 1820. Friedrich Wilhelm handed the reins of government to Count Münster. A constitution and representative assembly had been introduced on 25 April 1820 in which the free peasants were represented by twenty members. Duke Charles should have come of age on his eighteenth birthday but George IV extended his guardianship and regency by one year, and Charles did not succeed to the throne until 1823. Annoyed with George IV and his Brunswick government he refused to swear the constitutional oath and in 1827 carried out a *coup d'état* by declaring null and void all legislation passed during his minority. The result was a violation of the existing laws and a conflict with George IV and the Brunswick government. Austria and Prussia tried in vain to mediate with Charles, who challenged Count Münster to a duel which Münster refused. Mediation continued to fail in face of Charles's intransigence, but faced by the threat of action by the armed forces of the German Confederation in 1830, he gave in and withdrew the patent of 1827. But he was also in conflict with his own subjects who formed a consolidated opposition which gained momentum after the July Revolution. The estates demanded to be called together, Charles refused, and on 6 September 1830 the populace stormed his residence. This compelled Charles to call the Diet's 'Great Committee'. Once assembled it decided to remain in session until the Diet was called, to send plenipotentiaries to Berlin and Hanover and to ask Duke Wilhelm, Charles's brother to take over the government. All this was of doubtful legality but Duke Wilhelm took over the government with Prussian support. Charles was at best prepared to accept his brother as governor-general for life, but he also made further exorbitant demands. Wilhelm refused them and in effect overthrew his brother, and the army swore loyalty to him. So Brunswick was the only German land in which the reigning prince was expelled and replaced by another as a result of a popular mass movement.

The Bundestag in Frankfurt had tried to prevent this development but Charles had refused all the suggestions offered him as a way out of his self-made predicament. The question that remained unsolved was which of the two Brunswick princes possessed the right of succession. The Bundestag could not make up its mind, which meant that neither of the two brothers, both still bachelors, could find a suitable wife, and this led to the extinction of the Brunswick line of the Guelphs. But stability returned to Brunswick under Duke Wilhelm and he transformed it from a feudal into a constitutional state.

Kur-Hesse under Napoleon had been part of the kingdom of Westphalia. It was restored to its original state in 1813. But the constitutional question resulted in a struggle between Elector Wilhelm I and his subjects. His successor Wilhelm II began a course of reform. He gave the country a modern administrative structure, but Kur-Hesse's joining the Central German Commercial Association was extremely disadvantageous to its economy. In addition, the population was over-taxed and consequently plenty of explosive material had accumulated by 1830. Events in Brunswick had their repercussions in Kur-Hesse and Wilhelm II reluctantly called for the Diet to assemble. Meanwhile the populace took to the streets, forming burgher militias. They were joined by the peasants who stormed the residences of their landlords and burnt the records which listed their feudal dues. The government tried to restore order by proclaiming a general amnesty.

In contrast to the situation in Brunswick, it had not only been the bourgeoisie which had led popular dissatisfaction but also the lower orders of society who pursued their own social and economic aims. The Bundestag in Frankfurt immediately recognized the inherent danger in this development and requested the states bordering Kur-Hesse to assemble troops to intervene if necessary and suppress any uprising.

Grand Duke Ludwig II of Hesse-Darmstadt proclaimed a state of siege for his territory. But Wilhelm II managed to convince the Bundestag that order had been restored and that all concessions had been revoked.

In the meantime the Diet had been assembled and on 5 January 1831 a constitution was accepted which contained major concessions by Wilhelm II. But this was not the end. Wilhelm II had entered into a liaison with a Countess Reichenbach who because of her extravagance and influence on him was requested to leave. To avoid popular pressure Wilhelm left Kassel for Hanau. A delegation of the Diet gave him the choice of parting company with the Countess or resigning his office. He chose the latter and a Co-Regent, the electoral prince Friedrich Wilhelm, stepped in his place until such time as he was prepared to return to Kassel. As Wilhelm failed to do so the full power of government was transferred to Friedrich Wilhelm.

In 1831 he introduced a constitution which has been described as the most radical in the whole of the German Confederation. This introduced a one-chamber system in which princes of the ducal house, heads of mediatized families, knights and sixteen deputies from each of the cities and rural districts were included. Eight of the deputies had to have property qualifications, the other eight not. Both prince and members of the Diet had to swear an oath to the constitution, and had the right to initiate legislation. Taxes could only be levied with the agreement of the Diet, which also enjoyed control of the budget. A whole catalogue of basic laws guaranteed freedom of religion, person, property and so on. The judiciary and administration were separated. Conscription was introduced and the bureaucracy as well as the army were sworn in on the constitution.

Perhaps the constitution was too liberal for its time because during the three decades in which it was in operation (until Kur-Hesse ceased to exist) there were continual constitutional conflicts.

Saxony was the one country in Germany which had the largest gap between its social and political structure. It was already being industrialized and the Leipzig Fair was an established institution. In contrast to most other German states it had no popular representative assembly, only an assembly of the estates of the kingdom made up of nobility, clergy, knightly estate owners and the cities. Even before the July Revolution public protest manifested itself on religious issues since the dynasty was Catholic whereas the mass of the population was Protestant. Also in the Chemnitz area workers protested against exploitation by factory owners. The call for the abdication of King Anton was beginning to be heard when the moderate constitutional forces silenced the radicals and channelled discontent in a constitutional direction. On 4 September 1831 a constitution was introduced which in its main features was little different from those existing elsewhere in Germany.

Hanover until 1830 was governed by Friedrich Wilhelm, George IV of Great Britain. As in Saxony the old feudal constitution remained in force at first. But the Governor-General, the Duke of Cambridge, introduced a constitution by way of royal patent of 7 December 1819 which was a compromise between the old assembly of the estates and a representative assembly. The First Chamber combined nobility, pre-lates and knights, the Second Chamber the representatives of the cities. The franchise was exercised not by the burghers but by the magistrates. Free peasants were also to be represented but it took more than a decade before they were admitted.

Little wonder therefore that the disturbances of 1830 originated with the peasants, followed by the townspeople, who resented being ex-cluded from exercising the franchise in their own right. Hopes were raised by King Wilhelm IV who came to the throne shortly before the July Revolution, but public unrest continued, culminating in a rising of students in Göttingen. The students had appeared on the public stage for the first time since the dissolution of the *Burschenschaften* in 1819. The Duke of Cambridge, who had become Viceroy, advocated a more liberal regime and a constitution emerged representing a conservative-liberal compromise, with the conservative elements clearly predominating. The competence of the two-chamber representative assembly was severely limited and the royal prerogative extended. Parliamentary censure was not allowed. After the death of Wilhelm IV in 1837 he was succeeded by his brother Ernest Augustus, Duke of Cumberland. Thus the personal union between the Crowns of Great Britain and Hanover was dissolved because the Salic law of succession did not allow a female ruler to take the throne. Ernest Augustus was an arch conservative, who had made his name as a Tory in the House of Lords in the struggle against the Whigs. His first action in Hanover was to prorogue the Diet, and on 1 November 1837 he revoked the constitution of 1833. This meant of course that the constitutional oath taken by civil servants was no longer valid. Seven professors of the University of Göttingen, Wilhelm Eduard Albrecht, Friedrich Christoph, Dahlmann, Georg Gottfried Gervinus, Jacob Grimm, Wilhelm Grimm, Georg Heinrich Ewald and Wilhelm Weber protested publicly against this unconstitutional act. They were dis-missed from their posts, but soon found places in other German universities. The whole of Germany from Bavaria to Prussia took the side of the 'Göttingen Seven'.

Inevitably the Bundestag in Frankfurt was involved. Hanoverian deputies appealed to it about the violation of the constitution. Bavaria, Württemberg and Baden demanded an examination of whether Hanover had violated the *Wiener Schlussakte*. A long tug-of-war ensued which was not concluded until Ernest Augustus introduced a new constitution on 6 August 1840. The opposition of the Hanoverians in general and of the 'Göttingen Seven' in particular had not been in vain.

Luxemburg was most immediately affected by the July Revolution. It had neither a constitution nor its own administration. It was a fortress of the Confederation garrisoned by Prussian and Dutch forces. The revolution in Belgium brought about the secession of the Walloons from the Dutch and extended to the Walloons in Luxemburg. A provisional government in Brussels declared Luxemburg an integral part of Belgium and called upon its citizens to abandon the Grand Duke. The Dutch envoy at the Bundestag asked for the represssion of revolution by German forces. The Bundestag was at a loss about what to do and this gave the new regime in Belgium time to consolidate itself. Austria, Prussia, France, Great Britain and the Netherlands had declared that none of the five powers would view intervention by the German Confederation in Luxemburg as foreign interference. But the Belgians promised support to the Luxemburg Walloons in case of German intervention, a direct challenge to the German Confederation which now mobilized an intervention corps. But it never came into action. At the London Conference in August 1831 Luxemburg was divided, the Walloon parts coming to Belgium while the eastern part, including the fortress of Luxemburg, remained part of the German Confederation. The arrangement was subject to the settlement of issues between Belgium and the Netherlands which were not completed until 1839. Finally on 19 April 1839 the division of Luxemburg came formally into force.

All in all events since 1830 had shown that inside the German Confederation political activism was rising and reaching levels of radicalism hitherto unprecedented. It was by no means a unified movement but one of groups and groupings which represented a virtual political sub-culture. The intellectual centre of radicalism was 'Young Germany', made up of writers like Börne, Heine, Büchner etc., committed to republicanism and operating in the main from outside Germany, particularly from Paris. It was not identical with 'Young Europe' led by Mazzini, but members of one were often members of the other, for example Dr Ernst Johann Hermann von Rauschenplatt, a former university professor, and Dr Philip Siebenpfeiffer, the son of a tailor, who had studied law.

The first national democratic manifestation since the Wartburg festival was the Hambach Festival of 27 May 1832. Since the Carlsbad Decrees had made political assemblies subject to police permission and supervision, this was circumvented by declaring the event a festival. Behind the Hambach Festival was the German Press and Fatherland Association in the Palatinate with Siebenpfeiffer as one of the main leaders. This association was one of the prototypes of German political parties. Its aim was the restoration of German national unity under a democratic and republican constitution. The association spread from the Palatinate into Hesse, Nassau and Frankfurt. In Bavaria its danger was recognized and it was forbidden. It carried on in secret with the motto 'Against legitimacy, for the sovereignty of the people'. Up to 30,000 people from all over Germany attended the Hambach Festival, following their colours of black, red and gold. A good many speeches were made in favour of a united Germany but most of them avoided the question of how this was to be achieved. Only the liberal radical Dr Daniel Ludwig Pistor called for force and revolution. A committee was elected which renamed the Press and Fatherland Association the German Reform Association.

The Hambach Festival was a godsend for the reactionary forces in the Bundestag to carry out repressive measures against the national democratic movement. Metternich put pressure on Bavaria to prevent any recurrence and appealed in much the same vein to Prussia. The member states quickly followed his initiative. A state of siege was proclaimed for the Rhineland and Palatinate but this could not prevent local disturbances. These measures had already been preceded in 1830 by a sharpening of the Carlsbad Decrees, hitting mainly the press and the universities. After the Hambach Festival measures were introduced which reduced the rights of petition of parliaments as well as curtailing their rights in budget approval. In addition a Watch Commission, was established to keep an eye on politcal activities in all the member states. As already mentioned, foreign powers intervened as well, notably Great Britain.

The situtation deteriorated further when the *Burschenschaft* of Heidelberg University tried to carry out a revolution in Frankfurt against the Bundestag. It was very much a dilettante affair, and had consequences out of all proprtion to the action taken. The Confederation intervened with military force. Another consequence was the formation of a Central Office of Political Investigation which was to investigate 'conspiracy directed against the public order in Germany'. By 1842 more than 2,000 suspects had been arrested. By that time the Central Office had been dissolved. The actual judicial prosecution and trial were matters for member states, and although there were numerous acquittals, there were also many prison sentences.

In January 1834 the Closed Council met in Vienna, but Metternich did not have an easy time, as numerous German states, such as Bavaria and Württemberg, counselled moderation. A secret protocol containing sixty articles was adopted, a measure which really violated the Constitution of the German Confederation. The articles were designed to whittle down the powers of representative assemblies and the ultimate arbiter was a new Court of Arbitration. On the whole the effect of the protocol was minimal.

Chapter 3

EIGHTEEN FORTY EIGHT

The three decades following the Congress of Vienna were a period in which, unperceived by many, deep changes took place in Germany's intellectual climate, in her political structure and her social and economic conditions. Things were in a state of transition, social *classes* were in the process of development, and the demands of the emerging middle class could no longer be ignored. Feudal relics remained and seemed firmly entrenched, but at the same time a working-class consciousness began to emerge. The peasantry still existed as a separate stratum in society: its value system had as yet not been urbanized. But generally speaking the demand for personal autonomy was being articulated, especially in such sectors as the economy and the creative arts. To this was added the demand for a *laissez-faire* economy, and with growing industrialization and commercialization a new upper social class with a belief in free competition began to emerge. Finally, public opinion, even if only 'printed opinion', introduced to the general public issues for debate.

This nascent middle class had as yet neither obtained its fully defined sociological shape nor full political equality and participation in the decision-making process. This was especially the case in countries without a constitution such as Prussia and Austria. The latent tensions created by this development demanded to be resolved, yet in the decade before 1848 the situation was aggravated by the blocking of constitutional advance for fear of precipitating revolution. Metternich's belief in the *status quo* had been elevated to the constituent principle of the European order, regardless of the fact that instead of containing or reducing the pressures it increased them until the dam burst. At the same time, although hardly noticed by contemporaries, the five-party system came into being which in essence continued until 1933, namely Conservatism, moderate Liberalism, democratic Radicalism, political Catholicism and revolutionary Socialism.

The German monarchies tried to block the evolution of political parties for the sake of the principle of 'monarchical legitimacy': they would only create unnecessary divisions and disunite the country. Like the Founding Fathers of the American Constitution they found no word more abhorrent than 'party'. Wherever parties appeared they were proscribed and driven into the political underground.

Most present-day discussions about German political thought in general, and constitutional thought in particular, proceed from a 'liberal' or Anglo-Saxon theory of the state and contrast it with the German idealistic tradition cast in the Hegelian mould. One may wonder what purpose such comparisons serve, whether in fact they help our understanding of modern Germany history at all. The differences they reveal seem all too inevitably the root of the evils that led to the destruction of Germany and large parts of Europe in our own time; but they ignore the profoundly different objective conditions that favoured the growth of democracy in the British Isles and the USA. One such simple factor, regularly ignored, is that of geography. Alexander Hamilton once remarked that the amount of internal liberty in a state was closely related to the amount of pressure, or the lack of it, from without. Great Britain's island position, and even more so the position of the United States, favoured the healthy growth of democracy much more than was the case in the heartland of Europe, once a mighty empire until it was fragmented and dismembered. Such comparisons also ignore the different historical traditions and experiences which in the one case led to consolidation, stability, strength and democracy, in the other to discord, fragmentation and weakness which for two centuries turned Germany into the battleground of Europe. That under such circumstances the German idea of freedom would be different from that of other more favourably located nations was inevitable. Kant defined liberty as the privilege and ability to dedicate oneself to the fulfilment of duty — the practical application of his categorical imperative. Under the impact of Napoleonic oppression Fichte had carried Kant's idealism one stage further in arguing that the state represented the focal point of the national community, towards which the attention of each individual component should be directed. Subsequent representatives of German political and constitutional thought worked from the objective unchangeable premises they discerned about them, from the real world, not from a daydream of the world they would have wished for. No doubt, in specific political and economic areas, Great Britain exercised a deep influence upon German thinking, particularly within the Prussian Reform Movement. But this influence was adapted to specific needs; it could not change the objective conditions, and Germany's neighbour to the west, France, throughout the nineteenth century hardly offered an example worthy of emulation. But these objective conditions alone ensured that, to mention just one label, 'Liberalism' meant different things in Great Britain and in Germany, in spite of the fact that J. S. Mill's *On Liberty* borrowed heavily from Humboldt's *Treatise on the Limits of the Effectiveness of the State.*

With this in mind we should now turn to the growth of the political parties.

THE FORMATION OF POLITICAL PARTIES

The oldest of the five-party constellation was *Conservatism*, with traditions reaching back to Burke and his *Reflections on the Revolution in France*. In Germany their most articulate voice was Adam Müller's, who viewed the state as an organic growth in which everything and everybody had its own natural place. Hegel's concept of the state could be used to support these conditions. But Conservatism was far from a uniform group, in Prussia as well as in the rest of Germany. In Prussia it was supported by Crown Prince Friedrich Wilhelm (later Friedrich Wilhelm IV), but even within his circle there were groups at odds with one another. The basis of Conservatism was the rejection of rationalism as the *sole* political principle or its application to theology. In this it not only opposed liberal and democratic ideas but also the principles of enlightened absolutism, and Hegel's philosophy. Conservatism was characterized by a traditionalism which believed that what had been formed and shaped since time immemorial was worth preserving, come what may. This in itself was a source of division among Conservatives, between those who wished to preserve everything and those who wished to preserve only that which had withstood the test of time, and who therefore were open to ideas of reform. The 'monarchic principle' and its preservation was one label which Conservatives of all shades shared. On practical political issues, such as the future of Germany, opinions were again divided. Those Conservatives who deserve to be called reactionaries because of their extremism defended particularist principles to the last: they recognized the historically-justified predominance of Austria within Germany. Yet there were Conservatives who supported Prussian hegemony and thus came close to the position adopted by the Liberals. For reactionary Conservatives the national state was suspect, since it involved the nation or, more crudely, the mob. The most prominent among them in Prussia were three brothers, Leopold, Ludwig and Otto von Gerlach, the philosopher Friedrich Julins Stahl and the historian Heinrich Leo. Stahl for instance argued that both state and law were of divine origin, as was the monarchy. His Christian-Conservative teachings really became the bedrock of one branch of Prussian conservative thought. Even the young Bismarck was associated with this group for a time. The moderate Conservatives had what we would now call a 'social conscience'. Property involved responsibility towards those who lacked it. Lorenz von Stein for instance was one of the first advocates of the transformation of the monarchic state into the social state. He argued that it was the state's function to examine and improve social conditions, a current of thought in which the principle of 'reform from above' was inherent. It was in itself nothing new since it was a policy practised actively by the Prussian state from 1712 to 1815 but allowed to lapse temporarily under the impact of the ideas of *laissez-faire*. This group enjoyed close affinity with the National Conservatives who supported national representation and the creation of a federally structured and united Germany. The most prominent of them was the historian Leopold von Ranke, and politically the most effective was Joseph Maria von Radowitz, the confidant and adviser of the Prussian Crown Prince. There was still another group difficult to define which supported national unity, but unity under military autocratic auspices, a group which for a time exercised considerable influence on Otto von Manteuffel who was Prussia's Prime Minister between 1850 and 1858.

Nearly as old as Conservatism was the political *Catholicism* which profited considerably from the wave of religious revivalism that swept Germany in the wake of the French Revolution. Since political parties were proscribed, political Catholicism organized itself in Germany in the form of various associations for welfare and other purposes. Members formed their own parliamentary groups a 'Catholic Party' was spoken of informally when Catholics throughout Germany protested against Prussian policy in the Cologne affair (see above p. 9). Joseph von Görres was their most articulate publicist. The demands of the Catholics included full autonomy for the Church within each state and the right to represent their opinions publicly especially on issues such as mixed marriages which they opposed as strongly as the new demand for civil marriage and divorce. Politically they tended towards a 'Greater Germany' under the auspices of the Hapsburg Empire. The most active of their groups were the Görres Circle and the Catholic Conservatives in Prussia under Prince Felix Lichnowsky. There was also a liberal wing, liberal in the sense that its representatives supported constitutional and representative institutions as well as free trade. Its motto was 'Everything for the people through the people'. The most outstanding representative of this group was Max von Gagern, a convert from Protestantism. But Catholicism also had its social wing supporting the idea of the social state, its members being fervent advocates of the abolition of child and female labour, a maximum working day of fourteen hours, support for artisans against exploitation by industry, and support for agriculture. Wilhelm von Ketteler was one of their most prominent leaders.

The German *Liberals* had come under both French and Anglo-Saxon influences. They viewed the state as a community but at the same time not as a society. Therefore the question of the relationship between individual and community was always foremost in their discussion. In contrast to Liberalism outside Germany, German Liberals like F.C. Dahlmann continued to develop further the idea of the organic state, originally a monopoly of the Conservatives. They abhorred the contractual theory of the state but considered it as an autonomous entity. Only within the state could the individual fully realize and maximize his inherent potential. Neither monarch nor people was sovereign but only the state, a sovereignty institutionalized within a constitutional order. Every nation needed its state – nations without states were considered unhistorical. They were therefore the most fervent propagandists for a Germany unitary state. Originally 'greater German', by necessity they become supporters of the 'little German' solution. It was the recognition of *Realpolitik*, a term coined by the Liberal August Ludwig von Rochau. In essence Liberals in Germany as elsewhere were anti-democratic since they feared nothing more than the *demos*.

The constitutional Liberal Group had its power base in northern Germany but also enjoyed considerable support in the Rhineland, the Hessian states and Baden. They were fervent supporters of the constitutional monarchy and the separation of power. Intellectuals, particularly university professors, were strongly represented in it, men like the Grimm brothers, Arndt and other members of the 'Göttingen Seven'. Hegelians, like David Friedrich Strauss, also found their home in this group.

The Parliamentary-Liberal Group stood to the left of them, aiming at full parliamentarization of the German state and states. They were monarchists but not supporters of monarchic legitimacy. They were deeply divided over the question of franchise, one part opting for universal and equal franchise, the others supporting a class franchise.

German political *Radicalism* had no firm base: its members could be found among the political Catholics as well as among the Liberals. Those who were democrats could be found on the left wing of the Liberals, while the proponents of socialist and communist ideas could be found in German revolutionary Socialism. They espoused the principle that all power derives from the people and therefore fully supported the absolute equality of universal male franchise. They could trace their ancestry back to Rousseau as well as to Jahn or to the radical who was most probably behind the assassination of Kotzebue, Karl Follen, the leader of the German Radicals in the second decade of the century. They were found among the *Burschenschaften* and in 'Young Germany'. Forced to operate largely from abroad, many were exiles in Zürich and Paris. Men like Siebenpfeiffer made way for the writer Robert Blum in Saxony and the lawyers Gustav von Struve and Friedrich von Hecker in Baden. Most Radicals came from the educated bourgeoisie and directed their egalitarian theories against this sector of their society.

Their political position was marked by an either–or attitude; either monarchic sovereignty or sovereignty of the people. They denied the existence of any other possibility. Germany was to be a centralized unitary republic, run by a government elected by parliament on the basis of equal and universal male franchise.

Since there was little chance that their ideas could be realized in their lifetime it comes as no surprise that poets and writers formed a disproportionately large part of their leadership; Hoffmann von Fallersleben, the author of 'Deutschland, Deutschland über alles', Ferdinand von Freiligrath and Georg Herwegh were but a few of many. In group terms they were divided into a moderate Left and an extreme Left, the difference between them being a matter of degree rather than principle.

Revolutionary Socialism was the product of Germany's industrialization. By 1848 large parts of Germany were still agrarian but for decades the process of industrialization had been under way in Silesia, Saxony, the Rhineland and Westphalia. Berlin had already become the largest centre of manufacturing industry in Germany. The social consequences were immense since this transformation brought with it the creation and steady rise of an urban industrial proletariat, recruited from what had once been the peasantry; smallholders whose produce was no longer sufficient to guarantee them even a subsistence existence; journeymen who found too many of them were in their respective trades ever to succeed in becoming full masters; day-wage labourers; and even small traders. Values had changed: the agrarian feudal land system had still acknowledged the estate owner's responsibility for his peasants, even in hard times, a responsibility abandoned with the acceptance of the principles of Adam Smith. Free trade and free competition were the maxim now, to produce and buy cheaply and sell at the highest possible prices were the new watchwords. To keep down wages was one of the best ways to compete not only in the German market but also in the international one. One of the results of the reforms of Stein and Hardenberg was a major demographic movement, a drift of population from the countryside to the industrial cities. The city promised peasants an easier life, more chance of success and much better opportunities all round. They had been accustomed to women working and to drawing children into the labour process at the earliest age. Much the same applied in the manufacturing industries. For the industrialist the harder the competition and the greater the need for capital to reinvest in further industrial expansion, the greater the temptation to cut his wage-bill by reducing wages.

Besides the economic incentive for moving from country to town, towns and cities provided far more opportunities than the rural countryside: opportunities for those who spotted and took them of quick upwards social mobility. There were better means of communication, and better facilities for further education. A rising birth-rate ensured that the reservoir of available workers was never exhausted. But side by side with these new opportunities there were also greater risks. Times of boom alternated with times of depression. The once stable rural community was replaced by the atomization of human relationships in urban centres. A process of social decomposition set in which, in the view of early socialist thinkers like Fourier, would inevitably lead to social revolution. Robert Owen in Great Britain preached, and to a more limited extent also practised, his gospel of practical social reform and Utopian communism. In France Pierre Proudhon popularized the slogan that 'property is theft'.

In Germany Lorenz von Stein advocated reform through a monarchy aware of social problems and capable of dealing with them. Johann Karl Rodbertus, a Pomeranian estate owner and later a Minister of Culture in Prussia, advocated the neutralization of social and economic conflict by state institutions. The threat of revolution should be defused by revolution from above, but this did not imply that the forces of bourgeois democracy were prepared to extend the same political rights to the working classes. It is significant that in the parliaments of 1848–49 in Frankfurt, Berlin and Vienna, not a single working-class representative was included. The only hearing given them was at the 'Democrats' Congresses' in 1848, but this merely divided the working class into bourgeois-Democrats and socialist Democrats. The former were deeply suspicious of the latter, who demanded social democracy which implied rule by the unpropertied class – a Utopian demand when two thirds of Germany was still agricultural land. Considerable impetus came from German émigré groups in Switzerland and France. But even these were far from being of one mind. The *Bund der Geächteten*, the League of the outlaws, split and led to the formation of the new *Bund der Gerechten*, the League of the Just, led among others by Karl Schapper, a former student who after 1839 and a stay in London was a member of the Communist movement. Within a decade he had given up his internationalism and returned to the nationalist fold, becoming a pronounced opponent of Marx. Another early émigré revolutionary was Wilhelm Weitling, a former tailor journeyman who broke with Marx at an early stage. He was by far the most important and significant early German Socialist: even before Marx he was postulating the inevitability of class conflict and therefore demanding social revolution – only such a revolution would produce a perfect society.

But it was Marx, the former student of Hegel's work, and Friedrich Engels, a German who owned extensive manufacturing industries in Britain, who gave the *Bund der Kommunisten*, the League of Communists, a real impetus with a social, economic and political theory of revolution, the first scientific basis Socialism possessed.

In 1846 Marx and Engels founded the *Kommunistische*

Korrespondez-Komitee, the Communist Correspondence Committee in Brussels. A year later, in June 1847, the first Communist Congress took place in London under Engels. The slogan 'Proletarians of the World unite!' was adopted and in October of the same year Engels was entrusted with drafting the programme of the Communist movement. The result was the Communist Manifesto beginning with the sentence that the history of human society has been the history of class struggle, an assertion which Engels himself later considered untenable. History was nothing other than the dialectical process of the struggle between the bourgeoisie and the proletariat. But the Communist Manifesto went further than that: it provided the tactical programme for the proletariat during the revolution of 1848. This revolution was to bring about first the bourgeois revolution and a bourgeois society. The working class was not to take the offensive, but in the first instance to support the bourgeois revolution. Only in the course of a second revolution, this time conducted by the proletariat, could proletarian rule be established. At this stage both Marx and Engels and other revolutionary Socialists were ahead of their time, because on the whole the German workers' political movement was still relatively deeply entrenched within the current of the German national unity movement. Nor did in 1848 a specific working-class *class consciousness exist any more than did that of a middle class.*

THE GERMAN STATES ON THE EVE OF 1848

Meanwhile, after the constitutionally stormy early 1830s, calm seemed to have returned to the states of the German Confederation, largely because of the re-establishment of autocracy. Debates in *Bavaria* were preoccupied with the arguments between the Liberals and the clergy. From the early 1830s the Catholic church had been recapturing the position which it had lost under Montgelas. Though not in principle a supporter of the clergy, after the unrest of 1830 Ludwig I looked at the Church as a pillar of support against the forces of revolution. The Church, that is to say its supporters in parliament, backed demands for further cash grants to the King for his architectural pursuits. In return Bavaria's public life was increasingly clericalized, as exemplified by the 'kneeling - decree' which compelled all Bavarian soldiers including Protestants not only to attend Catholic church parades but also to kneel before the sacrament. It was the work of the arch-conservative Minister of the Interior Karl von Abel, and it aroused widespread public debate and dissent, so much so that in 1845 Ludwig I had to annul it.

The Constitution was the subject of the debate between the Conservatives, who wanted to transform parliament into an assembly of the estates, and the Liberals, who successfully opposed any such step. But by 1847 Ludwig I fell out with his Conservative minister over the King's private life. Lola Montez, the dancer, had managed to gain the heart of the philandering King and extended her personal influence into politics. The clergy demurred, but not openly until the King decided to make her a Countess. The precondition for this was Bavarian citizenship which required the counter-signature of the minister of the interior. Abel, supported by other ministers, opposed this step and was summarily dismissed. In other words the government fell because it found itself unable to sanction the King's act. Abel's successor, the Protestant Georg Ludwig von Maurer, was prepared to provide his counter-signature and Lola Montez received the title Countess Landsfeld. It caused a public scandal, directed against the King and his new Countess and, when Joseph von Görres died on 29 January 1848, the occasion was used by Munich students for public riots which forced Lola Montez to flee the city. By the time the March revolution of 1848 broke out, Bavaria was in the middle of a constitutional crisis.

Calm had also returned to *Württemberg*, but until 1848 government was carried out by the Secret Council of King Wilhelm I and not by the responsible ministries. Because of the King's reactionary attitude many Liberal members in the Diet would not take their seats. After the election of 1844 many of them returned, aware that political abstinence would hardly further their cause. The government tried to some extent to meet the Liberals by partially lifting press censorship, but Metternich overruled them. By 1847 Württemberg was in the throes of an economic crisis which temporarily pushed political differences into the background. Genuine starvation led to public demonstrations that the King had to use the army against them. Württemberg, like Bavaria, was in a state of crisis in early 1848.

In *Baden* reactionary and liberal forces were finely balanced in the government until 1839 when the reactionary Foreign Minister Friedrich Karl von Bittersdorf began to dominate. To counter the opposition he invoked the prohibition of leave of absence for two parliamentarians coming from the civil service and produced a fully-fledged parliamentary row which destroyed his ministry. New elections in 1842 brought the Liberals an absolute majority in the Second Chamber. There was evidence that the government had tried to tamper with the election results and this produced an overwhelming vote of condemnation by the Second Chamber, the first such vote to be recorded against a German government. For most of the time following this, however, parliament was more preoccupied with religious issues arising out of controversies between Catholics and Protestants and less with constitutional affairs.

Hesse-Darmstadt, the territorial bridge between southern and northern Germany, also pursued a very conservative course, strengthened by the marriage of Princess Maria to the Russian Crown Prince, the future Czar Alexander II, in 1841. In 1830 Prince Emil had suppressed public risings with the help of the army, and since then there had been an air of disquiet. The government under Karl du Thil, leading minister since 1829, had on the one hand suppressed any sign of a popular rising, but on the other been prepared to make concessions to those convicted for 'Demagogerie' by reducing their sentences or giving them an amnesty. Du Thil managed to have his men strongly represented in both chambers, though many of them, such as Hans von Gagern and Prince Karl von Leiningen were supporters of the German unity movement. The government's policy towards the opposition was very similar to that in Baden and as in Baden religious questions reared their head with the emergence of an ultramontane party. New life was brought into the Second Chamber by the election to it of Heinrich von Gagern, another supporter of German unification in 1846. It appeared contradictory when he strongly opposed the introduction of a new and unified legal code, but this in effect meant the abolition of the *Code Napoléon* in the Hessian provinces on the left bank of the Rhine, and what Heinrich von Gagern was defending were the existing civil liberties, civil marriage, etc., which he felt were threatened by a potential police state. He quickly emerged as the head of the liberal opposition which was in continuous opposition to the government until the spring of 1848.

Throughout southern Germany, therefore, a liberal parliamentary opposition existed, but it was divided between the moderates and the radicals. The more the moderates consolidated their position, the deeper the rift became with the radicals. Both of them, the moderates under Heinrich von Gagern, the radicals under Siebenpfeiffer, had their own newspapers and pamphlet literature. The first large public assembly was held by the radicals at Offenburg on 12 September 1847. Though the aim of many of them was the establishment of a German Republic, they kept quiet on this subject because of the police authorities, and demanded instead the abolition of the Carlsbad and subsequent decrees, the introduction of freedom of the press, assembly and association, a German parliament elected on the basis of an equal franchise, the introduction of a progressive income tax, equal opportunity of entry to the institutions of higher learning, trial by jury, and the replacement of bureaucratic administration by self-government.

These demands challenged the moderates to formulate their own programme at the Heppenheim Rally on 10 October 1847. Men like Friedrich Bassermann and Karl Mathy came from Baden, David Hansemann from the Prussian Rhineland and Friedrich Römer from Württemberg. Altogether they amounted to eighteen moderate Liberals. They came out in support of a German national government and national representation, and suggested that the German *Zollverein* should provide the basis for this with the inclusion of the German part of the Hapsburg Empire. The monarchical principle was adhered to. On the other hand the question of civil liberties was hardly touched upon, and social problems were only mentioned marginally.

In *Prussia* the unresolved question inherited by Friedrich Wilhelm IV from his father on acceding to the throne in 1840 was that of a Prussian Constitution. Time and again the demand was made for the promise of 22 May 1815 to be honoured. At first the King adopted a very negative stance. On 4 October 1840 he clearly stated that he did not intend to solve the problem in the spirit of the promise given in 1815. He did not wish that 'a piece of paper should intervene' between himself, King by divine right, and his people, 'like a kind of second providence, to govern us with its paragraphs'. To him a constitution was directly associated with the event he hated most, the French Revolution.

But neither could he ignore the opposition, which came primarily from Liberals in the civil service in East Prussia, like Theodor von Schön, one of his own most prominent civil servants and from representatives of the prosperous bourgeoisie in Prussia's western provinces, such as David Hansemann, Ludolf Camphausen and Gustav Mevissen. In Königsberg the general practitioner Johann Jacoby published in 1841 a pamphlet entitled 'Four Questions Answered by an East Prussian'. In it he demanded the participation of the people in affairs of state not as a favour but of right. Jacoby made contact with all the prominent representatives of the opposition. This was cause enough to institute criminal proceedings against him and he was sentenced to two and a half years' imprisonment, but he appealed and the Chamber Court acquitted him.

The press played a highly important part in Prussia, mainly due to Friedrich Wilhelm's relaxation of censorship. Pictures, cartoons, drawings and books were exempt from censorship, and a 'Censorship Court' was founded in 1842 as a protection against the arbitrary rulings of individual censors. But when immediately after this relaxation the King found himself confronted by a tidal wave of caricatures and satires he soon changed his mind and censorship, though in a less severe form, was reintroduced.

In the meantime the money supplied by the Rothschild loan had run out and the need to float public loans forced Friedrich Wilhelm IV to make concessions towards greater constitutionalization. At first, in 1841, he had thought he could circumvent the problem by supporting the greater development of the provincial Diets. These were to be advisory bodies meeting every two years to discuss affairs and to deliberate partly in public. They were also to create committees which were to meet while the provincial Diet was not in session. On 18 October 1842 these committees were called to Berlin as a 'United

Committee', a kind of substitute for a general parliament. But Friedrich Wilhelm still refused to go the whole way towards a parliamentary system. Membership of the provincial Diets as well as of their committees was to be based on a system of representation of the estates. Thus the United Committee was made up of a total of 98 members, consisting of 46 nobles, 32 burghers and 20 propertied peasants.

Finally the King could no longer resist financial pressure (funds were needed to build a railway from Berlin to Königsberg) and on 3 February 1847 he published a decree which set up a Prussian Diet, the United Diet, while still maintaining the United Committee as a permanent delegation responsible for the state debts. The United Diet was to meet as often as the state needed it, such as when new loans were required, or for the introduction of new taxes or the increase of existing taxation. The United Committee was, in the absence of the United Diet, to meet every four years. Both Diet and Committee had the right to agree or to refuse loans and taxation as well as participate in the legislative process, but only as much as the provincial Diet did already. This of course meant that as far as legislation was concerned their function was restricted to a purely advisory and consultative role. While the United Diet was to represent the three estates, the higher nobility, such as the princes, were to deliberate separately as a kind of Upper House, the *Herrenhaus*.

Friedrich Wilhelm's decree proved to be too little too late, but was better than nothing. On 11 April 1847 the United Diet was opened in the White Hall of the royal palace in Berlin. An important novelty in the gathering was that its proceedings could be fully reported by the press, something hitherto unknown in Prussia. But more importantly, the members of the Diet, under the protection of the law and irrespective of social standing, could and did speak out and criticize their King. The Diet included 237 members of the nobility, 182 representatives of the towns and 124 representatives of the propertied peasants, while the Upper House was made up of 70 princes and counts.

The King's opening address caused a *furor:* 'no power on earth will succeed in causing me to change for a constitutional one, the powerful relationship between the prince and the people, existing as it does because of its natural origin and by virtue of its inner truth'. The majority of the members of the Diet immediately demanded full constitutional rights.

THE OUTBREAK OF REVOLUTION

This is in essence the German background to the revolution of 1848, which spread from France in February 1848 and affected the south German states first of all. It seems a paradox that precisely those German states which had representative institutions, developed over the past three decades, should have been drawn into the maelstrom of revolution earlier than the non-constitutional states like Prussia or Austria. Metternich's prophecy, that partial concessions would inevitably lead to greater demands by the liberal and democratic forces and bring about a complete upheaval in the social and political balance of power inside Germany, seemed justified. In the earlier phase not only the bourgeoisie but groups of students, artisans and small entrepreneurs, workers and peasants came to the front. The social-revolutionary element was certainly there and the question arose whether the revolution of the masses could be held back or absorbed by the educated bourgeoisie. The risings which took place in March 1848 were completely uncoordinated (this was, indeed, one of the reasons for the failure of 1848 in general). In the Black Forest, in Thuringia, Nassau, and Franconia peasants rose, plundering noble estates, chasing civil servants from their seats of power, destroying machines, locomotives, railway lines. In Rhine-Hesse and Kur-Hesse particularly Jews were attacked, because the peasants to escape feudal dues had to borrow money at exorbitant interest rates to pay off their former feudal masters. In the university cities like Munich, Marburg and Göttingen student riots took place.

But this uncoordinated spontaneity soon lost its initial fervour as the moderates came to the fore, their programme already forming the nucleus of political parties. They did not want to revolutionize the state but merely change the form of government by revising the constitution. Only Baden maintained a revolutionary radical core for some time.

As we have already seen there was already plenty of unrest about. In *Bavaria* the moderates led by Prince Karl von Leiningen, the president of the First Chamber, signed a burgher address to the King containing eight points. Freedom of the press, a people's militia, the army to swear loyalty to the constitution and new elections for the Second Chamber according to a democratic franchise, represented the core of their demands. Ludwig I proved obstinate and insisted upon the inviolability of the monarchical principle. The mob roamed through the streets of Munich, storming the arsenal and arming itself. Ludwig now saw no other way out: he changed the government and made partial concessions, but the reappearance of Lola Montez on the political stage and the rise in the price of beer kept the masses on the streets until Ludwig I abdicated on 20 March 1848 in favour of his son Maximilian II. Maximilian swore an oath to the constitution fulfilled all the demands put forward, abolished the remaining feudal relics, introduced legal and judicial reforms and by August calm was restored.

Württemberg too was in a state of crisis. A Constitutional Party under Römer established itself as did a Radical Democratic Party. Their demands were in essence much the same as those put forward in Bavaria. King Wilhelm I, hoping for Prussian and Russian support, was not prepared to yield at first but on 2 March 1848 he conceded most of the demands. The revolutionaries were not satisfied, especially after the more radical revolution in Baden had spread to Württemberg. Castles went up in flames which consumed the manorial rolls recording the feudal dues of the peasants. To appease the forces of revolution Römer was appointed Minister of Justice and Head of the new government and the demands conceded included the swearing by the army of loyalty to the constitution. But calm did not return immediately since a 'Republican Club' in Stuttgart adopted the demands of the Baden radicals. The Württemberg moderate liberals moved decisively against them, while the King entertained schemes to return eventually to the *status quo ante*. The May elections of 1848 produced a complete defeat for the forces of the right and the constitutional Liberal Party gained a majority. But the King did not call parliament together until 20 September 1848.

Prior to the March revolution political parties had developed furthest in *Baden*. Here the question was whether Radicals and Liberals could join in concerted action. This appeared difficult since the masses had taken the law into their own hands, managing to get even army and police formations to join them. The demonstrators managed to enter the Second Chamber where they demanded the revocation of the Carlsbad Decrees and cancellation of feudal rights. The Radicals, led by the lawyer Hecker, got as far as having their demands put on the agenda of the Second Chamber by Karl Mathy. They were accepted, including the demand for ministerial responsibility to parliament. Irrespective of these concessions Grand Duke Leopold could not find the means to halt the revolutionary movement. He begrudged the concessions already made, but on the other hand he wanted to avoid unnecessary bloodshed and refused a Prussian offer of assistance. However, the Radicals under Hecker continued to gain the upper hand, supported by bands of irregular forces. On 8 April 1848 Mathy, by then a member of the Baden government, had the radical Josef Fickler arrested, and Hecker, making his way via Alsace and Switzerland to Constance, proclaimed a republic on 12 April 1848. This was the final break between the moderate Liberals and the Radicals. The ensuing April revolution was essentially an agrarian one directed against feudal lords and the Jews. But the Radicals were also divided among themselves. Masses of irregulars could not compensate for united leadership. Forces of the German Confederation intervened and by the end of April 1848 the first revolution in Baden had been defeated, most of its leaders escaping abroad. Some 3,500 cases of treason and breach of the peace came before the courts which handed down very severe sentences.

In *Hesse-Darmstadt* the revolution caused Grand Duke Ludwig II to appoint his successor as Co-Regent. Du Thil was dismissed and his post taken over by Heinrich von Gagern as Interior and Exterior Minister and head of the cabinet. All the reforms demanded were quickly conceded. But large-scale peasant and artisan violence directed against state officials and Jews and the destruction of railways, engineering shops, locomotives and steamships could not be brought under control before the end of August.

Nassau was an almost completely agrarian country populated by smallholders, who also carried out their revolution against the government. They demanded much the same things as were demanded elsewhere but added that the domains of the Duchy should become state property. The Liberals who gained power there soon found themselves under pressure from the Radicals and only Austrian and Prussian forces through a Confederate, executive action, restored law and order. Most of the radical leaders escaped abroad.

Kur-Hesse had been the most liberal and democratic among the constitutional states. Yet revolution occurred there too. The March demands were also raised there and, once conceded, normality returned.

The city of *Frankfurt* had restored its old patrician system of government in 1816 and was further removed from any constitutional form of government than the other south and south-west German states. Liberals and Radicals united in demanding the arming of the people, trial by jury, freedom of the press and assembly, and representation within the Diet of the Confederation. In addition they demanded the revocation of the Carlsbad and successive decrees, amnesty for political crimes and complete equality of citizenship. Supported by the masses a deputation handed over the demands to the Burghermasters von Heyden and von Schweitzer, who undertook to submit the petition via the Senate of the city to the legislative assembly. The masses were in no mood for procrastination. They stormed the town hall and were expelled by the militia with difficulty. The Senate granted freedom of the press and political amnesty but refused complete equality of citizenship.

Saxony, which was one of the German states undergoing industrialization, had prior to the March revolution been subject to severe economic depression. Moderates and Radicals were joined in an uneasy alliance, united only by their common opposition to the reactionary government of King Friedrich Augustus II. They submitted the March demands to the King, but Robert Blum, the leader of the Radicals, also demanded a change of government, and succeeded in this. The revolution had begun in Leipzig and then spread to the royal residence at Dresden. The King abolished censorship and called both chambers together for 20 March 1848. This was delayed until 18 May, and then the constitution was changed in accordance with the March demands which, among other things, introduced equal and universal male franchise.

The same concession was made in *Saxe-Weimar-Eisenach* and in *Saxe-Altenburg*, although *Saxe-Meiningen-Hildburghausen* was only prepared to grant an indirect universal franchise. *Saxe-Coburg-Gotha* adopted the March reforms and remained free from any revolutionary agitation. In *Anhalt-Dessau-Köthen*, which did not possess a constitution, it was intended that the assembly of the estates would deliberate over one. Here the Radicals were strongly organized and their pressure caused nobility to be abolished and the constitution contained the phrase that 'all power derived from the people'. This made it the most progressive constitution in Germany until it was revoked on 4 November 1851. *Anhalt-Bernburg* devised its own constitution but finally had one imposed upon it by Duke Alexander Karl.

In *Hanover* moderation prevailed in spite of King Ernest Augustus's conservative regime. Despite radical demands from Osnabrück, the power base of the Radicals, they gained little. The King read the signs of the times correctly and introduced a revised constitution in September 1848 which lifted censorship, allowed the creation of civic militias and extended the franchise for the Second Chamber to include employees but not domestic servants. In *Brunswick* the one-chamber system existed, which included nobility, burghers and peasants. Duke Wilhelm accepted the March demands and, draped in colours of black, red and gold, he had himself publicly celebrated as *Wilhelm der Deutsche*. *Oldenburg*, too, was a state without a constitution and as a result of public pressure Grand Duke Paul Friedrich Augustus ordered the election of a committee which was to draft one. He lifted censorship and in principle agreed to a representative constitution. Ministers were to countersign any legislation. The first Diet was elected in May 1849.

Friedrich-Francis II reigned in the Grand Duchy of *Mecklenburg-Schwerin* and Grand Duke George in the Grand Duchy of *Mecklenburg-Strelitz*. Both territories shared a common assembly of the estates. This was assembled and dissolved by Friedrich-Francis II. They were the only German territories which still existed on a feudal basis and the estates imposed severe restrictions upon their rulers. Hence it was difficult to transform them into a constitutional territory. The burghers of the cities and the agrarian population demanded a representative assembly and a constitution. Reluctantly Friedrich Francis called for an extrordinary session of the Diet; freedom of the press was conceded and on 23 March he promised a constitution. The estates were to be abolished and replaced by a representative assembly. This constitution came into force on 15 July 1848 and the Diet met for the first time on 31 October 1848 on the basis of universal and equal franchise.

Hamburg had had a constitution as a Free Hanse city since 1528 although this was somewhat antiquated by 1848. Initially the March revolution achieved nothing more than the lifting of censorship. But on 17 August 1848 Hamburg's political association demanded that the Senate call a representative assembly, to which the Senate agreed. The elections held towards the end of 1848 brought a surprise victory for the Radical democratic parties. They then deliberated about a constitution but since the Radicals could not agree on whether the American or the Swiss constitution should serve as a model, this did not come into being until 28 September 1860. *Bremen* was similarly structured to Hamburg and Lübeck but in contrast to the former it replaced its ancient *Bürgerkonvent* with a modern constitution on 18 April 1848. In *Lübeck* a constitution had already been accepted by 8 April 1848, though like most other constitutions it was subsequently revised in the 1850s.

In *Prussia* revolution began on 3 March 1848 with a mass demonstration of workers in Cologne which spread throughout the Rhineland. Three days later similar demonstrations took place in Berlin. Friedrich Wilhelm IV was forced to act. To prevent outright revolution, as was taking place in France, David Hansemann advised the King to turn to the people and to introduce moderate reforms. He should also not only support the cause of reform in Prussia but give a lead to the liberal burghers of Germany as a whole by supporting national unification, in other words reform of the German Confederation. In Hansemann's words: 'I beg your Majesty to understand the momentous importance of the time and to put yourself at the head of German Liberty and Independence.'

Afraid of revolution, Friedrich Wilhelm at first concentrated troops in Berlin despite the demands of demonstrators for their withdrawal. Then on 18 March 1848 he published a new decree in which he called a meeting of the United Diet for 2 April, promised to replace the German Confederation by a German Federal State, a German military constitution, a German Navy, a Prussian constitution and freedom of the press. But his confidant (and Prussia's envoy to the Diet of the German Confederation), Joseph Maria von Radowitz, had already been trying for some time to get action on the German question. It had become more and more apparent that in the long run the call for reforms of the German Confederation could not be ignored. Late in the previous year Radowitz had drafted a memorandum concerning the future of Germany. This was 'greater German' in conception but in practical terms suggested what amounted to a division of power between Prussia and Austria. In case other members of the Confederation obstructed it, Radowitz thought a suitable alternative would be to have a bilateral agreement between Prussia and Austria (the way in which the existing *Zollverein* had been negotiated). According to his plan the House of Hapsburg would restore the

German Imperial Crown while Prussia would be given supreme command over the military forces of the German Confederation. Austria was to be coerced by moral arguments to adopt a more positively German attitude. Radowitz had travelled to Vienna to discuss the matter with Metternich, but the latter received the plan without enthusiasm. All that was agreed upon was to convene a ministerial conference in Dresden; but before this could meet revolutionary events had overtaken it and Metternich had been overthrown.

Friedrich Wilhelm's proclamation of 18 March coincided with the recommendation by the Bundestag of the German Confederation to its member states to grant liberty of the press and adopt black, red and gold as German national colours.

As with previous measures, Friedrich Wilhelm's proclamation was again too little, too late. Berlin's population, clamouring for the withdrawal of troops, roamed through the streets and outside the palace. During a melée with the troops two shots were fired, allegedly by accident. Though no one was hurt, the masses felt betrayed by the King and the shots were the signal for revolution in Berlin. Hundreds of barricades were erected and bloody street battles ensued. In Berlin in particular the revolution was carried out by the workers, a fact confirmed by the young Rudolf Virchow, the brilliant doctor and future formidable parliamentary opponent of Bismarck. In a letter of 1 May 1848 he wrote to his father: 'You are quite right, essentially it has been the workers who have decided this revolution, but I also believe that you in the provinces do not fully realize that this revolution was not simply a political one, but essentially a social one.'

At first Friedrich Wilhelm IV was at a loss to know what to do. He found the bloodshed repellent, and his wife and several of his advisors pressed him to relent and concede the demands of several deputations of burghers to withdraw the troops from the city. He was aware that the stance he had adopted as the reformer of the German Confederation was hardly compatible with the forcible suppression of his fellow Germans. At midnight on 18 March he drafted a new proclamation appealing to his 'dear Berliners' to return to normal life and to clear away the barricades, in return for which he gave his royal word to withdraw his troops. Friedrich Wilhelm found considerable opposition to this course from the military party led by General Karl von Prittwitz, commander of the Berlin garrison. His suggestion was for the King and his family to leave Berlin and then put down the rising from outside. But Friedrich Wilhelm rejected this advice.

When news arrived on the morning of 19 March that several barricades had been cleared, the King ordered that troops should be withdrawn wherever the barricades had been removed. Confusion ensued, resulting in the total withdrawal of the troops, leaving the King alone in the palace without any military protection. The masses followed close on the heels of the withdrawing troops into the city, and the military party, as a rejoinder to the King's refusal to take its advice, decided to let him stew in his own juice.

Jubilation and rejoicing echoed through the streets of Berlin; the revolution had won, or so it seemed. The King's brother, Prince Wilhelm of Prussia, the future King and Emperor Wilhelm I, was held responsible by the masses for the bloodshed and had to flee the city on a 'temporary mission' to England. In accordance with the example already established in Paris, a mourning procession carrying the coffins of the victims arrived in the inner courtyard of the palace during the morning of 19 March. King and Queen were forced publicly to pay their last respects to the fallen revolutionaries. For the first time the Prussian monarchy had been humbled by its own subjects and when the 216 dead were buried the King again had to pay his respects from his balcony. The revolutionaries now formed a militia to protect the King in place of his army, and this was quite successful in re-establishing order. But further concessions by the King were necessary. On 20 March a general amnesty was declared for all persons convicted of political crimes. One of the King's ministers, Heinrich von Arnim, advised him to divert public attention away to the German question by publicly supporting the German national cause: this would be sure to win him the support of the masses. Hence on 21 March, draped with a black, red and gold sash, Friedrich Wilhelm rode through the streets of Berlin delivering speeches to the citizens' militia, the university and the city deputies. He promised to put himself at the head of the movement for German unity without any ambition for ruling Germany himself. He then issued a manifesto containing the famous sentence; 'Prussia henceforth merges with Germany'.

It was rhetoric, no doubt well-intended but devoid of any substance. The Prussian government was in such a shambles that it was incapable for a time of significant action within Prussia, let alone on a German national level. To re-establish some semblance of order at the top a new group of ministers was appointed, headed by Ludolf Camphausen, a Rhinelander, and including as Minister of Finance David Hansemann, another Rhenish liberal. The ministers were to discuss the drafting of a Prussian constitution, and one of the early results was the convening of a Prussian National Assembly elected by general and direct elections. It met for the first time on 22 May 1848.

THE FRANKFURT ASSEMBLY

All this demonstrated that the Prussian government, like the governments of all other German states, was being pressed by the movement for German unity which had been gathering force since 1840. At the

Frankfurt Bundestag of the German Confederation Radowitz became the spokesman for the reform of the German Confederation. But his original vision of reform from above had been made impossible by the outbreak of revolution in Berlin and Vienna. The idea had gained ground among the educated German bourgeoisie that national unity would have to be established by action from below, that is to say through the election of a National Parliament. The concept of the national state was inextricably interwoven with that of a National Parliament. Therefore one of the first demands raised in the individual German states was for the calling of a National Assembly based on free elections. Opinions were divided over the question of what position this National Assembly should occupy, and what the electoral system should be.

The democratic Radicals desired a sovereign National Parliament which alone would decide Germany's future constitution. In fact it aimed at the complete parliamentarization of Germany. This was opposed by the Liberals who feared a dictatorship by parliament and the divisive effects of party political pluralism. Therefore they were intent upon placing an independent executive above parliament through the election of a Head of State. The central power of the Reich was to be the guarantor of liberty against parliament and of national unity against the multi-party system. In constitutional terms it desired a separation of power. But how was parliament to be elected, through direct or indirect elections, equal or limited franchise? Should it alone have the power to draft the constitution and thus all future legislation or should it have a veto power against the Head of State? Should the Reich's central power be monarchical or republican? If it was to be monarchical should it be an hereditary or an elective monarchy? All these and many other questions were as yet unresolved, as was the question of whether Germany should be a unitary or a federal state.

Already in February 1848 Friedrich Daniel Bassermann, a liberal from Baden, and Heinrich von Gagern from Hesse had appealed to the German states to take the necessary steps for the calling of a National Assembly. But without awaiting the formal responses the leaders of the national cause in south-western Germany decided a few weeks later to create the preconditions for the election of a German parliament. On 5 March 1851 representatives of liberal and democratic groups in south-west Germany met at Heidelberg to take the necessary decisions. They were determined to lay the foundation for German unity, but they were also divided, one group, including von Gagern, advocating the restoration of the German Reich, while Radicals like Hecker and Struve wanted a German Republic. But despite this division they decided that a second assembly, the *Vorparlament* or Pre-Parliament, representative of all Germany, should assemble in Frankfurt. A committee of seven was to convene it.

The Bundestag of the Confederation was in a state of confusion. It created a political committee to assess the situation and the position of the Confederation and to recommend such measures as it thought necessary. On 1 March, in accordance with the committee's recommendations, it published a declaration in which it declared itself the sole legal organ of Germany's national and political unity. This was followed by the lifting of press censorship and finally on 8 March it declared itself in favour of the revision of the Constitution of the German Confederation, and adopted the old colours of the Reich – black, red and gold. Initially the envoys at the Bundestag acted on their own initiative. They created a Committee of Seventeen to prepare a new constitution and at the same time called for a Congress of German Princes at Dresden. Since a number of states, including Bavaria and Württemberg, refused to participate, nothing came of this. Moreover, as by the end of March most German governments had been reconstituted, envoys now received their instructions from their bourgeois cabinets, and were recalled and replaced.

Thus there existed a curious parallelism in Frankfurt: there was both the Committee of Seventeen and the Pre-Parliament which convened there at the end of March. The latter pursued a unitary course, the former a federal one, and of course there was still the Bundestag. Rivalries between these three organs were endemic and the Radicals particularly feared that the Liberals would squeeze out the democratic Radicals by cooperating with the other two institutions. The Radicals' sole power base was in the Pre-Parliament and they endeavoured to raise it to the status of sole German executive body and thus eliminate both the Bundestag and the Committee of Seventeen. But the Liberals, who dominated the Committee of Seven, submitted a constitutional programme consisting of four points: first, the appointment of a Supreme Head of the Confederation and a responsible ministry; second, the transformation of the Bundestag into a Senate consisting of representatives of the individual member states; third, the election of a National Assembly by direct elections in which there was to be one deputy per 70,000 of population; and fourth, the transfer of external affairs, trade, customs, traffic and communications, civil and criminal law, the protection of basic human rights and the entire higher judicature into the hands of the Confederation. However, since Austria was not included in the Pre-Parliament, the drafting of a new constitution seemed unlikely. The Radicals under Struve replied with their own programme which included the abolition of standing armies and of the professional civil service, the sequestration of monasteries and convents, the separation of church and state, the removal of the hardships afflicting workers and the division of Germany into *Reichskreise*. This implied the abolition of the monarchy and its replacement by a freely elected parliament headed by three elected presidents, all united in a federal constitution based on the American example. Gagern immediately opposed this scheme, describing monarchy and popular sovereignty as the foundations of German unity. The Radicals

for the time being did nothing, hoping to be overwhelmingly represented in the future German parliament. Both Radicals and Liberals
agreed on the principles for its election. The electoral territory should
extend beyond the boundaries of the German Confederation and
include East and West Prussia. The question of the inclusion of the
province of Posen was left open since the majority there favoured a
restoration of the Polish state. Only those provinces of Austria should
be included which were already part of the Confederation. such as
Bohemia and Moravia. Schleswig as well as Holstein should participate. Deputies were to be elected directly but provisions were made
which allowed governments under certain circumstances to conduct
the election indirectly. Those elected had to have the majority of votes
in constituencies of 50,000 inhabitants, but individual states with a
smaller number of inhabitants were to form a single constituency.
Universal and equal manhood franchise was to be granted. The Pre-
Parliament insisted on electors having 'independent status', but since
no definition of this status was provided, this led to considerable
inequalities during the election. Furthermore it was suggested that the
Pre-Parliament remain in session once the National Assembly had
come together in Frankfurt. This move was, however, defeated by the
Liberals by 356 to 142 votes. But the Radicals did not give up. They
demanded the exclusion of all those envoys to the Bundestag whose
presence was considered undesirable. This move too was defeated,
since most states by then had replaced their envoys. This brought the
split between the Radicals and the Liberals out into the open. Hecker
and forty of his supporters left the Pre-Parliament in protest.

Under the influence of this development the Diet of the Confederation on 2 April 1848 revoked all exceptional legislation enacted
since 1819. Amongst this repressive legislation were the infamous
Carlsbad Decrees of 1819. Then it was decided to dissolve the Pre-
Parliament, but a Committee of Fifty was to be kept in existence so as
not to lose control until the National Assembly convened. In it the
Liberals and the moderate Radicals but not the extreme Radicals were
represented.

The Bundestag agreed to the demands made by the Pre-Parliament
and the Election Law for the National Assembly on 7 April. To carry
out the elections was left to the German states. A uniform election
date was not set, but provision was made that elections had to be
carried out so that the National Assembly could convene in Frankfurt
on 1 May 1848. However, they were not carried out until 3 May in
Austria. A great problem was caused by the definition of 'independent
status' of the electors. Prussia, Hesse-Darmstadt and others were very
liberal in its interpretation. Only those who received public assistance
were excluded. In Baden and the Thuringian states no attempt at
interpretation was made, which left it up to the local authorities to
decide who was 'independent' and who was not. In Saxony and other

states labourers, domestic servants and farmworkers living with their employers and fed by them we excluded. In Austria, Württemberg, Hanover and Kur-Hesse all day-wage labourers, servants, journeymen etc. were excluded from the franchise. Bavaria limited the franchise to those who paid a direct state tax. It was also up to the states to decide whether to use the secret or open ballot. With the exception of Austria most German states used the secret ballot. Also the question of direct or indirect election had been left open. Only Württemberg, Kur-Hesse, Schleswig-Holstein, Frankfurt, Hamburg and Bremen used direct election. Elsewhere votes had to be cast in favour of electors who in turn elected the deputy.

COMPOSITION OF THE ASSEMBLY

Although personalities were elected rather than parties, the nucleus of political parties, as we have already seen, existed. But they were not strictly organized parties with their own infrastructure and organization, but at that stage were simply movements in a constant state of flux. There were associations calling themselves liberal or Radical, and there were clubs who put forward their candidates under various labels. But in the main it was the *Honoratioren*, the patricians of the cities and rural communities, who put themselves or their candidates forward. Estate owners, large farmers, higher civil servants, heads of municipalities, clergymen, judges, lawyers, university professors, teachers, doctors and factory owners dominated the scene as well as the intellectuals. The basic distinction was between the *Honoratioren* and the *Agitatoren*, the agitators who were mainly the intellectuals of the free professions, such as writers and journalists. But the main weight remained with the *Honoratioren*. Austria's Conservatives were intent upon maintaining the Hapsburg Empire's traditional position while the Austrian Liberals were at first supporters of the 'greater German' idea. Bohemia, Moravia and Slovenia absented themselves from the election, since they did not consider themselves Germans. Prussia's vote was predominantly conservative, Saxony's democratic, as was that of Königsberg, Stettin and Breslau. Berlin returned a liberal Centre and a radical Left. In the Catholic Rhineland the clergy exercised great influence but since no specifically Catholic party existed much of the vote benefited the Radicals while the Rhenish cities returned Liberals. Bavaria, under clerical influence, returned 'greater Germans' from its main provinces, while Franconia and Swabia returned Liberals and Radicals.

The National Assembly consisted of 585 deputies but they were never present in full strength. At the opening session on 18 May 1848 about 330 deputies participated. Gradually attendance increased, reaching the 400–500 mark, and only in the decisive winter months of 1848–49 was the full attendance approximately reached. With 312 members, officials and civil servants were extraordinarily highly represented. If one adds university professors and teachers and those in the service of the state or community they made up considerably more than half of the representation. The Frankfurt parliament has been called a parliament of civil servants (a trend that was maintained throughout the parliamentary history of Germany: even now the largest proportion of deputies in the Bonn parliament comes from the civil service). But this did not mean they received or obeyed instructions from their governments: on the contrary they were Liberals or Radicals. Representatives of business amounted to only 12.5 per cent. They had adopted a wait-and-see attitude and came to the fore only a few decades later. Labourers were not represented at all (there were only four artisans). None of the deputies could have claimed to be a labour leader, although the German labour movement was just about to leave its infancy stage. In other words in spite of the revolutions, the events of 1848 had not shaken Germany's social structure. The Frankfurt Assembly was also an educational elite: 570 of its members had completed an academic education.

The deputies were divided into three main groups, though the lines of division between them were highly fluid; Conservatives, Liberals and Radicals. No Catholic party existed but practising Catholic members of all three groupings formed their own Catholic Club. Every deputy had a free mandate, though deputies sharing identical views on various issues tended to cooperate and to decide which way to vote beforehand. Parliamentary discussion was not influenced by pressure from without. Parliamentarians did not have to watch the opinion of their constituency; they did not express the opinions of the media but their own personal opinions which made for a great openness of parliamentary discussion.

Each of the three main groups was subdivided into a number of sub-groups which crystallized around an issue or set of issues. These groupings were not called by any political name but by the hotel or inn where they lived. The Conservatives were the 'Milani' group, the two Liberal groups were called the 'Kasino' and the 'Württemberger Hof'; two other Liberal sub-groupings the 'Augsburger Hof' and the 'Pariser Hof', and so on. The 'Milani' group was small but comprised a number of eminent men. They rather favoured the 'greater German' solution, in opposition to the Conservatives in the Prussian Diet, and many of them when they returned to Prussian politics could be considered Liberals. The Prussian Conservatives insisted on the integrity of the Prussian monarchy and army, while the Bavarian Conservatives defended the independence of southern Germany from Austrian and Prussian hegemony. The Austrian Conservatives spoke up for the maintenance of the Hapsburg Empire and its dominating influence in

Germany, Italy and the Balkans. The Conservatives of the other German states were also in favour of German federalism.

The liberal centre was the strongest of the three main groupings, but it was divided into two wings. The right wing (*Kasino Partei*) opposed the Conservatives because of their 'greater German' federal solution, and also the Radicals because of their revolutionary social aims. The majority was in favour of Prussia's leadership in Germany. The left wing (*Württemberger Hof Partei*) aimed at strong popular represen-tation and making the ministries of the Reich responsible to it. They aimed at a parliamentary monarchy under 'greater German', auspices. There were various other Liberal sub-divisions which eventually joined either one or the other of the two wings.

The Radicals, or the democratic Left, were unanimously dedicated to the 'greater German' solution, to strong centralized unitary govern-ment and a territorial reorganization of Germany into provinces. They demanded the inclusion of Schleswig in the Reich but on the other hand wanted to exclude the non-German territories of Austria and Prussia. They rejected hereditary monarchy. They were also divided into two wings; the moderate Left (*Deutscher Hof*) under Robert Blum supporting the creation of a German Republic but ready to compromise over this issue, and the left wing (*Donnersberg*) who were supporters of a republic. The leaders of the latter had participated in the Baden revolution. These two wings also developed splinter groups, some becoming more radical and others more moderate.

ISSUES AND INSTITUTIONS

When the National Assembly met in the Paulskirche at Frankfurt on 18 May 1848 Heinrich von Gagern was elected President of the Assembly by 305 out of 397 votes. The question immediately facing it was whether it had the sole right to create the constitution, or did it possess that power as a constituent part of the individual German states? The assembly decided in favour of the former as was shown in Gagern's opening speech. In May 1848 the German princes were in no position to oppose this claim. But dynastic particularism was now replaced by parliamentary particularism. Increasingly the parliaments of the German states insisted that Frankfurt did not have the sole right of decision but that the individual parliaments would also have to agree to a future German constitution. This in turn led to divided opinions among the Frankfurt Assembly. Also the question of a Federal Ex-ecutive immediately arose and the assembly opted for the suggestion already made in April, namely to create a Federal Directory of three, in which Prussia and Austria would each have one member while the third constituent part should consist of the Closed Council of the Bundestag excluding Austria, Prussia and Bavaria. This conclusion was not acted on because the Committee of Fifty opposed it, feeling it had been ignored. Various other solutions were debated until finally on 24 June Gagern cut the debate short by suggesting the election of a *Reichsverweser*, a Reich Regent. He recommended Archduke Johann of Austria for the post. By suggesting that solution he went against his own party who were still considering various plans for a Directory, as well as against Prussian ambitions for hegemony in Germany, although the appointment of a *Reichsverweser* did not exclude the possibility of the imperial Crown ultimately going to Prussia. His suggestion met with the approval of the democratic Left and the liberal Centre-left, as well as with the general approval of most supporters of the 'greater German' solution. By a law enacted on 28 June all executive power was handed over to the *Reichsverweser* and this was accepted by 373 votes to 175. The next day Archduke Johann was elected as *Reichsverweser* with a majority of 436 votes. A deputation travelled to Vienna and he accepted the nomination on 5 July. On 12 July he attended the National Assembly and then the Bundestag. On 15 July he formed his government, the first Reich government, on a provisional basis. Although ministerial responsibility was introduced, parliamentary government was not. The Reich Regent could appoint or dismiss ministers as he wanted. In the case of a vote of no confidence the government was not obliged to resign, but since the provisional government's only backing was in the National Assembly, and it was devoid of an extra-parliamentary base of power, dependence on the support of the National Assembly was essential. In all there were five cabinets. The first Prime Minister was Prince Karl von Leiningen who adhered to the line of the right and left wing of the Liberals. The Leiningen government resigned in September 1848 because of a resolution of the National Assembly against the conclusion of the Malmö armistice (see below, p. 63). The Austrian Schmerling then became Prime Minister and also Minister for the Interior and for Foreign Affairs. When the 'greater German' solution could not be realized by December 1848 he resigned and his office was taken over by Heinrich von Gagern. When the 'little German' solution also failed Gagern resigned on 9 May 1849, his place being taken by the Prussian lawyer and Conservative Maximilian Grävell who was replaced soon by Prince Wittgenstein. It was a pure minority government, which lasted until 20 December 1849 when the federal power was handed over to Prussia and Austria and the German Confederation restored.

However, we have rushed ahead of events. The institution of a central executive had in fact ousted the Bundestag. This was an act of doubtful legality, though it would have been of little concern had the revolution of 1848 succeeded. But it put the individual German states into a difficult position. By the summer of 1848 it was still too risky to oppose the National Assembly and they therefore diplomatically suspended the Bundestag and delegated its functions to the Reich Regent. Johann accepted this task but the National Assembly did not merely want to suspend the Bundestag but to dissolve it. However, the Bundestag would not give way and insisted on its suspension but not its abolition. It could whenever necessary resume its activities, if for instance the constitution failed to be enacted or the provisional central power dissolved itself.

THE FRANKFURT ASSEMBLY AND THE GREAT POWERS

One of the first major problems this new provisional government encountered concerned its recognition by the other powers in international law. Germany had transformed herself from a confederation of states into a Federal State and achieved the principle of national self-determination. Much of its internal strength would depend on its external success. That Czarist Russia would adopt a hostile attitude was foreseeable, but greater expectations were put on France. However, the German envoy to France, the Liberal Friedrich von Raumer, was not recognized as an official representative in Paris. A unified German state was anathema to a French Republic just as it had been to a French Empire or Kingdom.

Great store was put on Great Britain's attitude. Palmerston viewed the new state with ironic sympathy but the *Zollverein* was already enough of an industrial competitor without being reinforced by political unity. British public opinion was against it. Also the support of the German National Assembly for Schleswig-Holstein met with considerable hostility in Great Britain. No official German envoy was recognized at the Court of St James. The only Great Power which recognized the German Reich was the United States of America. In the meantime the individual German states continued to maintain their representatives abroad.

THE PROBLEM OF NATIONAL MINORITIES

In 1846 a fresh Polish rising had taken place, centred in Cracow and affecting mainly Austrian Galicia. The intention was to spread the rising to Posen, but the attempt was anticipated by the Prussian authorities who arrested its leader Mieroslavski and others. They were tried for high treason and sentenced to various terms of imprisonment. In the wake of the political amnesty Mieroslavski was released and he renewed the attempt that had failed two years before. The German population of Posen now faced the threat of being submerged by the Poles. To prevent this German districts were put under German administration with the intention of annexing them to the German Confederation, or for that matter to the Reich. The result was uproar and revolt among the Poles, which in turn caused adverse comment on Prussia and Germany from outside Germany's frontiers. During the course of the spring and summer of 1848 Prussian military forces quelled the rising and Mieroslavski escaped abroad. All this happened when Prussia had come round to supporting the idea of restoring the Polish state. Mieroslavski had nipped these good intentions in the bud and instead the Prussian government considered dividing Posen into a Polish and a German sector. The Polish part was to become the Duchy of Gnesen, have its own administration, and provide a special Polish contingent in the Prussian army. Abroad, especially in France, the fourth partition of Poland was spoken of. In the National Assembly the radical Left supported Polish independence and moved a resolution to reject the union of Posen with the German Reich. The resolution was accompanied by a speech in favour of national self-determination for the Italians as well. Robert Blum, who had moved this resolution, was opposed by the deputies of the German East and the resolution was defeated by 342 votes to 31.

Bohemia and Moravia also represented a problem stemming from the old Empire and the German Confederation. The leader of the Czechs, Frantisek Palacky (who had learnt Czech only late in his life), had rejected the invitation to the Pre-Parliament, arguing that there was no place in a German national state for Bohemians 'of the Slavic tribe'. Elections were held, but 48 out of 68 constituencies had boycotted them. Nevertheless, Bohemia and Moravia were represented in the German National Assembly by twenty deputies.

The problem of South Tyrol also made its first appearances on the political stage. The northern part of Southern Tyrol, the districts of Bozen and Meran, were German-speaking, the southern part with Trent and Rovereto Italian-speaking. The Italian-speaking deputies at Frankfurt demanded that they should be allowed to leave the German Confederation, but this was rejected by the National Assembly, which at the same time asked the Austrian government to ensure the cultural autonomy of the Italian-speaking south Tyrolians.

The Duchy of Limburg was part of the Netherlands but since 1839 was also part of the German Confederation together with Luxemburg. To apply the German Constitution there was demanded even by the Radicals. But the Reich Executive did not press the point when the Dutch government rejected this.

MILITARY AND NAVAL POWER

More important was the question of military power. If a united German army was to be founded the long-term consequences would be the mediatization of the German kings and princes. Thus Prussia opposed any united German army. Radicals and the leftwing Liberals in the National Assembly were against a standing army anyway: all they wanted was a kind of national militia, while the right-wing Liberals pursued a federal solution on the basis of a national army with contingents provided by the federal states but controlled at the top by a unified central command, unified military judiciary code, standardized arms and equipment, and capable of operating together in large formations.

The law of 28 June 1848 had put the supreme command over the entire armed might of the individual states in the hands of the *Reichsverweser*. But was it to be a national army, one structured according to federal contingents or an army as more or less existed already under the German Confederation? A War Minister had been appointed, the Prussian General Eduard von Peucker, but in essence he remained a War Minister without an army. The German states obstructed any interference with their own armies and then opposed a national army. Prussia was as much opposed to handing over its supreme command to the War Minister as was Bavaria. In the Constitution itself a compromise was found by formally subjecting the armed forces of Germany to the central power of the Reich. The states retained the right to appoint their own commanders, while the War Minister could appoint the higher commanders who commanded more than one contingent.

If public opinion was deeply divided over the issue of the army it fully supported the creation of a German navy. Germany was on the way to becoming a great trading power, hence the need for a navy. Overnight all kinds of associations sprang up advocating one. The National Assembly answered the call and created a Committee for Naval Affairs chaired by the Austrian Karl Ludwig von Bruck. The Ministry of Trade created a special Department for the Navy which was to be financed by contributions from the individual states. Prussia paid part of it and then went on to create its own navy. Both the Reich navy and that of Prussia were highly improvised affairs. They lacked trained officers, engineers and crews; they hardly had any shipyards and docks, but by May 1849 eleven corvettes and frigates and twenty-six gunboats were in service under the command of *Reichsadmiral* Karl Ludwig Brommy. But in the same way as the gains of 1848 were superseded, the German navy began to decline, and this continued until 1852 when it was sold off cheaply. It had led to international tensions. Palmerston said that he would consider any vessel flying the black, red and gold colours as a pirate ship, or words to that effect.

SCHLESWIG-HOLSTEIN AND THE ARMISTICE OF MALMÖ

This was a dangerous development against the background of events in Schleswig-Holstein. A popular Danish movement had demanded the incorporation of Schleswig into the Danish monarchy and Danish troops had occupied the territory. The Germans in Schleswig insisted upon their independence and formed a provisional government. Berlin was asked for aid and Prussia's King, after having proclaimed himself at the head of the movement for German unity, could do little but comply with the request. He also turned to the National Assembly and to the German princes for aid. At first he attempted to resolve the problem by peaceful means but Danish obstinacy made this impossible. The German National Assembly fully supported the Germans in Schleswig and war broke out. German Reich contingents and the Prussian army under the command of General Friedrich von Wrangel were used. But when Russia, Great Britain and France threatened to intervene on the Danish side, an armistice was concluded at Malmö on 26 August 1848 and Prussian troops withdrew from Schleswig. The provisional government was replaced by a mixed commission of Germans and Danes. Public disgust over this capitulation was widespread in Germany. The Radicals in the National Assembly called for opposition and in September the Leiningen government resigned in Frankfurt. But in the final analysis the National Assembly had no other choice but to ratify the armistice.

THE PROBLEM OF THE CONSTITUTION

In the light of these developments the final acceptance of a German constitution was of little or no consequence. Long before the National Assembly had assembled in Frankfurt, the Committe of Seventeen had begun working on a German Constitution. Their plan envisaged a constitution for all the territories which already belonged to the German Confederation, including Schleswig and Prussia's eastern provinces. They based their scheme on the 'greater German' solution. Part of the sovereignty of the member states was to be transferred to the Reich authorities and the Reich was to guarantee basic civil rights. The Reich's powers were to include international representation, the right to make war and to conclude peace, all matters concerning military affairs, customs and postal services, supervision of waterways, railways, telegraphs and patents. Reich legislation would include all sectors of public and private law in so far as this was necessary for its unity. Supreme power would reside in the Head of the Reich and the Reichstag; the executive would be in the hands of Reich ministries. At the Head of the Reich would be a German Emperor whose crown was to be hereditary and who would reside in Frankfurt. He would possess executive power for external affairs and appoint civil servants and officers of the army and navy, and open, close and prorogue the Reichstag, but all his actions would require a ministerial counter-signature. Ministers would be responsible to parliament and subject to its control. A two-chamber system would be introduced: an Upper House consisting of reigning princes and monarchs, and a Lower House, the Reichstag, elected every six years by the people through a general franchise. Enactment of any legislation would require the consent of both chambers. Basic rights would include the right of every parliamentarian to participate at the Reich or state level in the legislative process and in the raising of loans or taxation, and the right to impeach a minister. There would also be a Burghers' militia. All public burdens would be shared equally and there would be career openings to all offices based on talent. Liberty of the person, a free press, freedom of religion, the right to emigrate, freedom of association and assembly, and a guarantee of postal communication remaining secret were to be included. The constitution was to be guaranteed by the Emperor's constitutional oath, that of his ministers, civil servants and the army, as well by the princes and state civil servants. Changes in the constitution should be carried out with the agreement of the Emperor and backed by a two-thirds majority in both chambers. A Reich Court should be the Supreme Judge of the constitution.

While the Emperor was to be elected in the first instance, subsequent emperors were to be his heirs. But the difficulty was, who should be elected? During the spring and summer of 1848 the reputation of both the Prussian and Hapsburg Crowns had declined so much that it seemed impossible to reach a quick decision over one or the other. The fact that it was a federal constitution made it unacceptable to the radical Left, as was the feature of insufficient parliamentarization. (There was no provision for a vote of no confidence compelling the resignation of the government in power.) That both chambers were equal, and that in the Upper Chamber there should no longer be envoys instructed by their governments, made it unacceptable to the reigning monarchs. A further obstacle was that the Emperor would have an absolute veto against parliamentary decisions, which was contradictory to the principle of the separation of powers. Most German governments rejected this scheme. The rejection by Austria, Prussia and Bavaria was important. Prussia's rejection was decisive, since Friedrich Wilhelm IV insisted on the retention of the Imperial Crown by the House of Hapsburg.

With this rejection work began anew by a Permanent Constitutional Committee of thirty members who began with basic civil rights. This catalogue of basic rights was based on the then prevalent conception of a conflict between *state* and *society*. The aim was to overcome this conflict by incorporating civil liberties into the state by way of the constitution. The social question played hardly any role among men whose origin was still essentially urban or agrarian but not industrial. Commerce and competition would provide sufficient opportunity for upward social mobility. They were completely blind to the implications of the rise of modern industrial capitalism. As a result the civil liberties or basic rights guaranteed the liberty of the person, equality before the law, habeas corpus, abolition of the death penalty, freedom of opinion and of the press, freedom in matters of religion, autonomy of the churches, civil marriage to precede the church marriage ceremony, freedom of education, freedom of property, freedom of the judiciary from government interference, the right of municipalities to administer themselves, and finally the guarantee to national minorities within the German Reich of freedom to develop their cultural autonomy. These basic rights were guaranteed against federal or state legislation.

Inevitably they met opposition within the National Assembly and from various states. They were considered by many to have a strong centralizing effect which negated the federal principle. But nevertheless they were enacted as law on 27 December 1848, but a number of German states refused to publish them, including Austria, Prussia and Bavaria. However, the majority of states accepted them.

The next major issues concerned the equality of the franchise, the question of one or two chambers of representation and the power of executive veto. The radical Left was in favour of a one-chamber system while the majority of the Committee had suggested two chambers. The majority within the assembly also preferred a two-chamber system. The Conservatives hoped that they would soon regain their strength and would be able to maintain their position in the Upper House, where they would also represent the federal principle. Its members would be elected by the Diets of the member states. The Second Chamber, however, would be nationally elected. Under the influence of the Liberals it seemed at first that the franchise was to be limited to those economically independent, excluding journeymen, factory workers, day-wage labourers and domestic and farm servants. Others suggested the census franchise, i.e. making participation in elections dependent on the amount of taxes paid, because the citizen who paid more taxes possessed a greater right to participate in the affairs of state. For the same reason an open instead of a secret ballot was suggested. As to whether members should be elected directly or indirectly, direct election was accepted quickly, and the secret ballot was stipulated by a narrow majority of thirty-one. In order that the supporters of a 'greater German' solution should be able to maintain a common front a compromise was reached which granted the active and passive franchise to all male Germans aged 25 and upwards. Members were to be those who achieved an absolute majority of votes. If none of the candidates achieved an absolute majority at the first ballot, a second ballot was to be held; if that failed then a third ballot would decide between the two candidates who had obtained the most votes. The Election Law of 1848 was never applied because of the failure of the revolution, but Bismarck borrowed large parts of it for the Electoral Law of the North German Confederation and then for the Second Empire, and it remained in force until the end of 1918.

As to the executive veto power the question was whether that power should be absolute or suspensive. The absolute nature of the veto power was rejected by a coalition between right-wing and left-wing Liberals. In return for the support of the left wing in favour of the principle of the hereditary imperial Crown the right wing supported the suspensive veto by 385 votes to 127.

'GREATER GERMANY' OR 'LITTLE GERMANY'?

All the members of the National Assembly were in favour of German unity but only the Radicals supported a centralized unitary state. The Liberals were overwhelmingly in favour of a federal solution. But how federal should federal be? To the Prussian-Protestant Conservatives as well as those representing south German Catholicism, liberal federalism made too great an inroad into the sovereignty of their states. The final solution was in favour of a federal state with a strong central executive, but the smaller states also presented a problem since they feared being mediatized. This indeed was the intention of many members but since tempers grew hot over this issue the matter was dropped.

However, the most important problem was represented by Austria where Prince Schwarzenberg had taken over since the fall of Metternich. He suppressed the revolution and once again consolidated the position of the House of Hapsburg. It was his idea that Austria, including its non-German territories, should join the German state, as had been envisaged for Prussia. But that would have killed the idea of a federal state and meant the return to a confederation. Liberals and Radicals in Frankfurt were against it and Austria was given the choice of entry into the Reich while sacrificing the unity of its empire, or of maintaining its empire but being excluded from the Reich. Schwarzenberg temporized: Austria was neither prepared to enter the Reich under the conditions put forward nor was it prepared to be excluded. This played into the hands of the supporters of the 'little German' solution. Prime Minister Anton von Schmerling found himself compelled to resign and was replaced by Heinrich von Gagern, the leader of the 'little German' party, Austria still put forward the idea of a double federation between the Austrian and German empires, but it found little support. Nevertheless, over 260 members of the National Assembly were still in favour of the 'greater German' solution. In the meantime Austria negotiated separately with Prussia and received her support for an Austrian 'Roman-German' Kaiser at the apex of the new state.

Initially the Frankfurt Assembly had left open the question of who should bear the imperial Crown. The argument was first about whether it should be hereditary. This was rejected by 263 votes to 211. However, the majority of the German states supported the hereditary imperial Crown, but only Prussia came out strongly in favour of the House of Hapsburg.

The matter was resolved by Austria's action. On 7 March 1849 Emperor Franz Joseph dissolved the Austrian Reichstag in Kremsier (where it had retired in order to escape the unrest dominating Vienna) and imposed a constitution upon the Austrian Empire, emphasizing the unity of its German and non-German parts. This made it impossible for Austria to join a German federal state and destroyed the 'greater German' coalition in Frankfurt. Many of them became supporters of the 'little German' solution as the only remaining alternative and this meant the election of the King of Prussia as German Emperor with 290 votes in his favour and 248 abstentions. However, the 'greater Germans' persuaded Archduke Johann to remain in office until Friedrich Wilhelm had decided whether to reject or accept the imperial Crown. In Prussia opinions were divided: Conservatives like Gerlach and the *Kreuzzeitung*, Prussian particularists, were in favour of rejection; the liberal Centre and the democratic Left were in favour of acceptance, as was the third group, the 'greater German' party. Also Prince Wilhelm and his wife Princess Augusta supported acceptance since in that way Prussia could enlarge itself in Germany. Acceptance was counselled even among the close advisers of the King. Friedrich Wilhelm IV was no Prussian particularist, but neither was he a supporter of the national democratic movement. His political view was an idealized version of the medieval Imperial Crown associated with the House of Hapsburg. Furthermore he saw the National Assembly as essentially revolutionary in character and when the Frankfurt deputation led by Eduard Simson, then president of the Assembly, arrived in Berlin on 2 April 1849 the decision had already been taken. The King simply stated that a parliament had no right to offer a Crown, though when he met the delegation the following day he made his acceptance dependent on the agreement of all the other German princes. The same applied to the recognition of the constitution. This in effect was the end of the affair.

Had Friedrich Wilhelm accepted the Crown and the constitution come into force, this would have meant that from then on the highest power emanated from the Reich, Reich legislation taking precedence over the legislation of the member states. It would have been responsible for the conduct of foreign affairs, decided on war and peace and exercised supreme command over the army consisting of the contingents provided by the member states (states with populations under 500,000 would have had to attach their forces to the contingent of a larger German state). It would also have exercised supreme command over the navy. Its power of legislation would have included matters concerning the army and navy, railways and communications, customs, production and consumption taxation, postal and telegraph services, coinage, measures, weights and printing of paper money, the raising of Reich taxes, the preservation of internal order, the granting or loss of citizenship, associations and assemblies, recognition of public documents, health and welfare, civil, commercial and criminal law, the Reich civil service, Reich jurisdiction including army and naval courts, problems of violations of the constitution and all other matters arising for instance out of constitutional changes. Legislative initiative would have resided within the government and the two houses of the Reichstag. The agreement of both houses would have been necessary for legislation to be enacted. The government would have possessed a suspensive veto. Secret laws would have been prohibited.

The Reich's judiciary's functions were to be limited to specific constitutional and political matters, such as disagreements between member states, constitutional differences within the Reich as well as within a member state, constitutional complaints raised by citizens and the impeachment of Reich or state ministers. Furthermore all cases of treason were to be dealt with by it, as also complaints against the financial administration. Executive power was not to reside exclusively with the Reich. The police powers of the member states would have been retained. Internal administration would have been the concern of the member states except for military and naval affairs, administration of waterways, railways, the road system, and customs, tariffs, production and consumption taxation, commerce and shipping as well as finance. These were supervisory powers of the Reich which would have cut deeply into the competencies of the states.

The Supreme head of the state would have been the 'Emperor of the Germans' who would have enjoyed the rights already enumerated in the scheme of the Committee of Seventeen (see above, p. 54). The constitution said very little about the structure of the government. It did not mention a Prime Minister, nor whether the goverment should form a collegiate body. Equally little was said about the relationship between government and parliament. But it did subject the government to parliamentary control. Ministers could participate in the deliberations of both Houses, address them and provide the information required by parliament, or state the reasons why they could not do so. A minister could not be a member of the First Chamber, but he could be of the Second Chamber. The Reichstag was to consist of two houses, the House of the States and the House of the People. Whereas the former was a federal organ, the latter was a unitary national organ.

An oath on the constitution would have had to be sworn by the Emperor, by all members of the government, civil servants, the army and the deputies of the Reichstag. To protect the constitution there would also have been, besides the judicial protection, executive protection either by intervention by the Reich or in extreme cases 'for the preservation of the peace within the Reich', by executive action by the Reich. In addition there was a provision for proclaiming a limited state of siege in case of war or internal upheaval. Any change of the constitution would have required a two-thirds majority in each of the houses as well as the agreement of the Emperor.

All in all, especially as far as the relationship between the government and the representative assembly was concerned, the Constitution of 28 March 1849 was in many instances strikingly similar to that introduced by Bismarck in 1871.

RESTORATION

But while this was all in the making the powers of restoration gradually recovered. In *Prussia* it gave the agrarian Conservatives the opportunity to organize themselves politically. They met in Berlin on 18–19 August 1848, forming the so called 'Junker parliament', the first step to the formation of a Conservative Party. In other parts of Germany it was not only the Conservatives who became active. On 15 July 1848 there was a meeting of the first German General Congress of Artisans and Tradesmen, essentially members of the emerging lower middle class whose economic basis was threatened by the forces of industrial capitalism on the one hand and the proletarian socialism of the extreme Left on the other. Politically it opposed the republic and supported a German federal state. Catholicism, too, began to organize itself, making the maximum use of the new liberties of the March revolution, such as freedom of the press, association and assembly. While one group supported the separation of church and state, another opposed it and this for the time being prevented the foundation of a Catholic Party.

The bourgeois Left was increasingly worried that its representatives at Frankfurt would be absorbed by the liberal Centre, so the Radicals convened their first Congress of Democrats on 13 June 1848. Its members considered themselves as a 'democratic-republican counter-parliament', and acted as a pressure group on the Left in the National Assembly. The events of March 1848 were also a signal for the return of many of the radical émigrés, particularly the Communists. Marx, Wilhelm Weitling and Moses Hess were among those who returned, as well as many members of former secret societies. But their return was not coincidental with the rise of the German Labour Movement which originated from workers' associations, workers' educational institutions and workers' congresses. They wanted social reform by legal means, and on 11 April 1848 the 'Central Committee for Workers' was founded in Berlin, led by Stephan Born who had parted company with Marx. The term 'social democratic' now appeared for the first time. A Workers' Congress was held in Berlin from 23 August to 3 September, at which social evolution not revolution was demanded. It limited its discussion to economic and social questions and avoided any expression to support for a German republic. It drew up a list of social and economic demands to be submitted to the Frankfurt Assembly. Politically it demanded no more than the recognition of a workers' organization within the framework of the constitution, a demand ignored at Frankfurt.

Ironically enough it was the armistice of Malmö which was used in Frankfurt as a pretext for a second revolution. Radicals were numerous there. A workers' association was founded which was to be the spearhead of the Second Revolution. Its leaders demanded to be included in the National Assembly. Robert Blum rejected this as illegal, but in the meantime most parts of west Germany were again in revolutionary ferment, which stemmed from those *petit bourgeoisie* and labour strata not represented in Frankfurt. One of their leaders was the young Ferdinand Lassalle. The rising in Frankfurt was put down by Prussian and Austrian troops. More disastrous for the Radicals was the murder of the two deputies, Prince Lichnowsky and General Hans von Auerswald. Both had voted for the Malmö Armistice. These murders evoked revolution in Germany the like of which had not been witnessed since 1819. It forced the bourgeoisie on to the side of the Conservatives. A state of siege was proclaimed in Frankfurt and any attack on the National Assembly was declared treason. The Liberals now had to use the army against the democratic Left. But just putting down the rising in Frankfurt did not settle matters. In *Baden* a new rising took place led by Gustav von Struve, but this had been suppressed too by the end of September 1848.

As the revolutionary fervour of the preceding spring was beginning to evaporate by the autumn of 1848 one could see that in *Prussia* the discussions about a Prussian Constitution had produced little of any practical use. Prussia's Conservatives began to reassemble and form the Conservative Political Party. Their mouthpiece was the newly founded *Neue Preussische Zeitung*, carrying as a symbol on its masthead the Iron Cross and therefore popularly referred to as the

Kreuzzeitung. The founder of the party, Ludwig von Gerlach, represented a conservatism that was aware of the social problems confronting Prussia as a whole and which rested on the state and its prosperous propertied members. By late 1848 he had also come to the conclusion that the time was ripe for counter-revolutionary action. He urged the appointment of a soldier as Prime Minister. After renewed outbreaks of violence in Berlin the Camphausen ministry had resigned in June 1848 to be followed by the Auerswald-Hansemann ministry. Gerlach suggested as Prime Minister the General commanding Breslau, Count Friedrich Wilhelm von Brandenburg. The Prussian National Assembly protested, but the King replied by proroguing it, knowing that the military balance was now in his favour. On 10 November 1848, 40,000 troops commanded by General von Wrangel entered Berlin and disarmed the citizens' militia. When the Prussian National Assembly refused to consent to any taxation Frederick Wilhelm IV dissolved it, although he had no right to do so. On the same day, 5 December 1848, he imposed his own constitution upon Prussia. The National Assembly in Frankfurt protested against the events in Berlin, but to no avail. The method of imposing a constitution was tantamount to a *coup d'état*, it was 'reform from above', reform which included many features which Liberals had been demanding for decades. General and representative elections were planned and two chambers were to convene to discuss the final version of the constitution. But the full executive powers of the Crown were retained, especially the Crown's supreme command over the army. A vital feature omitted from the constitution was that the armed forces should swear an oath to it; a clause was included that civil servants should swear loyalty and obedience to the King. The First Chamber was to be elected from those who had reached their thirtieth birthday and were men of property. For the Second Chamber no property qualification existed, in other words the same franchise operated as that introduced in March.

Frederick Wilhelm's rejection of the imperial Crown was to all intents and purposes the end of the revolution begun in March 1848. Austria recalled the Austrian deputies on 5 April 1849, thus demonstrating its separation from the National Assembly and its constitution. However, the National Assembly still tried to get the constitution it had devised accepted by the governments of the German states. Prussia let it be known that it did not wish to pre-empt the issue by its own decision. As a result twenty-eight German governments accepted the constitution, mainly the smaller states like Baden, the various Saxon states, and others, which included the entire non-Prussian northern German states. But Prussia, Austria, Bavaria and Württemberg were missing and so was the Kingdom of Saxony. However, King Wilhelm of Württemberg was pressed by public opinion to change his decision and to declare his adherence to the constitution. In Prussia both chambers declared in favour of the constitution on 21 April 1849.

The King prorogued both chambers, now intent on revising his imposed constitution by introducing the three-class franchise which proved such a political liability for the whole of Germany until 1918. On 28 April 1849 he publicly rejected both the imperial Crown and the Constitution. The National Assembly cherished the illusion that by introducing new elections for a German National Parliament it could force the hand of Prussia and those as yet uncommitted, but that step severed the last link between Frankfurt and Berlin. On 10 May 1849 Gagern resigned; Maximilian Karl Grävell's and Prince August Sayn-Wittgenstein's ministries represented a mere aftermath. Prussia also recalled its deputies from Frankfurt and requested the *Reichsverweser* to dissolve the National Assembly. He refused, but could not stop Saxony, Hanover, and Baden recalling their deputies. The deputies were faced by the choice of accepting the nullification of their mandates or of revolting against their governments, and the majority opted for the former. That increased the voting power of the Radicals in the Assembly which decided to transfer from Frankfurt to Stuttgart where the government had accepted the constitution. This split and put an end to the National Assembly.

But the end was not to come before further revolutionary outbreaks had occurred. In *Prussia* one of the King's endeavours was to subject the *Landwehr* to line regiments. This led to a number of mutinies among *Landwehr* units in Berlin, Silesia, the province of Saxony, Westphalia and the Rhineland, which were suppressed easily enough. But henceforth it was all the easier for Friedrich Wilhelm and his successor to instil the *Landwehr* with the spirit of the line regiments. *Saxony*, in spite of the vote in favour by the two chambers, had not recognized the Frankfurt Constitution. King Friedrich Augustus II, supported by Prussia, dissolved his parliament. The result was the Dresden May revolution dominated by Michael Bakunin, the Russian anarchist. Among the revolutionaries fighting on the barricades was Richard Wagner. Most of the Saxon regular army was still in Schleswig-Holstein and many members of remaining units made common cause with the revolutionaries whose aim really was to smash the foundations of the Austrian regime under Schwarzenberg. A quickly-established provisional government immediately recognized the Frankfurt Constitution, but on 5 May 1849 the intervention of Prussian forces put an end to the venture.

In *Bavaria* the government was in outright opposition to the constitution, but a petition was circulated in Munich which collected 12,000 signatures in favour of acceptance. A counter-petition managed to collect 9,000 signatures. The Second Chamber recommended acceptance by a narrow majority whereupon Maximilian II dissolved his parliament. The reply to this step was the popular rising in the Rhine-Palatinate, a centre of German radicalism, which was again put down by Prussian forces. In *Baden* Grand Duke Leopold had accepted the constitution, yet in this Duchy the most serious of the spring uprisings of 1849 occurred. This was headed by the Baden army where the introduction of conscription had caused serious dissatisfaction. The soldiers freed political prisoners and on 13 May 1849 deputies of the democratic associations in Baden met at the second Offenburg Assembly. Their leader, the socialist Amand Goegg, argued that the constitution had come into force, and the German princes who had rejected it were guilty of high treason. It was argued that although Grand Duke Leopold had accepted it he had refused to do anything to compel the other princes to do the same. A provisional government was formed and Baden became the refuge for revolutionaries from all over Europe. The Prussian forces under Prince Wilhelm were already in the Bavarian Palatinate and in June 1849 intervened on the basis of the right of intervention sanctioned by the German Confederation as well as of a Prussian intervention specifically requested by Grand Duke Leopold. Baden was not pacified until 23 July 1849. Over 80,000 Badeners, a twentieth of its population, emigrated.

In the meantime on 18 June 1849 the rump of the National Assembly in Stuttgart had dissolved itself. However, the *Reichsverweser* and the Reich Ministry still continued in Frankfurt, though there was little to do. Their position had become untenable. On 30 September 1849 Austria and Prussia agreed to transfer the powers of the *Reichsverweser* to a Confederate Commission consisting of two Austrians and two Prussians, and with that the last vestiges of the Revolution of 1848 had disappeared.

WHY DID '1848' FAIL?

When assessing the Revolution of 1848 one is confronted by a school of historiography which conceives the task of historian as that of a political educator in the service of further emancipation and democratization and therefore describes its interpretation of history as the 'critical approach'. In its view 1848 failed because the Liberals had betrayed the revolution by ultimately moving towards the Conservatives. The division between Liberals and Radicals was crucial. In view of the radical and social revolutionary tendencies the Liberals moved towards the Right and, faced by the option of radical revolution or counter-revolutionary order, chose the latter and thus joined forces of reaction, a view which Karl Marx had already held.

To qualify this interpretation one has to look at the Liberal's policy and ask what realistic alternatives did in fact exist. No doubt the break between the Liberals and the Radicals, between Radicals, Moderates and Constitutionalists who prior to March 1848 had formed what for brevity's sake we can describe as 'the opposition', represents an important element – it is a break in which tactical questions, political aims, the social aims and attitudes held by the various social groupings, are closely interwoven.

Already by the summer of 1848 we notice that the revolutionary élan of the spring had disappeared. The Liberals had no intention of driving the revolution further: instead they favoured orderly evolution. They stopped short before the thrones, they did not want to turn the sovereign power of the people against the princes and after initial resistance they had accepted the Malmö Armistice. An important factor explaining this attitude was the threat of a 'red Republic', of which there was much talk. That threat sufficed for them to cousel moderation. They lacked a decisive will to power. As the spectrum of political radicalism began to widen, so the Liberals, without abandoning any of the beliefs and aims they held, moved to the right. The thesis of the 'critical school' has it that this was an 'either – or' question, that there was no middle way for the Liberals to pursue. This ignores the fact to the Liberals could and did pursue a policy directed *against* the further radicalization of the revolution as well as *against* the forces of counter-revolution.

Certainly the fear of a 'red Republic' played a major role in this. After all Engels, in January 1848, with regard to events in Switzerland at the time, had written:

> Fight on you merry gentlemen of capital. For the time being we need you. You must remove the remnants of the Middle Ages and the absolute monarchy, you must destroy patriarchalism, you must centralize, you must transform for us the more or less unpropertied classes into real proletarians, into recruits for us. As reward you will be allowed to rule for a short time . . . but don't forget the hangman is already waiting for you at the door-step.

One must add to this the fact that in 1848 the German bourgeoisie was far from being a homogeneous group. It did not consist exclusively of Rhenish merchants and industrialists and an academic intelligentsia but was supported by peasants as well as the *petit bourgeoisie*. Hence the rejection of radical revolution is not reducible to mere class interest. The Liberal's preference for a qualified franchise, the census franchise, is only in part explained by reference to the interests of property. The plebiscitarian dictatorship of Napoleon III as well as Bismarck's use of universal male suffrage show quite clearly that in mid-nineteenth century Europe equal and universal franchise did not necessarily benefit the liberal-democratic constitutional state.

Moreover, Liberals and Radicals had quite different aims. The former aimed at a liberal constitution in which the participation of the bourgeoisie and the security of the individual had a clear priority, and at the separation of powers. The aims of the Radicals were diametrically opposed to this. In the ideas of the French Revolution the Liberals saw liberty endangered by the permanent rule of the majority over a permanent minority and the dominance of an abstract equality – the kind of fears James Madison had voiced not so long before. Where this was to lead to was at that time not even history. Just as in our own time the shadow of Hitler is still present, so at that time were the excesses of the French Revolution, which continued their influence for most of the century. Ultimately the Radicals argued that the revolution in Europe could achieve its aims only by means of dictatorship.

Quite part from these different aims and fears one will have to turn to the actual political reality of the day and ask what alternatives existed and what chance was there for their realization. The first thing to note is that in spite of their vociferousness the Radicals were in a minority. Events in Baden or Saxony, in Cologne or Berlin, do not change this fact. Three quarters of Germany's population still lived on the land and not in cities. The peasants were largely satisfied with the measures the governments introduced in March 1848. The mentality of the majority was still moulded strongly by particularist and monarchist sentiment, which very much came to the fore in the summer of 1848. Even the moderate Republicans accepted that fact and were prepared to operate within the framework of a constitutional monarchy.

Nor did the Radicals any more than the Liberals represent a socially homogeneous group. All social analyses, Marxist and non-Marxist alike, demonstrate this deficiency, particularly among the lower strata of German society. In other words, the modern class society in Germany was still in the process of development, hence the ambivalent political attitudes of all social groups.

The aim of the extreme Radicals was the completion of the revolution by militant radicalization. We look in vain for a strategy of calculable chances of realization. Popular risings had no chance of lasting success, indeed they produced the spectre of civil war and, more seriously, that of Russian intervention. The Radicals had no means of meeting and defeating the forces of counter-revolution. Marx and Engels as well as Robert Blum have pointed to the only strategic alternative: a great national-democratic war against the epitome of despotism – against Czarist Russia which might have had, as in France in 1793, a revolutionizing and radicalizing effect. But France in 1793 was a relatively well-centralized state. Germany in 1848 was still very much the opposite. But a war without or even against the Prussian army turns this alternative into a mere illusion.

The policy of the Liberals, of evolution rather than revolutionary confrontation appears to have been the more realistic. In the early phase of the revolution the old powers had quickly been pushed back and had made substantial concessions. From then on it was a question of maintaining what had been achieved and not risking a civil war, a Russian intervention or a dictatorship. Hence the extensive debates and discussions on basic civil rights, constitutionally guaranteed. That the Hapsburg Empire would fully recover its strength by the autumn of 1848 was not forseeable in the summer of that year.

What then caused the failure of 1848? The first great defeat of the Frankfurt Assembly was the acceptance of the Malmö Armistice, in spite of vociferous protests. Decisive here was the attitude of the Great European Powers to the revolution in Germany, especially that of Russia. The Liberals accepted the armistice not because they wanted to avoid any strengthening of the forces of the revolution, but because the alternative of a national war and a break with Prussia was not a realistic or for that matter desirable alternative. Not hostility towards democracy, but the realities of power were the decisive factor. As the German historian and prominent member of the Frankfurt Assembly Max Duncker put it at the Assembly: the Germany problem was not a question of liberty but a question of power. And that from a man who little more than a decade before had been persecuted and imprisoned for his 'subversive' convictions!

The first great victory of the forces of counter-revolution was achieved in Vienna, a fact quite unrelated to the differences between Liberals and Radicals in Frankfurt. The victory of the counter-revolution in Berlin was based on the reactivated strength of the old powers, but there exists not a scrap of evidence that political differences between the political groupings in the Prussian National Assembly, or the inclination of the Liberals towards compromise, ensured the success of counter-revolution. Of much greater weight is the drawing back of the strata of society that formerly supported the Liberals from the radicalization of the revolution, and the acceptance of the Conservative alternative: liberty in the form of anarchy versus law and order. But what applies to Berlin does not apply necessarily to the whole of Germany. Nevertheless three factors do apply to the whole of the country. First, a change in attitude, a change of mood evident not only in the bourgeoisie but also the petit bourgeoisie, and – very important – among the peasants. This change did not solely affect the Liberals but all the revolutionary groupings. Second, no one can say whether the Prussian army in view of the strength of reactionary power would not have carried out a counter-revolutionary *coup*, irrespective of the change in the public mood. Though the evidence is far from clear, there are indications which point in this direction. Third, it was not Liberal policy, the policy of finding a middle way, which had caused this change. Liberals were and remained decided opponents of counter-revolution. In Prussia they remained strong enough to force concessions under the imposed constitution, while the Liberals outside Prussia never accepted the Prussian *coup*.

No one can ignore a further factor making for defeat; the splitting of the revolution into particularist revolutions. This weakened the revolution as a whole, and favoured the forces of counter-revolution.

Finally, the last phase of the Frankfurt Assembly demonstrated the central and dominating significance of the 'greater German' and 'little German' problem, the problem of Austro-Prussian dualism and all its implications. It was not the differences between Liberals and Radicals but this dualism which shaped the alternative. The regrouping of the political alignments in the Frankfurt Assembly during the winter of 1848–49, the alliance of the anti-Austrian Radicals with the pro-Austrian 'greater German' Moderates, the rigorous demands of Schwarzenberg – all this demonstrates that in the end the problem of this dualism determined the fate of the revolution of 1848 in Germany far more than the conflict between the political groupings.

'Greater Germany' as demanded by Schwarzenberg would have transferred the major problems of the *multi-national* Empire to what was to become a German *national* state. A united Germany, as envisaged in 1848, could well do without that problem. The Austro-Prussian dualism, the particularist traditions in Germany, the strength of both Austria and Prussia, these were forces that could not be countered by either Liberals or Radical Revolutionaries. Added to this must be the attitude of the Great Powers which has been referred to. After all, the treaties emanating from the Vienna Congress had given them the right to intervene in Germany. This factor could never be ignored. Compared with that, the split between Liberals and Radicals is of purely secondary importance. Also – and it bears repetition – from a German social-historical perspective, German society was in a stage of transition in which the forces of revolution did not represent the majority, not even among the peasantry and rural communities still amounting at that time to two-thirds of the entire German population, not including the Hapsburg Empire.

The Frankfurt Assembly was a parliament without power. The double task of creating a new state and devising a liberal constitution produced problems which were insoluble without it, and the monopoly of power still lay in the hands of the supporters of reaction.

Nevertheless, the Frankfurt Assembly, in spite of its failure, had, to paraphrase Duncker, laid the practical and constitutional foundations for Germany's unification. It displayed, in its thankless task of defining institutionally and constitutionally what Germany should be, more intellect and education, more moderation and self-effacement than one sees in any German Reichstag after 1871. This in itself constitutes no mean achievement. Failure and defeat are not necessarily always the fault or guilt of the defeated.

Chapter 4

THE ERA OF REACTION

Friedrich Wilhelm IV, in spite of his hostility to the constitutional experiment of 1848 in Frankfurt, continued to believe in the need for reform of the German Confederation and a greater degree of German unification. As an initial stage in this process he envisaged the creation of a federation of the north German states under Prussia's leadership.

THE ERFURT UNION AND THE OLMÜTZ PUNCTATION

On 26 May 1849 Radowitz concluded a treaty with Saxony and Hanover who were joined by twenty-eight of the smaller German states, but not Württemberg and Bavaria. It amounted to the furtherance of the aim he had already been pursuing prior to 1848: the creation of a federal state under Prussian leadership associated closely with Austria by a Treaty of Union. Radowitz worked out a constitution in great detail, making provisions for a parliament with an Upper House consisting of German princes and a Lower House. In March 1850 the *Unionsparlament* convened in Erfurt in Thuringia to discuss the new constitution. Radowitz had by now been appointed Prussia's Minister for Foreign Affairs. But neither Friedrich Wilhelm nor Radowitz were able to dispel Austria's suspicions. Austria's Prime Minister, Prince Schwarzenberg, demanded that the Diet of the German Confederation, the Bundestag, be convened under Austria's presidency. It was boycotted by twenty-two members of the 'Erfurt Union'. The ensuing struggle for supremacy in Germany between Prussia and Austria was further complicated because it had begun to involve the Schleswig-Holstein question as well as constitutional conflict in Kur-Hesse, where the ruler's taxation was challenged by the population. The German Confederation was preparing to support

Hesse with armed intervention and Prussia mobilized in response. Austria, supported by Czar Nicholas I, issued an ultimatum to Prussia demanding the end of mobilization and the dissolution of the 'Erfurt Union'. Radowitz and Prince Wilhelm of Prussia were in favour of risking war. Prime Minister Friedrich Wilhelm von Brandenburg and the Minister of War, General August von Stockhausen, declared that Prussia could not take on both Austria and Russia. In the end Friedrich Wilhelm decided in favour of Brandenburg and Stockhausen but, typically, said he hoped they would not come to regret their decision. Radowitz resigned and Brandenburg communicated Prussia's decision to demobilize to Vienna. When Brandenburg died suddenly on 6 November 1850 Otto von Manteuffel took over his office as well as that of foreign affairs. In the Prussian Diet Manteuffel declared, 'The strong is taking a step back, but is keeping his aim firmly in mind, and is looking for ways and means by which it can be achieved in a different way.' On 29 November 1850 Manteuffel and Schwarzenberg signed the Olmütz Punctation which agreed upon the demobilization of Prussia's forces and those of the German Confederation and for the time being put an end to Prussia's bid for supremacy in northern Germany. The *status quo* was restored; Russia had now become the umpire in Central Europe. Prussian Conservatives like Ernst Ludwig von Gerlach argued: 'Unity between Prussia and Austria is German unity. Prussia's and Austria's disunity amounts to the tearing up of Germany and the downfall of Prussia, Austria and Germany.' Prussia returned, in the words of Marx, like a 'rueful sinner into the fold of the reconstituted Diet of the Confederation'. From 15 July 1851 Prussia's representative in Frankfurt was Otto von Bismarck. Using this position he did all he could to obstruct Austrian policy, saying, 'If they put a horse at the front, we will put one at the other end pointing in the opposite direction.'

THE PRUSSIAN CONSTITUTION

After Friedrich Wilhelm IV had dissolved the Prussian Diet in 1849, conservative voices in Prussia could be heard calling for the complete abolition of the constitution, but Friedrich Wilhelm wisely decided to retain it and, with a newly elected Diet, to revise it. As a first step, because of the revolutionary situation which still existed in Germany, he extended the range of the application of the proclamation of a 'State of Siege' without consulting the Diet. But his main aim, after the dissolution of the Second Chamber, was to make sure that new elections would not lead to a chamber of the same composition. The King therefore imposed the three-class franchise on the Second Chamber, a measure which was supported by the Liberals in Prussia who had viewed the general universal male franchise with considerable scepticism. This reduced to a minimum the political participation of the lower strata of Prussia's society. The new election law of 30 May 1849 completed the counter-revolution in Prussia. Only the Left in Prussia spoke out against it and refused to nominate any candidates for the election. The first elections were held on 17 July 1849 and both chambers assembled on 7 August 1849. The democratic Left, which had never been represented in the First Chamber, was now missing in the Second Chamber, where Conservatives and the right Centre, mainly Liberals, dominated. Work began on revising the constitution, which was accepted by both chambers on 17 and 18 December 1849. At first the revisions did not go far enough for Friedrich Wilhelm IV. He objected to swearing an oath to the constitution. His advisers overcame this objection but he still insisted on a number of alterations, and finally on 2 February 1850 the revised constitution was proclaimed. Four days later he delivered his oath to it, still insisting on the 'divine right' and the 'monarchical principle'.

The Crown remained hereditary and the principle that 'the King can do no wrong' prevailed. Ministers were responsible to the King and had to counter-sign any governmental action. This of course made the King dependent on his ministers since they could not be compelled to carry out his orders. They had to make their own decision on the basis of constitutionality and their own conscience but, although they were accountable to the Diet, they were not responsible to it. Sole executive power resided in the hands of the King; he was the Supreme Commander of the army, and the army and navy, apart from budget appropriation, were outside the competence of parliament. The same applied to foreign affairs. The King participated in the legislative process: he exercised legislative power together with both chambers. The King could issue the executive decrees necessary for the implementation of laws enacted by parliament. He also had the right to initiate emergency legislation such as proclaiming a state of siege and other measures when parliament was not sitting. But as far as the state of siege was concerned its actual proclamation was delegated to the State Ministry, or, if need be, to the local military commander. As far as the King's judicial functions were concerned, he could only grant pardons or reduce sentences handed down by the courts.

The State Ministry was headed by the Prime Minister. As such he was not the superior of the other ministers but simply a *primus inter pares* within a collegiate cabinet. The constitution neither mentioned the Prime Minister nor the number and types of ministries. Since they were appointed or dismissed by the King this was outside the competence of the constitution. This system basically operated in Prussia from 1848 until 1918. The Chancellorship emerged only with the North German Confederation in 1867. All ministers had direct access to the King; they swore an oath to the constitution as well as an oath of loyalty to the King. The question of whether the two chambers, or Parliament, would be able eventually to reduce the ministers to parliamentary dependence was unresolved. The constitutional struggle between 1859 and 1866 arose over this issue.

The King also had a close body of advisers for various sectors, the civil cabinet and the military cabinet (later a naval cabinet also), who were outside parliamentary control. The military cabinet, originally part of the War Ministry, managed to emancipate itself from the ministry and was thus outside parliamentary control. The constitution provided for conscription into the army, which was to be a people's army, but, contrary to Friedrich Wilhelm's previous assurance, it was including the military appropriations, was subject to parliamentary approval.

By 1854, after the various changes and arguments, the First Chamber, the *Herrenhaus* was to consist of princes of the royal house who were of age. But their attendance was subject to royal order. Since no Prussian king ever issued such an order no Prussian prince ever sat in the *Herrenhaus*. Furthermore there were the high nobility, such as the heads of the two Hohenzollern branches of Hechingen and Sigmaringen, twenty-two mediated nobles and fifty-one other Prussian nobility. In addition to these the King could appoint holders of high-court offices and, for life, members of the civil service or the officer corps as well as representatives of such organizations as the Protestant Cathedral Chapters, noble agrarian associations, members of the universities and cities. By 1911 there were in all 347 members in the *Herrenhaus*, 260 nobles and 87 burghers.

The Election Law of 30 May 1849 introduced for the Second Chamber the three-class franchise which remained in force until 1918. All male Prussian citizens who had attained their twenty-fourth birth day and who did not depend on charity possessed active franchise and had the right to vote while those who qualified for the passive franchise, i.e. candidates to be voted for, had to have attained their thirtieth birthday. The Prussian election system was a general one, but indirect and unequal. The country was divided into constituencies, each of which elected its deputies. Deputies were not elected directly: instead *Wahlmänner* were elected who then proceeded to elect the deputies. The original voters, the *Urwähler*, were divided into three classes, the first class paying the most in taxes, the third class the least. Each of these classes elected one third of the *Wahlmänner*. The system was based on the argument that the higher one's income the greater one's social and political responsibility. Opponents of it argued that 'property is no virtue, property is mostly not even a merit, property is only a very comfortable fact'. The worst aspect of the election system was that it was based not on secret but on open ballot. Only the French revolutionary constitutions had so far prescribed the open ballot, as a means of revolutionary terrorism.

The Second Chamber had 352 seats. When this law was introduced the predominantly agrarian areas of Prussia gained the most, but with growing industrialization and great shifts of population into urban centres, changes took place in favour of the new industrial middle class and the Conservatives had to give way to the Liberal opposition. Another result was that this franchise system caused great passivity: many of those belonging to the third class did not bother to vote. In the elections of 1849 only 31.9 per cent of the electorate went to the polls; in 1903 only 21.6 per cent, while in the elections of the Reichstag from 1871 onwards the trend went in the opposite direction, the poll averaging 75.8 per cent. Bismarck severely criticized the system but did nothing to change it.

Both chambers were called, prorogued, closed or dissolved by the King. They did not possess the right to assemble of their own volition, but the King had to call them at least once a year in November and as often as circumstances required it. The power of dissolution was an effective weapon against an oppositional parliament. No deputy could be a member of both houses, but civil servants and officers could be members without requiring leave of absence. Deputies were paid expenses and fees for attendance. They also had to swear an oath of loyalty to the King, an oath to fulfil their duties and an oath on the constitution.

The function of both houses, together with the King, was to introduce, debate and enact legislation. Each chamber could introduce legislation. The *Herrenhaus* had to accept or to reject the annual budget as a whole, while the *Abgeordnetenhaus*, the House of Deputies or Second Chamber, could introduce changes, but for them to be enacted required the assent of the King and the First Chamber. The most important power the Second Chamber possessed was the power of the purse. If the Second Chamber did not accept the budget it could not be enacted. The King could have recourse to emergency legislation. A literal interpretation of the constitution meant that in case of rejections all payments by the state would have to cease and thus put an end to effective government. There was no provision in the constitution by which government could carry on in cases of disagreement. The 'gap' in the constitution was bound to have serious consequences once a budget failed to get the assent of the Second Chamber.

The Prussian Constitution also contained a catalogue of basic civil rights and duties, ensuring equality before the law, liberty of person and of religion, freedom of opinion, assembly and association, security of property and judicial protection. The Christian denominations were assured their liberty, which particularly benefited the Catholic Church, while the Protestants were subject to supervision by the King as head of the United Reformed Church. The Catholic Church could communicate freely with Rome. In education the liberty of research and teaching was guaranteed and elementary schooling made compulsory; teachers in state schools became civil servants. The independence of the judiciary was decreed and its competency clearly defined.

THE POLICY OF REACTION

At a national level from 1841 Austria tried to resolve Austro-Prussian dualism by putting Prussia firmly into second place. Prussia, represented by Bismarck in Frankfurt, viewed this development with suspicion and opposed it where it could. But both states were agreed over the issue of combating liberal and democratic tendencies in all the member states of the German Confederation. On 23 August 1851 the Confederate Diet compelled the member states to set up institutions and ensure that conditions existed which would safeguard law and order and avoid situations which threatened the Confederation's general security. Hence all institutions created since 1848 would have to be scrutinized to see if they agreed with the Confederate Law, and if obstruction was met special commissions of the Confederation would be put into operation. Examination of such cases was a matter for the 'Committee of Reaction' comprising Austria, Prussia, Bavaria, Saxony and Hesse-Darmstadt. Furthermore, misuse of the freedom of the press should be prevented and special legislation for this was to be introduced. Papers and periodicals which expressed atheist, socialist or communist views and aimed at the overthrow of the monarchy were to be suppressed. Thus the establishment of a strong executive power for the Confederation was tantamount to the restoration of the Carlsbad Decrees. The Committee of Reaction began its work in October 1851. It examined all the constitutions, electoral and press laws of the member states, and most of them had to change their constitutions, with the exception of Bavaria.

In *Prussia* the cabinet under Manteuffel from 1850 to 1858 pursued a strongly reactionary course, without, however, acting unconstitutionally, though some of the conservatives planned just that: to do away with parliament and replace it by an assembly of the estates. Nothing came of that nor of the plan to revise the constitution yet again. All that was achieved was a restoration of the provincial estates. The reconstitution of the State Council was considered in this context but abandoned since it would have made sense only within the context of a *coup d'état*. However, the political police under the Berlin police president, Karl Ludwig Friedrich von Hinckeldey, became an important instrument to combact subversive activities. But it can be said that his unscrupulous policy affected democrats as much as it did the conservatives, particularly the Gerlach party. The press was strictly supervised and a central office for press affairs was established within the Ministry of the Interior. The mouthpiece of the arch-conservatives, the *Kreuzzeitung*, was interfered with so much that its editor resigned.

A number of political trials took place but in fairness to the Prussian judiciary it must be said that it did not allow itself to become the instrument of the political police. They acquitted a large number of cases, even individuals accused of having participated in the Baden revolution of 1849. A great source of embarrassment was the Cologne Communist trial of 1852. Eleven members of the Cologne Communist Association were accused of high treason. The evidence the political police submitted had come from London and Paris but most of it turned out to be police fabrications. Yet four of the accused were acquitted, and the rest, including Hermann Becker, the future Lord Mayor of Cologne and member of the *Herrenhaus*, were sentenced to varying short terms of imprisonment.

The Protestant Church was also used as an instrument of reaction. Its schools especially were to be institutions for the indoctrination of patriotism and piety. Subjects taught in elementary schools were reduced to the three Rs.

In this environment Prussia's political parties began to reform themselves: the Conservative Party, small but influential, and the *Wochenblattpartei*, Liberal Conservatives under Moritz August von Bethmann Hollweg, which had split from the Conservatives. It supported the constitution and opposed any interference with it, while it also adhered to the cause of German unity. The Liberal Party was only a shadow of what it had been in 1848–49: it opposed Manteuffel.

Since the marriage of Friedrich Wilhelm IV remained without issue his brother Prince Wilhelm von Preussen was the successor to the throne. He was renowned as an arch reactionary in 1848–49 and during the 1850s he opposed both the foreign and domestic policy of Prussia from his military command at Koblenz. He castigated the dominance of bureaucracy and clericalism, but there was little he could do in practice before being called to the highest office himself.

In *Bavaria* moderates prevailed in the Second Chamber. Leaning strongly on Austria its various governments opposed Prussia's bid for dominance. In terms of domestic policy the struggle, as in Prussia, was directed as much against the ultra-Conservatives as against the democratic Left. But towards the end of the 1850s conservative and reactionary currents increased, blocked only by the outbreak of the constitutional conflict in Prussia. Prussia's hardline conservatism led in Bavaria to a return to more liberal policies.

Württemberg's King Wilhelm I had introduced a one-chamber system on 1 July 1849 and entrusted it with the revision of the constitution. The result was that the Liberals had to make way for liberal

Conservatives whose job it was to restore the kingdom's public institutions, whose reputation had plummeted. The new assembly met on 1 December 1849: the Radical Democrats with 44 seats had a strong majority compared to the Liberal Centre which supported the government, but had only 20 seats. Attempts at cooperation failed and the King dissolved the assembly, since it was out of the question that it should pass constitutional revisions. A new conservative government under Joseph von Linden was appointed pursuing a pro-Austrian policy and, since the assembly called by Wilhelm in 1849 had proved unworkable, the Linden government carried out a *coup d'état* by calling an assembly of the estates. The Liberals accepted this; the Democrats protested in vain, but participated in the elections of 1851. The government party of the Right was supported by the Liberal Centre while the Democrats, the *Volkspartei*, could only muster 18 seats. Thus Württemberg returned to the conditions prevailing prior to March 1848. Linden's reactionary policy, however, increased and the opposition Liberals and Democrats began to cooperate, combining themselves in 1859 into the Progressive Party.

In the Grand Duchy of *Baden* the state of siege proclaimed in 1849 remained in force until 1852. Prussia's influence there was strong. Prussian troops only left the Grand Duchy in November 1850. Two years later, after the death of Grand Duke Leopold, his second son Friedrich succeeded to the throne, and lifted the state of siege. The initial phase of his reign was marked by conflicts with the Catholic Church which were not settled until 1860. For the rest of his reign he backed German unification under Prussian auspices and conducted a liberal domestic policy aiming at healing the wounds of 1849.

Hesse-Darmstadt under the Grand Duke Ludwig III was in endemic conflict with the Radical Party. The Liberal ministry under Karl Heinrich Jaup held elections in December 1849 in which Liberals supporting the government maintained their majority in the First Chamber while the democratic opposition had a two-thirds majority in the Second Chamber. The Grand Duke replied by dissolving both chambers. Jaup was a supporter of the 'little German' solution and as such was in favour of Hesse-Darmstadt's joining the Erfurt Union. He was opposed by the 'greater German' Conservatives under Prince Emil who cooperated with the Conservatives of Kur-Hesse. Their cooperation ensured the fall of Jaup and determined the policy of both Hesses for the following decade and a half. Jaup's successor, Karl Friedrich von Dalwigk, joined the Austrian course in German politics and internally returned to a form of absolutist government.

In the Kingdom of *Saxony* the King by means of a *coup d'état* restored the assembly of the estates in place of parliament. The University of Leipzig protested loudly, but to no avail. Twenty-one professors including four heads of faculty were suspended. Then on 15 July 1850 the Diet was reconvened as it had existed before 1848 and

nullified most of the constitutional regislation, returning to the constitution of 1831 – a clear breach of legality. This course was continued
after the death of King Friedrich Augustus by his successor King
Johann whose Prime Minister, Count Friedrich von Beust, further
consolidated the reactionary policy he had begun under the old King.

Hanover's King Ernest August followed the pattern of Saxony,
though he did not abolish the two chambers but merely dissolved
them. In the judicial sphere a reform policy was continued, which
amounted to a significant contribution to a future German judicial
constitution, but precisely these reforms caused the King to change
governments. King Ernest Augustus died in 1851 and was succeeded
by George V. The jurist Eduard von Schele headed the new cabinet in
which two actions were opposed to one another. The Catholic Ludwig
Windthorst and his supporters opposed the interference of the Confederation in Hanover's constitutional affairs while ministers like
Count Wilhelm von Borries wanted to overthrow the existing constitution. Schele, a supporter of the former faction, was in favour of a
moderate revision of the constitution. Failure to achieve this led to the
resignation of his cabinet in 1853. The new ministry under Eduard von
Lütcken was determined not to come to terms with the newly elected
chambers in 1854 and instead opted for a constitutional revision with
the support or even the intervention of the Confederation. This they
did effectively but by unconstitutional means. Lütcken had operated
within the existing institutional framework, but his successor Count
Eduard Kielmannsegg had the Second Chamber dissolved and nullified all constitutional progress made since 1848. However, one of the
consequences was a revival of liberal opposition of German national
unity vintage and the creation of the *Nationalverein*, supporting
German unification.

In *Kur-Hesse* the democratic one-chamber system was abolished
and replaced by two chambers with a franchise requiring a high
property qualification. The Liberals, at first in disarray, by the late
1850s had regained their strength and the revised constitution of 1852
was revoked once more by the end of 1859.

The *Mecklenburg* constitutional assembly of 31 October 1848 had
been made up of one tenth Conservatives, one third Liberals and one
third Democrats, the remainder having no political affiliation. They
had agreed on a franchise which severely curtailed its general application and equality. Nevertheless they still introduced a constitution
which Grand Duke George found too liberal and he dissolved the
assembly, an act which the Strelitz Duke was not empowered to do. He
rejected any objections, by the subjects of both Mecklenburgs. The
government of Strelitz and Mecklenburg's nobility took the issue to
court with the result that the Constitution, the State Basic Law, of
1849, was declared as illegal as was the Constitution of 1849. Thus in
constitutional terms Mecklenburg returned to the political status

which had existed in 1755. It restored the estates, and subsequent endeavours, even between 1871 and 1914, to give Mecklenburg a constitution failed.

ZOLLVEREIN AND MITTELEUROPA

Meanwhile, the Diet of the German Confederation had been deliberating about a German navy on the same contingent basis as applied to the army. It produced almost endless arguments and counter-arguments so that finally it was decided to dissolve the existing German navy.

The question of the *Zollverein* was of greater importance. The Austrian Minister of Trade, Karl Ludwig von Bruck, endeavoured to enlarge it by Austria's accession, thus creating *Mitteleuropa* from Trieste to the North Sea. The move failed because of Prussia's opposition. At that time she was pursuing the plan leading to the formation of the Erfurt Union, which would have excluded Austria. Although the Olmütz Punctation prevented this from happening, Prussia's opposition to Austria's admission to the *Zollverein* remained. First Prussia took recourse to delaying tactics. She wanted to keep intact the one group in Germany in which Prussia had gained dominance to the exclusion of Austria. Hanover in 1851, followed by Oldenburg in 1852, signed a treaty with Prussia which made them members of the *Zollverein* from 1854 onwards. Since, however, prior agreement of the other members would have been necessary, Bavaria in particular was piqued and together with Saxony threatened to form a south German customs union with Austria. Prussia countered that according to the Treaty of Accession, Bavaria could not leave before 1854 and it invited the member states to a conference in Berlin for 1 April 1852. Austria responded by calling a customs conference in Vienna. Prussia refused to participate. But the majority of the member states sent their delegates to Vienna. Austria submitted three alternative proposals: (a) the conclusion of general trade treaties, (b) a complete customs union including Prussia and Austria, (c) a customs union excluding Prussia. The delegates could not agree, since the first two proposals were considered unrealistic while the third would have meant a considerable risk for those taking this step. All that was agreed on was that Bavaria, Saxony, both Hesses and Nassau would meet at a conference in Darmstadt on 6 April 1852. There they agreed to act *en bloc* in future negotiations of the *Zollverein*.

This they did at the Berlin General Conference of the *Zollverein* between April and September 1852. Prussia insisted successfully on first renewing the *Zollverein* and entering into negotiations with

Austria. Saxony could not afford to leave the *Zollverein* and by 26 November 1852 Prussia had already made new treaties with Hanover, Oldenburg, Brunswick and Thuringian states. She managed to conclude a trade agreement in 1853 with Austria on the 'most-favoured-nation' basis to last for twelve years. One of Austria's main motives for doing this was the emergence of Napoleon III in France and the fear of an era of renewed instability in Europe. Also in 1853, after the Austro-Prussian trade treaty, the *Zollverein* was extended by including further members. Only Austria, Liechtenstein, Limburg, the Mecklenburgs, Holstein and the Hanseatic cities of Hamburg, Bremen and Lübeck were still outside it.

At the turn of the decade in 1859–1860 Austria reapplied for membership in the *Zollverein*. But Prussia pointed to the irreconcilability of the high-tariff policy followed by Austria and the free-trade policy pursued by the *Zollverein*. Austria was annoyed, and became even more so when Prussia, between 1860 and 1862, negotiated a trade agreement with France, concluded on 3 April 1862, which Prussia then submitted to the member states of the *Zollverein*. The agreement opened the western European market to Germany, integrating it into the western European economic community. Austria felt rather embittered because by this treaty France also enjoyed 'most-favoured-nation' treatment. In a note to the members of the *Zollverein* it opposed Prussia's claim that by the agreement with France it had the right to introduce lower tariffs and thus overturn the whole customs system as it had existed hitherto; and also requested admission. Prussia rejected the demand and Austria was now determined to torpedo the *Zollverein*. It seemed to have a chance. Bavaria joined Württemberg and Hesse-Darmstadt and rejected the Prusso-French trade agreement, but Prussia replied on 26 August 1862 that its rejection was tantamount to declaring that the states concerned did not wish to continue the *Zollverein*. Agitation of political parties and interest groups was rife in Germany. The *Nationalverein* supported Prussia, as did the associations of industrialists. Bismarck, Prime Minister of Prussia since 1862, showed his most conciliatory side and called for a new General Conference of the German *Zollverein* from 24 March to 17 July 1863 in Munich. All those who assembled there were agreed in wanting to maintain the *Zollverein* but the south German states asked for a renewal of negotiations with Austria about its accession. A conference was held in Berlin from 5 November to 15 December which was already overshadowed by the problem of Schleswig-Holstein. The climate moved in favour of Prussia, which gave notice that it would leave the *Zollverein* by the end of 1865. In the light of this the member states resolved to come to a trade agreement with Austria, which they did on 11 April 1865; already, in the preceding year, on 12 October 1864, the new *Zollverein* Treaty had been ratified.

THE GERMAN CONFEDERATION AND EUROPEAN POLITICS

In the meantime the German Confederation had undergone several international crises; the Crimean War, the question of Neuenburg and the Austro-Italian War. The Crimean War drastically demonstrated the impotence of the German Confederation in the realm of international politics. Only Austria and Prussia were capable of acting, but Prussia was divided over the issue, the parties crystallizing around the pro-Russian *Kreuzzeitung* and the pro-British *Wochenblatt*. Both claimed the right to participate in deciding what Prussia should do, itself a sign that the constitutional state was coming into its own. Austria was equally divided, but both states opted ultimately for neutrality. Within Prussia the pro-Russian arch-conservatives seemed to make the running at first, which led to the dismissal of the Minister of War, Eduard von Bonin, who opposed intervention. His dismissal caused Prince Wilhelm to protest by means of two rather offensive letters to Manteuffel. From then on relations between Friedrich Wilhelm IV and the Prince of Prussia became estranged, and were never to be mended. But one fact which even the pro-Russian party could not ignore was that militarily Prussia was badly prepared. In this situation it formed a defensive alliance with Austria, a means to strengthen its policy of neutrality. Inside Prussia it neutralized the pro-Russian and pro-British factions within the chambers, while externally it aimed to prevent Austria from joining the Western powers, though Austria hoped to use the alliance in the interests of intervention. The other member states of the Confederation were asked to join this alliance, a step delayed by the vacillating attitude of the German middle states.[1] The war party in Vienna saw in this a strengthening of its own position, and Austria mobilized, much to the alarm of Prussia. Under Prussian pressure the Confederate Diet declared on 8 February 1855 that the danger of war had passed for Germany, which meant the member states would not have to mobilize their armies. Not that it mattered one way or the other. At the Vienna Peace Conference beginning on 15 March 1855, neither Prussia nor the German Confederation was represented, nor for that matter at the Peace Treaty of Paris on 30 March 1856.

The Duchy of Neuenburg (Neufchâtel) was situated in Switzerland but had since 1707 belonged to Prussia. In 1848 Swiss Radicals led the revolution there. No Prussian troops were garrisoned in the Duchy, and there was nothing the Prussian Crown could do about it. During the era of reaction Friedrich Wilhelm IV thought he could reassert his rights with the assistance of the European powers. Indeed Prussian rights in Neuenburg were recognized by the London Protocol of 24

May 1854, but this amounted to little, especially after a royalist *putsch* in Neuenburg was quickly defeated. Great Britain now took the part of Switzerland and pressed for an acceptance of the republican *fait accompli*, while Napoleon III and the German Confederation supported Friedrich Wilhelm. There seemed no other alternative than armed intervention until Switzerland was forced into a compromise under French pressure. The Neuenburg republicans were to release the participants of the royalist *putsch*, while the King of Prussia would renounce his rights to the territory, which he did on 19 June 1857. It was nevertheless a clear victory for the republican over the monarchical principle.

THE IMPACT OF ITALIAN UNIFICATION AND THE PRUSSIAN CONSTITUTIONAL CONFLICT

Since the rise of Napoleon III the Italian unification movement had gained new impetus which threatened the principle of monarchical legitimacy. Russia, the stout defender of this principle, had been alienated by Austria's attitude in the Crimean War and was therefore not prepared to back Austria when Italy went to war to recover Italian provinces from the Hapsburg Empire. Prussia had no interest either, and was intent on maintaining its good relations with Russia. Only Great Britain was at first inclined to support Austria, at least under Palmerston, but in 1858 when the Tories came to power Great Britain was interested in containing any conflict in Europe. The Franco-Sardinian alliance of 10 December 1858 was the overture to the war. Austria tried to get the support of Prussia and the German Confederation, and generally Germany's public opinion was on Austria's side, because it feared the threat of France. The slogan was that of defending the Rhine on the Po. But Prussia opposed German mobilization on behalf of Austria on the grounds that the territory of the German Confederation was not threatened by the conflict. The Prussian Chief of General Staff, Helmuth von Moltke, and Eduard von Bonin who had been recalled to his office of Minister of War, were in favour of Prussian intervention on Austria's side but were overruled. In the opinion of the Prince of Prussia who, because of Friedrich Wilhelm IV's illness, had taken over the regency, the condition of the Prussian army was not such to ensure victory. He was convinced that Austria would be defeated, in which case he hoped, at the head of a German army, to dictate a peace which would preserve Austria's Italian territories. This would put Prussia at the apex of Germany. The battles of Montebello, Magenta and Solferino confirmed his assessment of Austria's military power and caused the partial mobilization of the Prussian army for the purpose of armed mediation. But before that could come to pass Emperor Francis Joseph and Napoleon III made peace at Villafranca.

Solferina had driven home one message to Prussia, the need to reform its army, and this was an indirect trigger to the Prussian constitutional conflict. On 23 October 1857 Prince Wilhelm of Prussia had assumed the reins of government; a year later he was appointed regent and on 26 October 1858 he swore the oath to the Constitution. In spite of his conservative inclinations he was intent on ruling constitutionally and introducing a more liberal era. This meant the departure of the Manteuffel cabinet and the appointment of a new Liberal cabinet headed by Prince Hohenzollern-Sigmaringen. In his speech to the new cabinet the Prince of Prussia emphasized that he would combat anything which pursued political aims under the cloak of religion. The school system would require liberalization, and Prussia's higher educational institutions would have to regain their eminence. Prussia's military force would require changes so that it would become an effective weight in the scales of power. 'Prussia must make moral conquests in Germany, by wise legislation, and the elevation of ethical norms.' The address threw down the gauntlet to the arch-conservatives and the political clergy. Bismarck had to give up his post in Frankfurt and became envoy in St Petersburg. His position there was most precarious because Wilhelm's wife, Princess Augusta, utterly detested him.

But Prince Wilhelm was first and foremost a soldier and not a politician. He thought the military and the civilian spheres should be strictly separated from one another. In its original concept the military reform he envisaged was not a sacrifice of the reforms of Scharnhorst and Boyen but their further extension. The Prussian army was still the size it had been in 1817. Although the Prussian population had increased from 11 million in 1817 to 18 million by 1858, only 40,000 recruits were drafted annually, a mere two-ninths of the available 180,000. Conscription was just a piece of paper, and the way it was practised contained serious inequalities. The regular army was under strength and in case of mobilization had to have recourse to the *Landwehr* whose training during the past decades had been seriously neglected. (The *Landwehr* was not only the territorial reserve but also 'the peoples' institution' sacred to the Liberals.) The Minister of War von Bonin frustrated the first reforms and in order to get the appropriations accepted by the Diet he advised Wilhelm to make constitutional concessions. Wilhelm, however, insisted on reform without concessions. Bonin resigned again and was replaced by General Albrecht von Roon, an arch-monarchist and authoritarian. This did not mean a change in the liberal course of the Hohenzollern-Sigmaringen cabinet but a change in military policy. The new reform envisaged drafting 63,000 recruits annually, extending the priod of compulsory military service to three years, and increasing the army from 150,000 to 220,000 men. The *Landwehr* was not to be abolished but further integrated into the army. The total cost would amount to 9½ million Talers per annum, no great burden on the budget. The important question, constitutionally, was who had the power to reform the army, the Prussian Diet because of its legislative initiative or the King as supreme commander of the army, a position as yet still within the royal prerogative. The Second Chamber argued that the reorganization of the army affected the law since it involved changes in the Defence Law of 1814 and, even more important, it involved intrusion into the basic rights of both individual liberty and property granted by the constitution.

The government did not dispute the fact that army reorganization was a matter for the law, but the law was the existing Defence Law of 1814 and the King could operate within its framework as he saw fit. Roon's plans were opposed from the very outset by the Liberals in the Second Chamber. Although not opposed in principle to the increase of the Prussian army, they insisted that the conscription period be limited to two years and the *Landwehr* be kept as it had existed hitherto. The King, or rather at this time still the Prince Regent, rejected these demands outright and interpreted them as interference in his power of command, which of course included the army's training and organization. He had not forgotten the *Landwehr* mutinies and was intent upon separating civilians and military to ensure that the army would become an instrument absolutely reliable to the royal will, to be used for Prussia's external as well as internal security. Obsessed by the endemic fear of revolution, which he had already seen many times in his lifetime, he was convinced that only a period of three years' service would produce the type of soldier who was utterly committed to the Crown and Fatherland. Three years would ensure the transformation of a people's army into a royal army, a constituent but separate part of the state, with an ethos determined by the professional regular officer corps. Since 1848 Wilhelm had viewed the *Landwehr* with deep suspicion, believing Scharnhorst's creation was no more than a training battalion for revolution. The Liberals on the other hand considered the reform of the *Landwehr* as an act of discrimination.

In accordance with Wilhelm's speech from the throne of 12 January 1860, the Minister of War submitted a month later the draft for a military law which contained provisions for the reorganization of the army and a financial law which asked for the 9½ million Talers necessary for it. The proposed legislation was referred to a parliamentary committee which agreed to accept it on condition that the two-year period of service be retained and that the *Landwehr* remain part of the field army. The Prince Regent considered these conditions unacceptable, arguing that the law as such was not really necessary since the whole matter was in the sphere of his prerogative. The road of new legislation had only been chosen in order to meet the Diet half way. From a narrow constitutional angle this was correct: conscription and length of service had been settled in 1814, when it was also laid down that the peacetime strength of the army was to be determined by the conditions prevailing at the time. According to Article 3 of the Defence Law all regulations lay in the hands of the Monarch. This had not been changed by the constitution of 1850. For this very reason the actual reform had already begun before these two submissions were made to the Diet. *Landwehr* units had been transformed into regular army units. But all this involved more expenditure and hence recourse to the Diet could not be avoided. The Minister of Finance, Robert von Patow, submitted the Finance Bill for 9½ million Talers to be spent within the period 1 May 1860 to 30 June 1861. He called it a provisional measure to complete and maintain such reforms of the army as had already taken place, and if the Second Chamber refused later on to make any new grants everything could then be reversed. As such the Second Chamber accepted and enacted the Finance Bill. This was a dangerous compromise not free from the taint of duplicity on the government's side. Wilhelm immediately dissolved thirty-six *Landwehr* regiments which had become superfluous to his reorganization plan and raised thirty-six regiments of line infantry in their place. By the autumn of 1860 these had been given their names and colours, and they were all sworn in, after Friedrich Wilhelm IV had died and the Prince Regent had been crowned King in Königsberg on 18 January 1861. These military measures could hardly be reversed.

Wilhelm had also insisted that the old custom of paying homage would be retained at his coronation; however, a group of Liberal ministers in his government argued that such an act was not in accordance with the words and the spirit of the constitution. Reluctantly Wilhelm gave in, persuaded by the argument that the spiritual act of coronation would act as a substitute for the ceremony of homage. The constitution itself said nothing about the coronation, and only the first King *in* Prussia, Friedrich I, had had himself crowned in Königsberg in 1701. His successors had not followed his example: upon accession to the throne they were crowned in Berlin.

In his speech from the throne on 14 January 1861 Wilhelm proclaimed that the reorganization of the army was final and not provisional. He submitted no more bills except for a financial one, demanding 8 million Talers for 1861–62. The Liberal opposition refused to assent and Georg von Vincke, a former civil servant before he became a Liberal politician, demanded that a bill on the length of military service be introduced at the next session of the Diet. Again it enacted the money bill as a provisional measure but not before having cut it by 750,000 Talers. As usual on 5 June 1861 the Diet was prorogued and this gave the government new breathing-space.

The elections of 6 December 1861 brought a resounding defeat to the Conservatives whose number of seats shrank to 14, while the Liberals were the actual victors. They were, however, split into the *Old Liberals* with 91 seats and the *Left Centre* with 50 seats, while the Catholics gained 54 seats. Important in the constitutional context was the re-emergence of the radical left who had formed themselves into the German Progressive Party and gained 109 seats. The Progressives fought for the maintenance of the two-year period of military conscription and of the *Landwehr*. Wilhelm's speech from the throne announced the introduction of a Bill extending the period of service to three years. The Diet was not prepared to consent to this nor was it prepared this time to pass the annual budget and increase income tax. In place of a government demand for a blanket appropriation it demanded that each item of expenditure be specified. As the majority of the Diet supported this attitude, Wilhelm I dissolved the Second Chamber on 11 March 1862. At the same time he formed a new government under Prince Hohenlohe-Ingelfingen. General von Roon remained Minister of War. On 6 May 1862 new elections for the Second Chamber took place. The Conservatives' position was further reduced from 14 to 11. Not one of the ministers who had stood for election was successful. The Catholic faction which had supported the government's military reorganization was reduced from 54 to 28 seats. The Old Liberals also lost, their seats being reduced from 91 to 65. It was their death-knell: they split into a constitutional faction with their left wing joining the Left Centre. Thus the Left Liberals gained 96 seats while the winners of the election were the Progressives with 133 seats. Taking all the Liberal opposition forces together they amounted to 85 per cent of the Diet and a compromise with the government was thus no longer on the cards. This parliamentary failure brought Wilhelm to the edge of abdication by the autumn of 1862. He had already drafted his abdication in favour of his son Friedrich Wilhelm. Crown and parliament had reached a deadlock, the former unwilling to suffer any inroads into its prerogative, the latter determined to throw out the military budget and impose parliamentary government upon the Crown. What was at stake was nothing less than the subjugation of the Crown to parliament and the overthrow of the monarchical principle.

On the day Wilhelm had drafted his abdication, Roon cabled Bismarck in Paris where he had gone after St Petersburg, recalling him to Berlin. On 22 September 1862 Bismarck had his audience with the King in which he declared himself ready to fight for three years of military conscription, even if that meant governing without parliament if it failed to pass the budget. Bismarck was appointed Prime Minister. On 23 September 1862 the Second Chamber cut all army appropriations in the budget to the tune of 6 million Talers. Only ten Deputies voted for the King's budget. Bismarck reformed his cabinet, appointing the one with which he was to fight not only on the domestic scene but in external affairs as well.

Bismarck tried to compromise at first by offering three ministerial posts to the Liberals, but they were not prepared to accept the King's policy. Whether the Liberals missed their chance then is a matter of speculation: Liberals in Prussia's leading ministries would have been an important step, but precisely in what direction must remain a matter of conjecture.

Bismarck withdrew his budget proposals for 1863, even before those of 1862 had been passed. On 30 September 1862 he addressed the Second Chamber in words which left no doubt that when faced by the attitude of the chamber he would pursue an uncompromising course. He talked hard political facts devoid of any ideology and cant, but this failed to impress the deputies, who passed the budget for 1862, minus the military expenditure. The First Chamber rejected the Second Chamber's budget and passed the original budget instead. The Second Chamber declared this unconstitutional. In view of this situation the King closed both chambers on 13 October 1862. Bismarck now formulated his *Lückentheorie*, the theory of a 'gap' in the constitution, originally formulated by the *Kreuzzeitung*. First, the government was unable to reverse the changes in the army based on provisional appropriation without causing serious damage. Second, the government was therefore forced to govern the State outside the basis envisaged in the constitution, and it would have to conduct business without budgets approved by the Diet. Third, the government was well aware of its constitutional duties and would fulfil them until a budget was constitutionally passed. It would also ask for a *post factum* sanction of its expenditure. The government was acting in an emergency; it was not its desire to do away with the constitution, on the contrary it desired to return to it on the basis of a bill of indemnity when the situation allowed it.

Bismarck adopted the same attitude when the Diet met on 14 January 1863. When Rudolf Virchow, the famous pathologist and one of the leaders of the Progressives, attacked the government for acting unconstitutionally, Bismarck replied that what would have to happen in the case of a budget not being ratified was not provided for in the constitution. In the face of this *constitutional gap* it was the government's duty to prevent a standstill of all business. Government had to continue even if that implied expenditure without lawful parliamentary enactment. Wilhelm fully backed his position.

The Second Chamber now tried to get the matter resolved by the judiciary and for that purpose introduced a bill on ministerial responsibility which was to empower the courts to decide whether ministers acted constitutionally or not. It was passed with a large majority but had no chance of being passed by the *Herrenhaus*, the First Chamber, let alone by the King. On 10 February 1863 the government submitted a third draft on the subject of conscription. It tried to meet the opposition by reintroducing the first line of the *Landwehr* but insisted on three years' service. This in effect meant sacrificing part of the royal prerogative and if the Liberals had accepted it they would have assumed an important role in formulating military policy. Part of the Left Centre was in favour of acceptance although the bill transformed the annual military appropriations into a fixed *Aternat*, not to be voted again annually. The military budget would thus have been removed from Parliament's competency. But the parliamentary commission demanded a law on recruitment, a law on national service which would lay down the recruitment and service periods, and an organizational law which would detail the strength and structure of the army. Roon was not prepared to accept it, though he too was ready to compromise over the two-year period of service. But the compromise was rejected by the Conservatives, the Old Liberals and the left wing of the Progressives who explicitly demanded a change of government. It would only be prepared to discuss the military question on that basis. Roon now took a hard line: 'The government determines the strength of the army and you have the right to approve it.' The debate produced massive accusations against the ministers which made Bismarck declare that they were prevented from attending the Diet when it reassembled (after the session had been interrupted for one hour). He further made ministerial participation dependent upon a declaration by the chamber that it claimed no disciplinary powers over the ministers. No such declaration was forthcoming and the government withdrew its bill. The King supported his ministers. On 22 May 1863 the Second Chamber proclaimed that there was no basis for cooperation with the present government. It was supported by 239 to 61. In fact it was a vote of 'no confidence'. If the King had now changed the government this would have meant transition to parliamentary government but Wilhelm did no such thing: he refuted the chamber's right to force another government upon him and on 27 May 1863 he closed the Diet.

All this was watched with great attention by the Prussian and German press and the press debate reached proportions which caused the King and Bismarck to invoke Article 63 of the constitution which imposed censorship and proscription of papers and periodicals after they had been warned twice, 'because of endangering public welfare'. Even the royal family was divided over whether criticism was to be muffled. Crown Prince Friedrich Wilhelm in a speech in Danzig publicly expressed his disagreement with the government measure.

New elections on 28 October 1863 somewhat reduced the Liberal opposition but it still commanded 70 per cent of the seats. The press censorship law introduced by the government needed parliamentary ratification and was soundly defeated. For the first time the Second Chamber had compelled the government to revoke and withdraw its legislation. It also cut down the budget so that it was unacceptable to the government. Government without a parliamentary-approved budget was continued.

Bismarck was now thinking of political alternatives such as the introduction of universal male franchise in Prussia, which he expected would bring forth the support the government needed. He entered into discussions with the founder of the German workers' movement, the leader of the *Allgemeiner Deutscher Arbeiterverein*. Assessment of the weight attributed to these discussions differs but two things are beyond doubt. Firstly, under the leadership of Lassalle, who envisaged an alliance between the existing state of a united Germany and its growing industrial working class, the German working-class movement would have taken a different direction than under the initially revolutionary Marxist leadership of Wilhelm Liebknecht and August Bebel. This is confirmed by the fact that from the early 1860s onwards there is ample evidence of Bismarck's awareness of social problems and his recognition of the need for social reform which ultimately he was to carry out in the form of state socialism. Secondly, however – and this indicates that not too much weight should be placed on these conversations – Bismarck was a shrewd assessor of power. Lassalle's movement, at the time, was only a few thousand members strong, and hence was hardly likely to tip the scales in Bismarck's favour in the present constitutional predicament. Though correct at the time, this assessment on the other hand failed to recognize the long-term political potential of politically organized labour.

After the Diet had been closed in January 1864 the chamber did not meet throughout the year, while Bismarck hoped that tempers would cool. It reassembled on 14 January 1865. Once again a conscription law was submitted and rejected, as was a naval bill. The session ended with the Second Chamber cutting the budget, opposed by Conservatives and supported by the Left. The budget proposals of the Second Chamber were thrown out by the *Herrenhaus*. The King closed the session on 17 June 1865.

SCHLESWIG-HOLSTEIN

A new division was now appearing, that between the Second Chamber and public opinion, which became increasingly impressed by Bismarck's foreign policy, aimed at the consolidation of Germany. The issue which deeply stirred German national sentiment, that of Schleswig-Holstein, again came before the public eye. King Frederick VII of Denmark, yielding to the pressure of Danish nationalists and contrary to the London Protocol of 1852, separated Schleswig from Holstein, annexing the former and introducing a new constitution for the latter. The Diet of German Confederation called upon Frederick to desist. When the Danish government refused, the German Confederation decided to intervene, but the Danes stole a march on them by accepting a constitution applicable to Schleswig as well as Holstein which meant Schleswig's annexation and its separation from Holstein. Frederick died on 15 November 1863 without having been able to sign the new constitution. The following day, on the basis of the London Protocol, Prince Christian of Glücksburg was proclaimed King Christian IX, while at the same time Prince Frederick of Augustenburg issued a proclamation in which he announced his succession in Schleswig-Holstein as Duke Frederick VIII. Frederick found immediate support in Holstein and among national and liberal opinion in Germany. Both Prussia and Austria decided not to call on national support in Germany, though for different reasons. Austria's policy was the result of Napoleon III's plan to revise the treaties of 1815 according to the principle of national self-determination, a plan which the events in Denmark had given him occasion to voice again and which carried profound dangers for the Hapsburg Empire. What Austria aimed at in the Schleswig-Holstein question was the restoration of the previous personal union between the Duchies and Denmark. Bismarck, however, thought in terms of their annexation. Wilhelm I was initially very reluctant to follow Bismarck's advice on this, arguing that Prussia had no right to claim these Duchies. But Bismarck pointed out that Augustenburg's claims were equally doubtful, and that there was also another possible outcome to the situation, namely the creation of a new small state, which as far as Prussia was concerned would offer no guarantees over its future political direction. The wishes of German public opinion would best be met if Prussia, with the agreement of the German Confederation, leaving out Austria, declared war on Denmark and then placed Augustenburg on the throne. But that course would mean war with Austria and the intervention of the western powers. To act jointly with Austria would be the course most likely to prevent the formation of a European coalition.

In spite of the opposition of the Prussian Queen and Crown Princess Victoria, Wilhelm came to support the policy of his Prime Minister. Prussia therefore, jointly with Austria, pressed for action by the German Confederation against the Danish breach of the London Protocol. Great Britain and Russia tried to mediate but Danish national fervour forced the King of Denmark's hand and mediation failed. Prussia and Austria now asked the Diet of the German Confederation to demand that the King of Denmark revoke the constitution or else their forces would occupy Schleswig until their demands were met. This the Diet refused to sanction and Prussia and Austria decided to go it alone, concluding an alliance on 16 January 1864. They issued an ultimatum to Denmark and after its rejection Prussian and Austrian forces under Prussian command took the offensive. The reorganization of the Prussian army bore its first fruits. The Danish government first sued for an armistice and then for peace which was finally concluded on 30 October 1864. Denmark ceded Schleswig, Holstein and Lauenburg to Prussia and Austria, who already occupied them jointly. This was hardly a satisfactory conclusion for either, but it made it impossible now for the European powers to intervene and a question solely concerning Prussia and Austria.

In 1865 Lauenburg, as a result of the Austro-Prussian Gastein Convention of 14 August 1865, was brought into a personal union with the Prussian Crown, a step vigorously opposed by Virchow in Prussia's Second Chamber. He wanted it declared invalid because the Prussian Diet had not been consulted. His argument was constitutionally untenable since Lauenburg was not incorporated into Prussia but was merely united with the Prussian Crown. Although Virchow's resolution was accepted it was without practical consequence and alienated Germany's Liberals from those of Prussia.

After the peace of Vienna the territories in the joint possession of Prussia and Austria were a new focus for Prusso-Austrian differences. At the Convention at Gastein, Holstein was put under Austrian administration, Schleswig under that of Prussia. To resolve the Austro-Prussian dualism once and for all Bismarck first secured his flanks with France on the one side and Italy on the other, concluding an alliance with Italy on 8 April 1866.

The following day Bismarck demanded a reform of the German Confederation in Frankfurt. The wind was taken out of everyone's sails by his startling demand for a Federal Parliament elected by universal male franchise. In a still predominantly agrarian society the rural population could be expected to be a bulwark of conservatism.

Wilhelm I was not completely resolute in his attitude, but the fear of facing another Olmütz, which was simply unbearable to him as a soldier, proved decisive – rather war than that. Any thought of Russia and Great Britain mediating was quashed by Bismarck's proposal for a reform of the German Confederation. The Austrians armed frantically and Prussia demanded that this should cease. Austria gave in but since the Italians continued to arm Austria had no choice but to follow suit. There remained the problem of those German states hitherto uncommitted to either Prussia or Austria. In the Diet of the German Confederation, to avoid giving a definite response to Bismarck's reform proposals, the smaller German states asked him to submit them in greater detail for examination. Bismarck rejected these delaying tactics and demanded instead that a German parliament be convened before any discussion of the reform of the Confederation. If this demand was not met Prussia would consider its own reform proposals as having been rejected. That was on 27 April 1866, the day before Italy mobilized. Prussia followed suit on 3 and 5 May. Napoleon's intervention came to naught since the German states bordering France had more to fear from French than from Prussian or Austrian ambitions. In the Diet of the German Confederation Austria as well as Prussia declared that their own suggestions had been rejected and Austria added that it would submit the Schleswig-Holstein question to the Diet and to the estates of Holstein. Prussia declared this a breach of the Gastein Convention and General Manteuffel moved his troops into Holstein, which the Austrians evacuated. Prussia then declared itself ready to discuss the Schleswig-Holstein question but only in connection with its plans for the reform of the German Confederation, which now included the explicit exclusion of Austria. On 12 June diplomatic relations between Prussia and Austria were severed and Bismarck declared that Prussia considered every vote in the Diet for Austria as a decgaration of war. On 14 June four kingdoms voted for Austria: Saxony, Bavaria, Württemberg and Hanover; then Nassau, Frankfurt and Hesse-Meiningen followed suit. In southern Germany only Baden voted for Prussia, but Luxemburg and most of northern Germany voted for her. The struggle was short and quick. The battle of Königgrätz put an end to the German Confederation. In the final peace concluded in Vienna on 23 August 1866 Prussia gained and annexed Schleswig-Holstein, Hanover, Kur-Hesse, Hesse-Nassau and Hesse-Meiningen as well as Frankfurt. On the following day the German Confederation was formally dissolved. The Prusso-Austrian Peace Treaty of Prague had excluded the Hapsburg Empire from Germany.

THE SETTLEMENT OF THE CONSTITUTIONAL CONFLICT IN PRUSSIA

Against the background of these national events the constitutional conflict in Prussia continued but became increasingly unreal when considered in relation to the shift of power that was taking place in Germany. One issue occupying the Prussian Second Chamber early in 1866 was the question of the immunity of its deputies. Two deputies had publicly accused the Prussian Judiciary of being guilty of corruption. To prosecute them required their immunity to be examined. A court deliberately packed with Conservative judges pronounced that immunity applied to expressed opinions as a result of the process of thought and not to assertions and the spreading of facts. This was countered by a sharp resolution from the Liberals by 263 votes to 35. As far as the Left Centre and the Progressives were concerned they continued to reject any government budget as long as the existing government was in power. Because of this Bismarck closed parliament on 22 February 1866 on the orders of the King. It was about to be overtaken by events in Germany.

For more than four years Bismarck had succeeded in operating the *Lückentheorie* successfully. It was not his invention. The constitution did not specify what should happen if the legislative branches of government could not agree. The King was therefore the last arbiter and executive because sovereignty resided in him. This theory had been used during the early constitutional phase of other German states, at a time when the monarchical principle still prevailed. Even radical opponents of Bismarck accepted it and argued that it derived from the law of the German Confederation. It was not an invention of arch-conservatives. It did not concern simply the use of power but also the responsibility which a constitutional government as the executor of power carried. The monarch, the legitimate holder of the highest executive power, also bore supreme responsibility. The question was whether the Constitution of 1850 had established the parliamentary principle in Prussia in place of the ancient monarchical principle. Considering the extent of the royal prerogative, particularly in military and foreign affairs, the answer is clearly no. No constitution, written or unwritten, is without gaps and without ambiguities and ambivalence, as the evolution of every constitutional state has shown. But for the fundamental ambivalence in the American Constitution and in the answers which its Founding Fathers provided to the question of whether power resided in 'the People' or in the several states, there might never have been an American Civil War.

Arch-conservatives like Ludwig von Gerlach or Edwin von Manteuffel did not want to twist the constitution to suit their purposes: they wanted no constitution at all but a return to an assembly of the estates of the realm. They were prepared to risk a *coup d'état* but Wilhelm would have no part of it. Bismarck, contrary to the hopes of those who had called on him and contrary to the fears of the Liberals, was determined not to have recourse to open force and instead to return to constitutionality through a compromise. He hoped to do this by a policy of indemnity, by which parliament would sanction retroactively expenditure it had not previously authorized. Of course in the years of struggle, between 1862 and 1866, there was no thought of this being realized. But a change became noticeable in the spring of 1866: in May Bismarck stated that after the new elections he would ask for a bill of indemnity. He always made sure he could communicate with the opposition. The election took place on the same day as the Battle of Königgrätz, 3 July 1866. Public opinion clearly swung to Bismarck's side. The Conservatives increased their seats from 35 to 136; the Catholics maintained their position with 15 seats. The Old Liberals only gained 24 seats; the Left Centre and the Progressives, who together held 247 seats, were reduced to 148. The liberal opposition was dissolving under the impact of Bismarck's successes. The Old Liberals under von Vincke became government supporters. So Bismarck prepared his indemnity Bill, finding opposition not in parliament but among his ministerial colleagues, some of whom considered the measure superfluous, while others argued that the bill implied an admission by the government of having acted illegally. Bismarck persuaded them and the King that no such thing was implied and on 14 August 1866 the bill was introduced in the Second Chamber, together with the budget for 1866. The parliamentary commission accepted it with a few alterations but the debate in the chamber was nevertheless sharp, criticism coming from the Left Centre and the Progressives. However, as the debate went on the Progressives became divided over the issue and this ensured Bismarck a victory by 230 votes to 75. The bill came into force on 14 September 1866 and sanctioned all that had been done since 1862. Bismarck had used moderation and made no attempt to humiliate the defeated minority.

One issue, which had been at the very root of the original argument, was left open: the power of the royal command over the army. Bismarck could not compromise over this. But with the creation of the North German Confederation (see Chapter 5) the problem was transferred to a different level, to the Diet of that body.

The first Prussian election in which all newly acquired or annexed territories since 1866 participated took place on 7 November 1866. The Second Chamber now consisted of 432 instead of 352 deputies. The Conservatives, who had begun to distance themselves from Bismarck, gained only marginally; in percentage terms they actually declined. The new Free Conservatives, pro-Bismarckian, and National Liberals (the Liberals supporting Bismarck) increased in numbers, especially from the new provinces. They trebled their vote. The Left Centre was declining while the Progressives lost one third of their vote.

There was a wide party-political spectrum within the Diet, and the development of party-political pluralism rather than a two-party system was the result not only of Prussian but of German constitutional change, showing how heterogeneous were the historical and political traditions of the various German territories. It did not assist stability and from Bismarck's point of view to govern with continuously changing majorities was not an ideal position. He had to fight on different fronts at once. The Conservatives opposed his 'revolutionary' measures, such as those involved in sweeping away several dynasties like the Kingdom of Hanover. The National Liberals were opposed to the indemnification agreement with the House of Hanover by which George V received an annual pension and retained his residence at Herrenhausen and, in return, handed over 19 million Talers which he had transferred to Great Britain in 1866. The question of the immunity of deputies raised its head again and was not resolved. Arch-conservatives left the government and were replaced by moderates so as to appease the liberal Centre. In the cultural sphere Adalbert Falk was appointed Minister of Culture and was eventually to play his role in the *Kulturkampf* (see below, page 148). Essentially

Bismarck's new cabinet consisted of moderate Conservatives and Right-wing Liberals.

THE *ZOLLPARLAMENT*

Finally, the *Zollverein* needed further clarification. In the war of 1866 its member states had fought on opposing sides, and at the end of the war the annexed states automatically joined the *Zollverein*. The peace treaties regulated the re-entry of Prussia's opponents, such as Bavaria and Württemberg. The creation of the North German Confederation (see next chapter) changed the structure of the *Zollverein*. Article 33 of its constitution speaks of a unified customs commercial area surrounded by a common customs boundary. A whole number of enclaves were excluded which had no joint boundary with the Confederation, such as Hohenzollern-Sigmaringen and the Hanseatic cities of Hamburg, Bremen and Lübeck which were free ports. In 1867 Hamburg applied for membership for some of its territories and so did Lübeck. They were accepted in 1868. The North German Confederation had the sole legislative power for customs and tarriffs. Austria's exclusion from Germany also tied the south German states closer to northern Germany. Bavaria took the initiative and put forward a plan by Prince Hohenlohe-Schillingsfürst to create a close league of states between southern and northern Germany; Württemberg supported the plan but Baden's and Hesse's objections caused it to fail. On 3 June 1867 the south German governments and the government of the North German Confederation held a conference in Berlin. Bismarck submitted a new draft treaty which eliminated the veto power by any one state in customs and commercial matters. Legislative initiative would be transferred to the *Zollparlament*, the customs union parliament. There was also to be a *Zoll-Bundersrat*, extended to include members of south German states, while the King of Prussia would be the President of the *Zollverein*. The Presidency would prepare and negotiate trade and commercial treaties and generally supervise the laws of the *Zollverein*. Only Hohenlohe on behalf of Bavaria considered the treaty unacceptable but was told by Bismarck that he would rather do without the *Zollverein* than without the *Zollparlament*. Bavaria therefore finally accepted.

On 26 June 1867 all members of the North German Confederation and the four south German states, as well as Luxemburg, met at a new conference to conclude the new customs union which was to come into force on 1 January 1868. Bavaria still objected but had to give way. Whereas the old *Zollverein* had been a customs confederation, the new body was a federal customs union. Decisions by the *Zollparlament* were taken by majority vote; the veto power had been abolished. Only Prussia had the power of veto as the linchpin of the system, but never exercised it. The *Zollparlament* was elected on the basis of universal, equal and direct elections of all member states but its functions were limited to matters of trade, commerce and customs. The states of the North German Confederation had 297 deputies; Bavaria 48, Württemberg 17, Baden 14, Hesse-Darmstadt and Luxemburg 6 each. Elections took place in February and March 1868. In Bavaria the clerical-particularist factions gained 26 seats, while the National German Party gained only 12. In Württemberg the 'greater German Democratic Party gained 11 seats, the rest going to the faction supporting the government, while the National Germans scored nothing. But in Baden they gained 8 of the 14 seats, 6 seats being taken by the 'greater German' Democratic Party. In Hesse-Darmstadt the National Germans gained all 6 seats. The first *Zollparlament* was opened on 27 April 1868 by Wilhelm I, who in his speech underlined the fact that for the first time all Germany was united to discuss common economic problems.

In the following debate unitary and particularist tendencies clashed head on but, nevertheless, when in actual business they acted fairly efficiently. The *Zollparlament* met twice more in 1869 and in 1870. In essence it can be considered the prototype of the Bismarckian Empire and as such its psychological importance in the process of German unification was as great as it practical importance.

NOTE

1. The term 'middle states' is not to be interpreted in a geographical sense. It refers to that grouping of German states which, like Bavaria and Württemberg, opposed Prussian or Austrian hegemony in Germany.

Chapter 5

THE BISMARCKIAN EMPIRE

Prussia in its 1866 peace treaties with Austria at Nikolsburg and Prague was compelled, under French pressure, to exclude southern Germany from any reform of the German Confederation. Bismarck had to turn down several requests for membership of the North German Confederation. But in the peace treaties concluded with his former opponents he could nevertheless aim at strengthening the ties between northern and southern Germany. Bavaria tried to create some kind of confederation of the South but this was rejected by Württemberg and Baden. Since the Treaty of Prague had excluded the Hapsburg Empire from Germany proper, the south German states now faced the risk of having no military support or protection, especially at a time when France's demand for the left bank of the Rhine was renewed. This by necessity led them, despite the reluctance of Bavaria and Württemberg, closer to northern Germany and to Prussia in particular.

PRUSSIA'S TREATIES WITH THE GERMAN STATES

The peace treaty with *Bavaria* provided the greatest difficulties, as Bismarck had originally insisted on the line of the river Main which would have meant Bavaria losing part of its province of Upper Franconia. Also Grand Duke Ludwig III of Hesse-Darmstadt was not prepared to cede Upper Hesse and was supported in this by his brother-in-law, the Czar of Russia. Bismarck therefore had to moderate his claims, and as far as Bavaria was concerned the peace treaty contained only a minor frontier rectification and 30 million Gulden in reparations. At the same time Bavaria concluded an alliance with Prussia. *Württemberg* caused no problem at all: no territory was lost, only 8 million Gulden were required in reparations, together with

105

recognition of the North German Confederation and alliance with Prussia. Württemberg also declared that it would not join any southern confederation. *Baden*, together with its peace treaty also concluded an alliance with Prussia: its losses were 6 million Gulden in reparations. *Hesse-Darmstadt* had its province of Upper Hesse join the North German Confederation, but it lost Hesse-Homburg and Mainz was to be garrisoned by Prussian forces. The reparations were set at 3 million Gulden and on 11 April 1867 it allied with Prussia. These alliances were of a defensive character only, and were intended to serve mainly against a French or Austrian attack. At first they were kept secret but in March 1867 Prussia published them.

As far as the central German States are concerned only the peace treaty with Saxony is important. Originally Prussia had intended to destroy it altogether and annex it, but since this would have caused Austria to continue the war, these plans were abandoned. Instead, like the other states, it recognized the dissolution of the German Confederation and accepted Prussia's pre-eminence in the conduct of foreign affairs. It joined the North German Confederation and its army was put under Prussian command until it had been reorganized. It also had to pay 10 million Gulden in reparations.

THE NORTH GERMAN CONFEDERATION

The German Confederation had continued to exist through the two months of the war, which in constitutional terms was not a war at all but an executive action carried out by the German Confederation against Prussia. But soon after the outbreak Prussia had invited nineteen north German states to create a new confederation since it believed the German Confederation no longer existed. After the preliminary peace of Nikolsburg Bismarck, on 4 August 1866, sent a circular note to the seventeen states which had answered his original invitation to draft an alliance on the basis of the reform proposals Prussia had put forward before the outbreak of war. The temptation was great for Prussia to exploit fully the hegemonical position it had obtained, especially since liberal and democratic public opinion expected that Prussia would impose a unitary national constitution upon all Germany. However, Bismarck was neither prepared to force unity upon Germany against the will of its constituent member states nor to make himself dependent on Liberals and Democrats, which would have been the consequence of such a step. He stood by his federal principles, and in the years to come this was to make it easier for the south German States to join a unified German Empire. In the end there were twenty-three member states in the North German Confederation, although Luxemburg and Limburg left the original Confederation in 1866. Through treaties of offensive and defensive alliance the constituent governments declared their agreement to maintain the internal and external security of their states. They also agreed to draft a federal constitution in conjunction with a parliament yet to be elected. The elections were to be carried out on the basis of the electoral law of 12 April 1848; in other words part of the abortive constitution of the Frankfurt Assembly of 1848–49 was adopted. The armed forces of the allied states at the same time came immediately under the supreme command of the King of Prussia. It all amounted to a preliminary treaty for the creation of a federal state.

The parliament of the North German Confederation was not a constitutional national assembly but one of several bodies who would advise and agree on a constitution. This was to be a product both of agreements between member governments and with the respective parliaments. Since the North German Confederation had not yet come into existence it was necessary for all member governments to introduce the same electoral law, and this meant that the passing of the law was still subject to the approval of the individual states' respective parliaments. Prussia introduced its electoral law on 13 August and met opposition in parliament from the Liberals who expressed their disappointment at the introduction of the federal rather than the unitary national principle. They argued against the equality of the other states and expressed serious doubt on whether another parliament was really necessary. They believed the Prussian parliament was sufficient and could have its number of deputies increased. Right-wing Liberals, Conservatives and Catholics objected to the introduction of universal manhood suffrage and demanded that the parliament of the North German Confederation should have a purely advisory function. They wanted the last word to remain with the parliaments of the individual states. Obviously this was a contradiction, but together with many other contradictions it was the main feature in the work of unification because not only Conservatives of all German Lands tried to defend their particularist interests against a unitary state, but also Liberals and Democrats everywhere feared that their powers would diminish by the creation of a parliament which clearly stood above them. But in Prussia Bismarck, with a few minor changes, got his law through the Second Chamber: the *Herrenhaus* expressed fears about the democratic franchise but nevertheless passed it. A further demand for the payment of attendance fees to members of the future *Reichstag* was narrowly defeated.

For electoral purposes the territory of the North German Confederation was divided into 297 constituencies, 235 of them in Prussia, 23 in Saxony, 6 in Mecklenburg-Schwerin, 3 each in Hesse, Oldenburg, Saxe-Weimar, Brunswick and Hamburg, 2 each in Saxe-Coburg-Gotha, Saxe-Meiningen and Anhalt, and one constituency for each of the remaining small territories. One deputy had to be elected with an absolute majority for every constituency, even if this meant holding two elections.

The elections took place on 12 February 1867 and brought a resounding victory for the Liberal Centre, composed of Free Conservatives, Old Liberals, National Liberals and Liberals of other diverse vintages, who together obtained 180 seats and thus formed the majority. Conservatives, the Ultramontane Particularists and the Progressive and Democratic opposition, supported by one Socialist (August Bebel), and deputies of the Danish and Polish minorities, obtained 110 seats. *The Bundesstaatlich-konstitutionelle Vereinigung*, a coalition of Catholics under Windthorst and Guelphs under Hermann von Mallinckrodt, gained only 18 seats. The Liberal Centre elected the former president of the Frankfurt National Assembly, the Old Liberal Eduard Simson, as the President of the *Reichstag*, and Ludwig Windthorst, the Duke of Hohenlohe-Öhringen, a Free Conservative and Rudolf von Bennigsen, a National Liberal, for the two posts of Vice-President.

THE CONSTITUTION

Bismarck had already entrusted Max Duncker, the radical of the 1830s and 1840s, with the task of preparing a draft constitution. But the draft included too much centralization for Bismarck's liking and was not flexible enough to have any appeal for southern Germany. He wanted a more elastic flexible instrument. Several other drafts were submitted, but only that of Lothar Bucher, the former opponent of the Prussian government who had had to flee to Great Britain in 1850, returning in 1861, provided Bismarck with a basis to work on. The final version was discussed in the Prussian Crown Council which made some alterations before it was sent to the allied governments.

Bismarck attached an extensive explanation to it. Sovereignty was to reside within the Federal State, but the autonomy of the individual states was to be preserved within its framework and they were also to have the right to contribute to the political decision-making process. So as to secure their autonomy and cooperation the member states were to be represented in the Bundesrat which was to consist of the envoys of the states, bound by instructions from their respective governments, rather like the Diet of the former German Confederation. Prussia, together with the territories it had annexed, claimed 17 seats out of a total of 43. In other words she did not have a majority but could achieve it with a little support from other states.

Executive power was to rest with the Federal Presidency, which was to be held on a hereditary basis by the Prussian Crown. It was to represent the North German Confederation externally, make and sign treaties, declare war and peace. It was also to have the right to appoint federal officers to investigate cases in which a member state had violated the Constitution. Most important of all, the Prussian Crown was to exercise supreme command over the military forces of the North German Confederation. Yet the King of Prussia was not a federal monarch but, as President of the Bundesrat, simply a *primus inter pares*. The Presidency was also to appoint a Federal Chancellor who acted in the Bundesrat on behalf of the King, but no provisions were made for an actual federal government. Initially Bismarck did not intend to take the office of Chancellor himself. The Reichstag was to be a one-chamber body: Bismarck rejected the notion of an Upper House as existed in Prussia. It was to be the product of universal, equal and direct male suffrage. Civil servants were not to have the passive franchise. Bismarck, still smarting from the wounds of the constitutional conflict, wanted to see competence for military and naval affairs removed from the Reichstag, and all avenues that could lead to full parliamentarization carefully blocked.

The draft received a mixed reception from the envoys of the member states assembled in Berlin, who made demands ranging from greater centralization, the setting up of an Upper House and of a Supreme Court, to determination of the military budget by the member states. The Prussian Crown Prince, son-in-law of Queen Victoria, and especially the alleged supporter of liberal reforms on a grand scale, listened eagerly to plans for greater centralization which would have ridden roughshod over the diverse traditions and institutions of the member states. Bismarck overcame the major objections and, apart from minor alterations, the envoys accepted the draft constitution on 7 February 1867, subject to ratification by the states and then to its submission to the Reichstag.

The Reichstag met for the first time on 24 February 1867, and Wilhelm I, in his opening speech, emphasized that disunity had destroyed the greatness of Germany and previous attempts at reunification had failed because they had been based on unrealistic premises, but the work of unification had now begun on the basis of the existing situation. On 4 March Bismarck submitted the draft constitution to the Reichstag, demanding a quick decision because the alliances and agreements made in 1866 were to expire on 18 August 1867. Therefore, despite opposition from the Progressives, the majority decided not to refer the draft to a commission but to decide upon it in full session. In the debate there was opposition not only from Ultramontane Particularists and Unitary Democrats but also from the National Liberals and the Free Conservatives. Revisions were demanded on a number of important points, so much so that Bismarck had to ask himself whether the changed constitution still corresponded with the document agreed to by the envoys of the states. Conflict was never far below the surface and the serious question arose as to whether the constitution should not be simply imposed upon the Reichstag. Bismarck had to consider this option because the changes demanded affected the other states, not Prussia. It was Prussia's firm attitude which defended their interests. Bismarck wanted to avoid imposing the constitution, if it was at all possible. In the event, thanks to his powers of persuasion, the allied governments gave in on most of the points raised by the Reichstag.

The following issues were the main points of contention: the federal principle, the federal presidency, the Bundesrat, the office of Chancellor, the role of the Reichstag, legislative and external power, the power of military command, budgetary powers, basic rights and constitutional jurisdiction.

The Progressives demanded greater centralization to create a real state and not an embroidered version of the German Confederation, while Catholics, Guelphs, Danes and Poles defended the principles of particularism. Bismarck countered this opposition as best he could and gained a parliamentary victory based on a Free Conservative and Liberal majority. Opponents of the constitution complained about the lack of a strong central executive power. But Bismarck clearly realized that a parliamentary monarchy could only emerge on the basis of a strong unitary monarchy. Hence he successfully opposed the demands of the Left, defending the federal principle which he believed was a bulwark against democratic parliamentary tendencies, and the majority of the Reichstag followed him. The Particularists took offence at Prussia having seventeen votes in the Bundesrat. Although this did not amount to a majority, it was nevertheless two fifths. The National Liberals on the other hand argued that Prussia's weight was underrepresented since its population amounted to 25 million out of the 30 million in the North German Confederation. By that reckoning Prussia should have had five sixths of the votes. Since neither party was able to press its claims strongly enough, nothing was changed. The issue of the Federal Chancellor was more controversial. According to the draft constitution he was *de facto* to preside over the Bundesrat and conduct its business. As such he would have to receive his instructions from the Prussian Foreign Office while not being answerable to the Reichstag. This was strongly opposed by the Left, but the majority vote defeated their resolutions. However, the National Liberals' attitude on this question came very close to that adopted by the Progressives. They objected that the Federal Chancellor alone should conduct all the business of the Bundesrat. Instead of there being a responsible government, committees of the Bundesrat, free from public control, would form the actual government. Therefore Rudolf von Benningsen, head of the *Deutscher Nationalverein*, demanded the appointment of further ministers with ministerial responsiblity.

Bismarck opposed this too, but carried the issue by only a very narrow majority. However, Benningsen, assuming that ministries would be created and ministers appointed succeeded in subjecting the Federal Chancellor's actions to counter-signature by responsible ministers and thus make him responsible to the Reichstag. Bismarck let it be known that he would not oppose him, but this was the real reason why Bismarck decided to assume the Chancellorship himself rather than delegate it and instead of appointing ministers, nominated secretaries of state. The so-called *lex-Bennigsen*, by making the Chancellor answerable to parliament, transformed the federal-hegemoniol system of government of the draft constitution into a constitutional-unitary system. The office of the Federal Chancellor now became the supreme executive, together with the Federal Presidency, while on the other hand the Bundesrat was deprived of its decisive position within the federal executive. As far as the Reichstag was concerned, Bismarck thought he had done enough for it by introducing universal manhood suffrage and direct secret elections. But Conservatives and Ultramontane Particularists, as well as some National Liberals, attacked the electoral system, one of them declaring that it was the prelude to democratic dictatorship. Bismarck with great calculation countered by declaring there was no worse electoral system in the world than the Prussian three-class franchise. This was applauded and gained the agreement of the majority of the Reichstag. The powers of its members were also strengthened by the provision that its votes be cast by secret ballot. They were also to enjoy extensive immunity. The Reichstag, however, opposed the exclusion of civil servants from the passive franchise. By introducing the incompatibility between public office and parliamentary mandate Bismarck wanted to avoid the situation he had faced in the Prussian Diet where civil servants were frequently spokesmen for the opposition, especially as civil servants included university professors, for instance. But, as Windthorst pointed out, there were already 190 civil servants in the existing Reichstag, amounting to two thirds of its membership. Hence the incompatibility clause was omitted. The question of attendance fees produced similar controversy. The draft constitution wanted to avoid the emergence of professional party and parliamentary functionaries; instead the Reichstag should be filled by deputies still pursuing an active professional life outside politics. Bismarck's fear of the development of a professional parliamentary oligarchy was great. However, the Reichstag voted in favour of attendance fees by a narrow majority of 136 to 130. Bismarck, on behalf of the Bundesrat, vetoed this and a new vote abolished attendance fees. As far as legislation was concerned the Reichstag extended its legislative powers and acquired competence over matters of citizenship within the Federation and the member states; it also extended its powers over tax legislation from indirect to all direct taxation. Bismarck wanted the conduct of external affairs to remain the domain of the Federal Presidency. But the Reich-stag succeeded in introducing its power of ratifying treaties with foreign powers. This could be a potential power lever in the future if used in the right way.

As was to be expected, the question of command over the army and navy caused the most serious controversy. The National Liberals succeeded in getting agreement that legislation affecting these questions was to be a matter for the Confederation. But they com-promised and agreed that the presidency of the Bundesrat would have the decisive voice over military and naval questions, which in practical terms gave Prussia the power of veto over all bills intended to change the existing military system. Associated with this were the Reichstag's own budgetary powers over military expenditure. The draft consti-tution had envisaged an *Äternat*. The Reichstag Progressives and National Liberals in the Reichstag were particularly opposed to this. A compromise was accepted by which the peacetime strength of the army was subjected to review every four years and was to amount to one per cent of the population. The Prussian Chief of the General Staff, who was also a Reichstag deputy, tried to change this but was defeated. However, Bismarck used his power of veto. He made the entire constitution dependent on the agreement over the military issue. A compromise was reached in relation to the next four years, the same compromise which had already been accepted and then vetoed by Bismarck. Now he made his acceptance conditional on agreement that during those four years federal legislation would have to be introduced and passed to regulate the matter permanently. In the meantime the organization of the army continued as it existed and the military budget was not subject to annual appropriations. The Reichstag had a voice in military affairs, while at the same time the existing military structure continued without being a cause for constant conflict.

As far as the budgetary power of the Reichstag was concerned the draft envisaged budgets for three-year periods. Johannes von Miquel, a National Liberal, insisted on an annual budget, and the granting of a longer period only in extreme cases. The military budget, during the interim period of four years, was to be submitted to the Reichstag for information only. This was agreed to by the majority and by Bismarck.

Hermann Schulze-Delitzsch of the Progressive Party demanded a catalogue of basic rights similar to that of the Frankfurt Constitution of 1849, while the Catholics demanded a federal guarantee of the liberty of their church and the exercise of their religion. Bismarck opposed this demand, not because he was against such basic rights, but because he feared the unitary effect of such rights within the Confederation would erode the federal principle. After all, all the member states had constitutions in which these rights were already guaranteed. The Federal executive did not have its own administrative executive, so there was no need for such basic rights as protection against the

Federal Executive. They were simply alleged to be irreconcilable with federal structure. The majority of the Reichstag agreed with him on this point. Over the final issue, that of a Federal Supreme Court, Bismarck pointed out that differences about the constitution could arise only between member states, and the Prussian envoy Karl von Savigny elaborated on this by saying political arguments did not belong to the judicial sphere but would be dealt with within the Bundesrat. Finally, on 16 April 1867, the constituent Reichstag accepted the constitution by 230 votes to 53. Opposing it were the Poles, the Hanoverian Geulphs, the Progressives, the *Bundesstaatlich-konstitutionelle Fraktion* and the Socialist, August Bebel. It came into force on 1 July 1867. Unlike the American Constitution the Constitution of the North German Confederation was not ratified by the parliaments of the member states but accepted by their governments.

Northern Germany was now a powerful consolidated unit, politically as well as economically viable, with strong ties with the southern German states through the Prussian alliances with them. Prussia gained increasing influence over them, especially in the military sphere. The southern German states reformed and remodelled their armed forces on the Prussian pattern; arms and equipment were standardized throughout Germany; the military manual and military jurisdiction were patterned on those existing in Prussia.

THE SOUTH GERMAN STATES

However, public feeling varied considerably towards the North German Confederation in general and Prussia in particular. *Bavaria* made several attempts to create a South German Federation but always failed, mainly because of the opposition of Baden but also because Württemberg inclined more and more towards the north. The publication of the Prusso-Bavarian alliance in 1867 caused deep public misgivings, especially the provision that in case of war the Bavarian army would have to fight under Prussian supreme command. The Bavarian *Patriotenpartei* accused Prince Hohenlohe of weakness towards Prussia and he had to manoeuvre carefully since they had an absolute majority in the Bavarian Diet. The Liberals in Bavaria, on the other hand, accused Prussia of having allowed the German question to stagnate since 1866. When Hohenlohe faced two votes of no confidence in January 1870 he submitted his resignation to King Ludwig II. Even Bismarck's appeal for him to remain in office was to no avail. Hohenlohe was succeeded by Count Bray, who was both weak and uncertain, so that Prussia could no longer be sure of Bavarian adherence to the alliance in case of war. Only France's attitude brought about a profound change of public opinion in Bavaria in 1870.

Württemberg possessed a strong National Liberal party which expected German unification under Prussia. But the governing Conservative Party and the left-wing opposition rejected any move which would have led to Württemberg joining the North German Confederation. This attitude changed with a change of government in 1867 when Friedrich von Varnbüler retained the leadership but a number of pro-Prussian ministers were appointed. In 1868 the Minister of War, Rudolf von Wagner, introduced the Prussian military system based on conscription (but only for two years), the Prussian Dreyse rifle and army training manual. But here too the publication of the alliance with Prussia caused a great outcry. The government met this by stating that the decision over the *casus foederis* resided with the government, although this was a blatant lie. For the next three years opposition to the government increased, only to be brought to a complete stop by the events of July 1870.

Baden was the south German state where the cause of German unification was the most popular. Its previous support for Austria had been the result of a freak upheaval in the Second.Chamber and the 'greater German' attitude of its Foreign Minister, Ludwig von Edelsheim. After the conclusion of peace, Baden's new government under Karl Mathy, the former student revolutionary, pursued a course strongly aligned to that of the North German Confederation, which it wanted to join, and Bismarck's cool response caused some alienation. The military organization of the Baden army was modelled fully on that of Prussia.

LUXEMBURG AND LIMBURG

There was still one legacy from the pre-1866 period in the shape of Luxemburg which until 1866 belonged to the German Confederation and included the Duchy of Limburg. Limburg had already wanted to leave the Confederation before the crisis of 1866, but its request had been rejected. The Duchy of Luxemburg, however, still adhered to the Confederation after Prussia had destroyed it, because of fear of French annexation. Bismarck made no attempt to include either Luxemburg or Limburg in the North German Confederation, because neither of them wanted to be part of a German federal state and, in the case of Luxemburg, Napoleon would have actively opposed it. During the abortive Prusso-French alliance negotiations between 1866 and 1867 Bismarck declared that he would not oppose France's extension to territories of French nationality. Luxemburg therefore seemed a negotiable item although Moltke stressed the importance of the fortress for Prussia. Bismarck used delaying tactics which compelled Napoleon III to take the first step and propose to the King of the Netherlands the cession of Luxemburg to France. King William III was not averse to this idea. But Bismarck could not risk showing openly that he was in favour of Luxemburg being ceded to France. When the news that France might take it over reached the public, national feeling on both sides of the Rhine reached fever pitch. The French incited anti-Prussian demonstrations in Luxemburg; a diplomatic arrangement was now no longer possible. When the National Liberals in the Reichstag opposed the cession of 'ancient German land', Bismarck explained his reasons for not allowing it to become part of the North German Confederation. However, he advised the Dutch King to reject Napoleon's overtures since agreement to his demand would make a Franco-German war inevitable. At the same time he declared that the Duchy of Limburg had severed its connections with Germany. Napoleon was annoyed and was no longer prepared to accept the Prussian occupation of the fortress of Luxemburg. Public opinion in Germany forced Bismarck to insist on the right to maintain this even at the risk of war. The matter was resolved by the London treaty of 11 May 1867 which agreed to the neutralization of Luxemburg and the maintenance of personal connection with the Dutch Crown.

THE 'KAISER' ISSUE

The idea of turning the Presidency of the North German Confederation into an imperial position with a hereditary Emperor had already been aired on the floor of the Reichstag in 1867 but was rejected by Bismarck because at this stage he wanted to avoid giving offence to the Hapsburg Emperor and, more important, it seemed to imply strengthening the unitary at the expense of the federal principle. In the intervening years it was raised time and again, but early in 1870 Bismarck took it up again, then seeing in it a means and symbol of national integration. He prepared his ground first of all institutionally on 3 January 1870 by creating the Foreign Office of the North German Confederation to be headed by an Under-Secretary of State. Four days later he developed his plan to the Prussian Crown Prince, who was in close touch with the National Liberals and could therefore be expected to favour the idea, as well as to gain the support of Great Britain via his mother-in-law Queen Victoria. The Crown Prince accepted the idea fervently, though later he distanced himself, primarily because this was a question he wanted to solve himself. But in January 1870 he informed the British Ambassador, Lord Loftus, of this idea and he reported back to London. But the Crown Prince acted undiplomatically by also informing Loftus that Bismarck intended to overcome any difficulties over the military budget once it had expired by means of the 'Kaiser' issue which was highly popular in Germany. Bismarck was deeply disturbed about this diplomatic clumsiness. But the British Foreign Secretary, Lord Clarendon, was not averse to the idea of turning the Presidency into an Imperial title and expressed his surprise that this had not been done in 1866. But when Clarendon sounded out Paris, France protested. So for the time being Bismarck put the idea on ice, in spite of the fact that unexpected and unintended support came from Bavaria where the leader of the *Patriotenpartei*, Professor Nepomuk Sepp, argued that Prussia had done nothing for the benefit of Germany. If there was only one Germany, then Bavaria would be prepared to make sacrifices: 'Yes, even if a North German Regent, even if the King of Prussia himself, became German Kaiser, then the Patriotic Party would join with the Progressives.'

THE FRANCO-GERMAN WAR AND THE UNIFICATION OF GERMANY

The Hohenzollern candidature then intervened and its consequences resolved this matter. Its constitutional aspect is our only interest here. Strictly speaking, irrespective of what Bismarck's ultimate intentions may have been, it was a Hohenzollern family affair and the assertion that King Wilhelm I acted unconstitutionally by confirming the withdrawal of the Hohenzollern candidature is untenable. Formal acts of state of the King as President of the North German Confederation required the Chancellor's counter-signature, as did all written and verbal declarations which the King gave in his presidential role. The Chancellor was not entitled to interfere in the private affairs of the Hohenzollern family: his advice could only be given as a private person and not constitutionally as Chancellor. Therefore Wilhelm I was perfectly entitled to inform or express opinions to the French Ambassador in his role as the head of the family. Obviously the affair had diplomatic implications, since Bismarck supported the candidature, but this does not alter the fact that in principle it was a family affair which ultimately exploded into a diplomatic controversy which led to war because of France's insistence on being given guarantees in a matter which was already dead and buried as far as the House of Hohenzollern was concerned. Up to the point of Benedetti's last intervention everything had taken place within the framework of relationships between equal states. France's insistence on being treated as a superior power by demanding additional extraordinary guarantees was the straw that broke the camel's back. The Ems telegram, a very lengthy and detailed document, was edited by Bismarck for publication in a crisper and no doubt sharper form. France, which had been a source of serious disquiet to Europe in general and Germany in particular since 1859, mobilized and the Ems telegram together with French mobilization rallied German national feeling overnight. For the time being south German particularism was swept aside and, on 19 July 1870 when France declared war, Prussia did not stand alone but Germany as *one nation* rose to the occasion. France's attitude had infused the German unity movement with new vigour in the spring of 1870 when it was stagnating in South Germany. The crisis Bismarck feared over whether Bavaria, for instance, would honour its alliance obligations, never materialized. The parliaments of the southern German states could have refused war credits but enthusiastically granted them.

France's defeats at the hands of the *German* army provided new impetus to the urge for national reunification, a work that could not simply be achieved from above but was dependent on support from below. Some governments might have hesitated: their populations did not. Baden was in favour of joining the North German Confederation, as was Württemberg, though it wanted to see some rights reserved for itself. Hesse could do nothing but join. Bavaria, however, refused, and demanded a new federation with a new constitution. The alternatives were a new federal state and the dissolution of the North German Confederation or the maintenance of the latter and the accommodation of Bavaria by some sort of special alliance.

Bismarck was never tempted to exercise direct or indirect pressure over this issue. He refused to listen to the Unitary Liberals, who simply wanted the incorporation of southern Germany. Lasting unity could only be based on southern Germany joining voluntarily and he was therefore prepared to enter into a lengthy period of negotiation. This also included a readiness to make concessions to the peculiarities of the south German states. He was not prepared to make any deals over territorial concessions, and by the same token the unity established by the North German Confederation was beyond discussion. Bismarck resisted the Prussian Crown Prince's pressure after Sedan to use Prussia's army to enforce speedy unification. A policy of force was the worst instrument to achieve his objective.

Bavaria was the most important factor. Without Bavaria Germany would not be properly unified. Therefore Bismarck's main emphasis lay on winning it over. Unofficially at first he made contact with the Bavarian Prince Luitpold, conducting conversations which he continued with the Bavarian envoy Count Tauffkirchen. At the same time Saxony was persuaded to mediate between Bavaria and Prussia. Although Baden urged a quick solution, Bismarck held it at bay, hinting that it might help his endeavours in Munich. He had a memorandum worked out on the future shape of Germany which did not differ fundamentally from the North German Confederation. By September 1870 Bavaria took the initiative and declared itself ready to discuss the new formation of Germany. Initially Bavaria's idea was a constitutional alliance between southern and northern Germany. A series of conferences took place in Munich, the protocol of which did not envisage a total revision of the North German Confederation. It suggested changes in the existing constitution and the introduction of extensive reserved rights for Bavaria in the realm of foreign and military affairs. Whether Bavaria would join the Confederation or try to create its own remained unresolved. Bismarck was quite ready to concede special rights to Bavaria and on 27 September he struck a bargain with Tauffkirchen – the granting of reserved rights in return for the Imperial title for the Prussian Crown. In this way Bismarck let it be known that he would strongly favour the Imperial Crown being offered to Wilhelm by King Ludwig II. This was ostensibly to avoid the impression of the Empire being created by pressure from below. There was now no doubt that Bavaria's role was crucial and therefore Saxony began to oppose the special treatment it was to receive. But other German Princes, like Duke Ernest of Saxe-Coburg, sided with the supporters of a strictly unitary solution who wanted the Bundesrat to be replaced by an Upper House representing the princes and the Diets, an idea immediately rejected by Bismarck. He wanted to maintain the Constitution of the North German Confederation, though modified in a way which would reflect the new situation. To solve the problem, he intended to hold a conference of the German Princes at Versailles but as Ludwig II of Bavaria could not be persuaded to make the journey, envoys were to meet instead at a ministerial conference there. The negotiations were protracted, the main obstacle being Bavaria. Therefore Bismarck decided by coming to agreements with Württemberg, Baden and Hesse to try to persuade Bavaria to join in. Delays still occurred, but on 15 November the first treaties were signed between the North German Confederation and Baden and Hesse, determining the creation of the German Federation and a constitution for it. Bavaria, fearing isolation, gave up her demands for a double federation, and her envoys declared that she was ready to join a unified German Federation. In return Bismarck respected Bavaria's wishes. Bavaria signed on 23 November 1870, securing agreement that in the constitution any changes carried out by the Bundesrat would fail if fourteen votes were cast against them. Bavaria retained command over its own army in peacetime. A permanent committee for foreign affairs was to be established within the Bundesrat, chaired by a Bavarian representative. Two days later, on 25 November, a similar agreement was signed with Württemberg, as well as a military convention, by which the Württemberg army became part of the Federal Army. Treaties were completed with Baden and Hesse and the new state was provisionally called the German Federation under a Federal President. But all participants were aware of their common aim to restore the *Reich* under a *Kaiser*. *Kaiser und Reich* formed a slogan with wide popular appeal in Germany, especially among the Liberal Centre and the Democratic Centre, who saw in it the ultimate realization of the ideas of 1848–49.

In return for offering the Imperial Crown to Wilhelm I, Ludwig II of Bavaria demanded territorial and financial compensations. He endeavoured to obtain a stretch of land to connect the Bavarian Rhenish Palatinate with Bavaria proper, which could only be obtained at the expense of Baden. Bismarck turned this down, suggesting instead that after conclusion of peace with France Bavaria would be compensated with Alsatian territory. That ultimately this never happened was never forgiven by Ludwig II. On the financial side Bismarck proved more generous and treated it as the repayment of reparations received from Bavaria in 1866. But he ignored the fact that these had been paid by the Bavarian state, while the money Ludwig was demanding now was for his own private purse. He wanted it to support his extravagant policy of building a number of highly expensive castles and châteaus in the Bavarian countryside. The amount paid amounted to 5 million marks which Bismarck took from the *Welfenfond*, the funds of the Guelphs, over which Bismarck had personal control, sequestered by Prussia after the annexation of Hanover. An additional 10 per cent of the amount went into the pocket of Bavaria's envoy as a negotiation fee.

All the royal princes and the higher nobility in Bavaria were against the plan but Ludwig's need for funds was paramount. In his negotiations with Bismarck, the Bavarian envoy at the headquarters of Versailles, Count Holnstein, suggested that things could be speeded up if Bismarck himself were to draft the letter. He promptly did this and Ludwig copied it, with only a few small changes, and Holnstein handed it over to Wilhelm I. At the same time Ludwig issued a circular note to all German monarchs and reigning princes as well as to the Free Cities suggesting they join in his appeal to Wilhelm I. In the letter the point was stressed that as a consequence of the southern states joining the German Federation, Wilhelm's presidential rights now extended into southern Germany and he, the Bavarian King, agreed to this for the sake of the common interest of Germany. With this restoration of the German Empire, he trusted that Wilhelm would now assume the title of German Emperor.

All this had taken place completely without Wilhelm I's knowledge and when he received the letter he was deeply disturbed: it seemed to him it would dilute the value of the Prussian Crown. But with Bismarck's persuasion he finally agreed to accept the title.

The November treaties had still to be ratified because they were constitutional treaties in the sense that they created a German

Federation with a new constitution which replaced the North German Confederation. They also changed the constitution because the mere accession of the four south German states considerably weakened Prussia's dominant position and because all member states gave up most of their sovereignty which was now to reside in the Reich. On 24 November the Reichstag of the North German Confederation discussed the treaties and during the session the deputies were informed of the Bavarian King's letter to Wilhelm I. Only the Free Conservatives were unreservedly in favour of ratifying the treaties; the Catholics attacked the strong unitary-centralist tendencies; and the National Liberals argued against the extensive concessions made to the south German states. The Progressives and the Social Democrats (the Social Democratic Party having been founded in 1869) violently opposed ratification and were joined by the Guelphs, the Danes and the Poles. The latter argued that while they might be Prussian subjects they could never be German citizens. When the vote was taken after the third reading on 9 December 1870, the treaties with Baden, Hesse and Württemberg were accepted almost unanimously. But when it came to the ratification of the treaties with Bavaria a large number of deputies absented themselves, and of the 227 deputies present 195 voted in favour of ratification and 32 against it, including the Guelphs, the *Bundesstaatlich-konstitutionelle Fraktion*, the Progressives and the Social Democrats. It has been pointed out that precisely those parties which rejected the November treaties and with them implicitly the Bismarckian constitution for the Empire were the parties which in 1919 managed to push through the acceptance of the Weimar Constitution.

After the North German Confederation had ratified the treaties, they had to be ratified by the parliaments of the south German states. In *Baden* ratification was achieved with an overwhelming majority. In *Hesse* there were greater reservations but here too a large majority was in favour of ratification. Nor was there any serious resistance in *Württemberg*, where the elections of 5 December had brought the National Liberal 'German Party' an impressive victory, and on 29 December a large majority voted in favour of ratification. In *Bavaria* the First Chamber accepted the treaties with a large majority on 30 December 1870. Even the former opponents of the treaties, the royal princes, the Bavarian archbishops and bishops and the higher nobility voted for them. In the Second Chamber, however, a two thirds majority was necessary and in the course of the debate it seemed doubtful at times whether this could be obtained. The Constitutional Committee of the Second Chamber voted by 12 to 3 against ratification. The leader of the radical wing of the *Patriotenpartei*, Josef E. Jörg, argued that ratification would mean the subjugation of Bavaria under Prussian militarism and absolutism, its mediatization and the complete destruction of its independence. But Jörg did not put forward any alternatives – he had to admit that Bavaria alone was not viable and all that could be done was to resume negotiations with Prussia to conclude an indissoluble alliance with her and a renewal of the *Zollverein*. The Second Chamber realized that this amounted to six of one and half a dozen of the other, and the moderates within the *Patriotenpartei* together with the Liberal 'little Germans' had little difficulty from then on in swaying the Chamber in favour of ratification. When it came to the vote on 21 January 1871, there were 102 votes in favour and 48 against. The two thirds majority had been achieved by 2 votes. Ludwig II retroactively dated the ratification 1 January 1870.

The Emperor could now be proclaimed. The November treaties had produced a constitution for the Reich, though in essence it was that of the North German Confederation. The Crown had been offered by the princes to Wilhelm, and he now only had to accept it. The date of the proclamation was set for 18 January 1871, the day of the old Prussian coronation. However, a last obstacle came from Wilhelm himself, who insisted on being called 'Emperor of Germany' whereas Bismarck preferred the title 'German Emperor' because it was more in accordance with the federal structure of the Reich and more appealing to German national sentiment. As usual in the end Bismarck's wish prevailed.

The proclamation of Wilhelm I as German Emperor took place in the Hall of Mirrors at Versailles in the presence of the German princes, though no European reigning monarch attended. All attendants were in uniform: no civilians were present, nor had they been invited. In his speech, read out by Bismarck, Wilhelm accepted the Crown from the allied German princes and cities and promised to aid the growth of Germany not by military conquests but by the benefits of peace, and to pursue the welfare, liberty and ethics of the nation. The Emperor's first task was to appoint the supreme executive organ of the Reich, that is to say a Federal Chancellor. On 23 January 1871 the Bundesrat assembled, now increased by Bavaria's 6 votes, Hesse's and Baden's 3 each and Württemberg's 4, to a total number of 58. On the same day elections for the Reichstag were announced for 3 March, the day of the ratification of the preliminary peace between France and Germany. In these first elections to the German Reichstag the National Liberals gained 125 seats, the Conservatives 57, the Free Conservatives 37, the Liberals 30, the Progressives 47, the Catholic Centre Party 63, the Guelphs 7, the Poles 13, the Social Democrats 2 and the Danes 1. The parties supporting the founding of the German Reich had 192 seats, but to strengthen their position on vital issues they needed support either from the Conservatives, the Catholics or the Progressives.

THE BISMARCKIAN CONSTITUTION

The *Reichstag* met on 21 March and its first task was the revision of the Constitution of the North German Confederation. Bismarck had already prepared a draft. The first changes were to rename the Federation the Reich, but Bismarck insisted, against the objections of the Kaiser and in order to placate the Federalists, that the name Bundesrat be maintained and not changed to Reichsrat. In principle Bismarck thought that revisions should only be minor ones, an intention immediately thwarted by the Catholic Centre Party's demand to include basic rights into the constitution. In practice this meant those liberties which would guarantee the Catholics the freedom to exercise their religion, such as were contained in Articles 27 – 30 and 12 and 15 of the Prussian Constitution. This demand caused a major debate and its opponents, Conservatives, Free Conservatives, National Liberals and Progressives argued that it went further than the editorial work on the constitution which the Reichstag was to carry out, that it aimed at substantial transformation for which the time was not yet ripe. Moreover, the basic rights mentioned had been selected arbitrarily and would probably not correspond with the national interest. The Centre Party's move was thus defeated. By 14 April 1871 the editorial work had been completed and was accepted by the Reichstag with only 7 votes against, 2 Social Democrats, 4 Guelphs and 1 Dane.

The Constitution of the German Reich came into force on 4 May 1871 and thus replaced the November treaties. As an instrument of government it was as much a creation of statecraft as it was of legislation. Hence to approach it from a narrowly constitutional angle would tend to confuse rather than elucidate the complexity of its structure. The peculiarity of this structure is immediately evident in its preamble which speaks of 'the eternal union to protect the federal territory and its law, as well as to take care of the welfare of the German people'. This seems a legal paradox, because either the constitution was the product of a union of equal partners and in consequence a treaty, or it was a law, in which there was no room for a treaty. Theoretically at least the two approaches are mutually exclusive. But that such a situation is not unique is more than amply borne out by the constitution of the United States of America. The German Constitution can be understood only by recognizing that it did in fact embody two mutually exclusive structures of federalism and unitary state, of treaty and of law. The fundamental question which this left open at the time was whether the principle of democratic legitimacy had overcome that of monarchial legitimacy – and it is precisely in this ambiguity that part of the 'Bismarckian compromise' lies. Only conflict could produce a firm immediate answer – that is when the exponents of the different principles disagreed instead of cooperating. However, Prussia's major advantage in 1871 lay in possessing precisely those traditions, that framework of institutions, both administrative and military, which very largely integrated the two classes upon which the Reich was built: aristocracy and middle class. The rapid rise of the working class was not anticipated by Bismarck. As the Social Democrats had only obtained two seats this seemed to confirm his views. For the time being class conflict was not to be expected. The constitution of 1871 was the product of the German desire for unification and the aims of the German middle class as exemplified by the repesentation of the German people in the Reichstag on the basis of universal manhood suffrage.

Any proposed piece of legislation had to have the consent of the Reichstag and the Bundesrat before it could be enacted, and the Reichstag could also initiate legislation. However, unlike parliaments of today, the Reichstag was not overburdened by this task. Consequently in practical terms its main function was the exercise of those rights which allowed it to influence the Imperial administration, its main power resting on its control of the purse. From the point of view of the Reichstag the constitution was unitary and took the form of law. But at the same time, looked at from the point of view of the Bundesrat, the constitution was federal. Here the states of the Reich were represented, the monarchial principle was the important part of the constitution, and its legal aspect was that of a treaty. In order to prevent potential party strife from cracking a structure which no doubt appeared formidable to the outside world but was highly fragile to the experienced eye of Bismarck, neither foreign policy, nor the army, nor the government in the person of the Chancellor, were made subject to direct parliamentary control. By excluding such a large area from the direct interference of the Reichstag, its role (apart from controlling the budget) was restricted to that of a safety valve for potential discontent and an indicator of public opinion. Both of these, if necessary, could be taken into account by suitable action from above. No doubt the Imperial constitution was a very imperfect instrument, especially when measured against the constitutions of Anglo-Saxon countries. But at the same time it was not tailored to Bismarck's personal desires nor doomed from the start, as Germany's constitutional development up to 1918 was to demonstrate.

Beside the constitution as such, there were also constitutional laws which transformed the provisions of the November treaties into Reich laws, laws concerning the reserved rights of the southern German states and also the law concerning the reunification of Alsace and Lorraine with the Reich of 1873. Later constitutional laws included the annexation of German colonies and the legislation introduced there.

Bismarck's constitution rested on the support of German political Liberalism. He could not foresee that this same Liberalism would become responsible for Germany's transformation into an international world power, once industry had replaced agriculture as the main base of the German economy. And, as a leading industrial and commercial power, it was inevitable that it should also become a colonial power. A corollary to that was its rise as a naval power.

The Reich was a federal state, but the law of the Reich took precedence over that of the states. It initiated and enacted legislation, although its actual administration was left in the hands of the administrations of the constituent states. Foreign affairs were the exclusive preserve of the Reich, while the army was structured in state contingents, a feature arising out of the reserved powers of the south German states. In contrast, the navy was an institution solely of the Reich. In case of war all German armed contingents came automatically under the command of the Emperor. Furthermore the Reich possessed emergency powers in the case of a threat to internal public order. It could declare a state of siege.

It would be hard to prove that Prussia ever exercised its hegemony over the Reich and misused its powers. For two decades Bismarck taught his bureaucracy to put the particular interest second to the interest of the Reich. Nor could Prussia totally dominate the Bundesrat, where a vote of fourteen members was sufficient to veto any Prussian proposal. It is significant that it never became necessary to invoke this veto. The one aspect which publicly highlighted Prussia's hegemony was the personal union of the Imperial with the Prussian Crown and the fact that, with two exceptions, the office of the Reich Chancellor was combined with that of the Prime Minister of Prussia. But even a Bavarian, like Hohenlohe, could become that, and he was also Prussian Foreign Minister. Indeed with the growing industrial, economic and social complexity of the country, Prussian ministers often carried out Reich functions. The Prussian Minister of War, the Prussian General Staff and the Prussian Military Cabinet increasingly fulfilled Reich functions, but membership of these bodies was open to all Germans. The Prussian Minister of Trade in fact ran the economic policy of the Reich, and the administration of the Reich railways after 1879 was in the hands of the Prussian Minister of Public Works.

The reserved rights enjoyed by the south German states included in Bavaria matters of land settlement policy, its own postal and railway service, the King's military command over the Bavarian army in peacetime and his right to proclaim a state of siege. In addition there were other minor rights concerning taxation on beer and brandy. Württemberg retained its own postal system and reserved military rights, but not to the same extent as Bavaria. Like Bavaria, it retained its taxation on alcohol, but only Baden had the right to tax spirits. The supreme executive organ of the Reich was the Kaiser whose office was inseparably combined with the royal Crown of Prussia. While as King of Prussia he had to swear an oath to the Prussian Constitution, as German Emperor he had only to give his solemn pledge to the German

Constitution. Actually the German Constitution contained no such provision but Wilhelm I, Emperor Friedrich III and Wilhelm II gave such a pledge. Both offices were hereditary and the renunciation of the Prussian throne would automatically have involved the renunciation of the Imperial title. Nor was it possible to renounce the Imperial title and retain the Prussian Crown. If Wilhelm II, in November 1918, had followed the advice of some members of his entourage to hold on to the Prussian Crown while renouncing the Imperial throne that would have been unconstitutional. The Emperor in the Bundesrat, among his fellow German princes, despite his presidential power, was no more than a *primus inter pares*. Wilhelm I never tried to change this, while Wilhelm II adopted an attitude of treating his princes as vassals which caused much misgivings but basically was of no consequence and did not imply constitutional change. The Emperor's ordinances and decrees required the counter-signature of the Chancellor.[1] Wilhelm I and Friedrich III adhered strictly to this. Wilhelm II and his alleged 'personal regime', with the exception of the social legislation of 4 February 1890, never issued anything without ministerial counter-signature. Instead he talked too much, too often and, above all, too undiplomatically. According to the constitution, only the Chancellor possessed the right of responsibly advising the monarch. Nevertheless the Kaiser also had advisory bodies outside the constitution and the control of parliament: these were his Civil Cabinet, his Military Cabinet and later his Naval Cabinet.

The Civil Cabinet concerned itself with questions of personnel in the civil sector. It provided political information for domestic policy and administration. Its first chief, Karl von Wilmowski, also served the Emperor as adviser in affairs of the Reich and he enjoyed the confidence of both the Emperor and Bismarck. The Military Cabinet after 1871 dealt with personnel matters in the military sphere and extended its influence to the Reich level. While originally part of the Prussian Ministry of War, in the process of greater parlimentarization it had emancipated itself from that body together with the Prussian General Staff. It had also reduced the functions of the Prussian Minister of War, who as such was answerable to the Prussian Diet as well as to the Reichstag, to purely administrative rather than policy-making ones. This further consolidated the supreme power of military command exercised by Emperor and King. In 1899 a Naval Cabinet was added after the German government had decided to expand its navy. Since the navy was Wilhelm II's pet project it quickly gained influence far beyond that of merely dealing with the personal matters of the Imperial Navy, especially during the First World War when its influence on strategic questions collided with the Reich Naval Office and the Supreme Naval Command, the *Seekriegsleitung* (SKL), which had been created rather late in the day.

The choice and appointment of the Chancellor rested exclusively with the Kaiser and was independent of the Reichstag. But as the Reichstag held the purse-strings, no Chancellor could risk governing for long against its will. He was therefore dependent upon having majority support. In practice, it was the Chancellor who determined the political course of the state, though in constitutional theory it was the Emperor. The *lex Benningsen* (see above, p.111) had also been adopted by the German Constitution. Appointment by the Emperor made the Chancellor theoretically independent of parliament, but his responsibility to parliament also gave him definite independence from the Emperor. As the only minister of the Reich, he not only determined policy but also became head of the growing number of Reich offices, or ministries, which were directed by Secretaries of State responsible directly to the Chancellor. What had not been anticipated in 1871 soon became reality: the burden of work on the Chancellor became so great that he was no longer able to cope with it alone. Therefore in 1878 a law was introduced which allowed him to delegate work to the State Secretaries, including the right of counter-signing legislation within their competence. But in the Bundesrat the Chancellor could only be represented by a member of this body, i.e. such a Secretary of State had also to be a member of the Bundesrat. The law of 1878 was meant to apply to exceptional circumstances, but it quickly became the rule, and with it the appointment of Reich Secretaries of State similarly answerable to the Reichstag. In that way government by the Chancellor was transformed into a collegiate government under his leadership.

As already stated, the chancellorship went hand in hand with the office of Prussian Prime Minister, though these offices could be separated. This happened on three occasions. From January to November 1873 Albrecht von Roon took over as Prussian Prime Minister; between 1892 and 1894 Leo von Caprivi handed over the office to Botho Eulenburg, while during the chancellorship of Prince Max von Baden from October to November 1918 the office remained vacant. On none of these occasions did the separation really work. Bismarck came into conflict with Roon, as Caprivi did with Eulenburg, a conflict which in the end resulted in the resignation of both. The separation disturbed the harmony between the Reich and the Prussian government and it was therefore important to maintain the personal union of both offices. Reich State Secretaries were in many instances also made Prussian ministers. Bismarck's aim was to use these Secretaries in the Prussian government as a bulwark against Prussian conservative particularism. Constitutionally this argument was problematic, because as Prussian ministers they were colleagues of the Prussian Prime Minister, while as Reich State Secretaries they were subordinates of the Chancellor.

No Chancellor during his period of office was also a member of the Reichstag. Of the eight Chancellors of the Empire only four had been parliamentarians: Bismarck, Hohenlohe, Bethmann Hollweg and Hertling. But Bethmann Hollweg's parliamentary career had only been a very short one. The constitution did not explicitly state the incompatibility between holding office and membership of the Reichstag, but no member of the Bundesrat could be a member of the Reichstag. Thus Chancellorship and Reichstag membership were incompatible. This also largely applied to the Reich State Secretaries, many of whom were members of the Bundesrat.

Constitutionally the Chancellor was the only Reich Minister and the office to serve him as the *Reichskanzlei*, so named after 1879. Subordinate to him were the Reich Office of the Interior, in existence since 1867 but thus named after 1879; the Foreign Office which emerged from the Prussian Foreign Office; the Imperial Admiralty which combined the two former Prussian offices of the Supreme Command of the Navy and the Naval Ministry (after 1872 the Imperial Admiralty: in 1889 command and administration were separated again, the former going to Supreme Command of the Navy and the latter to the *Reichsmarineamt*, the Reich Naval Office); the Reich Post Office; the Reich Justice Office; the Reich Office for the Administration of the Railways; the Reich Treasury; the Reich Colonial Office, a late creation of 1907 before which date colonial administration was in the hands of the colonial department of the Foreign Office; the Reich Food Office, a 1916 creation of the war, and the Reich Office for Economy, also created during the war in 1917, which took over functions previously handled by the Office of the Interior and the Trade Office. The final creation of 1917 was the Reich Labour Office which was to deal with the immense social and labour problems caused by the war.

The Bundesrat was the federal component of the German Empire Its members were the envoys of the member states of the federation. Membership was not a right but a duty. Like the Reichstag it possessed the right of legislative initiative but for any legislation to be enacted required the consent of the Reichstag.

The role, function, significance and powers of the Reichstag have already been mentioned. Like the Reichstag of the North German Confederation it was the result of universal, equal, direct and secret elections by Germany's male electors. Indeed the electoral law of the North German Confederation became part of the German Constitution. As an elected body it was completely different from the Prussian parliament, based as it was on the three-class franchise. While Prussia had stood in the van of reform in Germany during the first half of the nineteenth century, in the second half it became the bastion not merely of conservatism but also of reaction. This was especially so after 1871 when the agrarian Junkers east of the Elbe feared being swamped by the forces of industrialization and democracy, as allegedly embodied in the universal manhood suffrage for the Reichstag. While, on the whole, the Reich policy of legal and social reform also applied to Prussia, the Prussian middle classes, especially the Liberals and the nobility, defended their franchise.

Every German male who had reached his twenty-fifth birthday could vote for the Reichstag. The active franchise was suspended for soldiers while they were serving with the colours but participation in elections was allowed even to those considered to be intending to subvert the constitution or for that matter the state. Thus even during the repressive anti-socialist laws of 1878–90 Socialists could vote, and Socialist deputies took their seats in the Reichstag throughout that period. The franchise was equal; property played no role. However, this period was marked by shifts of population from east to west and from rural to urban areas which resulted in an increasing maldistribution within each constituency. This, combined with the principle of the majority vote, led to a situation in which the votes cast resulted in rather serious inequalities. Thus in 1912 the smallest constituency of Schaumburg-Lippe had 46,650 inhabitants, the largest, Teltow-Charlottenburg, 1,282,000 inhabitants, yet each constituency elected only one deputy. This inequality was strenuously attacked by the Social Democrats. Elections were direct and secret, which led to a much greater participation in Reichstag elections than in Prussian ones. By 1873 there were 397 constituencies, in all of which an absolute majority had to be obtained. If none of the candidates obtained this, a second election was held between the two top candidates and if the vote was evenly divided, the decision was made by lot. If an elected candidate did not accept his nomination or if a deputy died, a by-election was held.

Bismarck took considerable notice of political parties: after all the majorities depended on them. As in the American Constitution (to the Founding Fathers parties meant factions and divisions), the German constitution contained no specific reference to political parties. But the Reich Election Law of 1869, in Article 17, expressly stated that those eligible to vote had the right to form associations and to hold unarmed public assemblies for election purposes.

Actually what was meant by this was the formation of *ad hoc* organizations for the elections, and the law did make a distinction between parties, which it described as political associations, and electoral associations. But in practice these *ad hoc* bodies were simply auxiliaries of political parties. Up to 1866 political parties had generally been forbidden, thought this prohibition was evaded and even officially ignored in many instances. After the end of the German Confederation political activity once again became more public and no longer secretive, and the electoral law of 1869 actually presupposed the existence of political parties. Without them no elections could have been carried out. Without this law there would have been no legislation assuring the freedom of assembly and association. The electoral law left it perfectly free for individuals to run as independents for election, or for groups not affiliated to any party to nominate their own candidate. But the electoral associations of the political parties really determined the elections and their outcome. They organized electoral coalitions, which were particularly important if a second ballot was necessary to decide the final outcome. The most famous electoral coalitions were made in the *Kartell* elections of 1887, when Conservatives and National Liberals supported each other and thus achieved an impressive victory. But it could also happen that at the second ballot there were two candidates standing, both of whom many voters had rejected; so unless one candidate stood down the only choice they could make was between the lesser of two evils. The system had one advantage in comparison with the British model, namely that party political fronts could not harden and petrify; the voters had a choice and the parties were compelled to make tactical compromises. Bismarck's support for universal manhood suffrage had been largely determined by his experience during the period of constitutional conflict in Prussia, where the three-class franchise did not favour the conservatives but the rising industrial and commercial middle class. However, he expected loyalty to Crown and Emperor from the 'common people'. He was to be disappointed yet again. In the first decade of the Reich the main beneficiaries in the Reichstag were the National Liberals, soon to be followed by the Catholic Centre and finally the Social Democrats, which in 1890 gained a fifth and then in 1912 more than a third of the votes. In 1881 the opposition parties gained 57.2 per cent of the vote and in 1912 61.1 per cent, a figure that would be even higher if one added the smaller opposition groups like the Guelphs, Poles, Danes and Alsatians.

The Reichstag was the natural representative institution. Within it there was a multiplicity of political ideas, ranging from Conservatism to revolutionary Socialism. Every deputy had the right of free speech and free decision. The Reichstag sat until 1888 for a three-year and from then on for a five-years period. Summoning and opening the Reichstag were exclusively reserved to the Emperor, as were its prorogation and closure. It did not have the right to call or suspend itself on its own. The term of each Reichstag was divided into sessions. Up to 1898 each term consisted of four or five sessions, between 1898 and 1918 of only two sessions. Legislation, petitions etc., had to be dealt with in one session. If this was not done, they had to be reintroduced in the next session. The dissolution of the Reichstag was an important weapon held by the government against the opposition, since it meant new elections. Five of the thirteen Reichstag terms between 1871 and 1918 ended in dissolution. The last Reichstag which was elected in 1912 and extended by one year in 1916 and again in 1917, came to an unconstitutional end because of the revolution. Virtually any reason could be used as a pretext for dissolution. In 1878 it was the argument over the anti-Socialist laws, demanded in the wake of the assassination attempt against Kaiser Wilhelm I; in 1887 the argument over the *Septennat* to extend military appropriations over a seven-year period; in 1893 the argument against army increases; and in 1906 criticism over German colonial policy in South West Africa. In all these cases the parties supporting the government won the subsequent elections.

The Reichstag determined its own agenda and elected its President and Vice-President from its members. The government and the Crown could not interfere in this. On 14 February 1912 the Reichstag elected the Social Democrat, Philipp Scheidemann, as its Vice-President. But he had to be dropped after he had refused on the instructions of his party to pay his respects to the Emperor as was customary. Reichstag sessions were held in public. In cases where the outcome of an election in a constituency was contested by one of the candidates, it was the Reichstag's sole right, together with the judiciary, to examine and decide the case. The police could not intervene in the Reichstag except when called in by its President.

Although most Reichstag members were members of political parties, the deputies had a free mandate, very much in accordance with Burke's letter to his Bristol constituents. Although they were on the threshold of the pressure of mass politics, it had not yet been crossed. However, each deputy depended on the party which supported him and party control over its deputies increased markedly as the Reichstag entered the twenieth century. Nevertheless the tradition of a free mandate was maintained and was carried over into the Weimar Republic by many deputies, notably by Gustav Stresemann and the Social Democrat Hermann Müller who ran the risk of separating themselves from their party base (see p.291 below). This change was accompanied by the transformation of the deputies into professional politicians. In the early 1870s their number was small and deputies continued their jobs in industry or banking, as judges, doctors, university teachers, employees or workers. It is difficult to trace when this change took place since most deputies gave rather misleading information about themselves, calling themselves by the profession they had once pursued. It had been intended to prevent the rise of professional politicians by not paying deputies attendance fees, but the parties and trade unions paid those who were elected and unable to maintain themselves independently. It required a change in the constitution, made on 21 May 1906, to revoke the law forbidding attendance fees. Attendance fees as such were not introduced but 'compensation' was provided from state resources, and deputies retained the right which had existed since 1874, to use the railway free of charge. There were no restrictions against holding public office while being a member of the Reichstag and deputies enjoyed full immunity.

Although the Chancellor was not responsible to Parliament he was still subject to its control and had publicly to give account of his actions. Military affairs, foreign policy, colonial policy and anti-Catholic and anti-Socialist legislation were subjects of heated debate and censure, as was the '*Daily Telegraph* Interview' and the 'Zabern Affair' (see pp.180, 183). It was always easy to rally majorities in the Reichstag to criticize the government. The right to discuss the budget and the right to petition and interpellate were extensively used, and it was the Chancellor's duty to be present and to try to justify his actions. As a member of the Bundesrat he had the right to speak from the floor. According to the constitution he had to accept petitions to the Bundesrat or the Chancellor, and these provided a further occasion to present grievances and complaints and raise them to the level of a general criticism of government policy. Interpellations had to be signed by at least thirty deputies and were formally addressed to the Bundesrat. The Chancellor had to reply to them and a vote was taken on whether the reply was satisfactory or not. A negative vote was tantamount to a vote of 'no confidence' but did not have the same consequences as in a fully parliamentary government. The deputies could not formally move a vote of 'no confidence' but only a vote of disapproval or censure. One of the many consequences of such a vote could be that at the next budget the Chancellor's salary was withdrawn, or other sensitive items on the budget refused. This happened to Bismarck who had two new ministerial posts cut from his budget in 1884/5. Parliamentary politics evolve on the basis of precedent, and what one notices if one actually reads the parliamentary debates on vital issues is the growing tendency towards a parliamentarization of the Reich government, one which was cut short by the events of November 1918. Chancellors needed their majorities, and if they could no longer provide them they were of no use to the Monarch. One of the reasons for Bismarck's fall is precisely the fact that in 1890 he suffered a heavy electoral defeat.

Reichstag and Bundesrat, not the Chancellor, had the right of legislative initiative, though he might use them to introduce legislation. The determination of the content of any legislation was also a matter for them. If the Bundesrat had drafted a piece of legislation it was the duty of the Chancellor to submit it to the Reichstag. The Kaiser had no rights in the legislative process; once a law was enacted it was his duty to proclaim and sanction it.

External affairs lay in the hands of the Reich executive, that is to say in the hands of the Kaiser. Both Bundesrat and Reichstag only possessed very limited influence in this area. The Bundesrat had it via the Committee for External Affairs, which had to be kept regularly informed by the Chancellor. But it had no power of decision and it only gained some influence during the First World War. The November Treaty of 1870 allowed Bavaria diplomatic representation in the German states and abroad, but in practice this right was only exercised in the realm of cultural affairs. The Prussian Foreign Service virtually merged with the Imperial one. The diplomatic representations of the North German Confederation were after 1871 divided into embassies and missions. Ambassadors and envoys were tied to instructions issued by the German Foreign Office. Also the entire German consular service came under the control of the Kaiser. He could conclude treaties but these required the Chancellor's counter-signature. The same applied over the declaration of war and the conclusion of peace, and in the former case the assent of the Bundesrat was necessary. In the 1914 July crisis it was the Chancellor who really had to press the Kaiser for his agreement. The Reichstag could also intervene by using its control of the budget. Under the impact of Wilson's 'Fourteen Points', and his subsequent notes in 1918 the constitution was changed so that both the declaration of war and conclusion of peace required the agreement of both the Bundesrat and Reichstag.

The revenue of the Reich was derived from customs, consumption taxes and the income from postal and railway services. It did have the right to introduce direct taxation but it did not make any use of this right in the member states until the turn of the century. Since the income derived in this way was very low in the early years, the member states made annual contributions to the Reich on the basis of their population. With the introduction of tariffs in 1879 the income of the Reich increased considerably. If the annual sources of income exceeded the amount required in the annual budget, part of the contributions made by the states was returned to them. In 1904 financial legislation was introduced which changed aspects of the constitution. The main sources of revenue were now to come from customs and tariffs as well as from postal and railway services and other forms of taxation. Contributions by member states continued but were reduced by the amounts which the states transferred to the Reich from the Reich taxation they collected.

The execution and administration of Reich legislation was a matter for the member states. The Reich had only the right of supervision though some institutions, installations and territories came under the direct control of the Reich, as did postal, telegraph and railway services, the naval administration, the central banks, the Kiel Canal, Alsace-Lorraine and the colonial territories, state debts, social welfare legislation and the supervision of insurances and patents. The Reich bureaucracy developed quickly and proved highly efficient.

As far as the armed forces were concerned Article 63, paragraph 1 of the Constitution stated that the entire military power of the Reich was to form a unified army, which was to be under the command of the Kaiser in peace and war. But, as already stated, Bavaria was excepted and its army came under Imperial command only in case of war. The supreme command of the armed forces and Navy was outside parliamentary control. Apart from the determination not to infringe the monarchial principle and the royal prerogative, other factors favoured this arrangement, such as the relative political immaturity of the German parliamentarians and the weaknesses party strife was bound to introduce into an armed force of a country with no natural frontiers and ever open to attack as in preceding centuries. But while Bismarck wanted to see the army outside parliament's control he was by no means prepared to accept the interference of the army in politics. He always insisted upon the primacy of politics and, particularly during the war of 1870–71, had to fight some hard battles with Moltke before he finally won. This relationship began to tilt in favour of the military only after Bismarck's departure, when on the one hand Wilhelm II favoured this change and on the other hand Chancellors were either too weak to hold it back (Caprivi, Hohenlohe, Bethmann Hollweg) or agreed with it (Bülow). After Bethmann Hollweg's departure Germany was in effect run by the Supreme Headquarters of the Army under Hindenburg and Ludendorff. The army itself was based on conscription, which, under Caprivi, was reduced to two years' service. It was under the complete command of the Emperor, possessed a unified military jurisdiction, and uniform arms and equipment. Within the armed forces two main distinctions existed. These were the area of military command, which was removed from parliamentary control, and the administration of the armed forces by the Prussian Minister of War who as such was answerable to parliament. But parliament could still intervene by virtue of its budget power. This also applied to the Imperial Navy, the only Reich military institution whose finance was directly derived from the Reich treasury. On the whole the Imperial Navy enjoyed great popularity within the Reich and the Reichstag, mainly because it was not a specifically Prussian or Prussian-dominated institution. Opposition to it was vociferous but was limited to only a small number of Reichstag deputies. Members of the armed services swore an oath to the Crown, not the Constitution, and they therefore did not have to examine the constitutionality of the orders they received.

The protection of the constitution was a police affair, but the Reich did not possess a Reich police force. However, some kind of central office was necessary for the political police, a role taken over by the Prussian political police who were mainly responsible for the collection and evaluation of information. The anti-Socialist laws between 1878 and 1890 expanded its functions. After 1890 the political police no longer had any special powers. Freedom of the press existed fully after 1874. Organizations hostile to the constitution could be prohibited and were, as in the case of the Socialists. Constitutionally the Reich was empowered to carry out executive action against any of the member states, but this was dependent on the support of the Bundesrat. It only came into operation at a time when, in 1919, the Empire had ceased to exist and the Weimar Constitution had not yet been adopted. On the basis of the old constitution armed forces suppressed the Spartacist rebellions throughout Germany. The Kaiser could also proclaim a state of siege, in which case executive power was transferred from the civilian to the military commander. This was the case at the outbreak of the First World War. Its proclamation also included the suspension of such basic rights as that of personal liberty, the inviolability of one's home, the prohibition of extraordinary courts, freedom of association and assembly, the prohibition of the use of armed power internally without the prior request of the civil authorities.

The German judiciary did have the right to examine whether a decree, ordinance or law of the member states of the Reich actually corresponded with the Reich legislation. The principle of legality ensured the precedence of the Constitution and laws enacted by the Reichstag over decrees which had to correspond with either one or the other or with both. However, no case of any such examination ever arose.

As already mentioned the German Constitution had made no provision for political parties. Until 1866 they had been prohibited, but not electoral associations, and until the turn of the century supra-local or regional associations were proscribed, excepting electoral associations. Therefore the only supra-regional organizations of political parties were central committees at the provincial, Land or Reich level. They were subject to police supervision as were all associations, political or non-political. Only from 1899, with the introduction of the *le Hohenlohe*, could local and regional associations join central committees. The central committees could then combine and thus form national parties. Their activities were guaranteed by Article 17 of the Reich Electoral Law, and through the freedom of the press after 1874 they enjoyed the institutional guarantee of free party organization. The political parties of the empire evolved, so to speak, and became institutionalized. The Social Democratic Party started out as a revolutionary workers' party and by 1914 was a tightly organized and disciplined party which had been sufficiently integrated into the Empire to be prepared to grant war credits at the outbreak of and during the First World War. However, although access to direct executive power was closed to them, legislative initiative, the power of the purse and the power to control the government steadily increased their influence on the executive.

FUNDAMENTAL PROBLEMS OF GERMAN POLITICAL PARTIES

At this point in the development of a German parliament it is important to look at some of the fundamental problems inherent in the history of German political parties at the time, which continued to play a role right into our own century. Many contemporaries and critics, past and present, have pointed at the unique character of German political parties, compared with the political parties of other European states. This applies particularly to the extent to which principles, doctrines and ideas, indeed ideologies, played a role in them. Ideology rather than pragmatism is their main feature. Even debates on purely practical issues such as protective tariffs were discussed by German parliamentarians on ideological, even metaphysical, premises. This applied equally to Conservatives, Liberals of all shades and Socialists. This orientation towards theories and ideas often produced an ambivalent relationship to actual political practice. The Lutheran tradition is of profound influence here: the belief that the 'word' alone would triumph, and in the existence of a strict division between the realms of the divine spirit and of secular rule. Hegelianism, which influenced many of the early Liberals, had it that revolution in Germany was superfluous, because the Reformation had also been the Reformation of truth firmly anchored in the consciousness of the individual; ultimately it would also triumph in state, society and its institutions. In short, theory by the force of its own impetus would become reality, a conviction virtually shared by all German political parties and ultimately most pronounced in Germany's Social Democracy. Since *principles* reigned supreme, the virtue of *compromise* was considered almost akin to treason. Political debates in the Reichstag were conducted like scientific discussions without a thought being given to the political consequences. Even when shifts of political parties or groups to the left or to the right took place they remained ideologically bound. The reason for this can only be marginally indicated. During the formation of the German bourgeoisie there emerged two social groups with practical aims, but the intelligentsia and the educated bourgeoisie, groups which so far in German history had held no strong positions in the political process. Their freedom of action was limited to and constrained by the German particularist states within which they grew and operated; hence a German intra-party political consensus was still missing. Furthermore the influence of theology played a major role and thus by implication the German universities. Lutheran Protestantism had awakened religious energies in the individual but ultimately failed in organizing and chanelling them within the context of the church. Thus functionally these energies found little practical outlet other than in the form of an introverted spirituality which found expression in the religious revivalism of the first half of the nineteenth century. Theological and philosophical speculation dominated the German intellectual scene and if one looks at a wide range of personal biographies of German parliamentarians of the nineteenth century one finds more often than not that they are the offspring of parsons or had been students of theology. This furthered the process of legitimizing political ideas philosophically, and partially explains why theory and doctrine were of such great significance in Germany's political parties. Essentially static theories developed which were believed to transcend the changing pattern and development of life. However, at least since Hegel, the thread which connected philosophically-orientated political thought to the timelessness of a political 'ideal' also included the element of historical prognosis which ignored the present and aimed at an anticipated reality, a fundamental certainty about the specific character of the future. The reality, so frequently invoked, was an anticipated reality like that inherent in Marx's concept of the class struggle. To interpret the present and act politically under the dictates of a reality which as yet did not exist, was bound to misinterpret existing reality. Parties based on philosophical premises were inevitably tied to the fate of that philosophy and thus to the fate of the dissolution of metaphysics. But that decline and dissolution did not mean the end of ideology: in place of philosophy, history and historical philosophy stepped in, a trend already observable in mid-nineteenth century Germany. The experience of 1848–49 did not change the fundamental aims of the German Liberals or the means chosen to achieve them, it simply produced a new concept of the nature of politics. In spite of occasional compromises, principles still retained their absolute value: even *Realpolitik* could be sanctioned by ideological premises. Ideologically justified aims on the one hand and practical political action on the other nevertheless began to diverge. In this process lies the reason for the polarization which is one of the fundamental characteristics of the history of German political parties in the nineteenth century. But again it would be wrong to see in this divergence an end of ideology. Ideology degenerated into a crypto-ideology, the 'ideal' was hallowed by tradition, but after 1871, for the most part accepting the new state, new ideological conglomerates emerged in the form of *Weltanschauung*. Since these were closely interwoven with social, national and confessional group sentiments, they determined the behavioural pattern and the mental attitudes of the members of the respective parties. Thus crypto-ideologies of middle-class parties made them blind to the class struggle as a fact of political reality: to them it was an ideological perversion which could only be overcome by a national community. This further reduced the possibilities of practical political cooperation on issues that transcended class interest.

Political parties in spite of many objective changes continued to represent absolutes. The Liberals in their own eyes were the sole representatives of the ideas of the Enlightenment, corrupted neither by Junkers nor clergy, especially so before 1866 when the embryonic Catholic Centre or Socialist Party were still considered to be somewhat 'illegitimate' political parties. The Conservatives claimed for themselves the monopoly of a truly Prusso-Germanic tradition, and the

Socialists of alone being aware of and concerned with the social questions posed by the industrial revolution. But such absolute claims produced an adverse repercussion among the electorate: support for the bureaucratically efficient and incorruptible monarchic state, standing above the parties. Germany's political parties, in contrast to those in Great Britain, failed to integrate the nation. Constitutional provisions apart, which excluded them from the exercise of real political power, this is one of the reasons why for many decades they failed to play a dominant part in Germany's political life. Indeed this failure was one of the reasons why Bismarck was anxious to restrain their influence. Always aware of the inherent fragility of his structure, he tried to hold back the centrifugal forces of an excessive party-political pluralism. What results such an excess of pluralism could yield, the Weimar Republic was to demonstrate more than amply. After 1880 the parties of the Right accepted this fact, which in turn helped to increase the prestige of the constitutional monarchy.

A second factor characterizing and determing the history of German political parties is the religious divide. The Bismarckian Reich contained about 40 million Protestants and 24 million Roman Catholics, not counting over 600,000 Jews and 500,000 unclassifiables. In contrast to many other countries of western Europe Germany in the early nineteenth century did not have an aggressive anti-Catholic and anti-clerical movement, mainly attributable to the relatively enlightened position adopted by its Catholic hierarchy. Only the conflict between State and Catholic Church in Prussia in the 1830s produced something akin to a Catholic Party, and ultimately by 1871 the Catholic Centre Party which managed to obtain between two thirds and three quarters of the Catholic vote. The rising tension between modern state and Liberalism on the one hand and dogma-bound Catholicism on the other fortified the position of this party, which it managed to maintain and further consolidate during the *Kulturkampf* (see p. 140 below). But in the wake of the religious revival of early nineteenth century Germany, the rise of Pietism, to mention but one phenomenon, led to a division between positive, liberal and orthodox Protestants, with a corresponding impact upon the conservative–liberal conflict. One of the by-products of the *Kulturkampf* was the appeal by Prussian Conservatives and right-wing Liberals to the confessional loyalties and emotions of non-Catholics. Anti-Catholicism, especially among the National Liberals, can almost be described, at least for a time, as part of the party programme, in spite of the growing secularization of Germany and loosening of ties between Protestant Church and bourgeoisie.

A third factor marking German political parties cannot be over-emphasized: they were not only 'German' parties but also parties of particular German states, their particularist tradition going back for centuries. Hence the actual political experience of the representatives

137

of political parties had been limited by the horizon of a particular German state. In spite of the emergence and rise of German political currents during the late eighteenth century which transcended particularism, actual particularist reality operated against this especially since the German states were in competition with one another in terms of efficiency of their bureaucracies and in the realm of cultural attainments and economic prosperity. This particularism ensured that Germany, unlike France or Great Britain, lacked a natural geographical and political point of focus, one factor to which the failure of the revolution of 1848–49 as well as that of 1918–19 can be attributed. Hence, though political parties may have had identical names, Conservatism, Liberalism or Socialism were not necessarily one and the same in Prussia, Bavaria, Baden or Württemberg. Electoral analyses in Germany during the second half of the nineteenth century clearly demonstrate that regional traditions dominate over economic and social motives among the electorate, in spite of the fact that in the last decades of the nineteenth and the first decade of the twentieth centuries political parties were slowly becoming factors making for national integration. The year 1848 had stood at the cradle of German political parties, 1866–7 had given them shape, the national as well as the social question helped to form them anew, but the issue 'centralism versus federalism' was never resolved by them, neither in the Bismarckian Empire nor in the Weimar Republic.

The period of incubation of German political thought was that of domination by France, the idea of liberty being necessarily associated with national liberation. Thus the principle of the national state exercised a mediating function between the state governed by enlightened absolutism and the state based on a liberal constitutional order. Bismarck's solution met the then existing liberal demands half-way, a large part of the liberal bourgeoisie deferred its constitutional demands indefinitely so that Germany should become a national state again, a path followed finally also by the Catholic Centre once the *Kulturkampf* had been abandoned and an apparently much more serious danger had begun to loom on the horizon: the 'red danger' which from Centre to Right exercised the same integrating function which it had in 1848–9 upon the attitude then adopted by the Liberals.

Fourthly, the history of Germany's political parties was determined by the inner political structure of the German states, most of which operated on the principle of bureaucratic reform, political, social, and economic conflict being absorbed by reform from above. Reform carried out in time from above made it difficult for political parties to take the reins of government into their own hands rather than be integrated and institutionalized into the existing political order. Here of course the best example was provided by none other than Prussia. By reforming itself, by attracting the educated bourgeoisie into its administrative ranks, by having a relatively high social mobility in an upwards direction, especially when compared with the Hapsburg Empire, the acceptance of liberal elements into the fabric of state was bound to weaken liberal opposition. Hence, seen as a whole, there was no need for a revolution. The state would carry out the reforms and reform-minded liberals could hardly oppose them. After 1871 social reforms even appeared to integrate revolutionary socialism, as evinced by the German Socialist response to the events of 1914, a response that seemed beyond the bounds of possibility in 1879.

Lastly, there is the basic conservatism of the political structure of Germany, a conservatism which in many respects was not intent upon preserving everything for its own sake but was also prepared to throw overboard much that was not worth keeping. The preservation of the Prussian three-class franchise, thrown overboard only when it was too late, is the great but fateful exception to the rule. This conservatism determined the reality and the character of Germany's political parties. In the early constitutional period when parliaments and their deputies possessed a legitimate place and limited participation they had no real power or responsibility. Only gradually did deputies begin to mobilize their supporters and transform them into a political public. The constitutions which emerged from 1848 onwards were not, as we have already seen, their ultimate aim by any means, but provided a basis on which one could pursue its realization. The Bismarckian system, certainly from 1879 onwards, offered the basis upon which, though slowly and gradually, German parliamentarism could unfold – perhaps too slowly in the face of the rapid changes in the socio-economic environment, but even this point is debatable. From the 1890s onwards parties gained in power and the parliamentarization of 1917 18 was not simply caused by the war but was also the product of gradual development. Nevertheless this slow process made a party political career hardly an attractive proposition for talented careerists. Parties had little to offer: no patronage and certainly no hope of responsible political office. Without responsibility there was nothing to force parties into a policy of compromise, the rewards of which were at best meagre or even nonexistent. Hence party political perspectives were directed to this distant future or, as far as the ultra-conservatives were concerned, determined by the maintenance of the *status quo* which was elevated to a constituent principle of state. This made it all the easier for ideologies or crypto-ideologies to operate freely and untrammelled, thus leading to the positions of polarization mentioned previously.

In essence that section of the German population which had actually supported the emerging political parties had been the educated bourgeoisie together with a substantial part of the German nobility. The early period was one in which Germany – the German states – was still economically backwards, and with some reservations it can be argued that there existed a discrepancy between a premature political maturity on the one hand and a still backward socio-economic development on the other, something that changed profoundly during the second half of the nineteenth century. The industrial revolution transformed a society of estates into a class society, a transformation which, so it seems, the majority of the members of Centre-to-Right parties resented or refused to acknowledge. Consequently this sector of German society was unable to keep pace with the transformation. Hardly had a liberal constitutional state been achieved, according to the maxims of the early phase of German liberalism and constitutionalism, when it was already being confronted and overtaken by the social question. And the fear of radical and revolutionary socialism mobilized the conservative instinct in these originally progressive political groupings and parties. Therefore the easiest way to confront the problem was to accept reform from above. This meant in part to give up the previous position of opposition to the existing state, in part to accept the norms of conservatism and a self-denying ordinance to transform newly-gained economic and social power into political power. Germany's political parties reflected and adjusted to this process, as in the end did Social Democracy. On the question of revolution or evolution, the majority of Germany's Social Democrats opted for the latter rather than the former.

Germany's political parties, then, and this characterizes them already in 1871, carried an excess of ideological baggage, made no easier by the religious divide and, in the long term perhaps even more important, their particularist traditions. Added to this must be the inner structure of the German states and an innate conservatism which further hardened in the face of the surprise of being a unified state, while its society in the face of Germany's economic transformation was more divided than ever before. On the one hand it was too much of a success within the course of a few decades to have become the major European power, on the other that success was considered too fragile to be exposed to the full blast of party politics. The traditional German parties, those we have seen in the process of formation in 1848–49, by the end of the century on the whole sided with conservative attitudes since this course seemed not only to serve their own material interests but, and this is a factor often ignored in our own cynical age, also appeared to ensure the survival of what had been at issue during most of the nineteenth century and which had finally been achieved: German unity.

GERMANY'S POLITICAL PARTIES

At the outset the five major party-political tendencies, Conservatism, political Catholicism, national Liberalism, democratic Radicalism and revolutionary Socialism, were fluctuating movements with many cross-currents.

The Conservatives originated from opposition to Bismarck and his endeavour to unite Germany, a development they expected would take place very much at the expense of Prussia and the conservative position there. After 1871 they were the first major opponents of Bismarck. But in 1873 the Conservatives split: the New Conservative faction supported the Chancellor while the Old Conservatives remained in opposition, their mouthpiece still being the *Kreuzzeitung*. In 1876 the conservative supporters of the government organized themselves into the German Conservative Party which tried to rally all conservatives throughout the Reich. It demanded an end to the *Kulturkampf* and a social policy which would ensure domestic peace. While the Old Conservatives disintegrated, the New Conservative faction was absorbed and between 1879 and 1890 the German Conservatives were a pillar of support for Bismarck's policy. They welcomed the end of the *Kulturkampf*, supported the introduction of tariffs and social legislation and at first closely collaborated with the Catholic Centre Party. This alliance collapsed when the Centre Party unleashed its struggle over the *Septennat*, the military budget based on a seven-year period. As a result the German Conservatives turned towards the National Liberals and their *Kartell* policy from 1887 to 1890. Bismarck's dismissal forced them into opposition, especially because Caprivi reduced tariffs, a serious blow to the economic interests of the Prussian conservatives. Already during the *Kartell* period an oppositional faction under the leadership of Hanover Kleist-Retzow, Wilhelm von Hammerstein and the anti-semitic court chaplain Adolf Stoecker had come into existence. In 1892 this group toppled the German Conservatives' leader Otto von Helldorf and in the same year adopted a new party programme the *Tivoli-Programm*, by which it returned basically to the same course as the Old Conservatives, affirming support for the monarchy but opposing any further parliamentarization. In addition it clamoured for high tariffs, support for agriculture and increased supervision of the private money market, banks, bourses and the like. In effect it became purely an interest group which now opposed the social legislation which it had previously supported. But this programme was not radical enough for Stoecker and in 1896 he founded his Christian Social Union, pro-labour but anti-semitic. This failed to gain any significant foothold and ultimately disintegrated. After an initial flirtation with Chancellor Bernhard von Bülow the Conservative Party moved into opposition to him and contributed to his fall. They opposed Bethmann Hollweg from the outset. But they were a declining party whose strength ultimately lay in the Prussian Diet and not in the Reichstag.

The Free Conservatives were also an offshoot of the Old Conservatives and on the whole were remarkable for their moderation. While supporting the government they did not surrender their independence. Among their members were renowned intellectuals such as the historian Hans Delbrück and the sociologist Max Weber The party's main efforts were directed to finding a *modus vivendi* between agrarian and industrial policy. While opposing the Socialists, industrialists like Wilhelm von Stumm and Gustav Krupp von Bohlen und Halbach represented a progressive patriarchal attitude to the workers which they practised themselves in their own industries. They operated at the parliamentary level in alliance with the German Conservatives and the National Liberals but, surprisingly enough, lacked any firm party-political organization. In terms of parliamentary seats they were not a strong force: the highest number of seats they ever obtained was 57 in 1878, declining by 1912 to 14.

Stoecker's Christian Social movement has already been mentioned. His Christian Social Workers' Party attracted artisans rather than labourers and even these were not in sufficient number to give him any political weight. For a time he enjoyed the support of the future Wilhelm II but this hardly helped. Bismarck at first saw them as a serious danger because of their militant nationalism and anti-semitism, and at one stage he considered invoking the same legislation against them as against the Socialists. But when they made a very poor showing at the polls the problem resolved itself. An offshoot of Stoecker's movement was the National Social Association of Friedrich Naumann, a Liberal with a social conscience, but he was no more successful than the other splinters of this movement.

The Pan-German movement must also be included among the Conservatives, although it was never a political party, nor did it ever possess over a million members as A.J.P. Taylor claims. At its highest point in 1906 it had 18,000 members and its journal never sold more than 5,800 copies. Among its members were liberals and conservatives, renowned academics and industrialists, and its programme was colonial and commercial expansion as well as naval increases. It was created in 1890 in response to Caprivi's agreement with Great Britain when Germany gained Heligoland in return for Zanzibar and East African territories. Among its supporters from industry was Alfred Hugenberg, then a Krupp director, and the industrialist Emil Kirdorf. Academic supporters included the zoologist Ernst Haeckel and the geographer Friedrich Ratzel. The young Stresemann was also a member until 1918. As a pressure group they only gained weight during the First World War in the formulation of German war aims but even Kaiser Wilhelm II greatly disapproved of them.

The Centre Party (Constitutional Party) was founded in December 1870 out of the various groups of political Catholicism. At the meeting of the first Reichstag it had 57 seats. Basically it was a conservative party and only Bismarck's *Kulturkampf* forced it into active opposition. Its leadership came into the hands of Ludwig Windthorst who, as a Hanoverian and thus a 'Prussian by compulsion' was from the outset hostile towards Bismarck. The party's power base was the local Catholic People's Associations which by 1890 were to merge into the People's Association for Catholic Germany. As a Hanoverian Windthorst was a strong particularist. The *Kulturkampf*, instead of reducing the Centre Party, increased its number of seats in the Reichstag by 1878 to ninety-three. In that year Bismarck, faced by the rising tide of Socialism, tried to rally all the conservative forces in the Reich and therefore began to terminate the *Kulturkampf*. This allowed the Centre Party to move away from its position of radical opposition, and with its support Bismarck carried out most of his economic and social legislation. Windthorst, against the advice of the Catholic clergy, in 1886–87 caused the struggle over the *Septennat*, a struggle which he lost. In March 1890 Bismarck hoped for a *rapprochement* with Windthorst but this was another reason for the Chancellor's dismissal. From then on the Centre adopted a pragmatic position, opposing or supporting the government according to the issue involved. It voted for the codification of German civil law in 1896, supported the Navy Bill of 1898, the Military Bill of 1899 and the second Navy Bill in 1900. Under Bülow the Centre Party filled the Reichstag presidency, voted for new tariffs in 1902 and for the financial reform bills of 1904 and 1906. In 1906 it supported the third Navy Bill but opposed the government's policy in South West Africa, opposition which led to the dissolution of the Reichstag. This was primarily the work of the Centre Party deputy Matthias Erzberger who led the attack on the government without prior agreement with his Centre Party colleagues. Although the elections of 1907 brought the Centre Party gains (from 100 to 105 seats), the Conservative–Centre coalition was broken and replaced by a Conservative–Liberal one with which Bülow managed to get along until 1909. Under Bethmann Hollweg the Centre Party supported the government's army and navy bills. It refused to co-operate with the Social Democrats, although they, together with the Centre and Progressives, had a majority in the election of 1912. The three parties, which ultimately presided over the birth of the Weimar Republic, only cooperated over the 'Zabern affair'. In the course of its history the Centre Party transformed itself from a purely Catholic party to an interdenominational one in which Protestants also found a place.

The National Liberal Party was founded on 28 February 1867 from Liberals throughout Germany whose common aim was a united Germany, and between 1867 and 1878 it provided the main support for Bismarck's policy. It had 178 seats in the Prussian Diet and 155 in the Reichstag of 1874, so it was by far the strongest single party. It propagated free trade, interdenominational schools, a strong army and navy, as well as being the major supporter of a German colonial policy. Its power base was the local Liberal Associations headed by a central committee which elected the party chairman. Among its most prominent members were Rudolf von Bennigsen, Eduard Simson and the historians Heinrich von Treitschke, Theodor Mommsen and Heinrich von Sybel. Bismarck's change from a free-trade to a tariff policy in 1878–79, his introduction of the anti-Socialist laws, and his social legislation, led to tensions within the National Liberals and to a crisis from which the party never fully recovered. Bismarck tried to win them round by offering Bennigsen a ministerial post, but he refused, fearing rightly that this would isolate him from the party. The Army Bill of 1880 further divided the party but Benningsen attempted to reform and reorganize it, a task he delegated to Johannes von Miquel. For a time the latter succeeded. The party began to support social legislation, policies to aid agriculture and the extension of the anti-Socialist laws. In 1887, together with the Conservatives, they formed the *Kartell* which supported Bismarck. Although it never obtained its 155 seats again, in the Reichstag of 1887 it still had 99. Three years later, however, they were reduced to a mere 42. The collapse of the *Kartell* in 1890 deprived the National Liberals of their key position in the Reichstag. Divided now between free traders and protectionists, the party was split over Caprivi's trade treaties which were intended to reduce tariffs and create a central European free-trade area. Miquel became Prussian Minister of Finance in 1890 which meant that he had to relinquish his seat in the Reichstag. He gradually moved more and more towards a conservative position. Despite their reduced representation in the Reichstag, the National Liberals supported all the army and navy bills up to 1914.

The German Progressive Party, founded in 1861, initially suffered heavily from the loss of those members who made their peace with Bismarck in 1866 and became the National Liberals, but the remainder represented a hard core of opposition to Bismarck. They only supported him during the *Kulturkampf*, except for a small group led by Eugen Richter. They were free-traders, opposing tariffs, come what may, as well as social legislation, and fought equally hard against the Social Democrats and increases in the army and for an extension of the budgetary power of parliament in military matters. They mostly failed, but what held them together was a good organization based not on committees but associations which was so strict as to raise complaints from within the party about increasing dogmatism. It was a party for the petit-bourgeoisie at a time when most of the academics and men of property had gone over to the National Liberals. In 1875 Eugen Richter emerged as their leader, the first professional politician in Germany who had the ability to run his party, so much so that he was accused of dictatorship, an accusation which ultimately split the party.

The secessionists from the Progressives, which included Richter, joined the German Free-Thinking Party, the left-wing Liberals, which had been founded in 1884. Richter became its leader but its members were not prepared to accept his tight discipline. Its programme did not differ significantly from that of the Progressives and its policy was based on hope, namely the accession to the throne of Friedrich III and the eclipse of Bismarck. Since Friedrich, stricken with cancer, only ruled for ninety-eight days, their hopes were dashed. Even after their hopes had been shown to be futile, the party found no true unity, some voting for the extension of the anti-Socialist laws, others against. With the advent of Caprivi the left-wing Liberals believed that their day had come, but once again divisions could not be healed and Richter and his circle denounced any concession to the government. A further split in 1893 produced the Free-Thinking Association, but only 19 of the 66 deputies in the Reichstag joined it. It represented the left-wing Liberal élite, including Mommsen who had left the National Liberals in 1880, Georg von Siemens and Freiherr von Stauffenberg. In 1903 they were joined by Naumann's National Social movement. The large remainder of the left-wing Liberals adopted the name of Freethinking People's Party and were led by Richter.

There was also the German People's Party, with its power base in Württemberg and its traditions rooted in 1848–49. It was represented in the Reichstag until 1887 when it lost all its seats. Calling itself the Progressive People's Party it was refounded in 1910. In 1907 the various liberal splinter groups occupied 49 seats in the Reichstag and when they fused in the Progressive People's Party they obtained in the 1912 election only 42 seats.

The Socialist Workers' Party (SAP), or Social Democrats (SPD) as they were called after 1890, had its origins in Ferdinand Lassalle's *Allgemeiner Deutscher Arbeiterverein* (ADAV), the General Workers' Association, founded in 1863. Lassalle's death a year later was to prove fateful for the further development of the Socialist movement in Germany, which till then had operated within a national context. His successors, August Bebel and Wilhelm Liebknecht, were to lead German Socialism towards Marxist internationalism, the adoption of a belief in the class struggle and in change brought about by revolution. Bebel originally had opposed forming a Socialist party. As the only Socialist elected to the Reichstag of the North German Confederation, he had denounced the cession of Luxemburg as un-patriotic. He had also denounced the creation of the German Empire in 1871. The SAP was founded in 1869 by Bebel and Liebknecht at the Eisenach Congress. In its structure it was strictly democratic, the highest institution was the annual party congress which elected the party leadership consisting of five members as well as a committee of supervision consisting of eleven members. The party programme demanded the separation of church and state, the transformation of the standing army into a militia, the right of collective bargaining, freedom of the press and of association, abolition of indirect taxation, fixed maximum working hours, abolition of child labour, restriction of women's work, and state support for consumer and production co-operatives, the latter point being a departure from Marxist orthodoxy according to which state aid only delays the necessary revolution. The outbreak of the Franco-German War placed the SAP and the Lassalleans, led by Johann von Schweitzer, in a serious dilemma. The Lassalleans supported war credits in public, while the SAP abstained. Marx's advice was sought but he evaded the issue in his reply and instead demanded they protest against the planned annexation of Alsace-Lorraine. When the SAP did this, the party leadership landed up in prison since they had violated the state of siege proclaimed at the beginning of the war.

In the 1871 Reichstag election only August Bebel and another Socialist gained seats. Liebknecht was defeated. In 1874 three SAP members were elected to the Reichstag. In membership numbers the SAP remained far behind the ADAV. This was one reason for the SAP to press for fusion with the ADAV, which was achieved at the Gotha Party Congress of 22–27 May 1875. Though the party leadership changed formally, Bebel and Liebknecht remained the actual leaders. In the elections of 1877 they gained 493,000 votes and 12 seats. During the period of the anti-Socialist laws their vote slipped at first, but from 1884 onwards the SPD increased its vote, in 1890 gaining 35 seats. Roughly speaking during the twelve years of its proscription the Socialist Party trebled its vote and quadrupled its number of seats. After 1890 the party leadership was still in the hands of its founders, but in spite of nationwide organizational consolidation it was still as far removed from revolution or power as it had been in 1871. Against this background the revisionist movement, believing in evolution rather than revolution, had its impact upon socialism in Germany and other European countries. A division now appeared between the revisionists and orthodox Marxists. This was very much reflected in the 'Erfurt programme' of 1891 which, although it repeated the demands of the Gotha Congress can be divided into a social revolutionary and a reformist part. The influence of the emerging trade unions upon the labour movement was essentially reformist in character, but the question whether the SPD was a party of revolution or reform was never really resolved – not until 1918–19 when the bulk of the Social Democrats affirmed the reformist course, leaving revolution to the Independents, the Spartacists and ultimately the Communists.

The question of revisionism was therefore always in the forefront of the debate within the SPD from the 1890s until 1914. Bebel officially rejected revisionism in 1899, but he could not stop it from infiltrating at all levels of the party. Until his death he remained a committed revolutionary, to the extent that he did not shy away from treason by communicating confidential details of the Reichstag's Budgetary Commission to the British via Switzerland and explicitly calling upon them to meet the German threat. But irrespective of that Eduard Bernstein, the founder of the revisionist movement, was gaining ground. One feature which was also to trouble the SPD in the Weimar Republic was the fossilization of its leadership. New leaders did not emerge until the death of the old one. The danger of immobility was forever present. The first really serious electoral reverse suffered by the SPD came in 1907 when its number of seats was cut from 81 to 43. The 1912 election campaign resulted in a victory for pragmatism: the SPD conducted it with as much nationalist fervour as the National Liberals and gained 110 seats, making them into the strongest single party.

From 1890 onwards the SPD had also decided to participate in Land and communal elections and it was at that level that revisionism struck deep roots, especially in southern Germany where Social Democrats could be found in Bavaria, Baden and Hesse voting in favour of the budget. In Prussia, however, the three-class franchise was a barrier which the SPD could not overcome and its maximum number of seats never exceeded ten. The Social Democrats were the first of the German parties to mobilize the women's movement and guide it into their fold. Although women did not possess the vote, it was only a question of time until they had it. In 1914 the SPD had 175,000 female members amounting to 16.1 per cent of its total membership. The most prominent among them was Rosa Luxemburg, the representative of radical revolutionary activism, who eventually fell a victim to it. She was aided by Clara Zetkin and others.

One weapon available to the SPD was that of mass strikes but here opinion was divided between Social Democrats and trade union leaders. The latter considered strike action to be an extreme economic measure not to be used for political purposes. Bebel was in favour of political strikes but failed to get his views accepted. Rosa Luxemburg called for mass strikes as a means of direct revolutionary action but found little support among the moderates. Mass demonstrations were carried out in Prussia in protest against the three-class franchise, but yielded no results.

THE CONSTITUTIONAL PROCESS

Turning from the parties to the reality of the constitutional process of the German Reich, the question must be asked whether Bismarck's Constitution was in fact a Chancellor's dictatorship. It has often been argued that he had the constitution tailored to his personal needs, that using the nobility, the army, bureaucracy and industrial pressure groups he operated a pseudo-constitutionalism. This would be justified if Bismarck between 1871 and 1890 had ever tried to turn himself into the actual and real power behind the throne. On the contrary his period in office is marked by his endeavour to maintain the principle of monarchical legitimacy *vis-à-vis* the influence of parliament as well as the Reich offices. He considered governmental acts of the King and Emperor in spite of the requirement of his counter-signature, to be always the acts of the Crown. The possessor of power, as Bismarck frequently pointed out, was the Kaiser or the total number of governments of the German states, and not the Chancellor. Obviously Bismarck used his great powers of persuasion to win over the Kaiser to his point of view, as had been the case in his advocacy of moderate war aims in 1866 and again in 1870, the introduction of civil marriage and the conclusion of an alliance with Austria in 1879. At times he combined his demands with the threat of resignation. He needed the assent of the Kaiser in all important questions. On several occasions this was very difficult to obtain since the Empress always viewed him with suspicion and opposed him. This opposition was all the stronger since it was supported by Crown Prince Friedrich Wilhelm and Crown Princess Victoria, the daughter of Queen Victoria of Great Britain, who were close to the Liberals in the Reichstag and the Prussian Diet. All this constrained the Chancellor's power.

Originally the Chancellor was the only minister. This remained so even after the Reich Secretaries of State had obtained a limited right to counter-signature on 17 March 1878. He was the first among equals and not the head of departmental chiefs in the Prussian and German governments. Obviously he tried to determine both Reich and Prussian policy, but he made relatively little use of the power of instruction which he possessed *vis-à-vis* his Secretaries of State, with the exception of foreign policy which he considered his own domain. It was fully within his power to replace ministers or state secretaries when he changed course, as he did from advocating free trade to counselling protectionism.

In his relationship with the Reichstag, the latter's control of the purse imposed serious limitations to any excessive use of the Chancellor's powers. The charge that the Reichstag was too divided to represent a serious check on Bismarck's power is unfounded. A divided, weak and almost powerless Reichstag would make nonsense of the fact that throughout his period in office Bismarck had to endeavour to rally a majority of its members around him. Moreover the Reichstag contained a great number of highly skilled and experienced parliamentarians like Wilhelm von Kardorf, Heinrich von Helldorf, Rudolf von Bennigsen, Johannes von Miquel, Ludwig Windthorst, Albert Haenel, Eugen Richter, August Bebel and Wilhelm Liebknecht. He needed its support in his financial, defence and colonial policy, even in foreign policy, and when he could not obtain it he had to make do with compromises of one kind or another.

The Reichstag's best chance for full parliamentarization existed in the early period between 1871 and 1878 when the National Liberals were the strongest party and together with the Free Conservatives and Old Liberals very nearly amounted to an absolute majority. At that time Bismarck was compelled to follow what amounted to a National Liberal policy. He had to be ready to make concessions, because he was dependent on them. To the same degree as he was dependent on the National Liberals he encountered the hostility of the Conservatives, where erstwhile friends like Ernst Ludwig von Gerlach became his bitter opponents, and eventually there was a complete break between Bismarck and the Old Conservatives. The *Kulturkampf* reached proportions which Bismarck had not originally envisaged, not least because of the aims of the National Liberals. The introduction of a unified Code of Civil and Criminal Law for the whole Reich was in essence a product of the unitary National Liberals which went counter to Bismarck's conception of federalism. Here the legislative initiative of the Reichstag was put to very good use by the National Liberals, reaching its high point in the *Reichsjustizgesetz*, the Reich Justice Law, of 27 January 1877. Hence at no time can one speak of a Chancellor dictatorship.

THE *KULTURKAMPF*

This early period was overshadowed by the *Kulturkampf*. The German Constitution contained nothing that regulated the relationship between Church and State. It left these matters to the member states of the Reich. For the Catholic Church, whose symbiosis with the former Holy Roman Empire of the German Nation had been very close, the new German Reich was at first a potentially hostile power. And Liberals throughout the Reich felt the same way towards the Catholics as early as the 1860s when the Roman Catholic Church introduced the *Syllabus Errorum* in 1864 which contained a list of eighty 'errors' and to this added the dogma of papal infallibility and the Immaculate Conception. The Catholic Church's struggle against liberalism, socialism, the progress of science, and its demand for full church control over education and research reached almost totalitarian dimensions and was bound to create a forceful opposition front.

The member states of the Reich had guaranteed the Church full autonomy. The Constitution merely sanctioned the equality of all faiths, but the demands of the Church represented a serious challenge to this and since principles, not issues, were involved, confrontation rather than compromise was the result. However, the Church itself initially was far from unified. Three quarters of the German bishops had opposed the dogma of papal infallibility in 1868, as had about the same number of Austrian bishops, but they were outvoted when it came to the final decision on 18 July 1870. Infallibility implied the complete subjugation of the German Catholic Church to Rome, and this was not easily accepted by all German theologians. It was intended that teachers of theology, from university to school level, who expressed doubts about the new dogma, should lose their jobs, yet they were civil servants of the respective German states. Since 1841 there had been a Catholic Department within the Ministry of Culture of Prussia staffed by Catholics, to represent Catholic interests. The department had always been a thorn in the side of the Liberals, and with the new papal legislation it inevitably became involved in the controversy surrounding it. Therefore Bismarck proposed to abolish it and combine Catholic and Protestant affairs into a Department for Spiritual Affairs, a step carried out on 8 July 1871. But when a new German envoy was appointed to the Vatican in 1872 the *Curia* denied him its *Agrément*. This meant that diplomatic relations between the Reich and the Holy See had been severed.

More practical difficulties arose at Bonn where the Archbishop of Cologne, Paulus Melchers, tried to impose ths dogma of infallibility. When a number of theologians refused this they had the *missio canonica*, their right to teach, withdrawn from them. This was not only a contravention of the statutes of the University of Bonn, but also a direct challenge to the Prussian State since these teachers were its civil servants. The same thing happened at a number of other universities. The refusal of the individuals concerned ultimately led to their ex-communication, which according to past practice would have required the sanction of the Prussian State. The conflict did not stop there: it entered the army, because of the army field chaplains, and led to the suspension of the army's Centre for Field Chaplains, a step which the Kaiser only sanctioned very reluctantly. Eventually there was a full confrontation between the Catholic episcopacy and the Prussian government, since the bishops upon taking office had also given a promise of obedience and loyalty towards the laws promulgated with the sanction of the Crown. The issue was a question of which law had primacy, the law of the State or the law of the Church. The bishops insisted that in matters of faith the latter had precedence.

The Prussian State countered this problem by a whole body of legislation introduced by the Liberal Minister of Culture, Adalbert Falk. All these laws were repressive in character, except for the law introducing civil marriage. The legislation was fully backed by the Liberals and by a parliamentary majority. The *Kulturkampf* also involved the south German states who fought the Roman *Curia* with measures similar to those introduced in Prussia.

This is not the place to discuss in detail the legislation arising out of the *Kulturkampf*, except to remark that Bismarck had originally intended to conduct the struggle with limited means and aims but was drawn deeper into it than he had intended because of the Liberals. During the *Kulturkampf* the Catholic Centre Party moved into outright opposition and Bismarck identified them as *Reichsfeinde*, enemies of the Reich. The National Liberal Party, on the other hand, used it to try to capture greater political power.

FREE TRADE, PROTECTIONISM AND ANTI-SOCIALIST LEGISLATION

A change became perceptible when the doctrinaire Pope Pius IX died, to be replaced by the more flexible and conciliatory Leo XIII in 1878. This facilitated a new *rapprochement* between Church and State, but other factors also played a role. The crisis in the Balkans after 1875 ultimately led to the Congress of Berlin in 1878. There Bismarck noticed with alarm that France was trying to enlist the support of Austria-Hungary. Fearing an alliance between the two, he decided to take pre-emptive action by concluding an alliance between the Reich and Austria-Hungary, and this could hardly be achieved without relaxing the anti-Catholic legislation in Germany. A further and equally important motive was the development of the German domestic scene. Bismarck had seriously underestimated the pace of Germany's industrialization and the equally rapid rise of the German Socialist Party. Forever seeing the spectre of revolution on the horizon, Bismarck decided to rally all 'state-preserving' institutions to combat the threat of red revolution. The Catholic Church was bound to occupy an important place within such a rally of conservative forces. Hence on 14 July 1879 the Liberal Minister of Culture was dismissed and replaced by the Conservative, Robert von Puttkamer. Under him and the under-secretary, Gustav von Gossler, negotiations were conducted in Vienna with representatives of the Vatican. These led to agreement in principle between both parties and were followed between 1880 and 1885 by legislation which revised the repressive legislation of 1873.

Another important change of course in the years 1870–73 were followed by a period of industrial and agrarian depression which was world-wide. The German agrarian sector clamoured for protection against cheap grain imports from Russia, the United States and elsewhere, but politically this sector, represented by the Conservatives, was no longer strong enough to carry such a measure through by itself. It therefore allied with the National Liberals, the party representing heavy industry, which was equally clamouring for tariffs, and thus protection was introduced and carried by a majority in the Reichstag.

Before that, in 1877, Bismarck had tried to tie the National Liberals closer to the government by offering ministerial posts to Bennigsen and others. They refused, since this would have meant relinquishing their parliamentary seats. This ended Bismarck's ability to rely on a firm parliamentary front within the Reichstag. But the middle-class parties were still united enough, after two attempts on the life of Kaiser Wilhelm I, to enact the anti-Socialist laws on 18 October 1878 by 221 votes to 149.

Hegel, in his *Grundlinien der Philosophie des Rechts*, had already pointed out that when the bourgeois state developed into an industrial society there would be an inevitable division between those with property and those without. In Hegel's view it was the state's function to protect the economic and social position of those without property by state intervention. From this was derived the notion of a 'social kingship', and the idea was taken up by Lassalle. Social reform had always been an ingredient of Prussian government policy ever since the days of Friedrich Wilhelm I. It was the institutional absorption of social and economic conflicts. To attribute Bismarck's social legislation to mere opportunism, to a stick-and-carrot policy towards the members of the Social Democratic Party (a policy which together with his later colonial policy has been described as one of 'social imperialism' to integrate the working class into the Reich) ignores the ample body of evidence available. This shows that Bismarck from the earliest days of his political career had recognized the social problem and considered it the state's duty to intervene on behalf of the underprivileged. The first discussions about social reform and social legislation actually antedate the anti-Socialist laws. Nevertheless it was inevitable that once these laws had been passed, social reform legislation would be an adjunct.

The first assassination attempt on Wilhelm I of 11 May 1878 was wrongly attributed by the majority of German public opinion to the Socialists, and Bismarck immediately suggested legislation against them which was limited to the Bundesrat or the local police proscribing Social Democratic associations, assemblies or publications. The Reichstag rejected the bill by 251 to 57. The Centre Party voted solidly against it, out of fear – since the *Kulturkampf* was still going on – of creating a precedent which could be used against itself. The second attempt to assassinate Wilhelm I took place on 2 June 1878 and was made by a Dr Nobiling. It was sufficiently serious for the Kaiser to have to delegate his functions to the Crown Prince until 5 December 1878. The background of the attempted assassination has never been fully explained except for establishing that Nobiling was associated with the anarchist wing of the revolutionary socialist movement. Any direct connection with the Socialist Party could not be proved. But this second attempt enabled Bismarck to have the Reichstag dissolved on 11 June and new elections took place on 30 July 1878. The Right increased its votes, the Centre maintained its position unchanged, while the other middle parties and the Left sustained losses. On 13 August Bismarck submitted a new anti-Socialist bill to the Bundesrat which supported it. In the Reichstag on 18 October 1878 the law was accepted by 221 votes from the two Conservative factions and the National Liberals against 149 from the Centre, the Progressives and the Social Democrats. It was directed against social democratic and communist associations, assemblies and publications and the collection of money on their behalf. Any organization, assembly or publication which aimed at the overthrow of the existing order of society was proscribed, but proscription was dependent on the socialist pursuit of revolutionary aims. This meant that the law was limited in scope and time, and until 1890 was extended several times. The legislation assumed that socialist leaders might revise their aims and opinions, in which case the law would no longer be needed. For the same reason there was no general proscription of socialist associations, assemblies and publications. The law was flexible enough to be handled according to the circumstances prevailing. Punishments could be money fines or imprisonment up to one year, prohibition of residence in certain areas or cities, and proscription of certain professional pursuits. This was aimed at printers publishing socialist publications, or bookshops selling them, and restaurant owners who made their premises available for socialist assemblies. The heaviest sanction the law foresaw was the proclamation of a minor state of siege for one year, which provided that assemblies required police permission (excepting election rallies), that publications should be sold openly in public places, that dangerous persons were banned from residing in a particular district and that the possession, carrying, import and sale of weapons could be forbidden. The anti-Socialist law was to last for two and a half years but as early as 1880 Bismarck had it extended until 1884, when it was extended for a further two years. The third extension until 1888 was only carried by twenty-seven members of the Centre Party voting in favour of it. The fourth extension, which also envisaged fiercer laws, was planned to last until 1893. The Reichstag removed the additonal repressive measures and passed it in its old form until 30 September 1890, when it expired. The attempt to have it extended for a fifth time was a contributory factor in Bismarck's dismissal.

The execution of the anti-Socialist laws varied from Land to Land, Prussia and a number of other German states handling it fairly strictly, others less so. The first three years were the harshest, to be followed from 1881 to a harsher application when the polls had shown that the Social Democratic Party membership was not to be separated from its leaders.

When the anti-Socialist laws actually came into force the Socialist Workers' Party had been closed down by the Berlin City Court in March 1876. Therefore the Socialists did not organize a central

153

administration, relying solely on local party associations. After the passing of the laws local associations, trade unions, workers' support associations, educational institutions, cultural associations, sports associations and women's assocations were affected. The socialist leadership, however, did not disappear but went underground, holding its congresses and meetings outside Prussia or abroad. Socialist trade unions were dissolved but in order for the newly enacted social legislation to function properly the cooperation of organizations representing the workers was highly desirable. For that reason the laws originally also applying to trade unions were considerably relaxed. During the mid 1880s when Germany began to recover from the depression there were demands for higher wages and strikes followed. While Puttkamer accepted the right of collective bargaining he insisted the strikes would have to be carried out without disturbing the public order. Implicitly Puttkamer recognized the right to strike, as long as it was for economic reasons. The strike movement increased towards the end of the decade. From 1 January 1889 to the end of April 1,000 strikes took place in the Reich involving 400,000 strikers. The executive refrained from any counter action. Wilhelm II in May 1889 received a deputation of striking miners and assured them that he would consider their requests favourably, provided that the strike movement rejected socialist attempts to overthrow the existing order. The anti-Socialist laws considerably affected the freedom of the socialist press. In the summer of 1878 the Socialists had more than fifty newspapers. Almost all of them were proscribed, but they soon emerged again under different innocent cover-names. One had scarcely been prohibited before another appeared with a different title.

The most extreme sanction of the anti-Socialist laws, the proclamation of a minor state of siege, was invoked on six occasions. However, throughout this time the Socialists were still represented in the Reichstag by their deputies and were returned by the electorate in increasing numbers. Also, as already mentioned, while still paying lip-service to revolution, from the 1890s onwards the Social Democratic Party was in the process of transforming itself into a reformist party, moving away from its revolutionary principles.

Bismarck's social legislation was to provide a model for the rest of Europe, but he was unable to carry it out without opposition, especially from the liberal doctrinaire bourgeois Left under Eugen Richter. But the measures for sickness insurance and benefits, accident insurance and old age and invalid insurance, were all passed between 1883 and 1889, to be extended by further legislation under Wilhelm II in 1891–92.

From 1878 onwards Bismarck had to govern in the Reichstag with varying majorities, especially in the years between 1881 and 1887. The Conservative and National Liberal majority of the 1870s was reduced to 125 seats. It was much easier for him to gain a majority for the anti-socialist laws and their subsequent extensions than for his social legislation. In 1884 the three parties of the Right increased their number of seats to 157 but the opposition, Progressives, Centre and Social Democrats, had 197 seats. To some extent this problem was neutralized since the opposition to Bismarck was divided against itself and unable to unite under a common programme. Bismarck may well have prevented the timely transition to parliamentary government, but when one looks at the parties of the Reichstag the possiblity of the formation of a government majority in the 1880s can be firmly excluded. Conservative confessionalism, as expressed by the Centre, Manchester-Liberalism as espoused by the *Freisinnige*, the Free Thinkers and the Progressives, and the international Marxism of the Socialists, made any coalition impossible. Their parliamentary and electoral successes were successes of negation.

None the less in the end Bismarck did get his majorities, be it on issues such as Hamburg and Bremen joining the *Zollverein*, social legislation, tariffs or the annexation of colonies. But he obtained them on an *ad hoc* basis and could not rely on any firm backing. The composition of these majorities was often very curious. The Social Democrats, who had voted against social welfare legislation, supported the building of the Kiel Kanal, and this at a time when the anti-Socialist laws were still in full force. But Bismarck also suffered his defeats: the state monopoly on tobacco was defeated, as was that on spirits – all potential sources of additional income for the Reich – as well as the *Septennat* army bill of 1887.

This last defeat led to the dissolution of the Reichstag and new elections which Bismarck hoped to win with the backing of the *Kartell* composed of Conservatives, Free Conservatives and National Liberals, but it formed a far from solid basis. The Conservatives tended to incline towards the Centre rather than to the National Liberals over many issues and after 1888, with the deaths of Kaisers Wilhelm I and Friedrich III and the accession of Wilhelm II, they expected Bismarck's fall. The *Kartell* served election purposes only and did not bring stable support for the government, although Bismarck got the *Septennat* bill through the Reichstag with it.

This instability alienated Bismarck from a Reichstag based on universal manhood franchise. He saw his task as the consolidation of the German Reich, the integration of a social and political multiplicity into one state. He believed the parties endangered this aim more and more. He criticized parliament for its negative attitude, yet countered the opposition's demand for parliamentarization by his insistence upon the constitutional monarchy which was irreconcilable with parliamentary government. It is hardly surprising therefore that his thoughts turned not towards the abolition of the Reichstag but to a change in its constitution, replacing parties by interest groups, professional and industrial: a conflict of genuine interests could be resolved more easily than conflicts based on ideological principles.

Constitutional questions affected the German states no less than the Reich. *Prussia* was subjected to administrative reforms following its annexations of 1866: new *Kreis* constitutions were introduced, a process completed by 1888. Provinces were reorganized, each headed by an *Oberpräsident* advised by a provincial council. Cities were equally subject to administrative change. Within the Prussian government Bismarck tried to revive the State Council as an extra-parliamentary institution. Wilhelm I opposed this since it contradicted the existing constitutional arrangement. But Bismarck managed to get his way and the State Council was restored on 20 April 1884. Though never abolished, it ceased to meet after 1895.

More explosive was the endemic demand to reform the Prussian three-class franchise. Such a reform was at first opposed by the Free Conservatives and the National Liberals, though not by the Conservatives until the late 1870s. Its most vociferous critics were the Centre and the Socialists. In spite of various patchwork reforms and lengthy debates on the issue, nothing was changed fundamentally until 1918.

CONSTITUTIONAL PROBLEMS IN THE GERMAN STATES

Bavaria had its problems with its King Ludwig II and his extravagant passion for building which by 1886 reached such proportions that expenditure could no longer be met from the Wittelsbach treasury. Numerous bankruptcies resulted for firms involved in the King's projects, leading to a conflict between the King and his ministers. Munich psychiatrists attested the King's insanity. His civil list was cut and Ludwig appealed to Bismarck but he could offer no help. Ludwig was removed and his uncle Prince Luitpold appointed Regent. Ludwig himself, together with his physician Dr Gudden, drowned in Lake Starnberg on 13 June 1886. Under Luitpold electoral reform was carried out. So far the vote had been limited to those paying direct state taxation. In 1906 the equal, direct and secret ballot was introduced. After the death of the Prince Regent in 1912 his son Prince Leopold was appointed Regent and in 1913 formally crowned as Ludwig III. Strictly speaking this was a constitutionally illegal act, since Ludwig II's brother Otto, also detained because of insanity, was still alive: it might have been better to have waited until his death. Hence Ludwig III never lost his reputation as a usurper.

In *Saxony* the three-class franchise was introduced in 1896 as a bastion against Social Democracy, the sole case in Germany between 1871 and 1918 of a return to reactionary practice. But by 1909 it was abolished again in favour of a general franchise. In *Württemberg*, too, the change of the electoral law in favour of more equitable representation was the most salient feature between 1871 and 1918. *Baden* remained a bastion of National Liberalism but also the first German state to accept Social Democracy as an equal partner, so much so that in 1910 Social Democrats voted for the budget. In *Hesse* electoral reform was also at issue and found a solution acceptable to all parties in 1911. The two *Mecklenburgs* were the only states without a constitution. This caused great debate, leading in the Reichstag to the demand that the Reich intervene. Bethmann Hollweg refused, however, and until the November revolution of 1918 the Mecklenburgs continued to be run by an assembly of the estates. In *Brunswick* after the death of the bachelor Duke Wilhelm the elder line of the Guelphs became extinct and the succession reverted to Duke Ernest Augustus of Cumberland, the son of King George V of Hanover, who had been dispossessed in 1866. Like his father he opposed the annexation of 1866 and the creation of the German Empire in 1871; it was therefore impossible for someone to occupy the throne who opposed the legal foundations of the Reich and its constitution. Hence a regency council of five was appointed, but the question of deciding the succession to the throne was left to the Reich. The Bundesrat refused to accept Ernest Augustus and instead appointed as Regent first Prince Albrecht of Prussia (1885–1906) and then Duke Johann Albrecht of Mecklenburg (1907–13). The three-class franchise prevailed in Brunswick. In the meantime Ernest Augustus renounced the succession for himself and his eldest son in favour of a younger son also named Ernest Augustus. He succeeded to the throne in 1913 and married Kaiser Wilhelm II's daughter Victoria Luise of Prussia. But he did not renounce his claim to Hanover. Similar problems were also encountered in *Lippe-Detmold* and *Schaumburg-Lippe*, but were ultimately resolved.

There was a far more important and explosive problem over the land annexed from France in 1871, *Alsace-Lorraine*. At first it was occupied enemy territory, then on 9 June 1871 it was declared a *Reichsland*, under the immediate administration of the Reich. Sole power was to reside in the hands of the Kaiser, who during the early phase exercised his executive power together with the Bundesrat. The Reichstag's function was limited to political control. A civilian *Oberpräsident* was installed in Strassburg directly subordinate to the Chancellor. A first step was the replacement of the highly centralized French administrative structure by a decentralized German one. The *Oberpräsident* had emergency powers, including the proclamation of a state of siege. Initial problems concerned French anti-German agitation, the question of those who opted for French nationality, the language and the schools. The deputies for Alsace-Lorraine had voted against annexation in the French National Assembly and this attitude was prevalent at all levels of society during the first years. A well organized protest movement was formed but was quickly suppressed. The Franco-German Peace Treaty allowed all French citizens to opt for their French nationality until 1 October 1872. They were then compelled to transfer their place of residence to France, though they were allowed to hold on to their property in Alsace-Lorraine. About 10 per cent of the population opted for France but of 160,000 only 50,000 moved, which meant that the remaining 110,000 automatically became German citizens. Lorraine was predominantly French-speaking, while Alsace spoke German. In both Alsace and Lorraine the French had made their language the only official language and the one to be used in education. The Germans for their part began a Germanizing policy. From 1 October 1873 German was to be the sole language in all primary and higher schools; it also became official language, except in communes where French was the predominant. Compulsory primary education had already been introduced two years before. In a predominantly Roman Catholic area the *Kulturkampf* left its mark, though the Church there acted very moderately so as to reduce the possibility of conflict. In April 1871 an assembly of mayors of Lower Alsace had demanded the institution of a University at Strassburg, a request which was met by the founding of the *Reichsuniversität* in Strassburg in 1872.

The German Constitution was formally introduced on 1 January 1874 and opened the franchise to the Reichstag to all Alsatians and Lorrainers. In 1874 an Alsace-Lorraine Land Committee, composed of members of representative organs at district level, was founded as an advisory body for any legislation affecting the *Reichsland*.

In party-political terms the new province was divided into two parties. The 'protest party', consisting of a clerical and radical liberal wing, opposed annexation. They regularly lost in local elections but won in Reichstag elections. There was also the 'autonomist party' which accepted annexation but demanded autonomy for the province. In the 1874 election the 'protest party' won all 15 seats with the clericals gaining 10 and the radicals 5. In their first appearance at the Reichstag they protested against the annexation and opposed the right to invoke emergency law in Alsace-Lorraine. The German government replied that the French law of a state of siege had meant the immediate transfer of power from the civil to the military authorities, whereas the Germans had not introduced military power but had invested the civil authorities with the power to take emergency measures, which was in fact a milder practice than that of the French. Bismarck also argued that annexation of the province had been necessary to form a bulwark 'against the irruptions', made 'over the past 200 years by this passionate and warlike people' against Germany.

With the appointment of a *Statthalter* for Alsace-Lorraine the functions of the *Oberpräsident* were fused with his office, as were the functions of the Reichs Chancellor Office for Alsace-Lorraine, which was then abolished. A Ministry for Alsace-Lorraine based on Strassburg was created, with a Secretary of State at its head. The Land Committee continued to exist in its advisory capacity, and in addition a State Council appointed by the Kaiser was introduced. The Land, which was not yet a state, had a representative institution in the Land Committee. But Alsace-Lorraine was not represented in the Bundesrat; furthermore the Reichstag could interfere with legislation for Alsace-Lorraine, as could the Bundesrat. All this was held in Alsace-Lorraine to be discriminating. Tensions, initially high, began to subside in the course of the years, except during the Boulangist crisis in 1887 and over the introduction of compulsory passports and visas required by foreigners, especially French military personnel, entering the *Reichsland*. From 1890 onwards normalization of relations set in and the consolidation of the German position culminated in 1911 with the granting of a constitution for Alsace-Lorraine. By this the Emperor exercised supreme powers in the *Reichsland*, powers delegated to the *Statthalter*. The decree extending delegation of power by the Emperor to the *Statthalter* required the counter-signature of the chancellor, as did the act of appointing a *Statthalter*. The Ministry for Alsace-Lorraine remained its leading officials being appointed by the Emperor, but with the counter-signature of the *Statthalter*. The Land Committee and the State Council were replaced by two chambers. The First Chamber consisted of members holding high office or those elected by their corporations such as universities and cities. The right to examine elections was held by the judiciary. The Second Chamber was elected on the basis of universal, free, equal and direct franchise. Emergency powers were reserved for the Kaiser. From a constitutional point of view Alsace-Lorraine was rather more advanced than Prussia. In the elections to the Second Chamber in 1911 none of the radical opponents was elected. Of the 60 seats the Centre won 24, the Social Democrats 11, the Liberals 7, the Bloc of Lorraine 10 and the Independents 8, a development also reflected in the Reichstag elections of 1912.

THE EASTERN PROVINCES

Alsace-Lorraine was complemented in the east by Prussia's Polish provinces, which took on a new role in 1871 when its citizens became Germans. Poles were represented in the Prussian Diet and in the

Reichstag. In 1871 they held 13 Reichstag seats, in 1890 these increased to 16, and in 1918 to 19. Most of the Polish votes came from West Prussia and Posen. In East Prussia they once obtained one seat and in Upper Silesia they began to emerge only after 1903 when a vast influx of Polish labour into its industrial area produced a minority problem. Up to 1873 Polish coexisted with German as the official language, but in the course of the *Kulturkampf* in 1873 the clergy's right to supervise school instruction was abolished and in the previous years German had been made compulsory for religious instruction in grammar schools. In 1873 German became the language of instruction for all primary schools except for religious instruction. This rallied the Polish clergy solidly against the Germans. In 1883 the Poles in the Prussian Diet moved to readmit Polish in the grammar schools, but they were defeated. As already indicated, in the course of industrialization Prussia's Polish provinces experienced a mass influx of Polish labour from the Russian as well as the Austrian Polish provinces. This was considered a threat to the German position there and consequently in 1885 Prussia expelled 30,000 Poles of Russian or Austrian citizenship. In December of the same year 155 Reichstag deputies made up of the Centre Party, *Freisinnige*, Social Democrats, Alsace-Lorrainers and Poles, supported an interpellation asking the Reich government what steps it intended to take against the measures of the Prussian government. Bismarck reacted by saying that the Reichstag had no authority to control the exercise of their sovereign rights by member states.

One of the major methods of Germanizing the Prussian provinces of Poland was the purchase of large estates, their division and the settlement of German farmers on them. The Poles countered by creating their own cooperatives and banks and buying the land before the Germans could do so. In 1886 Prussia assumed the power to appoint all teachers and civil servants. Where it still existed, school instruction in Polish was abolished, a measure designed to strengthen Polish resistance even further. During the 1890s, however, both the Polish clergy and the nobility found their positions threatened by the Polish irredentist movement which led to a *rapprochement* between them and the Prussian administration. To further this development Caprivi tried to relax the situation by concessions on the schools, language and settlement issues. The Poles were divided between the 'radicals' and the 'court party', and the radicals dominated. The move divided the Germans also, Caprivi being more and more opposed by the German Conservatives and some of the Liberals, and this helped to bring about his fall. Under Chancellor Hohenlohe the anti-Polish course was resumed and legislation for the German settlement policy in West Prussia and Posen was speeded up. The 1894 readmission of the Polish language in primary school instruction was revoked in 1898. Under Chancellor Bülow the Germanizing policy hardened further, but he was also intent on using culture as one major avenue of influence, founding new museums, libraries, theatres, the Academy in Posen and the Technical University in Danzig. But in 1906 the Poles reacted by a school strike in which 60,000 Polish pupils refused to answer in German during religious instruction. This strike movement lasted until the summer of 1907.

A new measure of expropriation of Polish land was to be enacted in the Prussian *Herrenhaus* but it met formidable opposition because of the state's interference in private property. It only finally passed the Diet in a very emasculated form but nonetheless it became part of both law and constitution. Polish public assemblies now had to conduct their meeting in German except in areas where the Polish-speaking population exceeded 60 per cent. Bülow's successor Bethmann Hollweg tried a more moderate course but quickly came into conflict with the main organ of the Germanizing policy, the *Ostmarken-Verein*, which accused him of weakness. Bethmann Hollweg assured them he would not reject expropriation, and on 2 May 1912 he submitted a law to the Prussian Diet proposing to make 100 million marks available for the purchase of land in West Prussia and Posen. The law was accepted by both houses of the Prussian Diet, but by the eve of the First World War the attitude once again changed. Advocates of compromise on both sides were hindered by having to take notice of Russia. Caprivi, who considered conflict with Russia inevitable, could make concessions to the Poles, and the more Russia moved towards France and Great Britain, especially between 1909 and 1914, the greater the readiness on both sides to find a *modus vivendi* for Prussia's Polish provinces.

THE COLONIES

Bismarck had been originally averse to Germany joining in the scramble for overseas possessions since he expected such a move to lead to complications for Germany in Europe. But, like the later naval policy, the movement for German colonies was the product of the German middle classes, especially its commercial, industrial and scientific sectors. Among the political parties it was the National Liberals, the Free Conservatives and parts of the Centre Party as well as the *Freisinnige* People's Party which supported it. Even a small number of Social Democrats were in favour. The Conservatives were the last to support it. Wide-ranging popular organizations were founded to foster it such as the *Deutsche Kolonialverein* in 1882 and the *Gesellschaft für Deutsche Kolonisation* in 1884, which fused into the *Deutsche Kolonialgesellschaft* in 1887. Between 1884 and 1885

German South West Africa, the Cameroons, Togo, German East Africa, German New Guinea and German Samoa were annexed. At first Bismarck hoped that they would administer themselves without any great cost to the Reich, but eventually the state had to intervene directly. During the first stage the Central Office for the Administration of the German Colonies was part of the Foreign Office. From 1907 onwards the Reich Colonial Office was headed by a Secretary of State. At first *Reichskommissare* and later Governors were appointed to the individual colonies. Command of military forces lay in the hands of the Chancellor and through him in those of the Secretary of State, the only case in the constitution where the power of military command was in the hands of the civil authorities. The *Schutzgebietsgesetz* of 1886, the law concerning the colonial territories, stipulated that the Kaiser exercised the protective power and that the territories were subject directly to the Reich. In terms of international law the German colonies wers domestic and not foreign soil. The law which applied was German civil and criminal law. Laws enacted for them required the counter-signature of the Chancellor or the respective Secretary of State. The military forces stationed in them were police forces, their core being officers and NCOs from the army and navy, seconded from the armed forces of the Reich to serve in the colonies. Germans settling in the colonies had the same rights as in Germany. The natives were subject to their tribal laws except in instances when the law determined it differently.

EMPEROR FRIEDRICH III

When Kaiser Wilhelm I died on 9 March 1888 he was succeeded by his son Emperor Friedrich III. At that stage he was already fatally ill and he asked Bismarck to remain in office. Bismarck agreed, provided the Emperor would not suffer 'foreign influence' in the conduct of foreign policy nor any parliamentarization of the government. Friedrich accepted and on the day of his accession confirmed the Chancellor and all Prussian ministers in their offices. During his short reign of ninety-eight days the anti-socialist laws were prolonged until 1890. This had already been passed by the Reichstag and only needed the Kaiser's signature. He at first refused until it was pointed out to him that according to the constitution the Kaiser did not possess the power of veto. Another point at issue during this period was the proposed marriage of the Emperor's daughter Princess Victoria to Prince Alexander von Battenberg. Alexander had become the ruler of Bulgaria with Russian support in 1879, but soon fell out first with Czar Alexander II and then with Alexander III. Since 1882 he had been courting Princess Victoria, but he was vehemently opposed by Bismarck who wanted to maintain strict neutrality in Balkan questions. Wilhelm I had already refused to consent to the marriage in 1884. Prince Alexander was deposed from his throne in 1886 and in March 1888 the Empress Victoria tried to get the marriage project going again. But she was opposed by her son Crown Prince Wilhelm and Bismarck, since Russia would see in it an act of provocation. Bismarck won.

The only change carried out by Friedrich was the dismissal of the Conservative Minister of the Interior, Robert von Puttkamer. He did so without prior consultation with the Chancellor, a move out of keeping with constitutional practice. The Empress, who had been the driving force behind this dismissal, was unable to suggest a possible successor, and the office remained vacant until the death of Friedrich.

It is often argued that Friedrich's death prevented the liberalization and parliamentarization of Germany. But nineteenth-century Liberals in Germany as elsewhere were something different from what they are now. They were the main supporters of the idea of imperial expansionism, the 'big Navy' and the opponents of universal franchise. Moreover the Empress herself was trying to expand the power of the Emperor beyond the limits set by the Constitution. The Chancellor was to be completely subordinate to the Crown, and not to the Reichstag. It is therefore more than doubtful that the course of German history would have run a fundamentally different course had Friedrich achieved a full reign.

NOTE

1. Neither the Bismarckian nor the Weimar Constitution made any provision for a 'Vice-Chancellor'. However, in practice, by way of the 'Deputy Law' of 1878, the Kaiser could upon the Chancellor's suggestion appoint a Vice-Chancellor who solely deputised for the Chancellor, or appoint one of the Secretaries of State, usually that of the Interior, to this more-or-less improvised office. They had the right of counter-signature and were answerable to the Reichstag, but were never Reich Ministers.

Chapter 6

THE GERMAN EMPIRE UNDER WILHELM II

Wilhelm II inherited a Reich which appeared to be a strong consolidated body at least on the surface, and to the outside world. The previous pages have demonstrated that it was far from consolidated internally. It was in the process of consolidation, a process which could hardly be achieved in less than three decades, and it was still far from completion by 1914. Externally, Germany's geographic position made it continually vulnerable to threats from west and east, but because of this it possessed a strong army and this part of his legacy should therefore be examined first.

THE ARMY

It is often asserted that the German army was an extra-constitutional body, yet already as early as 1850 the Prussian Constitution contained detailed provisions regarding conscription, the use of the army internally, the military judiciary and parliamentary powers over the military budget. In the Bismarckian Constitution conscription, the army's peace-time strength and military expenditure were to be regulated by Reich laws; the extent of the monarch's power of supreme command was also clearly defined, including his power to proclaim a state of siege for the restoration and maintenance of public order. Supreme command resided with the Kaiser and that was laid down constitutionally: this exercise of command was not subject to ministerial counter-signature, nor did the army swear an oath to the constitution. But this did not exempt the army from control by the constitution, since its funds had to be voted by the Reichstag. Although the power of supreme command was outside its control the period 1871 to 1914 actually shows the increasing inroads the Reichstag made into military affairs by its legislative initiative, control of the purse, resolutions, interpellations and discussion. Issues that occupied the Reichstag ranged from the location of garrisons to training, armament, the role of cavalry in a modern war, disciplinary matters such as the ill-treatment of soldiers by their NCOs, duelling within the officer corps, and the use of the army in cases of civil unrest. Time and again the Reichstag intervened, opposed of course by the Chancellor and the Minister of War who argued that these matters were outside its competence, an argument which increasingly lost its weight. The government's refusal to answer on such issues caused such public furore that in the end it was considered expedient to answer the questions. In the period of increasing military expenditure between 1893 and 1913 the Reichstag's influence grew in almost equal proportions. Military jurisdiction was subject to regulation by Reich law, except in Bavaria. But the Emperor also had the right to issue military decrees as part of his power of command and these were outside the control of the Reichstag.

During the course of the nineteenth century the trinity of the military leadership had emerged. As already mentioned the Ministry of War at first also included the Military Cabinet and the General Staff, but with increasing parliamentarization both the Military Cabinet and the General Staff emancipated themselves from the Ministry of War and came under the direct authority of the monarch. It cannot be said that they were equal in status, since the Military Cabinet and the General Staff exercised a far greater influence than the Ministry of War over actual military policy-making.

The Minister of War was answerable to the Reichstag but his function by the end of the nineteenth century had become a purely administrative one. Although he had to defend the government's military ideas before the Reichstag he had little influence in actually shaping them. After Bismarck's dismissal parliamentary demands on him increased and he had to defend the official policy. This meant he had the political responsiblity in an area where his actual personal influence had been seriously reduced. Although he was officially the Prussian Minister of War, in fact he was also the Reich Minister of War.

The Military Cabinet had gained independence from the Ministry of War under General Edwin von Manteuffel by 1865. Originally, in so far as it was concerned with matters of personnel, it was still part of the War Ministry; in so far as it was an institution of the Emperor for immediate advice on matters of command, it was outside it. But this peculiar dual position was ended in 1883 when it was completely removed from the War Ministry. This lack of responsibility to any body other than the Emperor increased its power and for many members of the Reichstag it became the expression of royal absolutism.

The General Staff had already begun to emancipate itself from the War Ministry in the 1820s, but its Chiefs, including Helmuth Moltke in his early years in charge, did not have the right of direct access to the monarch. Moltke gained it in the war of 1866, but had difficulty in maintaining it in times of peace, nor was he particularly bothered by that. The struggle for the supremacy of the civil power over the military one was joined fully between Bismarck and Moltke in 1864, 1866 and 1870–71. Especially during the Franco-German War Bismarck was kept in the dark about military planning and actions, having to depend on newspaper reports for information. Bismarck finally brought the issue to a head and this caused Wilhelm I to issue an order to Moltke according to which all military information of importance available to the General Staff would have to be handed on immediately to Bismarck. During the conduct of operations Moltke demanded full equality with the Chancellor, which Wilhelm refused to consider. Moltke had to give in, but the conflict continued, surfacing again during the 'War-in-sight' crisis of 1875 and the Boulanger crisis of 1886–87 when Moltke was in favour of a preventive war, an idea rejected out of hand by Bismarck. Moltke's successor, Count Waldersee, was very much in favour of preventive war against Russia but was stopped by Caprivi. Wilhelm II parted company with Waldersee and appointed Alfred von Schlieffen as his successor. Between 1899 and 1911 Schlieffen and his successor the younger Helmuth Moltke (nephew of the elder one) pressed for increases in Germany's military strength but failed until after 1911. During the first and second Moroccan crises (1905 and 1911 respectively) Moltke privately expressed opinions in favour of a preventative war but received neither the hearing of the Kaiser nor that of the civil government.

However, the Schlieffen Plan designed for war against France and Russia remained a fateful legacy. It is often condemned as rampant militarism *par excellence*. This would be true if Schlieffen and his successor had not consulted and obtained the agreement of the civil authorities. Both Bülow and Bethmann Hollweg were fully put in the picture, including the fact that the execution of this plan would involve the violation of Belgian neutrality. They raised no objections.

The strength of the army was determined by the Reich law and was thus subject to the assent of the Reichstag. But in 1871 the parties concerned could not settle on an agreed figure, so that the peacetime strength of the army remained at the 1871 level until a law had been properly formulated and agreed upon. What Bismarck wanted to avoid was making the military budget subject to an annual vote which would have played havoc with long-term military planning. In 1874, mainly due to Bennigsen's readiness to compromise, the *Septennat* was laid down, which fixed the army's peacetime strength at 401,659 men from 1 January 1875 to 31 December 1881. In April 1880 a further *Septennat* was passed to run until March 1888, and the army increased by 26,000. Under the influence of the Boulanger crisis in 1886, Bismarck put forward the third *Septennat* in November 1886, but he was now firmly opposed by the Centre Party under Windthorst who demanded a *Triennat*. The result was the dissolution of the Reichstag, the election of 1887 and the *Kartell* victory which ensured the *Septennat* until March 1894 and settled the peacetime strength of the army at 468,406 men. But in view of increasing Russian and French armaments Waldersee demanded army increases. In 1890 the reservoir of potential conscripts amounted to 550,000 of which at the most only 190,000 were called to the colours. The War Minister, General Julius von Verdy, suggested increasing the army annually in order to correct this imbalance. Bismarck refused because that would have made the army budget subject to an annual vote by the Reichstag. Nor could Caprivi risk any serious reform and only managed to pass a supplementary law, a *novelle*, to the *Septennat* in 1890.

Three years later he tried again and found support from Wilhelm II to reduce the period of conscription from three to two years. While the strength of the army remained the same this would provide it with a higher number of trained reservists. The total strength of the army would be 600,000 men. But the Reichstag solidly opposed the bill. It was then dissolved and the June elections of 1893 brought a victory for the government. This bill settled the peacetime strength of the army at 479,229 including one-year service volunteers and NCOs. The *Septennat* was now replaced by a *Quinquennat*. In the meantime the General Staff continued to press for major increases in the forces, especially because of the conclusion of the Franco-Russian alliance of 1894, but without success. Only the darkening political horizons around Germany in 1911 brought new life into the issue of army increases. But it was opposed by the Secretary of State for the Reich Treasury, Adolf Wermuth, who argued that the money could only be raised by increasing indirect taxation. When he was overruled he resigned. Bethmann Hollweg was not in favour either, since army increases contradicted his policy of *détente*, and only the failure of the Haldane mission in 1912 and the Balkan Wars changed his mind. In 1912 the army was increased by 29,000 men with the approval of the Reichstag, although in the January elections of 1912 the SPD had become the strongest single party. But in December 1912 Moltke realized that the Schlieffen plan could only be carried out if the full potential of Germany's military manpower was used. He therefore demanded an increase of an additional 300,000 men. The Minister of War, General Josias von Heeringen, opposed this increase and the Kaiser sided with him. The raising of three new army corps was postponed for the time being. Within the Ministry of War and among other German senior officers it was also argued that the required number of officers would not be available for an increase of that size. This meant a large number of reserve officers would have to be appointed who came from what were considered to be socially and politically undesirable backgrounds. Nevertheless three years later under the pressure of war these three army corps were created and two thirds of the commissions within them went to officers of middle-class origin, because the German nobility had paid a heavy blood toll in the years 1914–15.

This period was marked by changes of attitude towards the military question by the parties of the Reichstag. The Centre Party, from being a party of opposition, gradually moved towards supporting the government on vital issues. This was also true of the *Freisinnige* Party which split, the splinter *Freisinnige* Association supporting the government on military issues. Even the Progressives began to rally to the government's side. The government on the other hand increasingly relied on the Reichstag, since under no circumstances did it wish for a repetition of 1862–66. The government could not overrule the Reichstag without running into serious problems. The Reichstag, by virtue of its budget powers, had become a real power factor. But the Army Bill of 1913 by no means mobilized Germany's full manpower potential. As a result of the increasing birth-rate, by 1914 there were 940,000 men eligible for conscription, but only 340,000 of them were drafted into the army as a result of the reform. On the eve of the war only 50 per cent of those eligible for military training had in fact been trained, as against 60 per cent in France. The war strength of army and navy amounted to 6 per cent of the population, as against 9.1 per cent in France. The German army on a war footing was 3,823,000 strong against 3,580,000 in France and 4,800,000 in Russia. These figures speak for themselves in any argument about Germany's aggressive intentions.

THE IMPERIAL NAVY

The new component that had joined the German armed forces since the accession of Wilhelm II was the Imperial Navy. A Prussian navy had existed since 1861, subject to the Crown and the War Minister who also became Minister for the Navy. Since 1 January 1872 it had become an institution of the Reich subject to the Imperial Admiralty, and it remained so until 1888 when Bismarck separated naval administration from naval command. In 1889 the Imperial Admiralty was dissolved and in its place came the Reich Naval Office, the Naval Cabinet and, following belatedly in 1918, the Supreme Command of the Navy, analogous to the divisions existing in the army. The Supreme Command of the Navy was the office of command; there was no naval General Staff. The Reich Naval Office fulfilled the same functions in the naval sphere as did the Ministry of War; the Naval Cabinet was the naval equivalent of the Military Cabinet. After a number of other changes the three most important naval institutions were the *Reichs-*

marineamt, the *Admiralstab* and the *Chef de Hochseeflotte*.

The *Reichsmarineamt*, founded in 1889, reached its zenith under Admiral Alfred von Tirpitz, though his position was not predominant. The Admiralty Staff, which was founded in 1899 and in 1918 became the *Oberste Seekriegsleitung* (SKL), the naval equivalent to the *Oberste Heeresleitung* (OHL), the supreme command of the army, was a planning institution and part neither of the naval administration nor the naval command. Even with the outbreak of war in 1914 it did not assume the strategic conduct of naval warfare until 29 August 1918 when the Supreme Command of the Navy (SKL) under Admiral Scheer came into being. The Chief of the High Seas Fleet was directly subject to the command of the Emperor. Only in 1918 was he also made Chief of the Admiralty Staff and Chief of the SKL.

' The expansion of the German navy under Admiral von Tirpitz is viewed by much of current historiography as an instrument of 'manipulation'. In fact the concept of manipulation is applied by a neo-Marxist school of historiography to the entire history of Germany between 1870 and 1918. Bismarck as 'the great manipulator' is *en vogue* – other motives than manipulation are dismissed with derision. The same goes for the building of the Imperial Navy which, so it is argued, was primarily aimed at domestic opinion to prevent the parliamentarization and democratization of 'Prusso-German constitutionalism'. This is alleged to have been the primary motive of the 'Tirpitzplan' (a term of relatively recent coinage). It is an interesting and original hypothesis subject to considerable discussion and dissent among historians. General agreement, however, exists that it was directed against Great Britain. Navalists had fully absorbed the lessons taught by the works of Admiral Thayer Mahan, and not only in Germany. German navalists in particular and large parts of the German public in general were fully aware of what they believed to be a strong current of Germanophobia in Great Britain during the mid 1890s, even before the ill-starred *Krüger-Telegramme*, which culminated in the demand *Germaniam esse delendam*. The immediate context within which navalism prospered, the geographic, economic, political and intellectual forces and factors favouring it, would deserve restatement rather than the postulation of a structural determinism which reduces the complexity of history to what in essence are monocausal explanations.

In 1873 the functions of the navy were to protect German commerce on the high seas, defence of the German coast and the development of an offensive potential. Under Wilhelm II the concept changed towards building an effective battle fleet. Since the naval budget was passed on an annual basis, and because of the length of time it took to build a battle cruiser and subsequent replacement, this was an unsatisfactory arrangement. A decisive change occurred with the appointment of Admiral von Tirpitz as Secretary of State of the Reich Naval Office in

June 1897. He went in for long-term planning and was one of the few military men in Germany who correctly read the signs of the times, especially in so far as they pointed to Germany's domestic development. Instead of seeing the Reichstag as a hostile force, he did all he could by his considerable powers of persuasion to win it over to his point of view. He won over most of the industrial pressure groups, many of which after all stood only to profit by it, and he exercised a powerful influence upon German public opinion, creating in Germany the equivalent of Great Britain's Navy League, the *Flottenverein*. His original aim was to create a navy strong enough so 'that a war, even for the most powerful naval enemy, would involve dangers which would put its own position of power at risk'. Naval hegemony was not the aim but a fleet which would make any potential enemy think twice before attacking it. However there are indications that by 1909 Tirpitz aimed at naval parity with Great Britain. He was aware that such a navy could only be created on the basis of a naval law which laid down the number, size, type, speed, armament and future replacement of the vessels. His first draft was opposed by Eugen Richter in the Reichstag as well as by the Prussian Minister of Finance, Miquel, on financial grounds. During the first reading of the naval bill Bülow made an intervention which most texts only partly quote: 'We do not want to put anyone in the shade, but we also demand our *place in the sun*'. The first naval law was passed in April 1898 and was intended to build a battle fleet within six years. But the duration of the law was not limited to six years: it allowed Tirpitz to keep the vessels in service after they had been built. What in fact Tirpitz had achieved was an *Äternat*. The naval bill of 1900 doubled the planned fleet, and these naval laws were supplemented by laws in 1906 and 1908, when Germany, following Britain's example, changed over to building dreadnoughts which required considerably more money. The Anglo-German naval rivalry was in full swing, and though attempts were made to come to a mutual arrangement, they failed. This was because Germany demanded as a precondition to any naval limitation a preliminary political agreement, amounting to Britain's neutrality in case of war in Europe, while the British demanded a preliminary naval agreement before any political arrangement. In any case Great Britain let it be known that it would only give assurances of neutrality in case of an 'unprovoked attack'. What precisely this means international lawyers are still discussing to this day. Naturally Germany was not prepared to make concessions on that basis; the British Foreign Office, which during the first half of the first decade of this century, according to the studies of Zara Steiner, was reorganized with staff who were essentially anti-German in outlook, saw Germany's demand as an implied bid for hegemony in Europe.

Thus even the Haldane mission of 1912 came to nought, although from then on both countries appeared to have accepted each other's position, and this resulted in a two-year period of improvement of

Anglo-German relations, the like of which had not been seen since the early 1890s. As far as Tirpitz's naval bill of 1912 was concerned, it was passed by as great a majority as the army bill, although the combined force of those parties traditionally opposed to the government had a numerical majority. This means that substantial parts of the opposition must have also voted for it.

WILHELM II AND BISMARCK

Having said this much about the most formidable part of the legacy inherited by Kaiser Wilhelm II and its further development, let us return to the constitutional developments in his reign. In contrast to his predecessors Wilhelm was much more a German than a Prussian; being half an Englishman did not help matters, either, nor did the extreme tactlessness he inherited from his mother. He was the exponent of the aims of the German National Liberal middle class, prepared to be open on social questions and interested in the progress of science. This was demonstrated by his creation of the *Kaiser-Wilhelm-Gesellschaft* for the advancement of the sciences, and his aims to modernize higher education and expand technical universities and other institutions of advanced and higher education. On assuming the throne he was determined to be a *Reform-Kaiser*, especially as far as the conditions of the working class were concerned. He expected in return their reconciliation with and integration into the state. On the other hand he cherished neo-feudal notions as far as his office was concerned, but his claims to 'personal rule' remained fictitious. He came to the throne on 15 June 1888, and at the opening of the Reichstag on 25 June twenty-two monarchs were present, headed by the Prince Regent Luitpold of Bavaria and King Albert of Saxony. Like his two predecessors he gave a solemn pledge to preserve and to protect the constitution.

His relationship to Bismarck at first was that of an admirer, but it was soon blemished when excerpts of the war diary of his father were published in September 1888. In these the then Crown Prince Friedrich claimed to have done most of the work leading to Germany's unification, while Bismarck's role was described as vacillating. Emperor Friedrich III before his death and, little more than two decades later, the dowager Empress, had transferred substantial parts of their private papers to Great Britain, hardly a loyal move to one's own or one's adopted country. The publication, which also revealed that Crown Prince Friedrich was considering the use of force against the south German states if they failed to join a unified Germany, was a serious embarrassment. It was the work of the clique that had surrounded the Emperor and his British-born wife and was designed to put a wedge between Bismarck and the younger Kaiser. Bismarck obtained Wilhelm's agreement to proceed against the person who had published the extracts on a charge of treason, but this roused public opinion against him on the ground of violating the freedom of the press. The courts however dismissed the case and any fears of suppression of the press proved to be unfounded. The next problem arose out of a scheme of Baron von Holstein of the Foreign Office and the Chief of the General Staff, Count Waldersee, to bring about a change in foreign policy aimed against Russia. Bismarck successfully foiled this, but it left an impression on the Kaiser.

The extreme *Kreuzzeitung* wing of the Conservatives was also continuing attacks on the *Kartell* parties on which Bismarck's parliamentary support depended. While praising the new Kaiser to unprecedented heights they directed their invective against Bismarck's policy without, however, achieving immediate success. But the major area of tension that developed was over the attitude to be adopted to the workers and social legislation. Bismarck had introduced the main body of social legislation, but by 1888 he had decided that for the time being no new laws were necessary, while the Kaiser aimed at further steps of reconciliation. The conflict between Kaiser and Bismarck came into the open during the miners' strikes in April 1889. Bismarck was in favour of non-intervention but Wilhelm intervened, and successfully at that. The Chancellor's intention was also to extend the anti-socialist laws for a further period. This was defeated in the Reichstag in January 1890, followed by elections in which the *Kartell* lost its majority. This double defeat at the hands of the Reichstag and at the polls shook Bismarck's position to its very foundations. Over the long term it was impossible for him to govern without a Reichstag majority, hence his thoughts turned, as already indicated, towards plans for changing its composition. The Kaiser himself was against the renewal of the anti-socialist laws. At a Crown Council on 28 January 1890, Bismarck argued that abandoning them would lead to public disorders and he went as far as to envisage proclaiming a state of siege and the use of troops on the basis of the existing emergency laws. The Kaiser, however, declared that at the beginning of his reign any bloodshed would be hardly desirable. Bismarck answered with a threat of resignation, insisting that voluntary withdrawal in the struggle against Social Democracy was the first step towards parliamentarization and doubting if he, Bismarck, would be the right person in office to see this happen. The Kaiser rejected Bismarck's argument but the split between the two was there. It was further increased by the Kaiser publishing two decrees enacting legislation for workers' protection. He did so without Bismarck's counter-signature, clearly a breach of the constitution. Bismarck should have replied to this by his immediate resignation, but he did not. It was the only occasion during his reign in which Wilhelm acted in this manner.

Bismarck was now faced by a Reichstag in which he had no majority, and as a last resort he tried to arrive at a *rapprochement* with the Centre Party. To this end he conducted negotiations with its leader Windthorst without arriving at conclusive results. If a compromise could have been reached, it would have implied the abandonment of anti-socialist legislation. The news of the secret negotiations between Bismarck and Windthorst led to open conflict with the Kaiser. The leader of the German Conservatives, Heinrich von Helldorf, informed the Kaiser that his party would not support the government if the conversations between Bismarck and Windthorst were continued. This strengthened the Kaiser's resolve to part company with Bismarck. He told Bismarck that he ought to have informed him about these negotiations and in fact should have asked for his agreement before they ever began. Added to this was a conflict stemming from a cabinet order of 1852 which obliged each minister to inform the Prussian Prime Minister of all important matters in his department and to forward his reports via the Prime Minister to the King, or to report in person to the King. This had become too cumbersome a procedure so that in practice it was the Prime Minister alone who reported to the King. Wilhelm now accused Bismarck of having forbidden his ministers to report directly to him. Bismarck went to some length to explain the position and he refused to submit a draft of a cabinet order which would replace that of 1852. Therefore on 17 March 1890 the Kaiser requested his resignation. Bismarck submitted it, listing in great detail the reasons for it. On 20 March 1890 the Kaiser announced his dismissal and appointed General Count von Caprivi his successor. Bismarck's dismissal document would also have required ministerial counter-signature, in this case by Caprivi, but Wilhelm, intentionally or unintentionally, made no attempt to obtain this.

CAPRIVI

Bismarck's departure is often described as a return to the pseudo-absolutism of the Hohenzollerns. However, it was not the result of the sole decision of the Kaiser, but agreed in consultation with several ministers and party leaders. That Wilhelm lacked any talent for actual personal rule was apparent to all those who participated in the crisis. After it there was no change in the relationship between executive and legislative institutions. Bismarck's successors had also had to respect the power of the Reichstag and, like him, they had to manoeuvre for their majorities. One important change which did occur was the attitude of the state towards social democracy and the trade unions.

The latter were now fres from any fetters and could develop fully. The Social Democrats still remained outwardly wedded to the principle of social revolution, but this was to change over the next two decades. To most members of the government they still remained potentially dangerous enemies of the constitution.

Caprivi's aim was to create '*klare Verhältnisse*', i.e. a clear, transparent situation both in the domestic and foreign spheres, less secret and more public policy. His first objectives were to reduce agrarian tariffs, to introduce a commerical policy which would favour Germany's foreign trade, to further strengthen workers' protection and to fight political subversion not by exceptional laws but within the body of existing legislation, and finally to reform the laws concerning schools in the spirit of demands made by the churches. But this anti-tariff policy turned the Conservatives into his enemies, while his school reform, though it aimed at confessional peace, failed in face of the Centre opposition.

Together with his post as Chancellor he had also assumed that of Prussian Prime Minister. But when Caprivi's school reform legislation was voted down in the Reichstag, the Minister of Culture resigned and this led to a whole series of changes in the government, the most important being that Caprivi handed over the office of Prussian Prime Minister to Count Botho Eulenburg in March 1892. By this action he created a rival, supported by the ultra-Conservatives. Bismarck from his country seat in Friedrichsruh launched a press campaign against him, directed especially at the series of commercial treaties which Caprivi was concluding with south-eastern Europe which aimed ultimately at a kind of customs union from the Balkans to the North Sea and the Baltic, a new version of *Mitteleuropa*. While his commercial policy proved a success, another crisis occurred over the army bill of 1893. After the Reichstag resisted any significant strengthening of the army, it was dissolved and the election of June 1893 strengthened Caprivi's position somewhat. He got his army bill through in a modified form, as mentioned above, and the *Quinquennat* replaced the *Septennat*. Actually Caprivi's position was less threatened by the Reichstag than by the activities of the camarilla around the Kaiser which included Eulenburg and Holstein. Their aim was to strengthen their influence and not necessarily the country.

The early 1890s were marked by the activities of anarchists in Europe. Assassinations took place in France, Italy and Spain. Wilhelm enquired whether Caprivi did not see the need for preventive legislation against anarchists. Caprivi did not think this necessary, especially since the member states of the Reich all had their own legislation which could be used for preventive measures if this was found necessary. Eulenburg, however, demanded preventive legislation by the Reich, but as Caprivi foretold, the Reichstag would not have any of it. In 1894 anarchism reached its highest point. The Italian Prime

Minister, Crispi, was the victim of a failed assassination attempt. The French President, Carnot, was murdered, as were several others towards the end of the decade, including the Empress of Austria. Bismarck lent his hand to a campaign for preventive legislation, but Caprivi would not budge. By the end of 1894 Wilhelm II was considering plans for a *coup d'état* similar to those of Bismarck in 1889–90. Caprivi solidly opposed the Kaiser's plans. He was not prepared to help; at most he would introduce a bill with moderate limitations on the freedom of the press and assembly. He had a draft worked out, while Eulenburg worked on another far more radical one. Both drafts were discussed in the Prussian state ministry and Caprivi's arguments carried the day, but Eulenburg would not give up, although he had initially to make a tactical withdrawal. A compromise between the Reich government and the Prussian government appeared in the offing, when the Kaiser was tactless enough to receive in Eulenburg's presence a delegation of the *Bund der Landwirte*, one of the strongest Prussian agricultural pressure groups, totally opposed to Caprivi's low tariff policy. Caprivi submitted his resignation. The Kaiser implored him to stay and asked him to tell Eulenburg that he had refused to accept his resignation. He did this, and Eulenburg himself submitted his resignation. The Kaiser hoped to hold on to both, when an article appeared in the *Kölnische Zeitung* which reported the exchange between Kaiser and Chancellor, and that both rejected any introduction of exceptional legislation. Caprivi was suspected of having inspired this article, an insinuation he completely denied. In the face of this the Kaiser saw no other way out than to part with both Caprivi and Eulenburg. In their place he appointed the *Statthalter* of Alsace-Lorraine, the Bavarian Prince Chlodwig Hohenlohe-Schillingsfürst, who once again united the posts of Chancellor and Prime Minister. Caprivi retired with dignity and it says much for his integrity that he completely destroyed all his papers – however much the historians may regret this action.

HOHENLOHE

At the parliamentary level Hohenlohe had no great problems during his chancellorship. Since the elections of 1893 he could muster a majority only if the Conservatives, the Centre and the National Liberals combined, or alternatively if in place of the National Liberals the government could obtain the support of the extreme right, the Reform Party. In the elections of 1898 Conservatives and National Liberals sustained heavy losses while the Centre maintained its position, but this did not lead to major change in the composition of the majorities. Hohenlohe's immediate legacy from Caprivi was the bill for preventive action against revolutionary action, the *Umsturzvorlag*. In its draft form it avoided being directed against any particular party: the majority of its provisions merely sharpened the laws already in existence. It also affected military jurisdiction and existing laws concerning the press, but it contained no provisions which affected the right of association and assembly. Yet even in that form it was rejected by the Reichstag in May 1895, though without affecting the position of the government seriously.

Much more important was the codification of the Civil and Criminal Laws of the Reich which had begun in 1873. On 21 October 1895 the commission dealing with the codification submitted the draft to Hohenlohe who referred it to the Bundesrat which made only minor alteration before forwarding it to the Reichstag. There, as expected, opposition came from the Social Democrats and also from the Centre because of the liberalization of the marriage laws. None the less, after a number of changes, it was passed on 1 July 1896 with a majority of 222 to 48. Only the Social Democrats presented a united front in rejecting it. On 1 January 1900 the new legal code the *Bürgerliches Gesetzbuch* (BGB) came into force. It amounted to a major achievement.

The Reichstag presented a somewhat uglier attitude when it was suggested that it should congratulate Bismarck on his eightieth birthday on 1 April 1895. The majority of deputies refused to do so.

Two scandals erupted involving the Secretaries of State Karl Heinrich von Boetticher and Adolf von Bieberstein Marschall in 1892 and 1896. During Bismarck's chancellorship Boetticher's father-in-law, a director of a Reichsbank branch, had embezzled one million marks, and Boetticher, who was then Vice-Chancellor, had reported this to Bismarck and had offered his resignation. Bismarck, however, wanted to hold on to Boetticher and used the Guelph fund to repay the sum. Boetticher himself contributed money from his own pocket. Apparently years later the Berlin political police supplied the information to the journalist, Maximilian Harden, who published the details in his journal *Die Zukunft*. But Hohenlohe kept Boetticher in his Prussian and Reich offices.

The affair concerning Marschall centred around a toast given by Czar Nicholas II to the Kaiser on the occasion of an official visit to Breslau: 'Je puis Vous assurer, Sire, que je suis animé des mêmes sentiments traditionelles que Votre Majesté.' A Berlin newsagency falsified the last three words of the toast into 'que mon père'. Since Alexander III had been a pronounced Germanophobe this assurance of friendship implied the affirmation of the sentiments of his predecessor, and the message was so interpreted by the entire German press. The mistake was rectified, but the *Berliner Wochenzeitung* reported that the falsification was a deliberate product of the German Foreign Office. It added that its source had given his word of honour that he had received it directly from the hands of State Secretary Marschall, who told him to place it in the papers, the intention being to fortify the pro-British course of German foreign policy by poisoning Russo-German relations. A judicial investigation was held which again involved the political police. Marschall emerged without blemish, but the Kaiser, who had originally supported Marschall, as he had Boetticher, considered them now too heavy a liability and replaced Boetticher by Count Arthur von Posadowsky and Marschall by Bernhard von Bülow.

One issue which virtually affected all the administrations was the building of the *Mittelandkanal*, a waterway connecting the Rhine, Weser and Elbe. Because of the Reichstag's opposition this hardly got anywhere and it was in fact only completed in 1938. But the army bills of 1896 and 1899 as well as the navy bill of 1898 had a relatively easy passage in the Reichstag.

The Kaiser's careless language, however, produced another crisis. The then Secretary of State for the Interior, Posadowsky, was to draft a law for the protection of the *Gewerbliche Arbeitsverhältnisse*. Its aim was to abolish the practice by trade unions in labour conflicts of compelling members to participate. Even before the draft had been completed, the Kaiser made speeches in Bielefeld and Bad Oeynhausen which suggested that all violations of this prohibition of the *Koalitionszwang*, the obligatory coalition of trade union members in strike actions, would be punished by forced labour. Hence when the bill was introduced in the Reichstag its opponents immediately called it the *Zuchthausvorlage*, the forced labour bill, and it was thrown out in 1899. Another piece of legislation originated in a murder trial in 1891 involving the Heinze couple who belonged to Berlin's underworld. the trial had revealed a considerable degree of moral degeneration and by 3 February 1899 resulted in a supplementary bill to the criminal law being introduced, the *lex Heinze*. It prescribed harsher punishment for procuring and similar offences, and in addition legislated against the sale of publications and performance of plays which would tend to offend public morality. This section was interpreted by the Reichstag as an attack against culture and artistic freedom and led to nationwide demonstrations against it. A new draft proved necessary which omitted the threats against the theatre, the visual arts and literature and in that form it was passed by the Reichstag.

By this time Hohenlohe, however, had had enough. He was the only Chancellor who gave up office without being forced to by a crisis. He was replaced by Count Bernhard von Bülow, previously Secretary of State for Foreign Affairs. During the first six years of his chancellorship he could rely on a majority in the Reichstag. He was tactful and flexible, qualities which the Kaiser himself lacked, and as a result the leaders of both Conservative parties, the Centre and the National Liberals, implored the Chancellor to exercise some restraint upon the

Kaiser's speeches. But Bülow, who did not wish to fall out with Wilhelm II at the very start, did nothing at first and tried to handle the matter in a different way, as shall be seen.

THE BULOW ERA

The Reichstag elections of 1903 brought no substantial changes in parliament. The old *Kartell* parties were reduced by one seat from 136 to 135 and were dependent on the support of the Centre. But new men were coming to the fore in the Centre Party, like Matthias Erzberger, who were inclined to cooperate with the Social Democrats. The last remnants of the *Kulturkampf* legislation were done away with, such as the most obnoxious features of the anti-Jesuit law; it was not completely abandoned until 1917. A minor financial reform was carried out, as well as the Reich Finance Reform Laws which passed the Reichstag in 1906. However, the attempt to transform the inheritance tax, which varied from Land to Land, into a uniform Reich Tax failed. The death of the implacable opponent of all governments, Eugen Richter, in 1906 made it possible to envisage that the government could perhaps reckon on the support of the *Freisinninge* Party instead of relying on the Centre.

To look for an alternative to the Centre soon became necessary, when Bülow in a supplementary budget in 1906 demanded funds to fight the rising of the Hottentots in German South West Africa. Erzberger, together with the Social Democrats and the minority parties, opposed it, whereupon Bülow had the Kaiser dissolve the Reichstag.

In the 'Hottentotten' elections of 1907 the strength of the Social Democrats was reduced from 81 to 43 seats. The Centre increased its numbers from 100 to 105, but Bülow had expanded the old *Kartell* by an extension to the left with the *Freisinninge* Party, and his bloc won an impressive victory with 220 out of 396 seats.

The bloc parties had conducted the elections with a great deal of nationalist fervour, but that alone was not responsible for their victory. The government could also show a fairly impressive legislative record between 1900 and 1906. Bülow had aimed at striking a fair compromise between agrarian and industrial interests, between protectionism and free trade, as expressed in his tariff laws of 1902. These, without giving up the principles that had guided Caprivi, made their application more flexible. The financial structure of the Reich was lifted from its desperate state when Bismarck departed on to a more solid basis by the minor Reich Finance Reform of 1904. Furthermore, the Reichstag deputies were appeased by the introduction of attendance fees. Added to this should be the supplementary naval laws of 1906 and 1908. Bülow managed to maintain this record from 1907 to 1909. The laws concerning association and assembly, up to now under the competence of the member states, were unified in the Reich Association Law of 1908 which eliminated any remaining restrictions. Women were allowed to participate in political assemblies and associations, but youths below the age of 18 were still excluded. Electoral and strike assemblies were exempted from having to give prior notice to the police. Furthermore the 'language article', which prescribed the use of German in public assemblies, was lifted for international congresses and suspended for twenty years in territories with mixed languages such as Prussia's Polish provinces, north Schleswig and Alsace-Lorraine.

Yet, like Caprivi, Bülow was exposed to greater dangers emanating from the camarilla surrounding the Kaiser than from the Reichstag. Within the former, however, divisions existed between Holstein and Eulenburg, while Afred von Kiderlen-Waechter had been pushed off to a post abroad. Eulenburg, despite having to leave his ambassadorial post in Vienna in 1902 as a result of an intrigue, maintained his influence with the Kaiser, while Holstein continued until 1906 to have a say in the shaping of German foreign affairs until he came to grief over the policy he pursued during the first Moroccan crisis. Bülow at first continued to maintain close contact with the camarilla. After he retired Holstein directed his whole desire for vengeance on Eulenburg, whom he considered responsible for his removal from office. Matters came to a head in November 1906 when Maximilian Harden published an article directed against Eulenburg and others whom he accused of exercising a harmful influence upon the Kaiser and furthering his 'personal regime'. He also threw out veiled hints pointing to Eulenburg's alleged homosexuality. The matter culminated in a civil lawsuit against Harden brought by one of those implicated, the Berlin City Commander Count Kuno von Moltke. Harden was supplied with ample material by Holstein which seemed to substantiate rumours in circulation for some time. He was acquitted. Now the state prosecution instigated criminal investigations against Harden which led to him being tried a second time. This time Harden raked up all the material at his disposal, which involved a number of highly placed persons, but the evidence was not conclusive and Harden was sentenced to four months' imprisonment. However, another trial emerged from this one, for perjury against Eulenburg. Under the impact of this trial Germany's Supreme Court, the *Reichsgericht*, quashed Harden's sentence and reduced it to a fine of 600 marks. Harden was prepared to carry on the fight, but Albert Ballin, the head of the Hapag-Lloyd steamship line, mediated and Harden withdrew his suit in return for a declaration by Moltke affirming Harden's honesty and patriotism, while Bülow paid him 40,000 marks from state funds to cover his 'expenses'.

All this took place in the full glare of German and international publicity. Bülow was asked awkward questions in the Reichstag, in reply to which he made no attempt to belittle the affair but denied the existence of any 'camarilla'. Eulenburg's sexual inclinations could not be hidden, but it did not come to a trial since a commission of doctors judged him unfit to plead. Judicially the matter only came to an end when Eulenburg died in 1921.

THE *DAILY TELEGRAPH* INTERVIEW

Bülow realized that irreparable harm had been done and that there was need to curb the influence of outside circles on the Kaiser as well as his public utterances. As he recognized, this could only be done by a greater degree of parliamentarization. It is in this context that the '*Daily Telegraph* interview' must be interpreted. When the Kaiser had visited Great Britain in 1907 he had stayed at the home of Colonel Stuart-Wortley and in the course of his stay discussed political questions, especially Anglo-German relations, with his host. When Wortley attended German manoeuvres in September 1908, the plan emerged, in the interests of improving Anglo-German relations, to put these discussions into the form of an interview.

The Kaiser agreed and Stuart-Wortley, with the assistance of a journalist, undertook the work. The final text was then sent to the Kaiser for approval. He agreed to it, but following his constitutional duty he forwarded the text to Bülow, who read it while on leave, remarked that a few minor changes were necessary and then passed it on to a junior official of the German Foreign Office who also read it. Since Bülow had raised no objections, he returned it to the Kaiser with the Foreign Office's approval. Far from serving to improve Anglo-German relations the effect was the opposite. The British saw in it further tactlessness of the Kaiser, while Germans of all parties, against the background of the Harden-Eulenburg affair, saw in it renewed evidence of Wilhelm II's 'personal regime'. As recent research shows, the whole affair was a trap which Bülow used, although he had not set it, to ensnare the Kaiser and thus ensure that in future he would be muzzled. The public did not know that the interview had been approved by the Foreign Office, any more than it knew that in 1896 it had been upon the instigation of the Foreign Office that the Kaiser despatched his telegram to Oom Paul Krüger. Nor did it know that his visit to Tangier in 1905 had been carried out against his own wishes under pressure from the Foreign Office. He had acted fully within the limitations of the constitution.

In a public declaration Bülow played the innocent and by implication put the blame on the Kaiser's shoulders, although he was prepared formally to accept responsiblity. He had achieved his aim: from all sides of German political opinion there were demands that the Kaiser should refrain from making public statements. Even the German Conservative Party demanded that the Kaiser should exercise self-restraint in future in his public utterances. This was a modest demand compared with the barrage that came from the Social Democrats and the Centre Party, who demanded full parliamentarization. The Bülow bloc still held together but the breach between the Kaiser and the Chancellor was complete. The Kaiser even thought of abdication. Then a coalition of those loyal to him formed itself in the Reichstag, not so much for the sake of the Kaiser but because of the opportunity they spotted to bring about Bülow's fall. They comprised arch-conservatives as well as Centre Party members like Erzberger. Bülow requested a formal audience with the Kaiser in which he apologized, but it was only a formal affair. When Bülow's law for an inheritance tax failed to pass the Reichstag, he asked to resign and the Kaiser readily agreed. Bülow left office with the conviction he would return as Chancellor in the not-too-distant future at the head of a fully parliamentarized government.

THE LEGEND OF PERSONAL RULE

Much has been said and written about the personal rule of Wilhelm II. It must be emphasized however, that he did not possess the power of sole decision, but required ministerial signature. The Kaiser could not act outside the constitutional framework, but, unfortunately, he could 'talk' outside it, though sometimes what he said has been separated from the actual context. For example, when visiting Munich, he was to sign the Golden Book of the city. As an act of politeness he asked one of the Bavarian Princes to sign first. He at first refused but under Wilhelm's pressure he did so. In a flight of humour Wilhelm then signed, adding the words *'Suprema lex regis voluntas'*. But there were more serious utterances, such as 'There is only one master in the Reich, I shall suffer none other', or 'I am the sole arbiter and Master of German Foreign Policy; the Government and my country must follow me, wherever I go', he said to Edward VII in 1910. Of course this was more wishful thinking than reality, but it was quickly taken up by his opponents who charged him with unconstitutional rule: in other words that contrary to the constitution, Wilhelm endeavoured to restore royal absolutism. Nothing could be further from the mark. His grandiloquent and irresponsible phrases did however disturb Germany's constitutional life. Far too weak to govern himself, he took refuge in pretence and thus caused unnecessary disturbance. But *utterances* that were outside the framework set by the constitution cannot be equated with unconstitutional *actions*. Nevertheless those utterances did him and Germany more harm than his actions. His personal intervention in the Ruhr miners' strike in 1889 in favour of the workers was clearly contrary to Bismarck's policy of non-intervention, and his two decrees of 1890 extending social legislation without Bismarck's countersignature were actions outside the constitution. He once entertained the idea of a constitutional *coup d'état*, but both Caprivi and Hohenlohe talked him out of it with no great effort. In the realm of foreign policy, the refusal to renew the Reinsurance Treaty with Russia, the Krüger Telegram, the journey to Tangiers, or for that matter the decision to go to war were not his *personal* decisions: far from it. German foreign policy was at no time directed by independent decisions made by the Kaiser. The assertion of 'personal rule' is at best a half-truth, and perhaps not even that.

BETHMANN HOLLWEG

Bülow's successor Theobald von Bethmann Hollweg had none of the experience in foreign affairs of his predecessor. His career had been pursued in domestic administration. Hence most of the legislation introduced and passed up to 1911 was of a constitutional and administrative nature, such as the further extension of the Reich financial reform, laws regulating economic matters and further progress in social reform. The watershed of Bethmann Hollweg's pre-war career was the Reichstag election of January 1912 in which the Social Democrats became the strongest single party. This in effect confirmed this party's integration into the existing constitution. Bethmann Hollweg could now obtain a majority only with the backing of the Conservatives, the Centre and the Liberals, but they were *ad hoc* majorities and did not form a solid bloc he could count on for support at all times. The first new session opened, as already mentioned, with *éclat*. Scheidemann, elected Vice-President of the Reichstag, refused to pay his respects to the Kaiser, as was customary, and this resulted in his losing this post.

THE ZABERN AFFAIR

Two crises marked Bethmann Hollweg's peacetime chancellorship. The first was in 1912 when, aiming at a *rapprochement* with Great Britain, he opposed Tirpitz to the extent of actually submitting his resignation. The Kaiser backed Bethmann Hollweg. More notorious, damaging and public was the 'Zabern affair.' Zabern, a small town in Alsace, was the garrison of two battalions of Infantry Regiment No. 99. On 28 October 1913 a subaltern officer, Lieutenant Günter von Forstner, who was still under age, while instructing his recruits told them that if they were molested while on town leave they could make use of their sidearms. He also added, 'If in the course of this you stab one of the *Wackes*, no harm will be done', and he promised 10 gold marks to anyone who did so, to which a sergeant present promised to add three marks. Quite apart from this challenge, the use of the term 'Wackes', a derogatory word in Alsatian dialect, had been expressly forbidden by a regimental order of 1903. Several of the Alsatian recruits reported this incident to the liberal *Zaberner Anzeiger* and to the *Elsässer*, a paper close to the Centre Party. They duly published this incident, which caused disquiet because Zabern was German populated, supported Germany and previously relations between the military and civilians had been excellent.

The incident made its way from the Zabern press into the press of the Reich, and the transfer of Forstner and the sergeant to some other area was demanded. The Regimental Commander, von Reuter, did not deny the incident but endeavoured to weaken its impact and was supported by the General commanding the XV Army Corps in Strassburg. Forstner, however, had become the object of public ridicule whenever he appeared in the streets of Zabern. On 15 November further news appeared to the effect that he had continued to use the term 'Wackes'. This was denied from Strassburg and three recruits who had denounced Forstner were arrested. Forstner, on the basis of the first incident, was sentenced to six days' confinement to his quarters, a punishment the public was not informed of, nor did it know that the *Statthalter*, Count (later Prince) Karl von Wedel, had recommended Forstner's transfer to the Commander of the XV Army Corps, General Deimling, which the latter had refused. Public discontent, ignorant of these moves, was further fuelled and in particular male youths insulted officers in the streets, causing the Regimental Commander to order that officers should only go out accompanied by armed guards.

In the Reichstag the Minister of War, General von Falkenhayn, declared that such insults could not be tolerated and refused to express an opinion about the punishment of Forstner since this was subject to the officer's immediate military superiors. Bethmann Hollweg announced that he would deal with the issue on 3 December. On 26 November the army for the first time arrested two troublemakers and, after checking their papers, released them. Two days later a demonstration of youths assembled at Zabern's *Schlossplatz* and Reuter lost his patience. He had them arrested but freed them again next morning. However, he instituted regular military patrols in the streets of Zabern for two days. On 1 December a Major-General Kühn, despatched from Strassburg, arrived in Zabern and withdrew all patrols. On the following day a new incident occurred which involved Forstner, who with the flat side of his sabre, injured a cobbler who had insulted him in the street. A few days later the two battalions were transferred to army training grounds and this ended the conflict.

In the Reichstag Bethmann Hollweg on 3 December argued that the 'King's uniform must be respected under all circumstances', but he left no doubt about the unlawfulness of the Zabern garrison's behaviour. None the less the Reichstag passed a vote of disapproval by 293 to 54 with abstentions. Scheidemann demanded Bethmann's resignation, but the opposition to the government then quickly disintegrated.

On 11 December the three recruits who had provided the newspapers with their information were sentenced by court martial to imprisonment for between three and six weeks. Forstner was also court-martialled and sentenced to forty-three days' imprisonment, a sentence quashed on 10 January 1914 by the Supreme War Court who acquitted him. On the same day Colonel von Reuter was also court-martialled and acquitted. This action was based on the existence of a Prussian cabinet order of 17 October 1820 which stated that suppression of internal disorders was a matter for the civil authorities but gave the military authorities the right to intervene without being called on if the Military Commander recognized that the powers of the civil authorities were not sufficient to restore order.

In effect the military hierarchy escaped unscathed while the *Statthalter*, Count Karl von Wedel, who had contributed immensely to the Constitution of Alsace-Lorraine in 1911, had to resign. The whole incident illustrated the primacy of the military in Wilhelmine Germany, but also the constitutional fact that a Chancellor, despite an overwhelming vote of disapproval amounting in effect to one of no confidence, could maintain his position in a constitutional monarchy, where Chancellors and Ministers, though answerable to parliament, could neither be appointed nor dismissed by them since this was a matter of monarchical prerogative.

However, what most historians dealing with the Zabern affair omit, is that one of its results was the abolition of the cabinet order of 1820 and its replacement by a service directive of 19 March 1914 which prohibited military intervention in civil affairs without a request from the civil authorities.

THE FIRST WORLD WAR

This is not the place to discuss again the origins of the First World War, except to counter the argument that in 1914 mobilization did not mean war and that therefore Germany should not have replied to Russia's refusal to stop total mobilization by a declaration of war, or for that matter declare war on France. As to the first point, as far back as 1892 at the conclusion of the Franco-Russian military agreement, the French Chief of Staff, General Boisdeffre, remarked to his Russian counterpart, General Obruchev, 'Of course you realize that from now on mobilization inevitably means war'. This was especially true of Germany because of its geographic position. As to the second point, President Poincaré had already in 1912 transformed the Franco-Russian defensive alliance into an offensive one, giving Russia a completely free hand. One can put the question the other way round by asking whether the European statesmen in 1914 would have been prepared to pay the price which the preservation of peace would have cost. Certainly as far as Great Britain and Germany are concerned the answer must be no. Great Britain was not prepared to endanger its imperial position in Asia by exercising a decisive restraining influence on Russia, for whose friendship the British Ambassador in St Petersburg, Sir George Buchanan, had early in 1914 stated that Great Britain must be prepared to pay almost any price. As far as the German leadership was concerned, it was not prepared to watch a further weakening of its Austro-Hungarian ally and in this way manoeuvre itself into complete isolation. Many incisive criticisms have been made of the Schlieffen plan but none has put forward an alternative for a country involved in a war on two fronts, cut off from its overseas supplies of raw materials and a third of its foodstuffs. Fighting defensively, that is fighting a war of attrition based on inner lines of communication, can only be risked successfully by countries with access to ample supplies of raw materials. All that Germany had was coal. Hence the only option was to fight a defensive war offensively even if that meant the violation of Belgian neutrality, an issue arousing much emotional fervour but used in Great Britain as mere window-dressing to win over for intervention those who were still undecided. Under the terms of the Treaty of 1839 guaranteeing Belgium's neutrality British obligations were not defined and there was no provision which obliged Great Britain or any other signatory powers to send troops to Belgium to make war on any power that should violate her territories. The British Foreign Office was well aware of this fact since in the last quarter of the nineteenth century precisely this question had been raised twice in the House of Commons and was answered thus. That it was also an economic war for Great Britain against a commercial competitor is shown by hitherto unprecedented actions in violation of international law such as the confiscation of all German private assets and German patents. That Belgium was only a pretext is also demonstrated by the German offer made in September 1914 via the United States to evacuate Belgium and make reparations to it. Great Britain was not interested: the issue was 'to root out Prussianism' – whatever that might mean.

It is interesting to note that during the July crisis Parliaments in both parliamentarian and constitutional states played no role whatsoever. Not until the preliminary steps had been taken did they move into operation and then their role was not one of decision but of acclamation. In Germany in the crisis the question was not who had the competency for mobilization or declaration of war; what was decisive was whether the whole nation, including the working classes, was ready to support the government or to oppose its actions. This was the essential constituent of the constitutional reality. That almost the whole of Germany rallied to the side of its government does not mean the nation was full of enthusiasm for war, but it was aware of the tightening grip around it; it was convinced of encirclement, and that the war to be fought was a defensive one. And this in a nation in which the Right, including the National Liberals, had a representation of only 26.3 per cent, while the bourgeois Centre and Left had 29.4 per cent and Social Democracy 34.8 per cent. Socialist internationalism proved an illusion: had there been any international solidarity of the working class the war would have been impossible. Only the integration of the working classes into their respective national societies created the foundation for the conduct of a war between the industrial powers of the world on a scale hitherto unprecedented.

The news of Russia's partial mobilization reached Berlin on 29 July 1914. When the news of Russia's total mobilization was received on 31 July the Kaiser at first would not believe it. German intelligence was even sent across the frontier to detach a poster announcing mobilization, and only then was the Kaiser convinced. The constitution made no provision for the proclamation of a state of imminent war, but since 1909 it had been included in all military plans as the preparatory step to mobilization. The Kaiser announced the proclamation of a state of war for the Reich excepting Bavaria. There, according to an agreement of 1913, King Ludwig III had to issue the same proclamation. Constitutionally this meant the transfer of the executive power to the military commanders, the tightening of the penal law and the suspension of basic rights such as those described earlier on. The agreement of the Bundesrat was necessary to declare war, but it was in fact faced by an accomplished fact, since the decision to this effect had been made on the morning of 1 August and the German Ambassador at St Petersburg, Count Friedrich von Pourtalés had been instructed to submit the German declaration of war at 13.00 hours on that day. The Bundesrat convened at the same time and unanimously supported the decision. Nevertheless, although von Pourtalés only handed over the declaration of war at 18.00 hours, it contravened the constitution.

Of immediate importance was to win parliament over to granting money for the conduct of war and to take up war credits. The government could declare war, but the effective means to conduct it depended on the agreement of the Reichstag and the Bundesrat. In this context the attitude of German Social Democracy was decisive. In the past they had almost always voted against military expenditure and army bills, but they had refused to bind themselves to using a general strike to avert war. Most Socialists were not pacifists but enemies of a war of aggression. Social Democrats and Liberals were united in their assessment that Czarist Russia posed the actual threat to peace. Russian mobilization clinched the issue for the Social Democrats and they rallied to the government. In previous years, various conservative politicians and generals had believed that measures would have to be taken against the Social Democrats in case of war. Those fears proved unfounded. But the attitude of the SPD leadership was not unanimous: the leader of the left wing, Hugo Haase, opposed war credits, while Eduard David of the right wing supported them. The decision was left open until Hermann Müller, who had been despatched to Paris to sound out the attitude of the French Socialists, returned. But even before his return the decisions were made; David won over a number of the right wing and the centre of the SPD in favour of war credits. When Müller returned on 3 August reporting that the French Socialists would vote for war credits in France the matter was finalized and war credits were supported by 78 votes to 14. The leadership also decided to introduce the party whip on this issue in the Reichstag.

In preparation for the Reichstag session of 4 August 1914, the government was anxious to have all the necessary measures passed with great speed. The legislation amounted to seventeen draft bills, already passed by the Bundesrat, of which the most important was the bill requesting war credits for 5,000 million marks. In addition emergency legislation not contained in the constitution had to be enacted, as well as an Enabling Bill, the first of its kind, which as yet had not been submitted to the Bundesrat. It was passed by the Reichstag and only then submitted to the Bundesrat. The Enabling Law meant that the Reichstag excluded itself from the passing of extraordinary emergency legislation in the economic sphere while the Bundesrat increased its power in this area.

WAR LEGISLATION

At midday on 4 August 1914 the Kaiser opened the Reichstag in the

Weisser Saal of the Berlin *Schloss* with a speech which emphasized Germany's determination to defend itself. 'We are not driven by the lust to conquer,' he said, and at the end he declared: 'I no longer know parties; I only know Germans!' The actual session began in the Reichstag building in the afternoon, where Bethmann described briefly the past developments and was sufficiently honest to be stupid enough publicly to refer to 'the injustice done to Belgium' and to propose restoration. Then the seventeen war bills were unanimously voted through *en bloc*. At the end there was a cheer for '*Kaiser, Volk und Vaterland*', and the Social Democrats for the first time rose from their seats and joined in. The legislation voted on consisted of the Enabling Law, war credits, five war finance laws, three laws for the protection of conscripts and serving soldiers, four laws concerning the war economy and three laws for social legislation during the war.

With the proclamation of the state of war the state of siege was automatically invoked which made the military commanders in the various districts the supreme heads of regional government in co-operation with the existing civil authorities. They had powers to issue local decrees, prohibitions, arrest, requisition and fix prices. Extraordinary war courts were instituted. By 1914–15 there were forty-six of them; the highest number reached was sixty. Each of them had five judges: two civilian judges, one of which presided, and three officers. Throughout the war they dealt with about 150,000 cases, but figures do not exist to show how many led to conviction, acquittal or dismissal.

Although Wilhelm II was the Supreme War Lord, ever since the *Daily Telegraph* affair he had withdrawn more and more into the background and continued to do so throughout the war. There was no single German military commander responsible for the overall conduct of operations nor one to whom all the local military commanders of the military districts were directly responsible. Germany lacked a central institution responsible for the difficult tasks of military administration. All there was was the General Staff, now called the *Oberste Heeresleitung*, which ran the war, while the military cabinet had neither the experience nor the competence to take over wide-ranging administrative functions. Only the Prussian Ministry of War under General Erich von Falkenhayn exercised such functions to a limited degree. But, since it was a Prussian institution and not a federal one, it could only issue guidelines to the other German states. In practice therefore beside the existing civilian federalism there now also existed a military one which was only ameliorated by the measures introduced by the war legislation of 4 August 1914 and in the course of the war by the creation of new offices like the War Office, the Reichs Economy Office and the Reichs Food Office. One should also add to these the office of the Supreme Military Commander, set up on 4 December 1916, which was the central authority in Germany to supervise the military district commanders and deal with complaints about them. Its head was the then War Minister, Hermann von Stein, followed in 1918 by War Minister Heinrich Scheüch.

The condition of a state of war did allow serious interference into personal liberties. Personal residence could be restricted and protective custody could be used against persons for their own protection or for that of the community. However, protective custody was severely limited to cases where a direct danger existed. The Reichstag was the only institution where an appeal could be raised against protective custody or against residence restrictions, and these powers were further curtailed by legislation introduced and passed in 1916.

Local military commanders supervised all associations and assemblies. They made very sparing use of their power to proscribe associations, while public assemblies were forbidden on numerous occasions. Press censorship was widely exercised by them, that is to say by their executive subordinates, which meant the police. In the main it was restricted to military matters or those affecting public security and order. During the first years of the war this power was exercised after publication had occurred, in other words editors did not have to submit their material to the authorities prior to publication. Trangressions could lead to reprimands or the confiscation of an issue of a paper or magazine. In October 1914 the *Oberzensurstelle*, the supreme censorship office, was established in which members of the General Staff, the War Ministry, the Admiralty Staff and the Reich Naval Office were represented. It laid down draft guidelines for the censorship offices throughout Germany and was also responsible for dealing with complaints against undue censorship. But it could not issue direct orders to the local military commanders. In August 1915 the War Press Office was called into being, subject directly to the OHL, but again its function was purely advisory. The OHL had its own news department which was far more effective in so far as it determined the kind of military news to be made available to the public. Of equal importance was the military news department of the German Foreign Office which became particularly effective under Erich Ludendorff. There were also press offices of the Reich Chancellery and of the Ministry of the Interior. Censorship was particularly effective in two areas; it suppressed the discussion of war aims by the extreme Right as much as pacifist publications or the 'peace without annexations' movement of the Left. Censorship of private letters also took place, although this was soon attacked by the Reichstag since the guarantee of secrecy of letters was one of the basic rights not suspended at the outbreak of war.

The Enabling Law passed in August 1914 allowed the introduction of emergency decrees by the Executive in times when parliament was not assembled, and had its precedent in Article 63 of the Prussian Constitution of 1850. This delegation of legislative power was a clear breach of the principle of the separation of powers. However, in practice this power was not used excessively and was limited by a number of factors. For one thing there was the Bundesrat which could block emergency legislation, for another there was the Enabling Law itself which was limited to measures to prevent economic damage. When the Reichstag was in session any emergency decree enacted had to be submitted to it and to be withdrawn if the Reichstag demanded it. Thus the Reichstag exercised a controlling and veto power even over emergency legislation. Most of the emergency decrees passed during the war, 825 in all, concerned the economy, currency and financial law, civil law, labour and social law and judicial procedure. In the economic sector the German and Prussian governments already had a long tradition of state intervention in the economy for the sake of the common weal. Existing state socialism was replaced by a war socialism whose legislative measures concerned the accumulation of reserves of foodstuffs and raw materials, import, export and transit regulations, price fixing, organizing food supplies, the establishment of central offices for the administration of the war economy and for the rationing and allocation of vital raw materials, and measures against the black market and excessive price demands. Taxation was increased on war profits; the stamp duty was converted into a turnover tax and the duty on spirits was raised. As far as the civil law was concerned no fundamental changes were carried out. In contrast to allied practice, enemy assets and property were not confiscated but put in the hands of state trustees. Wages in many sectors of industry were fixed and employees protected against being dismissed at short notice. Furthermore employees drafted into the army retained their social security rights during the war while every fit adult was compelled to carry a document showing that he was in employment. The measures concerning judicial proceedings were intended in the main to shorten and speed up the judicial process, and lighten its burden.

Since Germany, like all other belligerent countries, had only envisaged a short war no large-scale reserves of raw materials or foodstuffs had been accumulated. Through mobilization valuable manpower resources were withdrawn from industry and agriculture, the result was a serious decline in the output of both. In the iron and steel industry the output of August 1914 was only half that of the previous year and it only approached pre-war levels again in 1916. Food shortages were equally serious but bread rationing was not introduced until January 1915. Fundamental changes were required in the German economy, above all central planning and direction as advocated by Walter Rathenau and Wichard von Möllendorff. But their plans were only partially put into practice by the institution of the Reichs Food Office, mentioned above, the creation of an advisory body for food supplies by the Reichstag and a host of organizations dealing with various aspects of the economy for the duration of the war. The armaments industry was in any case a government affair; around 1914–15 60 per cent of arms contracts were awarded to private industry, 40 per cent to state-owned industry. The most important innovation was the creation of a war Raw Materials Department under Rathenau and Möllendorff. Under its auspices a number of war-material firms were created, each responsible for a specific sector: chemicals, metals, iron ore, etc. The greatest achievement of the Raw Materials Department was the securing of German requirements for ammunition through the technical development of producing nitrogen to replace saltpetre which had to be imported and could no longer be obtained due to the British blockade. A further important sector of the economy was the supply of energy, i.e. coal. The Rhenish-Westphalian Coal Syndicate which had been formed in 1893 under Emil Kirdorf was subject to government intervention when it threatened to fall apart in 1915. The government was prepared to compel it to remain in existence, a threat sufficient to keep the employers together, and a Reich Commissioner for Coal was appointed to ensure sufficient supplies of coal for the industrial and private sector.

The outbreak of war had also caused a profound transformation of the constitutional status of employers' associations and trade unions. The *Koalitionsrecht*, the right of labour to form unions, and the right to strike had already been in existence for half a century. When war broke out the trade unions immediately proclaimed the end of all strike activity and strike funds were made available to workers unemployed due to no fault of their own. They also took over the organization of bringing in the harvest. Although trade unions were not political associations, in practice they had been considered as such and working youths under the age of 18 were not allowed to join them. The trade unions had always objected to this. The government in 1915, under union pressure, expressly declared unions professional and not political associations. A bill was enacted by the Reichstag to this effect, but it did not lift the prohibitions against youths joining. Nevertheless the trade unions accepted the new regulation.

When the 3rd OHL under Paul von Hindenburg and Ludendorff came into being on 29 August 1916 its first priority was the maximization of industrial and agrarian output, the so-called Hindenburg Programme. Additional labour was required to achieve it and for that reason the OHL demanded that all able-bodied civilians including women were to be drafted into industry and agriculture. These demands were put into effect by the *Hilfsdienstgesetz* (War Aid Law), enacted on 5 December 1916, by which all males between 17 and 60 years of age, if they were not serving soldiers, were to be drafted into the war economy. No mandatory provisions for women were made because at the time there was still plenty of female labour available. All enterprises employing more than fifty men had to create workers' and employees' committees which were to act as arbitrators in case of labour disturbance. The law fully integrated the trade unions into the constitutional framework of the Reich. Industrial peace was secured until the formation of the Independent Socialist and the 'Spartacus' group (see below, p. 195) which organized mass strikes in opposition to the trade union leadership, i.e. to the largest body of trade unions – the 'Free Trade Unions' – but also including the Christian and the Liberal 'Hirsch-Dunker' trade unions. This strike in April 1917, organized in Berlin and most other industrial centres in central and southern Germany, had its greatest following in Berlin where over 200,000 workers went on strike, led by the Spartacist Emil Barth and the Independent Socialist Richard Müller. It failed after less than two days, primarily because of the intervention of the trade union leadership. As such the strikes were perfectly legal, since the right to strike had not been prohibited; even wildcat strikes were allowed. But what made this strike different was that it was a *political* strike, with demands directed not at the employers but at the government to supply more foodstuffs. Since, according to Emil Barth's own evidence, the strike was also to affect the German conduct of the war, it was a treasonable act according to the law.

Trade union membership had drastically declined until 1916. Whereas in 1914 a total of 2,371,705 members was recorded, in all trade unions by 1916 membership had declined to 1,203,378 and from then on was to rise again to 2,317,383. In other words even in 1918 the pre-war level of membership had not been attained, one reason of course being that many of the pre-war members were serving in the armed forces.

War had begun with Germany ostensibly unified. Bethmann Hollweg's aim was to maintain this unity and the fact that he enjoyed the support of the trade unions in the labour sector and that of the Social Democrats in the Reichstag illustrates that he achieved this aim. In spite of the increasing internal tensions within German Social Democracy, its Reichstag deputies voted time and again in favour of war credits. But the Social Democratic Left under Haase, Karl Liebknecht and Otto Rühle, supported from the outside by the agitation of Rosa Luxemburg, posed a serious threat to the continuance of this unity. And, as the short war became a rather long one, this opposition increased in strength and numbers. The first two war credits had been passed in the Reichstag without discussion. But from 1915 the Reichstag did resume discussion, which frequently deteriorated into sharp polemics particularly over the two main issues: war aims and the conclusion of peace. But the major parties agreed to postpone elections until the end of the war. Social Democrats now had access to public office: people like Adam Stegerwald, August Müller and Alexander Schlicke became officials in the economic departments of the Reich offices. Increasingly Social Democrats were commissioned within the army as reserve officers, hitherto the exclusive preserve of the German middle class. The only opposition which Bethmann Hollweg faced came from the extreme Left of Social

Democracy and the extreme right-wing Conservatives, as exemplified in the vote over the war taxation law in which twenty Social Democrats and three Conservatives voted against. It was Bethmann's endeavour to pursue reform without alienating the Conservatives but at the same time to put forward sufficiently advanced measures to maintain the support of Social Democracy; it was his 'policy of the diagonal' which in the end failed, because he fell between two stools and was toppled by the cooperation of the Right and Left.

THE PROBLEM OF DOMESTIC REFORM

The reforms Bethmann planned were of a constitutional, social and economic nature appealing to all parties in the Reichstag and to their voters. But they were only to be introduced after the end of the war. The Social Democrats were not prepared to wait that long over one major constitutional reform: the abolition of the three-class franchise in Prussia, which they were already demanding in October 1914. The least that Scheidemann demanded was that the government should decide a timetable on this point. The Conservatives saw in this demand an attack on the established institutions and their attitude was shared by the Prussian Minister of the Interior, Friedrich Wilhelm von Loebell. The 3rd OHL enjoyed wide popularity, reaching well into the ranks of the Social Democrats, and Bethmann was prepared to raise the issue of reform anew in the Reichstag, which culminated in the reform debate of 11 October 1916. What it achieved was the consolidation of the faction against the Chancellor on the Right, while Scheidemann went even further in his demands, calling for the full parliamentarization of the German government, a demand which by 1917 was supported even by the Liberals, notably by Gustav Stresemann. These demands raised violent objections in the Prussian *Herrenhaus*, which hardly helped to cool tempers. On 14 March 1917 Bethmann promised his reforms which, however, for the sake of maintaining domestic peace, could not be carried out until after the war. The February Revolution of 1917 in Russia removed the reason which had prompted the Social Democrats to support the war effort and provided a new impetus for calls for constitutional reform. Reform initiative was taken over by the Reichstag which created a 'Constitutional Committee' in which all supporters of constitutional reform were represented, from the National Liberals to the Social Democrats. In its initial discussions the committee proposed changing twelve articles of the constitution, which in the main aimed at altering the existing franchise for the Reichstag in such a way as to provide for a more equal representation and votes for women. A resolution demanding that a Reichstag majority should be able to dismiss the Chancellor was rejected within the committee against the votes of the SPD and the USPD. In spite of Stresemann's previous demand both National Liberals and Centre Party members still rejected the idea of full parliamentarization. The reform programme became the subject for the Reichstag debate on 15 and 16 May 1917, when Scheidemann threatened revolution if Germany's enemies renounced annexationist aims and Germany continued the war as one of conquest. The issue of parliamentarization showed that the parties of the Right and Centre still considered it with scepticism. A reduction of the supreme command power of the Kaiser was demanded while the powers of the Minister of War, who was answerable to the Reichstag, should be increased. But the Prussian Minister of War Hermann von Stein rejected any further extension of his powers.

Much the same subjects were discussed in the debates in the Prussian Diet. Wilhelm II had promised reform but in terms too vague for the Social Democrats. On 7 April 1917 the Kaiser promised in his 'Easter Message' reforms of the franchise in Prussia, including a reform of the Diet and the *Herrenhaus* to correspond more with 'the present times', but like his chancellors he stated that it could only be carried out after the end of the war. This was a hopeful sign and the domestic situation relaxed slightly. Work was begun on various drafts.

THE SOCIAL DEMOCRATS DIVIDED

In the meantime, as already indicated, attitudes within the SPD began to change. From the outset its left wing believed any German territorial annexations to be out of the question, and the war aims plans that began to circulate among parties, industrial and agrarian pressure groups and busy publicists, were solidly opposed. But the majority of the SPD were in favour of internal improvement rather than the radical abolition of the existing system. This was not the case with the left wing under Karl Liebknecht who voted against the second war credits bill; on 21 December 1915 twenty SPD deputies voted against war credits. The demand to expel them from the party was turned down, but eighteen of them began to form their own faction within the parliamentary party supported by socialist radicals outside parliament like Franz Mehring, Rosa Luxemburg, Hermann Duncker, Wilhelm Pieck and others who founded their own 'international group'. Apart from Liebknecht none of them occupied party office. Numerous other radical groups emerged under the common denominator 'the enemy is to be found in our own country'. State reaction against them was hesitant and mild. Though Liebknecht was drafted into the army he had to be given leave to attend Reichstag sessions. Only Rosa Luxemburg served a one-year sentence and in 1916 was taken into protective custody until the end of the war.

The first international conference of the socialist radical Left took place from 26–28 March 1915 at Zimmerwald in Switzerland, where twelve countries were represented. The British government refused to let its socialists participate. Altogether there were thirty-eight delegates, nine from Germany and another nine from Russia. Only two came from France. Clara Zetkin led the German delegation which was made up of radicals in no way representative of the forces of German Socialism. The conference issued a manifesto which declared war the consequence of imperialism and demanded the resumption of the class struggle in all countries.

Inside the SPD parliamentary party Liebknecht was manoeuvred into a position tantamount to exclusion. He was joined by Otto Rühle. It was an exclusion from the parliamentary party, not from the SPD as such. They were joined in March 1916 by a group around Hugo Haase, in all eighteen SPD deputies. Haase founded the 'Social Democratic Working Group', supported from the outside by Karl Kautsky, Kurt Eisner in Munich and others. At the same time the 'international group' assumed the name *Spartacus League* under Liebknecht's leadership. On 1 May 1916 the *Spartacus League*, supported by socialist youth organizations, mounted a demonstration in Berlin. Liebknecht exhorted the assembly – which was illegal as no previous permission had been obtained – with the cry 'Down with the war! Down with the government!'. He was arrested but because he was formally a soldier came under military jurisdiction. At a court martial in Berlin he was found guilty of attempted treason and resistance against the police and sentenced to two and a half years hard labour, a period which, according to his own evidence, he spent in relative comfort.

Obviously the danger now grew of a split within the SPD. Friedrich Ebert, Bebel's successor after 1913 as party chairman, tried to keep the party together and called a Social Democrat Reich Conference for 21–23 September 1916 in Berlin. The majority of the 451 delegates present supported the official party line. The Spartacus Group and the Social Democrats Working Group dissented. But a complete break was still avoided until December 1916 when the SPD supported legislation in the Reichstag over the state of war, War Aid Service (which aimed to increase the number of workers in the arms industry) and the German peace offer. The radical left wing convened its own conference where a minority declared in favour of a split with the SPD. Between the 6 and 8 April 1917 this culminated in the founding of the Independent Socialists, the USPD, which included the fifteen Reichstag deputies led by Haase and Wilhelm Dittmann. From March to November the USPD included twenty-four Reichstag deputies.

THE KAISER'S CONSTITUTIONAL ROLE IN WARTIME

From the beginning of the war the primacy of politics was under challenge. According to Clausewitz, political decisions should have precedence at all times over military ones, which would mean that in time of war as well the civil government should remain the supreme decision-making power. But the final days of the July crisis of 1914 had already demonstrated a departure from Clausewitz's principles, mainly because of the extraordinary situation of a modern techno-logical war. This raises the question whether there was a temporary or even a permanent military dictatorship in Germany during the war. Constitutionally the Kaiser fulfilled a double function as he possessed supreme political and military power. Were Wilhelm's decisions those of the imperial government or those of the supreme warlord of the German nation?

Constitutional complications would certainly have ensued if Wilhelm had actually carried out his double function and put the military authorities above those of the civil government. But the *Daily Telegraph* affair had left a lasting impression on him, and throughout the war he continued to retreat more and more into the background, leaving military functions to the military authorities and political questions in the hands of Bethmann Hollweg. If one can speak in constitutional terms of a 'military dictatorship', then it was one exercised not by the Kaiser but by the growing power of the military authorities, especially the OHL. It could only accumulate such power because the Kaiser failed in his constitutionally defined function as the supreme coordinator of military and political affairs.

Institutionally, although the Kaiser's 'Great Headquarters' existed, this was just one of the several military institutions. Indeed the Great Headquarters amounted to a collection of highly diverse military offices and staffs including the General Adjutant, the Civil, Military and Naval Cabinets, the OHL and, until 1916, the War Minister as well. The Admiralty Staff, which was to be elevated in 1918 to *Oberste Seekriegsleitung*, the naval equivalent of the OHL, was also part of it, as were the liaison officers and civil servants who acted as go-betweens, linking the Chancellor and the Foreign Office on the one hand and the Great Headquarters on the other. Initially the Great Headquarters was at Koblenz, then at Luxemburg and at Charleville. From April 1915 until February 1916 it was at Pless and then returned to Charlesville. In August of the same year it moved back to Pless until in February 1917 it moved to Bad Kreuznach and finally ended the war at Spa in November 1918. The Great Headquarters throughout that period failed to become an instrument coordinating the war on land and at sea. In other words there was no unified command.

THE PRIMACY OF THE MILITARY

At the outbreak of war the Chief of the General Staff, who in peacetime was only the Head of the Planning Section and had no power of military command, was entrusted by the Kaiser to conduct the operations of the armies in the field. By virtue of the general mobilization directives, which came into operation at the moment of moblization, the Chief of the General Staff was entrusted with full powers to issue, on behalf of the Kaiser, operational orders to all commanders of the field army. In that way he became Chief of the OHL. The first Chief of the OHL was therefore General von Moltke. This was until 14 September 1914 when he suffered a breakdown under the impact of the failure of the Schlieffen plan. He was replaced by the Minister of War, General von Falkenhayn, who held this post until it had become clear that his Verdun operation would have to be aborted. He was replaced, with much acclaim from the population at large and from the members of the Reichstag, by the victors of Tannenberg, Field Marshal Paul von Hindenburg, and his Quartermaster, General Erich Ludendorff. In spite of the ever increasing power of the OHL, the supreme power remained in the hands of the Kaiser: constitutionally the Chief of the General Staff had no power of command. Legally the Chiefs of the OHL were not supreme commanders; they only exercised supreme command by delegation from the Kaiser. Until 1916, besides the OHL, there was also the Command of Supreme Commander East (*Oberost*) and until then both Hindenburg and Ludendorff were subordinate to the OHL, a source of much conflict which ultimately the latter pair won.

The Kaiser, who was usually present at the Great Headquarters, received the situation reports. It was his task to coordinate and to arbitrate, a task he was not equipped for mentally or by training. Thus in practice the exercise of supreme command lay in the hands of the Chief of the General Staff. Falkenhayn, who already had it in effect, claimed this, and the tendency reached its full impact under Hindenburg and Ludendorff. Thus military supremacy represented the actual constitutional reality during wartime.

The appointment of the Chief of the General Staff to head the OHL superficially did not change the existing triad of General Staff, War

Ministry and Military Cabinet. In practice, however, the OHL eroded the powers of the other two members of the triad. The Minister of War's function was to supply arms and replace manpower. Until 1918 he became the virtual subordinate of the chief of the OHL. Nevertheless his functions also increased as the coordinator between the OHL, the civil administration, the economy, the industrial organizations and pressure groups and the trade unions. In principle the Minister of War had no power of command *vis-à-vis* the other military authorities because the field army as well as the Deputy General Commands Germany was divided into were not subject to him but to the Kaiser. Although the commanders of the General Commands were rather anxious to maintain their independence, ultimately the need for greater centralization led by 1916 to the predominance of the Minister of War who as such acquired not only considerable political power but also political responsibility. Both his political power and political responsibility were subject to the scrutiny of the Reichstag. The regular demand for war credits, the military budget and so on, were levers the Reichstag could use to intervene and instigate debates over shortcomings at home, in the occupied territories and within the army; and with the aid of these levers the Reichstag could rapidly increase its power of control. The handling and limitations imposed by the War Emergency Law were always especially a subject of parliamentary controversy. In spite of his attempt to exclude matters of military command, after the initial *Burgfrieden*, the formula for maintaining domestic peace, of 1914, the Reichstag increased its power and compelled the Minister of War to face its members' questions and answer them. The Minister of War could no longer use his last resort and say these matters were outside the competencies of the Reichstag. The attitude adopted over the Zabern affair could no longer be repeated. But instead of this process reducing the powers of the War Minister, it in fact increased them, since he represented the linchpin between parliament and the OHL.

The Military Cabinet, headed for most of the war by General Moritz von Lyncker, maintained its importance as the personal advisory body to the Kaiser. The Chief of the Military Cabinet had an important voice in the appointment to high military posts as well as in interservice rivalries or those between the military and the civil powers. Lyncker's was a decisive voice in the appointment of Falkenhayn as successor to Moltke, and that he lasted until 1916 was in no small measure due to Lyncker's backing. Hindenburg and Ludendorff were not particularly well disposed towards him, viewing him as something of a defeatist who discouraged the Kaiser. Finally, due to the OHL's pressure, Lyncker was replaced in July 1918 when it hardly mattered any more. The history of the Military Cabinet during the war amply demonstrates how far wrong are the accusations which describe it as an instrument of military absolutism and as unconstitutional. In reality for most of its time it represented a countervailing power to the OHL of considerable weight.

THE OHL UNDER MOLTKE AND FALKENHAYN

If one looks at the functions of the government and OHL within the existing constitutional framework, one has of course to begin with Moltke. Because of Germany's geographical predicament in the case of a two-front war and shortage of most vital raw materials, he was the protagonist of the defensive war offensively conducted. In the July crisis of 1914 he ultimately convinced a reluctant and pessimistic Bethmann Hollweg that once Russia had mobilized, the Schlieffen Plan would have to be put into effect with all its attendant conse-quences. He considered these to be minor, provided, of course, that the plan succeeded. He was not a military expansionist as such, but increasingly had come to believe in the inevitability of war, especially in the face of the massive Russian arms build-up which would be completed by 1916–17. Once Russia had mobilized Bethmann Hollweg left it to Moltke to take all the necessary measures. He had indeed abandoned his political responsibility to the Chief of General Staff, though it seems doubtful that events would have taken a dif-ferent turn if he had not. The real inherent threat in Bethmann's attitude was that the primacy of politics would be abandoned, a threat that finally became reality. Bethmann soon noticed the mistake he had made, but what had been done could not be undone, nor did this change with Moltke's departure and Falkenhayn's rise. Bethmann and Falkenhayn fundamentally agreed in their realistic assessment of Germany's military situation, and both opposed the blind optimistic hopes of victory and the annexationism of the middle-class parties in the Reichstag, successfully repelling the advances of industrial pres-sure groups and instead supporting the notion of a negotiated peace. But Bethmann began to develop a deep animosity towards Falken-hayn, inspired mainly by Hindenburg and Ludendorff. Between the Battle of the Marne and the sinking of the *Lusitania* four attempts were made to end the war, all four instigated by Germany. The first in autumn 1914 involved the German offer to withdraw from Belgian territory: it was rejected by the allies, who insisted that until Prussianism' had been defeated there could be no peace.

However, this was only a minor issue in the growing conflict between Bethmann Hollweg and Falkenhayn; much more to the fore, after the Battle of the Marne, was the question over which front should be considered the primary one, the east or the west. Falkenhayn, convinced of the impossibility of a general German victory, opted for the western theatre, thus meeting the vociferous hostility of Ludendorff and Hindenburg. Moltke, who had not retired but assumed the post of Deputy Chief of General Staff, heartily detested his successor and thus inclined towards *Oberost*, attempting to topple Falkenhayn and replace him by Ludendorff. Failing that, Moltke wanted to resume his old post. Bethmann Hollweg was unwise enough to allow himself to be involved in the faction against Falkenhayn, though he was careful not to mention anything to the Kaiser, who resented direct interference by the political authorities in the military sphere. But covertly he supported the intrigue against Falkenhayn.

Yet he agreed with Falkenhayn's endeavour, once the intial offer to the west had been repelled, to obtain a separate peace with Russia, which seemed promising after the German-Austrian victory at Gorlice-Tarnov, the only battle in the First World War in which a belligerent power actually managed to achieve a significant breakthrough against the enemy's front. They also agreed on a number of questions subsidiary to a peace in the east. But when Bethmann Hollweg made a vain attempt to get a negotiated peace with Serbia via Greek mediation and did not consult him, Falkenhayn demanded that the Chancellor should not repeat such moves in the future. Bethmann Hollweg replied by insisting that this was a purely political matter and his sole responsibility. He denied that the OHL had the right of criticism, consultation and agreement in the realm of foreign affairs. Falkenhayn insisted on his position and thus the issue of the relationship between civil and military power had been opened for the first time in the war as a matter of principle. Falkenhayn had the right to be informed about political matters affecting the military conduct of the war, but he was wrong in rejecting the primacy of politics in wartime. He was right again when he insisted that in case of conflict it was the Kaiser's duty to decide between the two. The conflict between the two men was temporarily covered up, but it continued to smoulder under the surface. Falkenhayn in 1914–15 dominated over *Oberost* and he maintained the confidence of the Kaiser, at least for the time being. But he also needed the support of public opinion and this quickly waned and disappeared when he could not produce military successes and instead inaugurated the senseless slaughter at Verdun.

THE RISE OF HINDENBURG AND LUDENDORFF

Against the background there was a wave of sympathy and support for Hindenburg and Ludendorff among the parties of the Reichstag. This cut across party lines from the right-wing parties to the Social Democrats, the enthusiasm arising out of their successes in the east. The

German public at large clamoured for their leadership. Both the Kaiser and Bethmann Hollweg were initially reluctant to entrust them with the highest military office, but they could not continually resist the pressure of the parties and the general public. In the end Bethmann Hollweg's attitude was determined by that of public opinion. At first Falkenhayn tried to counter this movement by suggesting a separate Supreme Command for west and east. If he had succeeded this would have reduced the OHL to the status of OHL western front. Bethmann Hollweg realized this and the support of the Kings of Bavaria and Württemberg gave him weighty allies in his struggle against Falkenhayn. The Military Cabinet under Lyncker still backed Falkenhayn, while the Minister of War joined the anti-Falkenhayn faction. As a temporary measure he deployed the tactical device of entrusting Hindenburg with the conduct of operations over the entire eastern front. The Kaiser grudgingly gave his consent, as he felt this surrender to public sentiment was the first step towards the abdication of the monarchy. But this did not put an end to the intrigues. The final decision was brought about by Romania's entry into the war on the side of the allies, an act considered in Germany as akin to treason since it was governed by a Hohenzollern Prince, Ferdinand I. Falkenhayn had foreseen this move, but expected it to take place later. The confidence of the nation and the army crumbled, and to restore it on 26 August 1916 the Kaiser dismissed Falkenhayn and appointed Hindenburg as Chief of General Staff and Ludendorff as his First Quartermaster. The change was deep and profound. Hindenburg now became *de facto* supreme commander of the field armies, while Ludendorff formally became his first adviser in the army command structure, and in the conduct of operations. This was followed by a thorough shake-up in the command structure and the personnel of the German generals. As far as Bethmann Hollweg was concerned it seemed as though the primacy of politics had achieved an important and vital victory. What he failed to see was that he had created a precedent by which he opened to the generals not simply the door to the highest military positions but also access to the political decision-making process, particularly in cases when the army could claim that the needs of war and the danger to the Reich should have precedence over all else.

The conflict between Bethmann Hollweg and Falkenhayn had in essence been about foreign affairs. In the domestic field such questions as the War Emergency Law, the war economy, the supply of food-stuffs, the arms industry and labour deployment had been left in the hands of the constitutionally established military authorities, especially the Minister of War. But Hindenburg and Ludendorff extended their direct influence into the German domestic sphere. They were determined on the total mobilization of Germany's material and man-power resources. One of their first interventions concerned the three-class franchise in Prussia which they wished to maintain. A little more than two years later they changed their minds on that – too late, alas. They supported the extension of the powers granted by the War Emergency Law to the governors of the military districts, and for the duration of the war they insisted on increased interference and stricter handling of the provisos which limited freedom of the press and the right of association and assembly. On the other hand they showed an innovating hand in running the war economy and universal labour conscription on the basis of a centrally directed 'state socialism.' They scathingly attacked the shortcomings which had been hitherto encountered and for which, by implication, Bethmann Hollweg was held responsible. The new measures ordered by the OHL in the realm of the organization of labour and the economy required the assent of the Reichstag and this was obtained.

In addition to all this the OHL also intervened in foreign affairs. Under Ludendorff's pressure the Secretary of State for Foreign Affairs, Gottlieb von Jagow, was replaced by the previous Under Secretary, Arthur Zimmermann. Also upon the initiative of the OHL on 5 November 1916 the 'Kingdom of Poland' was proclaimed, a measure which ensured the failure of any attempt at a compromise peace with Czarist Russia. At the same time inside and outside Russia socialist revolutionary circles were mobilized and financed with German money, culminating in 1917 in the journey by Lenin and his entourage from Switzerland across Germany to Finland and from there to Russia.

The OHL supported wholeheartedly the resumption of unrestricted submarine warfare. Whether this step was a political mistake or not is a debatable point. The United States at the outbreak of the war was facing a renewed economic slump and was saved from it by the needs of the belligerent powers in Europe. Since the combined naval power of Great Britain and France dominated the oceans, this meant that only the western allies benefited. Secretary of State William Jennings Bryan was an advocate of strict neutrality and even opposed loans to Great Britain and France. When President Wilson overruled him on this point, the former Counsellor in the State Department, Robert Lansing, took his place, stating that 'we have to finance our prosperity' by offering loans to the western allies to pay for raw materials, foodstuffs and war equipment. As a response to the British blockade of the Central powers, illegal in international law, the Germans announced equally illegally, that there existed a war zone around Great Britain in which ships would be sunk on sight. The sinking of the *Lusitania*, a British liner with American passengers plus ammunition on board, caused an outcry. Ultimately Germany refrained from unrestricted submarine warfare on condition that Wilson would exert sufficient pressure on the allies to allow foodstuffs through to the Central Powers. Wilson accepted the pledge and ignored the condition.

Hence, after the failure of the Verdun offensive and the continued stalemate on the western front, Falkenhayn and his colleagues concluded that the United States could hardly be more helpful to the western allies even if she were a belligerent power. Under Hindenburg and Ludendorff this conclusion was taken a step further by asserting that a resumption of unrestricted submarine warfare might well bring the USA into the war against Germany, but it would take her some time to organize herself militarily, and it would divert resources which would otherwise have gone to the allies. In the interval unrestricted submarine warfare was to be carried out to an extent that would force Great Britain to the negotiating table before the United States could bring her full weight to bear in Europe. This calculation did not lack its inner logic, but it ommitted one factor: there were not enough German ocean-going U-boats available to carry out unrestricted submarine warfare on the scale which would have ensured success. Though submarines were an expanding branch of the Imperial Navy, they had been sadly neglected in peacetime and in the early years of the war. On the other hand thousands of German sailors were cooped up in battleships in harbours, making occasional forays and sallies into the North Sea, at Jutland even achieving a surprising tactical victory without, however, changing the overall strategic naval picture. Unrestricted submarine warfare was resumed too late and with too little.

GERMAN WAR AIMS AND THE REICHSTAG

A major issue, central to the conduct of the war, and debated throughout it, was the war aims of the Central Powers in general and those of Germany in particular. The allies had adopted a simple aim, as formulated by Sir Edward Grey on 5 September 1914, which eliminated the chance of a negotiated peace and met the popular demand for the destruction of Germany and Prussian militarism. Large-scale aims were laid down in secret agreements. The details of these are outside the scope of this book, but they included a blank cheque to Russia to extend her western boundaries as she desired.

All the belligerent powers had entered the fray claiming to be fighting a defensive war; all of them had annexationist programmes which they either publicized or agreed secretly with one another. The demands made exceeded by far legitimate claims for compensation and security and thus they became annexationist programmes. German annexationism represented a wide range of often contradictory claims put forward by political parties, economic pressure groups and intellectuals, notably university professors. The German government under Bethmann Hollweg avoided giving public support to these aims, but it did not denounce them either. The first draft of German aims was laid down by Bethmann Hollweg in the 'Preliminary Notes about the Guidelines of our Policy at the Conclusion of Peace' on 9 September 1914, a time when Germany was at the peak of her military successes in the west. What it actually contained was a list of desiderata from the various Reich ministries – a list of wishes rather than a settled programme. The original impetus for its compilation had come from the German industrialist Walther Rathenau and the banker Arthur von Gwinner. Neither looked at German war aims in terms of territorial expansion. They wanted the establishment of a Central European market which western nations like France would have to join and which first of all could face Great Britain on equal,even superior, terms. Once Great Britain had joined it, it would form an economic power of a size and stability which could compete with the ever-growing economic power of the United States and the potential economic power of Eurasian Russia. Bethmann Hollweg's main aim, however, was the security of the Reich which in his view required a glacis in the west against the power which had used Germany as a battleground for two centuries. This glacis would contain the iron-ore area of Longwy-Briey and would supplement the Saar coalfield. He hoped to conclude a customs treaty with Holland, but he kept his options open over Russia and Africa. The core of his aims, however, was the creation of a Central European Customs Union, which would not have a constitutional apex, and would be based on the equality of all its members; Germany by her sheer economic and military might would implicitly exert economic predominance in Central Europe. Nothing was mentioned about the Balkan states, nor about access to the Near East. But the realization of his aims depended on the success of the Schlieffen Plan, and once it failed *Mitteleuropa* receded into the background.

In contrast to the Chancellor's notes there was a movement for annexations from the parties, industrial pressure groups and even the kings and princes of the federated member states of the Reich who each had their own programme and aims; there was an annexationist movement, but there was no official annexationist war aims policy. One of the most fervent of these groups was the Pan-Germans who exercised a much stronger influence during the First World War than they had before. Their leader, Heinrich Class, published his first war aims programme on 28 August 1914. Bethmann Hollweg immediately had it confiscated by the police. It was completely unrealistic, but enjoyed support from parts of German industry and among academics. Industrial pressure groups also had a spokesman in Matthias Erzberger, a member of the left wing of the Catholic Centre Party. Erzberger, who always had his ear to the ground, quickly detected the issues that would enjoy popular support and enhance his own personal standing: he was the epitome of an unscrupulous opportunist, so much so that ultimately the name Erzberger became a synonym for 'dirty politics'. He had established a good working relationship with the Chancellor and had been entrusted with the running of German propaganda financed by the German Foreign Office who established him in a luxurious office with ample staff. However, his activities had little to show for them except large expense accounts and extensive foreign travel. At the same time he was working for the Thyssen-Konzern, one of Germany's greatest coal, iron and steel combines, and even before the Chancellor had compiled his notes Erzberger submitted his own programme which reflected the desires of his masters in private industry: the annexation of Longwy-Briey and what amounted to an annexation of Belgium and the French coastal strip of Boulogne-Calais. In the east large territories were to be taken from Russia and put under German 'protection.' A Kingdom of Poland was to be established and in Africa he demanded the creation of a Great German Central Africa. There was little difference between his programme and that of the Pan-Germans. With some minor alterations it was also that of Krupp and Hugo Stinnes. They all demanded large slices of territory to ensure Germany's supply of raw materials.

After the Battle of the Marne Bethmann Hollweg could file away his notes ad acta, but practical politics stopped him from proclaiming this publicly since it would have been tantamount to admitting German defeat and would have strengthened the enemy's morale. Moreover, if, as Bethmann Hollweg always hoped, peace negotiations would take place round the conference table, such a programme would have been a severe liability and prejudiced any negotiations. From a domestic point of view, the public renunciation of war aims would have had serious effects on his own position: he would have had all the pressure groups and a wide spectrum of parliamentary opinion against him and this would conceivably have led to a situation where the Kaiser would have been compelled to drop him. Even in a system of monarchic-constitutionalism no Chancellor could maintain his post if continually faced by the opposition of the majority of the Reichstag.

But when the Reichstag resumed its regular sessions in December 1914 a war aims debate could not be avoided. The two conservative parties, as well as the National Liberals and the Centre, demanded territorial annexations in the east and west. The Progressives asked for somewhat less, but what they asked for was still substantial. Right-wing Social Democrats attacked 'annexationism' but did not in principle reject some territorial demands; only the Left rejected annexations outright.

The government was in a dilemma: it wanted to maintain the *Burgfrieden* and therefore tried to avoid a public discussion of contrary views on war aims. Before the session it tried to achieve this through consultation and persuasion of the leaders of each parliamentary party. The socialist Left, though ready to vote in favour of war credits, was determined to couple this with a public renunciation of annexations. If the socialist Left refused to keep quiet the bourgeois parties were not prepared to let it have its own way. Hence a debate could not be avoided. Since the Chancellor had been unwise enough in his speech on 4 August 1914 to speak of the 'injustice to Belgium' committed by Germany, the Social Democrats had a peg to hang their argument on. Bethmann Hollweg tried to retract that statement on 2 December 1914. The Social Democrats replied that the known facts since then did not justify such a retraction. From 'injustice to Belgium' it was only a small step to discussing 'real guarantees to Belgium', which from a socialist point of view excluded any territorial demands. The leader of the Centre Party, Peter Spahn, countered this by saying that the frivolous war imposed upon Germany should be fought out until a peace had been obtained which corresponded with Germany's sacrifices and would provide a durable protection against her enemies. Spahn spoke for more than two thirds of the Reichstag deputies. He did not mention 'annexation' but demanded compensation and security. Obviously this implied territorial cessions to Germany. None the less, for the time being the *Burgfrieden* had been preserved. But since public discussion of war aims in the press, pamphlets and other publications as well as in public assemblies had been prohibited by the War Emergency Law, the propagators of war aims had recourse to the perfectly constitutional means of petitions to parliament. Public rallies and advertising over aims could be prohibited, but petitions as such could not be suppressed, whether from an individual, from pressure groups or from a seemingly unorganized mass. In that way the parliamentary right wing could circumvent existing barriers.

The first such petition came from the six most important industrial and economic associations, the Central Association of German Industrialists (CdI), the League of Industrialists (BdI) in which Stresemann was acting chairman, the Farmers' League (BdL), consisting mainly of east-of-the-Elbe landowners, the German Farmers' League, the Association of German Farmers' Associations, and the Reich German Association of the *Mittelstand*. They represented the entire German economy and in party-political terms their spokesmen ranged from the Conservatives to the Progressives. In political terms this meant that a substantial part of German society was ranging itself against the government. These efforts were supplemented by the submission of memoranda from important individuals, among them Alfred Hugenberg, then a Krupp Director, Emil Kirdorf, founder of the Rhenish-Westphalian Coal Syndicate and member of the directory of the CdI, Hugo Stinnes, head of the Stinnes-Konzern, and August Thyssen. In addition Stinnes, Heinrich Class, chairman of the Pan-Germans, and Hugenberg mobilized important German intellectuals and obtained 1,347 signatures, over 1,100 of them representing the sciences, arts and higher civil servants. This figure included 352 university professors;

230 signatures came from representatives of industry and agriculture. Inevitably these petitions began to erode the position and authority of the Reich government, and caused tremors in a constitutional system based on the independence of party and association. These pressure groups did have their opponents, notably the group of intellectuals and ministerial civil servants who rallied around the historian Hans Delbrück. They did not reject war aims as such but advocated moderation. Party-politically they were represented by the Free Conservatives and the Progressives. They gave Bethmann Hollweg the support he badly needed.

Italy's entry into the war on the side of the Entente powers gave Bethmann Hollweg the opportunity to state in the debate of 28–29 May 1915 that the greater the danger the more Germany would have to hold out until she had obtained all possible guarantees and securities so that none of Germany's enemies, alone or together, would ever again risk a war with her. With the phrase 'real guarantees' Bethmann Hollweg had found a formula which provided a common denominator for most parties and which was flexible enough to allow numerous permutations. It pacified Left and Right alike. However, as we have already seen, dissension was rife within the Social Democratic Party. It was this which caused it on 9 December 1915 to introduce an interpellation asking the Chancellor under what conditions he was prepared to enter into peace negotiations and at the same time to renounce annexations. The Chancellor in reply stated that he had outlined the general war aims on 28 May, but he could not enter into public discussion about which guarantees the government would consider necessary, for instance in the case of Belgium. The longer the war lasted, the greater the guarantees that Germany would have to demand. On 5 April 1916 he became more precise, stating that Germany had entered the war to defend herself, but that there was no going back. It had not been Germany's or Austria-Hungary's intention to open up the Polish question: it had been opened by the result of battles. But it would now require a solution: after such overwhelming events the status quo ante could not be re-established. Great Britain could hardly assume that Germany and her allies would hand over the liberated peoples between the Baltic and the Volhynian marshes to the regime of reactionary Russia, be they Poles, Lithuanians, Balts or Latvians. Nor could it be expected that the territories occupied in the west would be handed back without complete security for Germany's future. Germany would create real guarantees to ensure that Belgium would not become an Anglo-French vassal state, directed militarily and economically against Germany. There too there could be no status quo ante: Germany did not desire neighbours which could close ranks once more against her to throttle her: she wanted neighbours with whom she could cooperate for their mutual benefit.

In other words the Russian Baltic provinces as well as Lithuania and

Poland were to become independent states, but by the very nature of their position they would depend on Germany. Belgium was not to be annexed, but to prevent it being a vassal of France or Great Britain it should accept its economic and military dependence on Germany. The Chancellor had most of the parties behind him; only a socialist splinter group opposed the notion of turning Belgium from a potentially Anglo-French into a German vassal.

Bethmann Hollweg had hoped to contain the opposition from Left and Right, but he was still too soft for the extra-parliamentary groups. Anonymous pamphlets were directed against the Chancellor, especially from the Right; but the 'German National Committee' headed by Count (later Prince) Karl von Wedel, former ambassador to Vienna and *Statthalter* in Alsace Lorraine, supported him. They used a proclamation to attack those who wanted a peace at any price and those possessed by the Pan-German annexation madness. Instead they advocated the extension of Germany's eastern frontiers and real guarantees in the west. The Committee did not aim at a peace without annexations and indemnities, but hoped to take the wind out of the sails of the extremists with its greater moderation. By tolerating the National Committee Bethmann Hollweg implicitly lifted the barrier which had so far existed on the public discussion of war aims. Hence the 'national' groups, among them the six industrial and economic associations, launched their counter attack against the Chancellor and made exorbitant war aims demands. The National Committee also tried to win over the Social Democrats to their side, many of whose members agreed with its aims. But the party leadership, aware of the many fissures in Germany's Social Democracy, did not want to add a further one. Under the pressure of its left wing, the party press and organization opposed any cooperation. Instead on 11 August 1916 they issued a proclamation affirming Germany's defensive war for the country's security, independence and economic viability, and on the 18th of the same month they submitted a petition in the Reichstag calling for an end to a war which had already raged for two years in Europe and caused immense sacrifice in blood and materials. The petition asked Germany and the countries allied with it to declare themselves ready to conclude a peace which would guarantee Germany's political independence, its territorial inviolability and its economic development.

To all intents and purposes the public discussion of war aims had now been given the go-ahead. It was useless to stop it since it was already flourishing in countless anonymous pamphlets, memoranda and circulars, especially from the extreme Right and Left, at a time when the parties in the Centre had been condemned to silence. The ban was officially lifted on 27 November 1916 but with reservations. It was inadmissible to use discussion to insult or disciminate against those who thought differently, to influence the conduct of the war, to cause differences among Germany's allies or neutral powers; territorial expansion should not call for demands in excess of those required for Germany's defence and maintenance, nor the evacuation of territories occupied by the German army without corresponding compensation. Thus it was believed that both extreme annexationists and pacifists had been contained.

Political parties and organizations of the Left were in fact in danger of being overtaken by pacifist radicals organized in the German Peace Society and the New Fatherland League. The German Peace Society, founded in 1892 and headed in 1914 by the Munich historian, Ludwig Quidde (who received the Nobel Peace Prize in 1927), had been subjected to severe censorship since the beginning of the war. Members like Professor Friedrich Wilhelm Foerster and the expert on international law, Walther Schücking, had been subject to police supervision. In November 1914 they had created the New Fatherland League and when it was proscribed in 1916 they continued under different guises. Until the creation of the USPD a number of Social Democrats were counted among its members, such as Rudolf Breitscheid, Kurt Eisner, Gustav Landauer, Ernst Reuter and Georg, Count Arco, whose brother was to shoot and kill Kurt Eisner in February 1919 in Munich. Their main aim was to combat the annexationists and they were the first inside Germany to blame their country for having caused the war. They received valuable aid in their agitation from two sources: the memorandum of Prince Lichnowsky about the pre-war Anglo-German negotiations, written in 1916, and the revelations of the former Krupp Director Johann Wilhelm Muehlon about the July crisis, written in 1917. Lichnowsky, whom even Friedrich Wilhelm Foerster described as showing greater empathy for the motives of British diplomacy than for understanding the position of his own country, wrote under the title 'My London Mission 1912–1914', a rather one-sided account which implicitly put the burden of guilt on Germany. He circulated a limited number of copies among friends under the seal of strictest secrecy, but one reached the hands of Captain von Beerfelde who worked in the political department of the Deputy General Staff in Berlin. He duplicated the memoir and sent it to pacifist circles in Germany and abroad. In 1918 a Zürich publisher printed it without Lichnowsky's permission. Beerfelde was traced and a court martial initiated. It was never completed because of the end of the war, at which time he was already a member of the Executive Committee of the Workers' and Soldiers' Councils, belonging to the radical left wing. The 'Muehlon Case' broke in 1917. This Krupp director had been employed since the outbreak of war by the German Foreign Office. In 1917 he published a memorandum in which he revealed Germany's support of Austria-Hungary's move against Serbia. He gave as his sources confidential talks he had with Gustav Krupp von Bohlen and Halbach and the director of the *Deutsche*

Bank, Karl Helfferich. He circulated this memorandum, based on unsubstantiated evidence, at home and abroad, and quickly left for Switzerland from where he attacked the German government with more vehemence than wisdom. But both Lichnowsky's memoir and Muehlon's memorandum became the stock-in-trade of German pacifism in the 1920s and in the final analysis they did more to discredit it than to benefit it.

Before these 'documents' broke on the German international political horizon the Central Powers had prepared a new peace move. Bethmann Hollweg had already on 9 September 1915 announced that Germany was ready for a peace with 'dignity and security'. The response was nil. The German government continued its efforts at unofficial levels throughout 1916 and also responded positively to President Wilson's peace initiative. Bethmann declared before the Reichstag that Germany had been the first and only power to show its readiness to make peace, but had only met with rejection. They therefore had only one alternative, to hold out and be victorious. The Social Democrat Scheidemann agreed with the Chancellor and expressed the hope that reason would ultimately prevail among the peoples of Europe and with it the rejection of any plans for conquest. With the advent of the 3rd OHL on 29 August 1916, the Chancellor hoped that the reputation of Hindenburg and Ludendorff at home and abroad would provide secure backing for a new peace initiative. Added to this was the campaign in Romania which was going very favourably for the Germans. The Austro-Hungarian Foreign Minister, Burian, very much shared Bethmann Hollweg's opinions about a joint peace initiative on his visit to the Great Headquarters on 17 October 1916. The German Chancellor first ensured the support of the OHL and the Kaiser.

As his first step the German Chancellor spoke before the 'Main Committee' of the Reichstag. Rejecting British versions of the origins of the war, he detailed the allied annexation plans. But at the same time he spoke in favour of the creation of a League of Nations, President Wilson's pet project. Preconditions for Germany's participation would have to be the Entente Powers' assurance not to create coalitions hostile to Germany, and to depart from a policy of encirclement, which had forced Germany to conduct a war of defence. The speech was published in the German press, clearly addressed to world opinion. In view of the international significance and importance of the speech, the party leaders represented in the 'Main Committee' kept quiet about their opinions, though these were divided over Belgium. Though nobody demanded its annexation and they were at one that Belgium must not become the 'gate of entry' for Great Britain, opinions were divided concerning the 'assurances' to be given. These ranged from maritime bases, mentioned by the Conservatives, to German powers of military, economic and political control, and to a rejection of the demand for 'real guarantees' by the Socialists. On 15 and 16 November the Chancellor again met Burian in Berlin, to discuss the conditions of peace. They were the maximum demands *subject to negotiation*. First of all there would have to be a restoration of the territorial *status quo* and a guarantee of the future inviolability of both German and Austro-Hungarian territories. Austria was prepared to cede certain territories to Italy, though not German-speaking South Tyrol. Belgium was to be restored as a sovereign state but giving guarantees, to be negotiated, to Germany. Germany would return the territories occupied by her to France with the probable but not certain exception of Longwy-Briey. Luxemburg was to return to Germany as a Federal State, in other words a return to the position she had had within the German Confederation. Austria-Hungary and Germany would demand the international recognition of ths newly re-created Kingdom of Poland. Some Lithuanian and Courland territories would go to Germany. Austria was prepared for a restoration of Serbia with some minor territorial losses. It also demanded territory from defeated Romania. Montenegro was to be divided between Austria-Hungary and Albania. Germany was prepared to give up its Far Eastern colonies in return for compensation in the form of colonial territory in Africa. None of the demands was a condition *sine qua non*: everything was negotiable. Thus, as it was expected that the French would demand Alsace-Lorraine, the Germans, by claiming Longwy-Briey, intended to use it to restore the status quo of 1914. Compared with the war aims of their opponents the Austro-German demands cannot be considered other than moderate.

WAR AIMS AND THE PROBLEM OF A NEGOTIATED PEACE

From the domestic point of view Germany's peace initiative was well chosen. Rumours, even details, already circulated in the Reichstag when the Auxiliary Aid Service Law and laws changing some aspects of the war emergency legislation were debated and passed by a broad majority made up of groups ranging from the Conservatives to the Majority Socialists. On 6 December the war against Romania came to its formal conclusion with the occupation of Bucharest. Emperor Francis Joseph had died on 21 November 1916, and his successor Charles I and Kaiser Wilhelm met at the 'Great Headquarters' in Pless on 5 and 6 December. Finally on 12 December 1916 Germany and her allies, through the mediation of neutral powers, handed over their identical formal peace notes to the Entente Powers, a step which Bethmann Hollweg announced to the Reichstag on the same day. The committee of the Bundesrat had already been informed about all the details; all the party leaders were informed on 12 December. Bethmann Hollweg hoped – indeed he pleaded with the party leaders for the sake of the impact of the peace note abroad – to abstain from a full parliamentary debate, at least for the time being. However, the Conservatives, the National Liberals and the left-wing Socialists insisted on a debate on the same day. Party unanimity could not be achieved; thus after the Chancellor's speech a vote was taken on the agenda in which the Extreme Right and Left lost. The Reichstag was prorogued. This was not a demonstration of the powerlessness of the Reichstag but a responsible reaction by its majority who for the sake of the peace initiative outvoted the minority. It was important for Bethmann Hollweg that the majority of the Reichstag refrained from a debate which more likely than not would have shown to the world the divisions among its parties. This would be interpreted by Germany's enemies as a sign of weakness and would have due influence on their evaluation of the German peace note. German constitutionalism on this occasion was secured by the ability of the Reichstag to act and to cooperate.

The note was well received in Germany, especially as it appeared to express the will of the nation. All the greater was the disappointment when the allies on 30 December dismissed it as an insincere offer because it did not contain specific conditions while they themselves wanted sanctions, reparations and guarantees. Perhaps the reference contained in the note about Germany's military victories was tactless, but that it was not sincere because of its lack of specific conditions cannot be sustained. Germany and Austro-Hungary and their allies acted on the assumption that the most important thing was to get the Powers around the table: once there one could barter and bargain, a practice usual in preceding centuries, and again in our own day and age in fashion since the threat of total extinction hangs over mankind. As far as Bethmann Hollweg was concerned, the groundswell of opposition to him which had viciously broken the surface on several occasions even before the war, began to gather force and speed once more.

While the Central Powers were still waiting for the allied response to their peace note, President Wilson, who had been re-elected on 7 November 1916, undertook his own peace initiative on 18 December 1916. The Central Powers answered in the affirmative, suggesting the opening of direct peace negotiations as soon as possible, but the allies in their note of 10 January 1917 replied that the time had not come yet to obtain a peace based on reparations, restitution and the guarantees which they desired. They demanded the return of provinces and territories torn from them against the will of their populations. Obviously Alsace-Lorraine was meant by this. They also demanded the restoration of Belgium, Serbia and Montenegro and the liberation of Italians, southern Slavs, Romanians, Czechs and Slovaks from alien tyranny and the removal of the Ottoman Empire from Europe. This of course implied the dissolution of both the Austro-Hungarian and Ottoman Empires. Furthermore territory captured from the Russian Empire was to be returned and the annexation of Russia's Baltic provinces was to be renounced. Poland was to be restored, its former Prussian and Austrian parts united with the Russian part and put under Russian rule. By the beginning of 1917 it had become clear that the peace initiatives had failed not because of German but because of allied annexationism. When Wilson on 22 January 1917 proclaimed his aim 'Peace without Victory' Germany answered by detailing to Wilson the war aims of the Central Powers which were somewhat less than those originally discussed between Bethmann Hollweg and Burian. But this move was virtually nullified by the German decision on 31 January to resume unrestricted submarine warfare.

The question of peace had returned to its original starting-point, the discussion of war aims. The Prussian Diet was the first to discuss the failure of the peace moves. Here the Social Democrat Robert Leinert described the rejection of the German peace offers as a challenge to the German people, strengthening its resolve to fight for a peace which would leave the country's frontiers unviolated, while at the same time rejecting any plans of annexation. The latter was opposed by the Free Conservatives who argued that what Germany had obtained militarily would, in so far as the military situation allowed it, remain in German hands, and whatever was to be handed over would have to be compensated for.

This was embarrassing to Bethmann Hollweg, since it implied that the German peace offer had been just so much window dressing. He therefore used the Reichstag session on 27 February 1917 to reject the demands made in the Prussian Diet. He insisted on a durable peace which would provide compensation for the harm suffered and which would secure Germany's position for the present and the future. Spahn, the leader of the Centre Party, argued that the Chancellor had dismissed the Social Democrat notion that each belligerent would have to bear its own costs, and he (Spahn) supported reparations and 'real guarantees' for a durable peace. Even Scheidemann, the Social Democrat, no longer renewed his demand of 'no annexations and reparations'; instead he emphasized the readiness of his party to support the defence of the country. Only the left-wing Social Democrat Georg Ledebour, while protesting against the excessive annexationism of the allies, demanded that Germany issue a self-denying ordinance rejecting the idea of any annexations and reparations, even before the beginning of a peace conference.

But the opposition to Bethmann Hollweg was growing. The German Conservatives and the right-wing National Liberals represented the core of the opposition in the Reichstag, forming the 'Independent Committee' where the Chancellor's opponents gathered. The reason for the distrust was the official German war aims policy and more directly Bethmann Hollweg's reluctance to resume unrestricted submarine warfare. Industrialists like Kirdorf and others, joined by some naval men, met at the Hotel Adlon in Berlin and drafted a petition to the Reichstag, indicting the Chancellor and demanding his dismissal.

THE FALL OF BETHMANN HOLLWEG

The outbreak of the Russian revolution had as a direct result that the German Majority Socialists turned towards an unequivocally anti-annexationist programme. Solidarity with the working class in Russia was to be demonstrated as expressed in their resolution of 19 April 1917. This was the beginning of a parliamentary crisis which was to end with Bethmann Hollweg's departure on 13 July 1917.

Twelve days earlier, on 9 April, the Kaiser in his 'Easter Message' had promised political reforms, especially over the three-class franchise in Prussia, by the end of the war, and from the point of view of the Prussian Conservatives Bethmann Hollweg had entered into an alliance with the Social Democrats, which for the extreme Right was the signal to move jointly against the Chancellor. The Independent Committee issued a reply to the Social Democratic peace resolution, defending the gains Germany had made, especially those in the east where they would be a guarantee against the infection of Germany by Russia's revolutionary disease.

Throughout 1916 the controversy over whether or not to resume unrestricted submarine warfare was one of the major problems faced by Germany's political and military leadership. The old antagonists of pre-war days Bethmann Hollweg and the Secretary of State for the Navy, Admiral von Tirpitz, once again confronted one another. Through the News Office of his department Tirpitz was encouraging the agitation in favour of resumption. Consequently the Chief of the Naval Cabinet reprimanded him and Tirpitz replied by submitting his resignation. On 15 March 1916 the Kaiser dismissed him from office. Shortly thereafter, on 6 April, the Reichstag passed a resolution in favour of resuming unrestricted submarine warfare. This even gained the support of the left-wing Liberals and most of the Social Democrats. However, both Kaiser and Chancellor were still against it and this amounted to a victory of the government over the Reichstag. The OHL under Hindenburg and Ludendorf were in favour of resumption, as were most deputies, who saw in it the only chance for victory after the Verdun débâcle. The Centre Party was one of the major driving forces in favour of resumption, but Bethmann Hollweg managed to stall because of his projected peace initiative. When his and Wilson's moves had come to naught, the full force of parliamentary and public opinion was let loose, demanding unrestricted submarine warfare as a counter-measure to Great Britain's blockade which was now seriously affecting the state of food supplies inside Germany. At the Great Headquarters the OHL and the Admiralty succeeded in changing the Kaiser's mind and unrestricted submarine warfare was finally officially resumed on 1 February 1917. Instead of resigning his post, the Chancellor stayed on, thus formally backing this decision. But his resignation would have been pointless since after all his efforts he really had no alternative plans.

In the meantime Austria-Hungary had resumed peace initiatives and only partly informed her German ally of these. But Count Czernin, who had replaced Burian towards the end of March 1917, clearly expressed his opinion that it was unlikely that Austria-Hungary could carry on the war much longer than the autumn of 1917. Bethmann Hollweg in his reply did not share Czernin's opinion. He pointed to the defensive successes in the west and on the southern front in Italy and those achieved by the U-boats, and he judged the general situation favourable. It was only a matter of holding out until the enemy came to his senses and to the conference table. The Austrian peace initiative came to naught, except for indicating to the allies fissures in and a potential collapse of the German-Austrian alliance and thus strengthening their resolve and morale. Consequently the Austrians had to lean heavily on Germany once again. This was expressed in the Kreuznach agreements of 17–18 May 1917, where Germany and Austria agreed on common war aims which were not substantially different from those agreed between Bethmann Hollweg and Burian the previous year.

The German Chancellor, because of the unstable relationship with Austria and the hopes he nourished for a separate peace with Russia, was anxious not to prejudice them by public declarations of German war aims. This was not the case with the Conservatives and the Majority Socialists. The Conservatives introduced an interpellation in the Reichstag asking the Chancellor to clarify his attitude to the Socialist peace resolution of 19 April 1917. The majority of Social Democrats asked the Chancellor in their interpellation what he considered doing in order to conclude, in agreement with Austro-Hungary, a separate peace with the provisional government in Russia on the basis of no annexations and reparations. For the first time Scheidemann's threat was added to this interpellation that if Germany were to continue the war for expansionist aims, there would be revolution in the country. Bethmann Hollweg once again averted crisis, but his position was weakening; his sole backing was the bourgeois Centre and the Majority Socialists. His majority dwindling, and without it, neither Kaiser nor OHL could have kept him in office.

On the initiative of the Dutch Socialists the Socialist international was to be reactivated at a conference at Stockholm on 4 June 1917. While the Western Powers refused exit visas to their Socialists, Germany was represented by Majority Socialists, the USPD and representatives of the trade unions. While the German Majority Socialists on the whole adhered to the official government line, the USPD publicly supported Germany making territorial concessions from her territorial position before the war. This amounted to a further sign of growing divisions inside Germany, but did no immediate harm to Bethmann Hollweg's position. Much more serious, however, was the growing collapse of the support he had so far received from the Catholic Centre Party. Especially instrumental in this was Erzberger, Chief of German Propaganda abroad, and previously a supporter of an extreme war aims programme. He was the Chancellor's close confidant and initiated peace feelers on his behalf with Russia in Stockholm. These, however, had to be aborted because of Ludendorff's intervention, a further sign that Bethmann Hollweg was losing his political grip. Erzberger was also sent to Vienna to counter Austrian moves for a separate peace, and was there convinced by Czernin's arguments of the hopelessness of the cause of the Central Powers. With his highly developed instinct for political changes Erzberger changed sides, but since the Chancellor could only be toppled with the backing of the OHL, he allied with Ludendorff against the Chancellor. The decision of the Majority Socialists to make a renewal of war credits dependent on an unequivocal statement by the government of Germany's war aims was further grist to the mill. A change of Chancellor was definitely in the air, but before his resignation could be forced a Reichstag majority had to be assured that would vote for war credits. Theoretically Bethmann Hollweg could have asked the Kaiser to dissolve the Reichstag. This would have meant the end of the *Burgfrieden* and new elections, which in present circumstances would have led to a defeat of the government. Bethmann Hollweg desperately worked to maintain a majority, concentrating his efforts on the Centre, the Progressives and the Majority Socialists. He had excluded the Conservatives and the National Liberals. In the negotiations between these parties Erzberger let it be known that he was planning a decisive move against the government, and choosing the Main Committee of the Reichstag as his platform. Here he launched his attack without prior warning of his intentions to the Chancellor, nor to his party chairman, Spahn. Though the deliberations of this committee were confidential, Erzberger managed to leak the general substance of the deliberations and his attack on the Chancellor in particular, which was welcome news, especially to Germany's enemies. Erzberger argued that unrestricted submarine warfare had failed, and that no military gains were likely on land. Germany would therefore have to undertake a peace move, and this would have to be initiated by the Reichstag. The committee was in a state of panic and prorogued itself. At the same time the Committee for Constitutional Reforms was in session, discussing the revision of the oversized constituencies and those reforms emanating from the Kaiser's Easter Message over the question of the franchise in Prussia. Opinions diverged and thus the two most important Reichstag committees were in disarray. To solve the crisis the National Liberals, Centre, Progressives and Majority Socialists, ranging from Stresemann to Scheidemann, formed the *Interfraktionelle Ausschuss*, the 'Inter-parliamentary Party Committee'. It lacked any constitutional sanction, but nevertheless became for the rest of the war the most important parliamentary organ of the Reichstag, foreshadowing the future government coalition of 1919. Initially the three major issues with which it concerned itself were that of the electoral franchise, parliamentarization, and the question of peace. Basic agreement was reached on the first issue, but on the second, the National Liberals, for whom this was the most important issue, insisted that no constitutional change was required, only an order by the Kaiser issued in the cabinet. Erzberger's actual intentions surfaced at this point: he wanted to bring back Bülow as Chancellor, the very man whom he had fought hammer and tongs a decade before. He let it be known that the OHL would support this move. The peace resolution was the most important issue for the Progressives and Majority Socialists. But unanimity could not be achieved at first since the Centre Party chairman, who was deeply annoyed by Erzberger's independent moves, reserved his judgement and was joined by the National Liberals. A sub-commission was called into being by way of compromise to draft a peace resolution. On the eve of 6 July 1917 Bethmann Hollweg received the spokesman of the Inter-parliamentary Party Committee, the Progressive Friedrich von Payer, as well as deputies of the Centre, the National Liberals and the Majority Socialists. He responded favourably over the issue of the reform of the franchise. He maintained his opposition to a premature commitment to a peace without annexations and reparations, since premature concessions would hardly improve the chances of a negotiated peace. Nevertheless Payer and Friedrich Ebert believed that the Chancellor would support their unanimous resolution since it was in their interest to keep him in power. The only changes they wanted to see were at the Secretary of State level. Nor could they suggest an alternative to the present Chancellor and Erzberger's candidacy of Bülow gained no favourable response from them. Those advocating full parliamentarization really faced the same problem of finding an alternative to Bethmann Hollweg. In a speech made to the Main Committee, the Chancellor caused disappointment because, while making no concessions to the Conservatives, he was not prepared to subject himself fully to the demands put to him the previous day. This produced the threat by the Majority Socialists that they would vote against the war credits to force the Chancellor's resignation.

Scheidemann's threat of revolution in Germany was taken very seriously by the Chancellor. The attitude of the OHL was crucial and Erzberger was in close contact with it. Ludendorff especially demanded an 'organic unity between the representatives of the people and the government'. His subordinates, military and civilian (among them Kurt Hahn, later the founder of the Salem schools), worked in this direction, and the parliamentarians, notably Erzberger, had not the slightest objection to the intervention of the army in the highest political decision-making process. Hindenburg and Ludendorff visited Berlin on 7 July to recommend a change of government to the Kaiser, suggesting Bülow as the new Chancellor. The Kaiser, however, had not forgotten the *Daily Telegraph* affair: Bülow's name was anathema to him. Furthermore he had been forewarned by the Chancellor, and therefore told his generals that this was a political matter and outside their competency. He also forbade them to discuss it with party leaders in Berlin. Without having anything they had to return to Bad Kreuznach. Hence, from a constitutional point of view, it was a paradox that it was precisely the Inter-parliamentary Party Committee which registered its disgust that the Chancellor had eliminated the role of the army in politics. They were now determined to render Bethman Hollweg 'harmless'.

Little unity reigned among the parliamentarians about anything else. The National Liberals and part of the Centre wanted to topple the Chancellor, while, with the exception of Erzberger, the peace resolution was secondary to them. The left-wing Liberals and the Majority Socialists wanted the peace resolution, and used the threat of the change of Chancellor as a form of pressure, while in reality they wanted to prevent it.

On 9 July the National Liberals almost unanimously decided not to support the peace resolution. They insisted on the parliamentarization of the government first; a new Chancellor was to declare that Germany was not waging war for territorial expansion, while the Reichstag was not to pass a relevant resolution but leave the peace initiative to the Chancellor. The other three parties rejected this suggestion because they wanted a weak government and a strong parliament; the role of the Chancellor was to be that of an executive organ of the Reichstag majority. In a renewed meeting with the Chancellor on the same day both Stresemann and Erzberger, having previously agreed on this, told him blandly that he was 'not the right man to obtain peace'. On the evening of the same day the Kaiser convened a Crown Council. The main issue was the franchise in Prussia whose immediate reform was demanded both by the Chancellor and Vice-Chancellor Hellferich. But the Prussian Cabinet remained divided on the issue. The opinion was 10 to 6 in favour of reform but no formal vote was taken. The Chancellor reserved the final decision for himself. On the next day the

Inter-parliamentary Party Committee resumed its deliberations about the peace resolution; a draft, the third, was agreed upon but the divisions between the parliamentarians persisted. In the end all that was agreed was to enter into negotiations with the USPD to seek its support.

On the following day, 10 July, the Chancellor reported to the Kaiser and persuaded him to proclaim the equal and secret franchise in Prussia. The Chief of the Civil Cabinet, Rudolf von Valentini, was issued with the order to draft the corresponding proclamation. One reservation which the Kaiser made was that prior to publication he wanted to hear the opinion of the Crown Prince. Bethmann informed Ebert of this and also indicated possible agreement about a peace resolution which, however, would have to have a large majority. He also declared his readiness in principle to call parliamentarians into responsible government posts. Far from resolving problems, this development put the Social Democrats in a serious dilemma. Entry into a parliamentary coalition government would have to be preceded by agreement between the Social Democrats and their bourgeois partners. In other words they would publicly have to disavow their guiding principle since 1871 – though they had done this on many occasions – of non-cooperation, and they would have to assume full responsibility for the conduct of the war if the projected peace resolution met with the same fate as Bethmann Hollweg's peace initiatives. If they refrained from participation, any government would be a minority government. Ebert therefore was rather reluctant to support the programme of parliamentarization, an attitude criticized by the right wing of the Social Democrats who favoured a cabinet of Bülow as Chancellor with Stresemann, Erzberger and Eduard David as his Secretaries of State. However, Ebert preferred to defer the issue of parliamentarization.

After the Kaiser had consulted the opinion of his eldest son, on 11 July 1917 he signed the decree preparing the introduction of the equal and secret franchise in Prussia. Simultaneously he turned down Bethmann Hollweg's request to resign and expressed his confidence in him. The Kaiser's decision was immediately subjected to severe criticism by the Conservatives and the National Liberals, the bulwark of the Prussian three-class franchise.

It seemed as though the parliamentary crisis had been overcome, but twenty-four hours later the joint cooperation of the Pan-Germans, the Conservatives, the Centre, the Majority Socialists and the OHL brought about the fall of Bethmann Hollweg, the very man who had just achieved the political reforms many of his present opponents had been clamouring for for decades. On the issue of peace there was no candidate in sight who was closer to the opinions held from Centre to Left. This also applied to the question of parliamentarization. Centre and Left contributed to his fall without being able to name a suitable successor, or even to exert any influence in his choice. This was one of the many instances in the history of the German Empire, and for that matter also of the Weimar Republic, of the complete lack of political maturity of Germany's political parties. They made their major contribution to the undermining of the Empire and were to repeat that sorry and fateful action little more than a decade later.

On that day, 12 July 1917, a delegation of the National Liberals led by Stresemann, Ludendorff's 'blue-eyed boy', declared to the Vice-Chancellor that the majority of the parliamentary party would demand the resignation of the Chancellor. Stresemann added that otherwise Ludendorff would submit his resignation. Erzberger, Payer and David had already been informed. When asked, Ludendorff gave an evasive answer. The action of the parliamentarians was supplemented by that of the Crown Prince who received representatives of the political parties from the Conservative Count Westarp to the Free Conservative Erich Mertin, as well as Erzberger, Payer and David. He questioned them about their attitude to Bethmann Hollweg. Though their motives differed, they were at one in expressing their desire to change chancellors, and he informed the Kaiser accordingly. Others also made their influence felt on the Kaiser's Civil Cabinet, Erzberger declaring that to keep Bethmann Hollweg in office any longer would make it more difficult to bring about peace. In the afternoon requests were received in Berlin by Hindenburg and Ludendorff for their resignation. As Bethmann Hollweg did not enjoy their confidence, they could no longer serve the Kaiser. Having been reprimanded only a few days before by the Kaiser for their interference in politics, they were now summoned to Berlin. In the meantime the Inter-parliamentary Party Committee had agreed on a peace resolution, which among other things stated that the Reichstag aimed at a peace of understanding and durable reconciliation among peoples and that territorial expansion by force, or political, economic and financial extortions were irreconcilable with such a peace. However, the National Liberals refused to sanction this resolution and left the Committee. The OHL also registered the most serious objections against the resolution. Confusion reigned: on the one hand there was the unholy alliance of most of the Reichstag parties to topple the Chancellor, on the other hand a peace resolution submitted by some of the partners of this unholy alliance but opposed by the OHL and the National Liberals.

Bethmann Hollweg was under no illusions and knew that his days were numbered. However, when Hindenburg and Ludendorff received the parliamentarians in Berlin on 13 July they were agreed on his overthrow but were fundamentally disunited about the peace resolution. Hindenburg was called to see the Kaiser and gave his and Ludendorff's opinion. Under the combined pressure of the OHL and the Reichstag majority Bethmann Hollweg submitted his resignation. He had had enough. As yet there was no successor. Erzberger's efforts in favour of Bülow were rejected by the Kaiser. The Bavarian Prime Minister Count Hertling refused on the ground of old age. Prince Max von Baden lacked support. There was no other alternative than to turn to second-rank officials and politicians and thus Under Secretary of State Georg Michaelis became the new German Chancellor. The Kaiser had preserved his prerogative, mainly because the parliamentarians were at a loss to suggest any alternative other than Bülow. They had had an opportunity but failed to take it. The tendency towards parliamentarization of government was stopped in its tracks for the time being.

MICHAELIS, THE REICHSTAG AND THE PAPAL PEACE INITIATIVE

Michaelis tried to resume Bethmann Hollweg's policy of the 'Diagonal', but he could not prevent the introduction and passing of the Peace Resolution of 17 July 1917. This was passed by 212 to 126 with 17 abstentions and 2 invalid votes. Only the Conservatives and the National Liberals voted almost unanimously against it. It yielded no practical results, other than providing the Entente Powers with an insight into the deep divisions within the German body politic, with its signs of faltering morale. It gave them renewed confidence in the pursuit of the war and their war aims, at a time when signs of war weariness and dissatisfaction had begun to show in their own armies. On the German domestic scene the passing of the resolution ensured a majority vote for renewed – in fact the ninth renewal – war credits of 15,000 million marks. Parliamentarization made no great progress. There were only two parliamentarians in the Reich and the Prussian administration, the National Liberal Paul von Krause in the Reich government and the leader of the Centre Party, Spahn, in the Prussian administration.

In the arena of party politics divisions appeared in the Centre Party. Erzberger's role in the overthrow of Bethmann Hollweg and the cooperation with the Social Democrats which he had inaugurated, though backed by the parliamentary party, met with anything but unanimous approval by the party at large in Germany. To defend his position he publicly read out the Czernin confidential memorandum of April 1917, giving the impression that it was general knowledge. This breach of confidence acutely embarrassed the Austrians; it also embarrassed the war effort of the Central Powers, especially since Czernin's prognosis had proved incorrect in so far as the military situation had been stabilized and looked better than during the previous spring. In other words, Erzberger further demoralized the home front and provided ample material for allied propaganda.

To some extent as a reaction to this defeatism, right-wing extraparliamentary bodies emerged, among them the German Fatherland Party whose most prominent member was Admiral von Tirpitz. Its founder was the Prussian civil servant *Generallandschaftsdirektor* Wolfgang Kapp, the son of one of the 1848–49 Democratic Radicals. The party quickly expanded its agitation on behalf of national solidarity and expansionist war aims. It became so radical that serving officers and civil servants were forbidden to join it.

Bethmann Hollweg had been unable to bring about peace, and the same problem now confronted Michaelis, who was provided with the opportunity of a solution in the form of Pope Benedict XV's peace note. The origins of the note go back to the very beginning of the war when Benedict had ascended the papal throne on 3 September 1914. His Cardinal Secretary of State Pietro Gasparri had for years endeavoured to bring the belligerents together for peace talks. Since the Roman *Curia* was not represented in Berlin the German centre for these efforts was Munich, home of the papal nuncio. During Bethmann Hollweg's chancellorship preliminary negotiation with the papacy had begun. Benedict's proposals were handed over in Munich when the new nuncio, Eugenio Pacelli, later Pope Pius XII, took up his post there. He declared to King Ludwig III that the Pope had no other concern than to bring about a speedy peace. Erzberger, then still the Chancellor's confidant, had various talks with him, and Pacelli talked with Bethmann Hollweg and the Kaiser who welcomed the papal initiative. Towards the end of July 1917 Pacelli negotiated in Berlin with Michaelis and Zimmerman, and submitted Benedict's seven-point programme. This was based on the return of the German colonies by Great Britain; the evacuation of the territories occupied by the Germans in France and Belgium; and Belgium's military, political and economic independence guaranteed by Germany, France and Great Britain. Some questions such as Alsace-Lorraine were left open; the Pope simply endeavoured to re-establish the status quo ante. Michaelis declared his agreement in principle: the German official response would be made after he had reported to the Kaiser and consulted with Germany's Austro-Hungarian allies. Before this was received on 1 August 1917, Pope Benedict issued his peace note to the heads of government of the belligerent nations. He called upon them to begin peace negotiations on the basis of the following conditions: precedence of the moral power of law over the material power of weapons; simultaneous and equal disarmament of all states according to rules and guarantees to be agreed; establishment of an obligatory court of arbitration for all inter-state differences; true freedom of the seas; general renunciation of all war indemnities; mutual return of occupied territories, especially the complete evacuation of Belgium and the securing of its political, military and economic independence *vis à vis* every power, as well as the return of Germany's colonies; and finally the examination of territorial questions such as those between Austria and Italy and between France and Germany in a spirit of conciliation and according to what was just and possible.

The note was intended to be secret, not least because of the knowledge of the secret agreements existing between Great Britain, France, Russia and Italy. But secrecy could not be maintained and through a breach of confidence it came into the hands of the Italian government. As the latter had not been included in its circulation, the British government believed it had to publish the note. Consequently the German reply was very much determined by the attitude adopted to the papal note by her adversaries. Michaelis and the new Secretary of State Richard von Kühlmann, were prepared to make concessions on the Belgian issue. Opinions differed, however, over whether Germany's concessions should be made in advance of the reactions of her opponents, or whether they should be made the subject of negotiation to obtain concessions elsewhere. In the end it was decided to adopt the latter course. But the British government declared that the solution of the Belgian question was a precondition for any peace negotiations, especially since Lloyd George's government was determined on an all-out victory. The Reichstag's peace resolution was ignored in the Commons except by a few Liberal and Labour members. The British government insisted on preconditions precisely to torpedo the papal peace move. Balfour let Gasparri know that progress towards peace was unlikely unless Germany would officially declare its readiness to restore Belgium and to assume the costs of the damage she had caused. The French government was at one with the British. The British envoy at the Holy See, Count Salis, was instructed not to express opinions furthering the peace move, whilst the French government adopted the attitude of rigorously countering any official papal peace move. President Wilson rejected outright a return to the status quo ante. He did not call for reconciliation but for the destruction of German militarism, the 'world's enemy'; he threatened retribution for Germany's irreparable guilt and called upon the Germans to revolt against their own government, so as to deserve her adversaries' mercy. Although this was really tantamount to the total failure of the papal peace move, the Roman *Curia* persisted. Pacelli addressed a letter to Michaelis asking for further clarification about Germany's readiness to restore and indemnify Belgium and the guarantees Germany would give for that country's independence. He did not mention the details of the British and French response; had he done so, it would have been the end of the game. Germany and Austria-Hungary decided not to get involved in individual issues, except by secret confidential means, but to get to the conference table and settle matters there without prejudice.

The Reichstag on the whole welcomed the papal move; disquiet was only expressed over Michaelis's exposition of the note and his adding the phrase 'as I understand it', which of course was a clause indicating reservation. In the Main Committee Michaelis emphasized that the Central Powers had not initiated the papal move, but that they welcomed it. But his previous phrase, 'as I understand it', still continued to give cause for debate. The bourgeois parties accepted Michaelis's explanation and declared the phrase a misunderstanding, but the Social Democrats did not. A new committee, the Free Committee, was installed which besides domestic questions also considered what response should be made to the papal note. Whilst they were deliberating, the Central Powers had already agreed a draft reply in which the Belgian question was deliberately not mentioned because this would raise a whole series of questions such as Alsace-Lorraine and the southern Tyrol. Michaelis submitted the draft to the Free Committee on 10 September 1917. He argued, in defence of the omission of any mention of Belgium, that this country was a pawn in any negotiations and it would lose its value if the cards were put on the table prematurely. Important diplomatic weapons could not be thrown away. The Free Committee agreed with the Austro-German response. A final decision needed the Kaiser's assent and he therefore convened a Crown Council for 11 September. He approved the reply and agreed to the omission of Belgium as well as to the decision not to answer this question prematurely. Belgium was no more than a tactical weapon for future negotiations. The OHL, which had previously insisted on the military control of Belgium by Germany, gave up their demand; only the Chief of the Admiralty Henning von Holtzendorff continued to claim the Flanders coast. Thus the Kaiser decided in favour of the restoration of Belgium and the return of the Belgian King. Issues such as the question of Flanders and Flemmish autonomy (substantial numbers of Flemings collaborated with the Germans – something to be repeated during the Second World War – in the hope of obtaining if not independence then at least autonomy within Belgium) should remain subject to joint German-Belgian negotiations. On the whole Michaelis's point of view had won the day and, a rare event, he had even managed to carry Germany's military leadership with him. The German note of 13 September expressed full agreement with the guiding principles of the papal note and most of its specific points. But it failed to put forward at this stage concrete suggestions or concessions on issues of detail. It was intended that this should be the preserve of preliminary talks and ultimately of peace negotiations. Pacelli was disappointed about the German response and argued that Germany would have to take two steps before the allies took one. But in view of the allied response to the papal peace note, of which the Central Powers were still ignorant, the matter was irrelevant. However,

Michaelis in a letter to Pacelli emphasized that the German government was not disinclined to give a declaration on the Belgian question, but the preconditions for it had as yet not been sufficiently established.

The real decisive obstacle to peace negotiations in 1917 was not Germany's diplomatic tactics concerning Belgium but France's claim for the 'dis-annexation' of Alsace-Lorraine. On 18 September, Prime Minister Paul Painlevé outlined French war aims before the Chamber and the Senate, and these were such as to put an end to any idea of a negotiated peace. He added to the slogan of 'peace without annexations' that of 'dis-annexation', a smart propaganda move, but one which also destroyed Germany's basic willingness to make some concessions over this issue, namely to return parts of upper Alsace in return for some territory in Lorraine.

THE FALL OF MICHAELIS

The peace moves were not merely moribund: to all intents and purposes they were dead. Their failure led once again to a political crisis in Germany and the fall of Michaelis. As long as the papal peace move kept alive some hope of ending the war, Michaelis enjoyed the support of the majority of the Reichstag. The end of these negotiations was accompanied by the dissolution of the Free Committee, the first sign of crisis. Now arguments started in the Reichstag as to who was to blame for its failure. Erzberger's post-war claim that it was Michaelis is not corroborated by the documents. The debate in the Reichstag was cut short by another event that took place in August 1917, the naval mutiny among ships of the German High Seas Fleet. Apart from action in Jutland and U-boat escorting duties the German Navy had been bottled up in its harbours. Only U-boats, mine-sweepers, torpedo-boats and 'commerce raiders' remained active. Boredom, sharp discipline, the hierarchical structure which is particularly pronounced in groups confined to or contained in narrow spaces, were at the root of dissatisfaction, which was actively fed from outside by the USPD, bent as it was upon revolutionary changes in Germany. It coincided in time with the USPD's increased activities on German factory floors and the creation of revolutionary cells. The USPD compiled for the Stockholm conference mentioned above a list of German naval personnel belonging to the USPD in order to create an impression. Its programme envisaged for the navy disobedience by the crews to orders issued by their officers, sabotage and strikes. The heart of the activities was IV Squadron stationed in Wilhelmshaven, and Admiral Reinhard Scheer's flagship *Friedrich der Grosse* was the centre of the conspiracy to mutiny. The naval leaders were the stokers Max Reichpietsch and

Willi Sachse who had their USPD contacts in Wilhelmshaven and Kiel. They visited USPD leaders in Berlin. These Reichstag members, among them Haase and Dittmann, claimed that they had only been listening to the sailors' complaints. But both Sachse and Reichpietsche stated that they informed them of their secret organization and of their plans: Dittmann warned them to be careful but agreed to give them full support. The first signs of unrest occurred in early July 1917 when the sailors on a number of ships of IV Squadron rejected the food they were given, objected to carrying out their duties and refused to take on coal. This incident was repeated during the second half of the month. When forty-nine stokers of the *Prinzregent Luitpold* were refused permission on 1 August to go to the cinema, they left their ship without permission, returning in the early hours of the morning. Eleven of their leaders were put under arrest, whereupon on 2 August 400 men of the crew led by the stoker Albin Köbis left the ship and marched to a restaurant where they held a protest meeting. The naval authorities at first treated these occurrences as isolated incidents until they discovered by accident a revolutionary plot spread over a whole number of ships. As a result Reichpietsch, Köbis, Sachse and others were arrested and court-martialled. The accused heavily implicated the USPD. Five were sentenced to death; others to various terms of imprisonment. Reichpietsch and Köbis were executed; the other death sentences were commuted to fifteen years' hard labour.

At the parliamentary level the issue was how far the USPD had been involved. The deputies in question all enjoyed parliamentary immunity. Ebert was disgusted when he was informed, describing the sailors' action as pure treason, but he doubted whether the USPD would have been stupid enough to take a hand in this mutiny. He assured the government that it could rely on his party.

Conflict was inevitable from the outset when the Reichstag reassembled on 26 September. In order to divert attention from the revolutionary attempts of the previous months the Majority Socialists introduced an interpellation complaining about the way in which the commanders of the military districts in Germany interfered with socialist assemblies while those of the Fatherland Party remained unmolested. They also objected to 'Patriotic instruction', a belated attempt to educate and indoctrinate recruits and soldiers in home garrisons with patriotic fervour. But discussion of the naval mutiny could not be avoided. In the course of the debate Michaelis made tactical errors, such as publicly placing the USPD outside the legitimate political body, making it in fact an enemy of the state. This rallied the Majority Socialists to the side of the USPD. The Secretary of State for the Navy, Eduard von Capelle, submitted documents which heavily implicated the USPD in the mutiny, but he went too far in this by making assertions which the evidence at his disposal at the time would not support. Ebert then defended the USPD, arguing correctly that if conclusive evidence was available there was a correct procedure to follow to rescind the immunity of the USPD members involved. In the final analysis the USPD had done nothing more than make propaganda in the army and navy for political purposes, which was the right of any party. After all the army and navy themselves had introduced politics through their 'patriotic instruction'. The Majority Socialists and USPD moved a vote of disapproval which was defeated by the Centre, the National Liberals and the Progressives. Whether this was a move to support Michaelis or merely one designed to gain time to find a successor is open to question.

From early October 1917 Michaelis's position became increasingly untenable: he had failed to bring peace and he had blundered over the mutiny issue. The Centre, National Liberals, Progressives and Majority Socialists formed a bloc to exert pressure on the Chancellor to resign voluntarily. The decisive move came in the session of the Inter-parliamentary Party Committee on 23 October. Here Stresemann expressed disatisfaction with the Chancellor, but Erzberger thought that the Kaiser would be unlikely to listen to party leaders over this issue. Instead he suggested that the chief of the Kaiser's Civil Cabinet should be informed in writing that any future Chancellor should acquaint the parties about his political programme prior to his appointment. Deputies of the four parties visited Rudolf von Valentini and pressed on him the need for a change of Chancellor. The demands in effect amounted to a parliamentarization of government: the Kaiser was confronted with the problem of whether to defend his prerogative by resistance or to abandon it and thus open the way for full parliamentarization. According to the letter of the constitution the deputies' action was clearly unconstitutional. By the same token the Kaiser's insistence on maintaining his prerogative was considered by most of the parties in the Reichstag as a *coup d'état*. Michaelis resolved the problem himself by requesting to be relieved of all his offices on 26 October. But once more there was the problem of a successor. Erzberger again lobbied for Bülow, but in vain. Hertling was once more approached to take over the chancellorship, but being a Bavarian he was considered unsuitable to be Prussian Prime Minister. So Michaelis was persuaded to hold on to the office for the time being.

HERTLING'S CHANCELLORSHIP

Before making his final decision Hertling asked for time to discuss matters with the party leaders in the Reichstag, in itself a constitutional novelty, to which, however, the Kaiser agreed. Hertling asked them to see him, but as it was Sunday most were not in Berlin. So he met

Erzberger first, who still backed Bülow. Other party leaders were only consulted in the following days. Opposition to Hertling was strong within the Inter-parliamentary Party Committee. He was called the candidate of the 'military party', an injustice if ever there was one. His experience in foreign affairs was limited, but the same could be said of his two predecessors. A more weighty argument was his objection to granting greater autonomy to Alsace-Lorraine. A decision was only reached when eleven Prussian Ministers and most of the Reich Secretaries of State implored Hertling to take on the office: it was not the Reichstag but the executive of the Reich and of Prussia which brought this about. Hertling agreed to a *de facto* parliamentarization of the Prussian cabinet: National Liberals and Free Conservatives were to be won over to carry out the introduction of the free and equal franchise in Prussia, an issue lost sight of during the crisis over Bethmann Hollweg. The Inter-parliamentary Party Committee changed its attitude when Hertling adopted a more positive attitude towards autonomy for Alsace-Lorraine. He gave the impression that he would accept the National Liberal Robert Friedberg into the Prussian government and the Progressive Friedrich von Payer as his Vice-Chancellor. The committee was anxious to avoid a clear break with the Crown while Hertling was already at this stage showing himself a master of delaying tactics. The separation of the offices of Chancellor and Prussian Prime Minister was abandoned on his demand and on 1 November Hertling was appointed to both. Once in office, though, he endeavoured to keep Helfferich as Vice-Chancellor, but the latter, who was alarmed by the growing influence of the political parties in the decision-making process, resigned and Payer became Vice-Chancellor after all. A decisive step had been taken towards parliamentarization. Michaelis and Hertling had been the candidates of the Crown, not of the parliamentary majority. Hertling's consultation with the party leaders was already a step in a new direction, but Helfferich's resignation and the appointment of a parliamentarian as Vice-Chancellor were fundamental differences from constitutional norms and practice since 1871. No wonder therefore that for the time being Hertling rejected any further parliamentarization. Accepting office also meant the loss of a parliamentary mandate. During his chancellorship he successfully opposed any further changes in personnel.

None the less he endeavoured to fulfil the four-point programme of the majority parties. The draft of the new Prussian electoral law had already been forwarded to both Prussian Chambers on 25 November 1917. He outlined his government's programme to the party leaders before submitting it to the Reichstag. In the Reichstag session of 29 November he emphasized his opposition to slavishly copying the institutions of foreign nations. What had to be done was what corresponded to the real requirements of the people to the German spirit and character. He refrained from touching on the issue of Prussian electoral reform because as a Bavarian he did not want to interfere. His programme was basically conservative, especially when compared with the slow but steady reforming zeal of Bethmann Hollweg. He promised further social legislation and to extend freedom of expression in so far as the national interest allowed it in times of war.

In the realm of foreign policy he was able to announce that the Bolshevik government in Russia had sued for an armistice. He considered the Soviet proposal a basis for discussion, but as far as Poland, Lithuania and Courland were concerned he insisted on adhering to the principle of national self-determination. On the question of peace and war aims he maintained continuity with his predecessors: from the first day of the war Germany's aim had been to defend the fatherland, the inviolability of its territory and its free and independent economic development. The government had welcomed the papal peace initiative: 'The responsibility for the continued slaughter, for the destruction of irreplaceable cultural values, for the mad self-emasculation of Europe, rests only with the powers of Entente. They bear the responsibility and they will have to carry the consequences.'

In the debate the Centre leader Karl Trimborn virtually repeated what Hertling had said, while Stresemann emphasized that the National Liberals wanted nothing to do with the peace resolution. Scheidemann, whose party had helped to put Hertling in office, neither opposed nor supported him, opting for tolerating the government but maintaining its reserve, leaving open the option of outright opposition. On 1 December the Reichstag passed the war credits with a large majority, only the USPD voting against. But nothing was said about the interpellation that had been intended originally and a vote of confidence in the new government, nor was any mention made about moves towards further parliamentarization. The unity between parties supporting the government showed cracks. The bourgeois parties moved that the Reichstag be prorogued, while the Social Democrats and USPD opposed, intending to keep the Reichstag in being for the important armistice and peace negotiations with Russia and to exert their influence on them. But the bourgeois parties supported by the Conservatives pushed through the prorogation. The Reichstag was to reconvene on 19 February 1918. Thus party political activity reverted back to the party leaders and the Main Committee of the Reichstag, which the Chancellor informed on 20 December about the peace negotiations with Russia. Hertling took great pains to cultivate the party leaders in order to maintain a countervailing power to the influence of the OHL. When Wilson announced his fourteen points on 8 January 1918, Hertling publicly declared his agreement in principle with them. He added that at no time had the annexation of Belgium been a part of German policy, but as long as Germany's enemies were not prepared to assure the territorial integrity of the Central Powers as a basis for peace discussion, Germany would have to insist that the Belgian question could not be separated from a general discussion. He rejected the cession of Alsace-Lorraine, and as far as the east was concerned peace would be made on the principle of national self-determination.

THE TREATY OF BREST-LITOVSK

Throughout the war Germany had actively aided the revolutionary movement inside and outside Russia. Lenin's *coup* was the fruit of these endeavours, one which was to be much regretted by the Germans later on. On 28 November 1917 Lenin suggested that all governments should enter into negotiations over an armistice and a general peace. This led to a German–Russian armistice and the beginning of peace negotiations. On 20 December Secretary of State von Kühlmann outlined the peace plan to the party leaders of the Reichstag. It envisaged the independence of Lithuania and Courland as well as of Poland. But in contrast to the OHL neither Hertling nor Kühlmann intended initially to create a second Baltic state made up of parts of Latvia and Estonia, nor did they sanction a Polish protective strip for the security of the German frontier; however, on the former issue Kühlmann changed his mind. The majority of the party leaders gave Kühlmann a free hand in the negotiations. The Central Powers endeavoured, on the basis of Russia's acceptance of the principle of national self-determination, to create a belt of formally independent states such as Poland, Lithuania and the Baltic States who in turn would depend on Germany for their support and security. The parties of the Right in the Reichstag and the OHL were perturbed by the Russian slogan of no annexations, no contributions; the Left opposed the creation of separate states which they declared was hidden annexation. The issue further divided the Majority Socialists and the USDP. The OHL put up a maximum list of demands, but its representative at the negotiations at Brest-Litovsk, Major-General Max Hoffmann, had extensive experience in the east and therefore refused to act as Hindeburg's and Ludendorff's mouthpiece. His line was that of the Hertling government. This is not the place to detail the negotiations whose outcome was the Treaty of Brest-Litovsk which contained fourteen articles, an economic agreement and other additional arrangements and was finally signed on 3 March 1918. It has often been cited as an example of the 'German mailed fist' and therefore as justification for the Versailles Treaty. One should contrast this opinion with that of an expert diplomatist and historian, none other than

George F. Kennan:

> I think this assertion deserves some modifications. In comparison with the settlements the Western Allies imposed, on the basis of unconditional surrender, after two world wars, the Brest-Litovsk Treaty does not strike me as inordinately severe. No reparations were originally demanded in the treaty itself. The territories of which the Bolsheviki were deprived were ones the people of which had no desire for Russian rule, least of all Russian Communist rule. The Bolsheviki themselves had never at any time had authority over these territories. It was a hope rather than a reality, of which they were deprived by the terms of the treaty. The settlement accepted by the Allies at the end of the Russian civil war – the arrangement that is, that prevailed from 1920 to 1939 – was considerably less favourable to Russia, territorially, in the Baltic-Polish region than that which the Germans imposed on Russia in 1918.

THE JANUARY 1918 STRIKE

While these negotiations were taking place, in January 1918 the first *political* strike in the history of the German Empire took place. Initiators and leaders of the strikers were not the trade unions but the USPD, the Spartacus League and other radical left-wing organizations. Preparations for it stretched back to the Russian October Revolution. The agitators could build on the dissatisfaction arising from the disappointed hopes for a quick peace in the east. Revolutionary shop stewards guided the masses in Berlin's armaments industries and those of other centres in Germany. Workers' councils were created on the Soviet model and the strike movement demanded peace without annexations, the participation of workers in the peace negotiations, more food supplies, the lifting of the state of siege, the release of all those convicted for political offences, the 'democratization' of Germany and the introduction of universal, equal, direct and secret franchise and ballot for all men and women in the Prussian Diet.

The three Majority Socialists, Ebert, Scheidemann and Otto Braun, joined the strike leadership with the objective, as they declared after the war, of counteracting the influence of the radicals. Not all workers supported the strike. The liberal 'Hirsch-Duncker' trade unions and the Christian Trade Union roundly condemned it, as did the 'Polish Association of Workers', consisting mainly of miners in the Ruhr.

The government appealed to the strikers and told them that their doubts about the promised political reforms were unfounded, and to the duty of every worker to do his job for the sake of the men at the front. But it also moved actively against the strikers, having recourse to the laws available under the state of siege. They closed trade union offices and prohibited all public assemblies. The Majority Socialists now blamed the government for the strike. Hertling explained his readiness to discuss social questions with trade union representatives. He rejected the request by Ebert and others to receive a strikers' delegation of nine. By 31 January, when the strike movement had spread, the military commander of the Berlin area announced a severe state of siege and appointed military courts. At a mass rally on the same day Ebert was reluctant to state whether he thought strike action was a suitable political instrument: instead he emphasized the duty of every worker to supply the soldiers at the front with arms. Dittmann on the other hand called on them to hold out. The police then dispersed the rally. On 2 February Ebert, Scheidemann, Haase and Ledebour had another meeting with the Chancellor and some of his associates. They demanded freedom of assembly, which Hertling rejected since this would hardly have helped to end the strike. The alternative for the strikers now was either an attempt at revolution or to call off the strike. This they did unconditionally; the severe state of siege was lifted and the prosecution of strike leaders was transferred from military to civil courts. The sentences imposed were sharp and sufficient to stop the agitation of the extreme Left for most of 1918.

However, the strike seriously shook the cohesion of the Reichstag majority, which since July the previous year had in any case become very fragile. Both bourgeois Centre and Left condemned the attitude of the Majority Socialists as contradictory to that maintained hitherto. Further cooperation would depend on whether the Social Democrats resumed the attitude they had adopted before the strike. This gave the SPD the choice of joining the radical Left or returning to the fold of the coalition. The crisis was resolved by the Vice-Chancellor, Payer, and Erzberger who persuaded the SPD to return to its original course. However, these negotiations were hindered by the case of Dittmann. He had been arrested during the strike while acting on its behalf, and he could therefore be tried despite his parliamentary immunity. Since he had already been involved in the naval mutiny of August 1917, he was sentenced to five years' fortress and two months' jail[1]. In the Reichstag the SPD's coalition partners refused to back Dittmann and when the vote was taken the SPD and USPD voted jointly against the majority of the Right, Centre and the Progressives. In the debate about the strike the government pointed to the Russian example and its determination not to allow a similar development in Germany.

ELECTORAL REFORM IN PRUSSIA

One of the major constitutional questions faced by Hertling was the demand to change Article 9 of the Constitution, which prohibited the simultaneous holding of a parliamentary mandate and government office. To lift this prohibition would have been a further step towards full parliamentarization. Hertling opposed change and he was unwittingly aided and abetted in this resistance by the Social Democrats. They feared being drawn into a coalition government, and thus being saddled with governmental responsibility, since this would widen the rift even more between the SPD and USPD and the extra-parliamentary radical Left. They went as far as accepting the Vice-Presidency of the Reichstag, while the new Centre Party leader Konstantin Fehrenbach became President. The Social Democrats, while supporting war credits in 1917, voted against the budget, but as a result of the January strike, to demonstrate their loyalty, they voted in favour of new war credits as well as for the extension of the budget beyond its date of expiry. Thereafter, as a gesture to the extreme Left, they returned to a position of obstructionism and in July 1918 again voted against the budget. Other issues which occupied the Reichstag were the reform of the constituency boundaries and of the Prussian three-class franchise. The redistribution and drawing up of boundaries had become necessary as a result of demographic changes that had taken place in Germany since 1869. This together with the consideration of the demand for proportional representation, was a task which had been shunned, particularly by the middle-class parties. Hertling nevertheless on 16 February 1918 submitted a draft which would divide Germany into constituencies, proceeding on the assumption of an average of 163,500 inhabitants per constituency. The 36 constituencies which contained more than double this average figure were considered oversized. Proceeding from this the draft did not favour a further division of these oversized constituencies, but allowed each to return a greater number of deputies on the basis of proportional representation. The total number of constituencies was to be reduced to 387, and the number of parliamentary seats increased by 44 to 441. The Reichstag accepted the reform by a large majority and it came into force on 24 August 1918.

In the social sphere Paragraph 153 of the *Reichsgewerbeordnung*, the Reich Industrial Order, had been eroded, and in effect for most workers freedom of association had been transformed into a compulsion to join a union; in other words the closed-shop system had been introduced by the back door. For decades employers had argued in favour of putting teeth into this paragraph, while trade unions and Socialists had advocated its complete abolition. Ultimately, with the exception of the Conservatives, all parties of the Reichstag favoured scrapping it and a law in this sense was passed.

However, these were mere bagatelles compared with the reform of the Prussian electoral system. Once the Kaiser had decided in favour of it, on 25 November 1917 three draft laws had been introduced in the

Prussian Diet, the essence of which was to grant the equal, direct and secret franchise to all males of 25 and over. Women were excluded. The democratization of the Diet also required a reform of the *Herrenhaus* which was to comprise a maximum of 550 members. Thirty-six seats each were to go to the mayors of big cities, the representatives of the landed nobility and the heads of big industrial enterprises; 60 seats were to go to the high nobility for life; town and country districts were to send 76 deputies, professional corporations 84, churches and universities 32 for twelve years. Finally the King was to enjoy the privilege of appointing 150 members, who enjoyed his particular confidence. and the remainder was to be made up of princes of the royal house The Diet and the *Herrenhaus* were to enjoy equal status, with equal legislative rights. To avoid a repetition of the constitutional conflict of 1858 – 66 the budget law was to be reformed by provisions which would prevent a 'constitutional gap' from recurring. The first reading caused protests against the introduction of the equal franchise in the Second Chamber with the Centre and National Liberals opposing. The Left was equally disappointed since it had favoured a plural and not a proportional franchise. It seemed as though a compromise had been reached in the committee stage, since the Centre, in order to maintain the July coalition, voted for the equal franchise, but in the second reading this was once again defeated. In its place the simple majority system was accepted. But the Prussian government was determined to push through proportional representation. Only in the fourth reading, when part of the National Liberals abandoned their previous position, did the government gain a majority, and this was also confirmed in the fifth reading. The reforms had then to be submitted to the *Herrenhaus*, where in spite of their support by the Kaiser, a policy of obstructionism prevailed. Hertling, time and again, tried to get a compromise solution but no decision was reached, and Prussian electoral reform was overtaken by events.

THE RESIGNATION OF HERTLING

The German government and the OHL persisted in their endeavour to carry out a decisive military offensive accompanied by a peace offensive. Part of the latter was Hertling's answer to Wilson's fourteen points mentioned above. But the main spokesman for the peace offensive was Secretary of State von Kühlmann. His speech before the Reichstag on 24 June was well received except by parties of the Right. By the end of June the German government had become aware that the series of offensives in the west, launched in March, would not succeed in their aims. Germany could no longer win the war; the question was now how she could get peace and on what terms. Because of this Kühlmann's speech, which expressed the desire for a restoration of the status quo ante in the west, was met with derision by Germany's opponents. Constitutionally he was out on a limb, because he had made the speech without informing Hertling beforehand of its contents. He should also have consulted the OHL as well as the leaders of the parliamentary parties, a practice which had existed since the outbreak of war. The OHL protested, accusing Kühlmann of dividing the front at home and in the field, while giving encouragement to the enemy. The final consequence was his dismissal and replacement by Admiral Paul von Hintze.

Other changes, though not associated with the Kühlmann affair, included the replacement of General Moritz von Lyncker as Chief of the Military Cabinet by Major-General Ulrich von Marschall. Profound changes also took place in the navy where Henning von Holtzendorff was replaced by Admiral Reinhard Scheer as Chief of the Admiralty Staff; Eduard von Capelle was replaced as Secretary of State of the Reich Naval Office by Admiral Ernst von Mann. The most important change was the establishment of the *Oberste Seekriegsleitung*, the supreme Naval Command (SKL), on a par with the OHL.

The defeats suffered by the German armies on 18 July and 8 August – which the German public and most of the parliamentarians were unaware of because of the strict censorship exercised by the army and Foreign Office – were the harbingers of change, the extent and effect of which could not be foreseen. All the government could think of was a new peace move, but the question was when. Ebert argued in favour of delaying it until the front had stabilized itself, adding that Hertling had no reputation abroad and, like his predecessors, he was not the man likely to bring peace. But he refused to participate in a coalition government. The only cabinet the Social Democrats would join was one made up of the parties who had backed the peace resolution of 1917.

The news of the collapse of Bulgaria and the subsequent unilateral Austro-Hungarian step of issuing a note to all belligerent powers on the question of peace negotiations acted like a bombshell on these deliberations. Scheidemann's response was to dismiss the Austrian step as an enormous error which, however, could only be rectified if Germany joined it: Germany's official reply was that the Reich would be prepared to join the 'exchange of ideas'. But any hope for an acceptable peace was dismissed by President Wilson when on 27 September in a speech in New York he rejected any compromise peace: the only solution was absolute victory.

Unrest increased in the Reichstag, aimed at replacing Hertling. Stresemann negotiated for a broad coalition government, possibly headed by Bülow. The Inter-parliamentary Party Committee embraced Wilson's idea of a League of Nations and proposed a resolution in favour of this body which should demonstrate to the world that Germany was ready to make peace. The parliamentarization of the German government was also a major topic discussed during these final weeks and months, but no one really had a replacement for Hertling on hand, and all parties were reluctant to risk a move which would tar them with the brush of defeat. The solution was not brought about by the government or the Reichstag but by the OHL, which because of the situation in south-eastern Europe demanded a change of government or its extension on a broad basis. Hertling had lost their backing. The army, not parliament, brought about parliamentarization: it demanded an armistice and peace offer based on Wilson's fourteen points. On 30 September 1918 the Kaiser signed the decree for parliamentarization. Hertling refused to participate, requested his resignation and the Kaiser assented. German monarchical constitutionalism had come to an end.

CRITIQUE AND COUNTER-CRITIQUE

This half century of the constitutional history of Germany is not easy to assess. Certainly its dismissal by the new generation of historians, not least in Germany itself, as 'sham-constitutionalism' is as facile as the characterization of the Empire as a mere 'ante-chamber' of the Third Reich is perverse. This latter view of German history, as an inexorable progress down the line to Auschwitz, has been rejected by historians such as David Calleo, David Blackbourne and Geoff Eley, and, in Germany, like Hans Bucheim, Thomas Nipperdey, Ernst Nolte and H.G. Zmarzlick, to none of whom the fashionable label 'conservative' can be applied.

A less doctrinaire judgement would, as Ernst Nolte suggests, want to consider the 'Second Reich' in the context of its own time, and in the manner in which it appeared to its European contemporaries. By those criteria, and in comparison with the other European powers, its record emerges in a rather more favourable light.

The protagonists of the notion of a German *Sonderweg*, a specific path taken by Germany distinct from that of Great Britain, the United States and France, ignore the fact that every nation has gone its own specific way. In France, from Voltaire and de Tocqueville onwards right through the nineteenth century, the French intellectual tradition displays an awareness of France's *Sonderweg*, a path leading into decadence. Voltaire had contrasted an intolerant and backward France with what were in his view 'progressive' states like England, Prussia and Holland; de Tocqueville's discourse on the Prussian Legal Code sees in it the model of a progressive constitution, pointing the way ahead rather than cementing the social and political status quo, an instrument of political and social evolution which made a revolution superfluous.

Yet precisely the absence of a bourgeois revolution in Germany is taken by many present-day historians as the major factor responsible for the direction German history took in our own age. The supporters of this hypothesis, however, use a rather narrowly defined concept of revolution in so far as to them it was a battle between the aristocracy and the bourgeoisie in the course of which the latter wrested political power from the traditional monarchy and put in its place a parliamentary democracy. But as Eley quite correctly observes revolution in Europe did not take that form, neither in England in the seventeenth century nor in France in 1789. The reference to the American Revolution one might consider as almost irrelevent, since in principle it was a conservative revolution for the protection of property. Those who are still tempted to invoke it should take note of what the Founding Fathers had to say about democracy and political parties in the US Constitution; they should take note of the writings of John Adams, George Washington, Alexander Hamilton, James Madison, and even Thomas Jefferson. In any case a thorough reading of *The Federalist Papers* would be a salutary exercise, with its prominent themes of the fear of revolution, the fear of the 'mob', and the dangers inherent in democracy which all too easily could lead to the rule of a permanent majority over a permanent minority.

The idea of the bourgeois revolution which triumphantly imposed its interests with a programme of liberal democracy belongs to the realm of historical mythology. However, when using a more broadly defined concept of revolution which is not limited solely to the narrow process of democratic reforms but also includes the entire complex of changes that brought forth, among other things, industrial capitalism, one must come to the conclusion that Germany in the nineteenth century experienced a successful bourgeois revolution, though the 'revolution from above' in the 1860s and 1870s constitutes a specifically German variety of this.

It took France more than a century to reconcile itself with its revolution and to establish a broadly accepted consensus on this issue. Certainly between 1815 and 1848 French liberal and radical thought did not view the revolution as having really suceeded; the model still continued to be Great Britain and Germany, though the image of Germany was the idealized portrait painted by Mme de Staël. The plebiscitary despotism of Napoleon III was considered by many French intellectuals as a relapse in tyranny, an insult and a challenge at the same time. Only in the aftermath of 1871 did broadly based changes begin to develop, yet even these did not take place without for a time dividing the French nation even further. The struggle against the Commune was bloodier than anything that the anti-Socialist legislation in Germany had seen. The struggle over the separation of church and state was more bitter and divisive than Bismarck's *Kulturkampf*, and left a legacy of danger which only began to unfold in the Second World War. The French intellectual and political tradition also produced that most dangerous aberration of nationalism, 'integral nationalism', a model, as Ernst Nolte has demonstrated, for both Mussolini and Hitler and a host of lesser lights. Throughout the latter part of the nineteenth century, until the eve of the First World War, Germany – the German Empire – still served as an example: the modernity of a German 'America' on European soil with a European tradition was considered dynamic compared with the stagnation of France. Even in the last days of the July crisis Jean Jaurès implored his listeners, 'Non, non, la France de la Révolution ne peut pas marcher derrière la Russie des Moujiks contre l'Allemagne de la Réforme.' Two hours later he was killed by an assassin. Whenever progressive states were discussed, the German Empire was part of them.

In Great Britain the image of Germany, certainly during the second half of the nineteenth century, was that of a highly progressive state. Many British radicals and for that matter a large part of the population deplored the fact that so many Englishmen allowed themselves to be subjected to the 'feudal system', which Cobden, for instance, compared with the caste spirit dominant in India. In Bagehot's constitutional theory the deference of the masses was one of the foundations of Great Britain's parliamentary system. One need look only at the correspondence of Queen Victoria with her daughter, the mother of Kaiser Wilhelm II, to see what alarm was caused by any step towards further liberal constitutionalization. She resisted, with all the power available to her, the eroding of her prerogatives, especially the command of the army. Palmerston, Disraeli and Gladstone in turn had to face the charge of being 'Bonapartists', the same charge as is levied against Bismarck today.

Many British conservatives admired the German constitutional system precisely because it was one of gradualism, preventing changes from developing too rapidly. German idealistic philosophy left its impact on nineteenth century British philosophers like E.T. Greene, Francis Bradley and Bernard Bosanquet because they were alarmed by the consequences of an untrammelled laissez-faire liberalism, especially in the social sphere. Because many of their liberal contemporaries held what they considered an incomplete and inadequate view of freedom, a freedom without responsibility to the common weal, which would lead to Hobbes's war of all against all, they argued that the 'night-watchman' concept of the state would have to be abandoned. It was to be replaced by certain boundaries, these being essentially all those points at which this self-realization begins to impinge on or even curtail the liberty of others. From this point of view the state's function was to control excesses and to arbitrate whenever necessary, in effect a state 'above parties'. In this context it was Prussia and the German Empire which served as a pre-eminent model. From it came the impulses for social reform, for educational and scientific advance. Even those suspicious of Germany's aims never looked at Germany as an underdeveloped backward country. In spite of often pronounced Francophilism, it was Germany which served as a model in the areas of social, industrial and educational advance.

No doubt today's radical German critics had set out with the best of motives, namely with the aid of the discipline of history to produce 'the mature, emancipated citizen'. Whether history is the suitable instrument for such a task may be debatable, but the fact remains that they have ended in the cul-de-sac of conspiracy theories.

This in turn has led to the failure of recognizing that from 1870 onwards one is dealing with a new age, with the beginning of a qualitatively new era. New industrial developments, technologies, methods of organization, the massive growth of the network of communication entered the scene, together with a new social and political consciousness among the hitherto silent masses of industrial workers and employees. It seemed as though man was on the threshold of controlling nature's forces. The critics miss all that as well as the emancipatory forces which have their roots in the Empire. We find no mention of the German youth movement, nor anything that would point to the developing and increasing role of women in German society. In the decades of the Empire they became an indispensable factor in industrial production, and the doors to higher education, to the academic professions and even to party political offices were opened to them. Legislation for youth protection and youth welfare have their origins in the Wilhelmina period.

If one ignores such factors and developments it comes as no surprise that Heinrich Mann's satire *Der Untertan* (translated into English under the title *Man of Straw*) emerges suddenly as a historical generalization from the pages of a 'problem-orientated structural analysis' of the German Empire.

If the Empire was a mere 'sham-constitutionalism', mere manipulation, what actually held it together? This question has rarely, if ever, been asked by the radical critics. The answer, one suspects, would be: manipulation. Yet Germany's Social Democracy, in spite of massive social advances, became the largest single party, in terms of members and in terms of votes cast for it by 1912; so the voters cannot have been as stupid as all that, mere objects of manipulation. The simple fact is that any state, any form of organized society, produces loyalty if within that state or society or both it is possible to achieve substantial durable gains for the benefit for all.

German monarchical constitutionalism had produced such gains, but taken by itself this form of government was transitional. In Germany the constitutional transition took place in the last days of September 1918.

NOTE

1. Fortress sentences were somewhat more lenient than jail sentences, the prisoner enjoying greater personal liberties.

Chapter 7

FROM PARLIAMENTARY GOVERNMENT TO REVOLUTION AND REPUBLIC

After resigning Hertling refused to continue in office until a successor had been found, so the main burden fell on his Vice-Chancellor, Payer. He consulted the representatives of seven parliamentary parties, the Centre, the Majority Socialists, the National Liberals, the Progressives, the German *Fraktion*, the Poles and the USPD. All rejected the formation of a broad coalition except for the National Liberals and the German *Fraktion*. But the three majority parties were prepared to take in the National Liberals. The Poles and the USPD rejected any participation. So a government was formed by the National Liberals, the Centre, the Social Democrats and the Progressives. The constitution still prohibited holding both office and a parliamentary mandate: to circumvent this, the new Secretaries of State were appointed on a temporary provisional basis only.

The parliamentarians once again displayed their immaturity when it came to selecting a Chancellor. It did not occur to them to suggest someone from their own ranks. The Social Democrats for instance refused to put forward a candidate of their own, ostensibly because he might not meet with the approval of the Kaiser but really because they feared it would alienate their voters. Thus the ball was back in the court of the Kaiser where Secretary of State Wilhelm Solf, the banker Max Warburg, Colonel Hans von Haeften of the OHL and Kurt Hahn backed the candidature of Prince Max von Baden. A man of liberal opinions who had served as a General in the Prussian army for over twenty years, he was largely unknown to the German public and to Germany's enemies he was merely another Junker. The parties had also to be won over to his candidature, something that was achieved in the Inter-parliamentary Party Committee in the first few days of October. At the beginning Max von Baden opposed full parliamentarization; instead he desired the support of the major party leaders for a Chancellor's and not a party government. In the realm of foreign policy he opposed annexations and favoured a negotiated peace, an illusory notion at that or any other time.

The parties demanded the dismissal of the Secretary of State for Foreign Affairs Paul von Hintze, the War Minister Hermann von Stein and the Chief of the Reich Chancellery Wilhelm von Radowitz. The Centre demanded the post of Vice-Chancellor for itself; the SPD that of Secretary of State for the Interior, new Reich offices(such as a Labour Office and Office for the Occupied Territories), and that the Press Office should be occupied by parliamentarians. Payer remained Vice-Chancellor, the Interior Office did not go to a Social Democrat but to the Centre leader Karl Trimborn, although the Socialists got the Reich Labour Office. Scheidemann also entered the Cabinet without a specific office. Max von Baden divided his cabinet into a general cabinet and a war cabinet which mainly included those secretaries who were without portfolio; in addition it included members of the treasury, foreign affairs and the new War Minister General Heinrich Scheüch. Moreover political Under Secretaries of State were appointed, and finally as a direct consequence of this the incompatability between holding government office and a seat in the Reichstag was abolished.

WILSON'S NOTES AND CONSTITUTIONAL CHANGE

On 29 September, while Hertling was still in office, the decision was made to sue for an armistice on the basis of Wilson's fourteen points. Max von Baden considered it an error and the OHL was prepared to postpone it if a government had been established by the evening of 1 October. The Chancellor realized that such a request would inevitably lead to an unconditional surrender. He preferred military resistance at any price, while at the same time being ready to enter a negotiated peace. Before he could make his attitude known the OHL informed the leaders of the political parties of the consequences of Bulgaria's collapse, culminating in the statement that Germany was no longer in a position to force the enemy to ask for peace. There was still time for a long-drawn-out resistance to ensure a bearable peace, but time must not be lost. A precondition of a German peace offer would have to be the establishment of a united front at home, in case it was rejected. The party leaders were highly alarmed, and Max von Baden could not count on their support to oppose a request for an armistice. At the Crown Council of 2 October he made known his objections to an armistice but Hindenburg handed over a memorandum which summarized the details already revealed to the party leaders. The OHL was prepared to make territorial sacrifices in the west, such as parts of Alsace-Lorraine, but rejected any changes in the east. However, the anxious political parties remained undecided, so in the end the decision to request an armistice was made by the civil and military authorities. A note went to Wilson asking for an armistice as a preliminary to peace negotiations based on his foureen points and such other declarations as he had made since then. Germany was not submitting to the dictates of the enemy but aimed at a negotiated peace. The decision was forced upon the Chancellor: it was not his. Therefore when he justified the request before the Reichstag on 5 October the convictions he expressed were not really his own but in the main those of the OHL. Wilson's reply of 8 October was dilatory. He asked whether Germany would accept his own programme on the understanding that peace negotiations would refer only to an agreement about the practical details of its application, whether the irrefutable precondition of evacuating the occupied territories was accepted, and finally whether the Reich Chancellor was speaking on behalf of those forces which had so far conducted the war. Wilson's first two questions really aimed at the evacuation of Alsace-Lorraine and the creation of a corridor which would give Poland access to the Baltic; the last made the democratization and parliamentarization of Germany a precondition to an armistice.

The German response was gloomy. Rathenau advocated a *levée en masse*, an idea quickly dispelled by Ludendorff. In its reply on 12 October the German government unreservedly accepted Wilson's conditions but added that Germany proceeded from the assumption that the allied governments were also making Wilson's points their basis for future negotiations. The consequence was that on 28 October the Kaiser and the German government introduced laws changing the constitution so as to correspond with a fully parliamentarized state. Henceforth the army and navy had to consult and obtain the agreement of the government to any action.

The peace feelers were seriously prejudiced by another 'Muehlon affair'. In Switzerland Muehlon published a letter written by Prince Max von Baden to Prince Alexander von Hohenlohe-Schillingsfürst the previous January in which he strongly criticized the peace resolution of 1917 and the parliamentary system in general. The Chancellor had to defend himself before the leaders of the parliamentary parties, conceding that this – that Germany's evolution should follow its own path – had been his opinion at the time, which he no longer held. He offered to resign immediately if they had lost confidence in him. Thus the crisis was settled, but not without serious repercussions on public opinion abroad.

The government had put their hopes on Wilson's moderation. His second note of 14 October completely destroyed any such illusion. Wilson confirmed that Germany should accept the American conditions unreservedly, but he said nothing at all about the attitude of the allies to the fourteen points. The note demanded Germany's subjugation to the dictate of the USA and her associated powers. The armistice would have to ensure the present allied superiority on the western front; Germany would have to cease all action contrary to international law, such as U-boat warfare. Finally the note stated that one of the conditions Germany must accept was the destruction of any arbitrary power which of its own volition could disturb the peace of the world.

Thus a change in the German constitution became one of the preconditions for an armistice. It was a crude interference in Germany's constitutional life. The peace settlement and German constitutional reform had become interconnected.

The shock to the government and the parties was severe, but the parliamentary politicians still put their faith in Wilson. The OHL now wanted to change course and fight to the finish, obviously intending to place the burden of responsibility on the civil power. Social Democrats like Scheidemann were naïve enough to believe that it was not Wilson's intention to get rid of the Kaiser, but rather to reduce him to a role such as that of the monarchs of Italy, Belgium and Scandinavian states. Max von Baden saw no other choice but to accept the note as it stood. In the cabinet session of 17 October the army leaders were consulted and Ludendorff now reversed his position and was much more optimistic, talking of reserves which in reality did not exist. U-boat warfare was given up, not without objections from the navy and the OHL. In the Chancellor's reply reference to abandoning U-boat warfare was avoided; instead mention was made of orders issued to all U-boat commanders to conduct the war on the basis of cruiser warfare, and not to torpedo passenger steamers. It also emphasized the constitutional changes that had taken place in Germany. The new government had been formed with the agreement of the people's representatives elected by democratic methods. The armistice and peace offer proceeded from a government supported by the overwhelming majority of the German people.

Wilson's third note destroyed any further illusions: even constitutional changes were no guarantee of a durable change in the system since the German people possessed no means to subject the military authorities to its will, the power of the King of Prussia remained undiminished, initiative still lay with Germany's rulers. Genuine peace negotiations could only be conducted with a government which truly represented the German people. In other words the Kaiser was not simply asked to abdicate but the abolition of the monarchy was demanded. Wilson had joined the issues of Kaiser and Peace into one. The government and OHL now quarrelled over which course to take. The OHL, and Ludendorff in particular, agitated for breaking off negotiations, although Hindenburg remained uncommited. On 25 October both saw the Kaiser in Berlin and Ludendorff expanded his argument in favour of continuing the war. No unanimity could be achieved and Ludendorff submitted his resignation which the Kaiser accepted. That of Hindenburg, which had also been submitted, was rejected. Ludendorff was replaced by General Wilhelm Groener. His departure gave the government more of a free hand, but it was again limited by the news that Austria-Hungary had asked for a separate peace. The German note of 27 October emphasized that the military powers had also been subjected to civil control. Wilson's reply of 5 November informed the Germans that the allied and associated powers were now ready to receive German plenipotentiaries, who would be presented with the conditions of the armistice which would guarantee the interests of the nations allied against Germany. The allies would have unlimited power to ensure and enforce the details of the armistice accepted by Germany.

The illusion of peace based on law was dispelled: it was clear that here was a peace based on armed might. The man 'too proud to fight', the 'Puritan in the Ivory Tower' had proved an expert in the basest form of international poker. His bid for the USA to become the world hegemonic power, a bid that seems to have escaped most chroniclers, was about to succeed, but it was cut short by disregard of public opinion at home and ultimately by fate. In October/November he had played a cheap hand of poker skilfully but nevertheless dishonestly. He was to continue to play this game at the Paris peace meetings and to leave the bloodiest imaginable legacy, one that he did not live to see, though he would have fully deserved to do so.

In the meantime reforms had been pushed through the Reichstag swiftly and passed by the Bundesrat, reforms which were constitutional changes. The Chancellor was made responsible to the Reichstag; military power was subjected to civil authority. Although the incompatibility between holding office and parliamentary mandate had been circumvented, it was nevertheless maintained, though again circumvented by Article 21. The new Article 11 of the Constitution made the decision for war and peace dependent on the agreement of both Reichstag and Bundesrat. A Chancellor could be dismissed by a vote of no confidence of the Reichstag. The Kaiser's actions, including his power of military command, required the Chancellor's counter-signature. Appointment, transfer, promotion or dismissal of officers required the counter-signature of the War Minister of the corresponding member Land of the German Empire. Also the long-fought-over reform of the franchise in Prussia was quickly achieved. The three-class franchise was abolished, and Prussia divided into new constituencies which resulted in more equitable representation. Alsace-Lorraine was a problem, since many of its inhabitants had come to support the allies because of their victories, while others, previously moderate, became radicals in the German cause. According to the Chancellor, Alsace-Lorraine was now to become a full member state of the Empire. He gauged feelings correctly by pointing out that the question was not 'German or French' but 'Independent or French' and he believed that Alsace would decide in favour of independence. The deputies from Alsace-Lorraine in the Reichstag asked for the proclamation of an independent state, but agreement was difficult to reach as some members wanted it to be returned to France while others preferred to wait and see. In the military sphere the Chancellor bore the responsibility before the Reichstag for all actions of the Kaiser. All important matters required his counter-signature or that of the Minister of War; this applied to the OHL as much as to the SKL. The question of the General Staff was a tricky one, because the General Staff was not *de jure* an executive but a planning organ. Hence both Hindenburg and Scheüch argued for the inviolability of the General Staff. The Chancellor decided to postpone his decision on this matter for the time being. Consequently in constitutional terms, in spite of the changes, by 28 October 1918 the General Staff and the *Seekriegsleitung* still remained independent agencies. Bavaria, Prussia, Saxony and Württemberg put the administration of their military contingents under the direct responsibility of the Reichstag and Bundesrat. This increased the constitutional importance of the four war ministers. Both the Military Cabinet and the Naval Cabinet were subjected to their respective ministers, losing their autonomous position, a position which the army had managed to preserve for over a century.

Gradually the war emergency laws were relaxed especially over press censorship. Widespread amnesties for political offences were granted, a process which had already begun in the later summer. Two of its beneficiaries, Karl Liebknecht and Kurt Eisner, were to show little gratitude. The commanders of military districts had their powers curtailed, now only being able to act in agreement with the Chancellor or a deputy determined by him. Laws regulating public assemblies were relaxed; prohibitions were only admissable if an assembly violated the penal code, or if it advocated war, the breaking of peace, or the disruption of public order. Press censorship was also eased.

These reforms, far from defusing the atmosphere, produced new tensions at a time of rapid organization of a variety of revolutionary groupings, prominent among them the USPD, the Revolutionary Shop Stewards, and the Spartacus League. They had little chance as long as the military forces remained firmly in the hands of their commanders. Therefore the revolutionizing of the army at home was one of the main aims of these groups. It is an incontrovertible fact that revolution did not break out among the armies of the western front which fought a tenacious rearguard battle, but among the soldiers and sailors at home, in transport and supply units, most of whom had never heard a shot fired in anger. However, the defeats in the west from July/August 1918 onwards left their mark on the front-line troops, and even more so at home. Training became lax, food universally bad, an accumulation of minor grievances developed into an explosive core which gave the revolutionary movement its chance.

THE NAVAL MUTINY AND THE KAISER'S ABDICATION

The revolutionary movement clamoured for democratization only until it had been achieved and thereafter called for what amounted to emulating the Russian example. By peace was meant peace at any price in the naïve belief that once the guns were silent, Germans, Frenchmen, Britons, Americans, Belgians and so forth would embrace one another and celebrate the universal brotherhood of man. There were also more concrete issues like that of the Kaiser. It is one of the ironies and injustices of history that while men like Hindenburg and Ludendorff maintained their public esteem throughout most of Germany, once things went wrong it was the Kaiser who was blamed. Having pushed himself during the greater part of his reign too much into the limelight he now had to suffer the consequences. That the Kaiser had to go was a fairly widespread opinion by October 1918, but that did not as yet mean the end of the monarchy, although his son 'little Willy' was equally unpopular. Could the monarchy be saved by the Kaiser's abdication? As Max Weber put it, 'If he goes now without outside pressure, then he goes with honour and the chivalrous compassion of the nation is with him . . . I admit openly that I have considered the way he has reigned with dislike. But in the interest of the imperial institution I cannot want the Kaiser to end his reign in dishonour.' The Chancellor wrestled with himself until he concluded that abdication was the only means of saving the monarchy. Revolutionary agitation projected the Kaiser as the one and only obstacle to peace, and not only the Kaiser but the institution of monarchy itself. The Social Democratic party leaders were in favour of keeping the Kaiser or at least the monarchy in spite of having professed republican creeds in the past. Wilson's notes escalated the issue of the Kaiser and resulted in revolutionary mass rallies demanding an end to his rule and to the monarchy. At first the Chancellor planned a regency, until the eldest son of the Crown Prince came of age, but illness prevented him from pursuing the plan further. On 29 October 1918 the Kaiser made his own decision by returning to Great Headquarters at Spa, where he felt more secure than in the revolutionary atmosphere of Berlin, without consulting the Chancellor. In the cabinet it was Scheidemann who on the same day said that the majority of public opinion expected they would get better peace terms if the Kaiser abdicated. Opinion in the cabinet was divided. The Chancellor adopted the position that abdication was up to Wilhelm himself. It could only be voluntary and this would preserve the Reich and army from any damage. Yet it was no longer a question of a voluntary decision: the Wilson notes, the pressure of the political parties, all this limited the area of free choice. As Scheüch put it, 'The abdication is an issue of force and remains one of force', meaning that whatever the Kaiser's decision, it was one made under duress.

The deliberations in Spa were overshadowed by one unexpected event, the mutiny of the German High Seas Fleet. The Supreme Naval Command had opposed the cessation of submarine warfare but in the end had been forced to give in. Hence since the beginning of October the High Seas Fleet had regained its operational freedom and Admiral Franz von Hipper had begun to plan a major operation in the North Sea. Initial suggestions of attacking the British naval forces in Scapa Flow were dismissed in favour of an operation into the Channel which would also support the German rearguard fighting in Flanders. Hipper had completed his plans by 24 October and on 27 October received the assent of Admiral Scheer at the Great Headquarters. As the French historian Charles Vidil, the first to publish the plan, points out, the German battleships and their reconnaissance forces, by their attack on the coast of Flanders and the mouth of the Thames, would force the main British fleet to leave Scapa Flow. On its long journey south it was intended that it should suffer heavily near the German Bight (the south-east corner of the North Sea) from newly-laid minefields and U-boats. It was hoped this would bring about a German victory. Both fleets were expected to meet at the tip of the Dutch island of Terschelling. Were the British to take evasive action the Germans did not intend pursuit: only torpedo and U-boats were to attack the returning Royal Navy units by night. Provisions were made for the return of the German forces: special sea lanes had been cleared by German minesweepers to allow a safe return into German bights and harbours.

It was not by any means a 'death or glory ride', a suicidal venture of the German navy to perish 'in honour'. If that had been true they could have made straight for Scapa Flow. Instead it was intended that the one force which was still completely intact should bring its full potential to bear on to the rearguard battle in Flanders. This planned action has often – mistakenly – been described as the 'Admirals Mutiny' against the new constitutional arrangements in operation in Germany, an opinion which even the earliest chronicler of the Weimar Republic, the former communist Arthur Rosenberg, has rejected. Scheer and his Chief of Staff Magnus von Levetzow submitted the basic outline of the plan to the Kaiser on 18 October. They emphasized that with the abandonment of submarine warfare the High Seas Fleet had regained its operational freedom and no longer needed to hold back. The Kaiser assented. The Chancellor was informed on identical lines and as a former general he must have fully understood the implications of 'operational freedom'. But he raised no objection or queries about the measures to be taken. He was not surprised when he heard of the outbreak of the naval mutiny, nor did he then express any disapproval of the admirals. In a proclamation of 4 November, signed also by the State Secretary of the Reich Naval Office, Vice-Admiral Ernst von Mann, and by Scheidemann, the Chancellor declared that the officers of the navy were loyal to the government and the accusation that they had abandoned it or were intending to do so was unjustified.

It is true that there was a good deal of loose talk among many officers on the German High Seas Fleet about a 'death or glory ride', 'a fight to the finish even if we perish' and similar rhetorical nonsense, hardly conducive to settling the minds of the crews now that the end of the war was in sight. Whether they would have reacted differently if the plans had been outlined to them must remain open to question. In any event the revolt on board the ships of the High Seas Fleet began. The leadership of this quickly passed into the hands of members of the USPD or sailors associated with it and was ultimately directed against the government. Naval crews took over their harbour towns such as Kiel, and naval officers, who resisted the removal of the imperial flag from their ships and its replacement by the red flag of the revolution, were killed. There was little the government could do except to send Secretary of State Conrad Haussmann and the Social Democrat Gustav Noske to Kiel. They immediately began negotiations with the soldiers' and workers' councils, which had just been formed; this amounted to a *de facto* recognition of the revolution. But Noske was seen to have acted very positively in trying to bring under control what he himself judged as a mutiny, and he was therefore appointed governor of Kiel.

In the meantime the problems of the Kaiser's position had not been resolved. On 1 November the Kaiser rejected the idea of abdication since it would be the beginning of the end for all the German monarchies – ironically enough it was not the Hohenzollerns but the Bavarian House of Wittelsbach that was to fall first. He rejected the idea of a regency. Both Hindenburg and Groener supported the Kaiser wholeheartedly. Various other plans were discussed but in due course dismissed. Berlin was also reaching crisis point with the Russian Soviet envoy supporting the radicals with money and propaganda. Groener arrived in this cauldron on 5 November and, sizing up the situation, he stated that the home front would ruin the army if there were no drastic changes. The foundation of the 'stab-in-the-back' legend had been laid. Ebert was in favour of a regency but Groener would have none of it, a mistake which he later regretted when he realized that his refusal caused the Majority Socialists to turn towards the USPD. The SPD now demanded the Kaiser's abdication within twenty-four hours. Chancellor Max von Baden replied by submitting his immediate resignation. This put the Kaiser as well as the SPD under pressure. The Chancellor supported the Kaiser's abdication and advised the calling of elections for a constituent assembly. The cabinet was also in favour of abdication as the only way to avert civil war in Germany. The Kaiser at first decided to return to Berlin at the head of his troops to restore order, but this idea was quashed by the news that King Ludwig III of Bavaria had abdicated during the night of 7 – 8 November, leaving by the back door of the royal residence in Munich with a box of his favourite brand of cigars under his arm. On the evening of 8 November both Hindenburg and Groener decided that any action by the army inside Germany would be senseless. Fully-fledged revolution then followed in Berlin; army units, even élite ones, were no longer reliable and the Majority Socialists left the cabinet. In order to decide the future of the Kaiser frontline commanders were consulted. They replied by expressing loyalty to him, but added that the army was now tired and wanted peace: it would not march against the revolutionaries at home, not even if the Kaiser led it. It was the end of the monarchy. The Kaiser was constitutionally still Supreme War Lord, but the declaration of the frontline commanders amounted to nothing less than that the army no longer considered him as such. They would obey their generals on the way home, but no further. The final decision leading to the Kaiser's abdication is surrounded by too much intricate controversy to be detailed here. But Groener's report from Berlin and the report of the frontline commanders, as well as Groener's blunt conclusion to the Kaiser that he no longer enjoyed the confidence of the army, were the decisive elements. By 2 o'clock in the afternoon of 9 November Secretary of State von Hintze announced the abdication of the Kaiser, while two hours before the Chancellor had already instructed the well-known newsagency Wolff to publish the news of the abdication in Germany. The Chancellor realized that none of his previous ideas could be carried out and he therefore decided to hand over office to Ebert, the leader of the Majority Socialists, who together with his party had joined the revolution in Berlin. Ebert is said to have been reluctant to accept office ('I hate revolution') but on the other hand he had to contend with the extremism of the USPD and other left-wing radical groups and therefore preferred to keep control in the hands of the Majority Socialists. Revolutionary attempts now swept through Germany and incapacitated the German political leadership, particularly in their relations with the allies. Had Germany maintained a defensive position on her western frontiers, in Churchill's words

'ready also if all negotiations were refused to defend herself to the utmost, and capable of inflicting two million casualties upon the invader, it seemed, and seems, almost certain that she would not have been put to the test . . . In the lull and chill of the winter with the proud foe suing for terms and with all his conquests already abandoned, a peace by negotiation was inevitable. Even in this last phase Germany need not have placed herself in the appalling position of yielding to the discretion of those upon whom she had inflicted the utmost injuries of hate . . . The faithful armies were beaten at the front and demoralized from the rear.

Germany, torn apart by internal strife, left the allies in the position of sole arbiters of her future.

THE PROCLAMATION OF THE REPUBLIC AND THE INSTITUTIONS OF THE 'REVOLUTION'

The span of time between the departure of the last imperial government and the coming into force of the Weimar Constitution was an interregnum, in which the administrative organs of the November Revolution dominated the political landscape. As in Russia the soviets, or councils, appeared everywhere. Firstly there was the *Executive Council*, made up mainly of Berlin's workers' and soldiers' councils, which failed to enforce its claim to exercise control over all the other councils in Germany. Represented in it were Majority Socialists, the USPD and members of the Spartacus League. The successor government formed with its agreement was called the *Council of People's Deputies*. Its chairman, Ebert, to tame the left, drew in the USPD members, Emil Barth, Dittmann and Haase, while Otto Landsberg and Scheidemann together with Ebert represented the Majority Socialists. On 9 November Scheidemann proclaimed the Republic in order to steal a march on radicals like Ledebour and Karl Liebknecht who made the same proclamation from the balcony of the Berlin *Schloss*. Ebert was also quick to ensure himself of the support of the army by leaving its control in the hands of the OHL, while the army via Groener promised to back the government. The Kaiser decided to seek refuge in Holland. His wish was granted and he formally abdicated on 28 November. The alliance between the army and Social Democracy was a marriage of convenience, a temporary arrangement for the attaining of specific goals which, once achieved, would leave the way open for separation. It was an alliance burdened on both sides by many prejudices and reservations. It has once more become fashionable to resurrect Arthur Rosenberg's interpretation to the effect that this alliance sealed the fate of the Republic. Those who support this argue that in the first six months of its life there was an alternative to restoration or revolution, namely a national assembly called by free elections in conjunction with the continuation of the workers' and soldiers' councils. Such a fusion would have allowed it successfully to transform the social foundations of the Reich and to democratize it.

This 'writing-desk perspective' sounds attractive enough but lacks a realistic assessment of the situation at the time. Whether one considers the Council of People's Deputies, the Central Council, or the Constituent National Assembly, their members did not work in a political vacuum without external pressures, which would have allowed experiments with various alternatives. The question that must be asked is whether in this atmosphere of civil war there was a third alternative between a Red Army and a *Reichswehr* for whose leadership the officers of the old army were required. Posing this question in order to judge the problem of the social revolution that had not happened, reduces it to an either/or situation: either a social revolution in league with the forces aiming at a proletarian revolution, or a parliamentary Republic allied to conservative elements such as the officer corps. The experiment of a third solution was and remains a phantom divorced from Germany's geographic, political and foreign policy situation. In view of the attitude being adopted then by the allies towards Bolshevik Russia it is more than doubtful that they would have remained mere observers of the German revolutionary spectacle. Wilson in fact would grant Ebert's request for food supplies from overseas only on the explicit condition that no revolutionary government would be allowed in Germany.

Furthermore, another reservation must be made. It is quite wrong to speak of a Council Movement in Germany. What it amounted to was a multitude of uncoordinated workers' and soldiers' councils, with widely differing and often mutually exclusive aims. What happened in Berlin's councils was of little relevance to those in Munich, as both were of little relevance to what took place in Stuttgart, Dresden or elsewhere. In addition the division of the revolution at first by the revolutionary mass movement, followed by a second purely proletarian attempt, is purely artificial. It is an after-the-event construction which seems to have been fathered by Trotsky's *History of the Bolshevik Revolution*. One cannot speak of the Council Movement as a single effectively-acting entity: for many of its members the first phase was tactically conditioned and included the second phase. But this does not apply to all councils, any more than does the assertion that it was the aim of the councils to replace party pluralism by a councils' dictatorship. Revolutionary radicalism was a matter of minor groupings dispersed throughout Germany. One cannot speak of a 'German Revolution'. Any analysis shows that Germany with its particularist and federal traditions lacked an epicentre for a revolution. In highly centralized states like France or Britain what happens in their respective capitals tends to affect the whole of the country. In 1918–19 as in 1848–49 such an epicentre was lacking in Germany, and events in Berlin had little effect on what happened, for argument's sake, in south-western Germany. There were a series of attempts at revolution throughout Germany, but these were entirely uncoordinated, differing in style and aims, moderate in Baden and in Württemberg, radical in Berlin, later in Munich and Dresden. This also explains the relative ease with which the central power liquidated the revolutionary attempts by force once it had decided to do so.

In order to exercise greater influence over the government on 16 December, the Executive Council called a gathering of the delegates of workers' and soldiers' councils. This led to the third revolutionary institution, the *General Congress of Workers' and Soldiers' Councils*, in which the Social Democrats had the majority. It could have become a revolutionary parliament but its most significant decision was to vote in favour of the election of a German Constitutional Assembly – despite the protest of radicals like Karl Liebknecht.

A fourth provisional agency was called into being, the *Central Council*, to supervise closely the activities of the provisional government. In effect it replaced the Executive Council, though this institution continued until the elections to the National Assembly. Thus in the interim period a four-sided struggle for power emerged, consisting of SPD, USPD, the Spartacus League and the army. Each of the Marxist parties divided into right and left wings, whereby the left wing of the SPD and right wing of the USPD and the left wing of the USPD and the right wing of Spartacus were closer to one another than to the other wings of their parties. In practical terms this meant six socialist currents against only two alternatives: parliamentary democracy or socialist revolution. It was the army which ultimately tilted the scales towards moderation.

THE ROLE OF THE ARMY

In November 1918, however, the army was still an unknown quantity. It withdrew in exemplary order from the occupied territories and from the left bank of the Rhine according to the terms of the armistice signed on 11 November. It was the army that had suffered serious reverses in the west but not a decisive defeat, an army which had not laid down its arms but taken them home, an army aware that the war could no longer be won, but nevertheless conscious of the fact that as yet it had not been beaten. They were tired of the war, as were their opponents, the Americans apart, and they had no objections to returning home. The OHL and the General Staff had remained unscathed. not a single signature of a German General adorned the armistice document. After the Kaiser's abdication only Hindenburg's orders counted in the army. They were obeyed up to a point – once the frontline troops reached their home garrisons they quickly dispersed and dissolved. It seemed as though the Ebert–Groener alliance of 19 November could not be honoured by the army for lack of troops, a fact demonstrated when army units were deployed to disperse revolu-

253

tionary upheavals in Berlin on Christmas Eve. The forces deployed were either passive or made common cause with the revolutionaries. From this moment the *Freikorps* was born, but another factor contributed to it as well. Article XII of the armistice compelled the German army in the east to hold their positions there until recalled by the allies, i.e. until they could be replaced by allied forces which were intended to intervene against Soviet Russia. But they would have none of it and flooded back, via the Baltic countries, to Germany. The allies suspected a conspiracy between the Germans and the Russians and threatened to impose sanctions. In point of fact it was the soldiers' council at Libau in Courland which first called for the creation of voluntary formations, of *Freikorps*, to hold back the Bolsheviks who were close on the heels of the retreating Germans; furthermore the new Poland threatened to make serious inroads into German territories. A military force was needed to suppress the revolutionary movements at home, to secure the eastern frontier and to replace the forces in the Baltic countries vacated by the German 8th Army. The OHL looked rather sceptically at *Freikorps* but there was no other solution. Recruiting-posters on behalf of the provisional government went up all over Germany calling for volunteers, and there was a particularly gratifying response from all over Germany calling for young soldiers and officers. Irrespective of later quarrels it was essentially due to the *Freikorps* that Lithuania, Latvia and Estonia also gained and maintained their independence. They drastically suppressed the revolutionary movements in Germany, notably in Bavaria. Here after the assassination of Kurt Eisner, whose party had already been rejected by the Bavarian electorate, a Soviet Republic was established and bloody terror prevailed. The *Freikorps* suppressed the Soviet Republic without much regard for the bloodshed caused, but the soviet experience radicalized political opinion in Bavaria so that it became a hotbed of counter-revolution and a refuge for nationalist revolutionaries. Without that background the emergence and rise of Adolf Hitler would have been unthinkable.

The Council of the People's Deputies enjoyed *de facto* dictatorial powers, while the directives of the Executive Council were generally ignored. The former gained this power essentially because the majority of the German people recognized it, backed as it was by the army and the administrative institutions of the former Empire. It was not only an executive but also a legislative organ. It made full use of the emergency powers contained in the Bismarckian Constitution, though formally this constitution was now a dead letter. It did not dissolve the Reichstag, but in effect eliminated it while the Bundesrat's functions were reduced to purely administrative ones. Within the Council Ebert was responsible for internal and military affairs; external affairs, justice and colonies were looked after by Haase, and Finance by Scheidemann who was succeeded by Landsberg on 19 November;

Dittmann was responsible for demobilization and communications, Landsberg for press and information, succeeded on 19 November by Scheidemann, and Barth for social policy. One of the Council's first actions was to lift the state of siege which had prevailed since the outbreak of war. Bavaria under Eisner insisted on maintaining and expanding the special rights it had possessed under the Empire. It argued that the Central Council had no right to lift the state of siege there and therefore it continued in Bavaria. For the rest of Germany its lifting meant the reintroduction of full civil liberties. Censorship of the press and the theatre was ended; freedom of religion was guaranteed and a general political and military amnesty proclaimed. Most of the emergency war legislation was lifted and the workers' protection legislation, which had been suspended during the war, reintroduced.

THE COMPROMISE STRUCTURE

During the early phase significant concessions by Ebert had already been made. The first has already been mentioned, the Ebert–Groener pact which safeguarded the army from undue interference by revolutionary organs. A second compromise, concluded on 15 November concerned the question of nationalization of industries and employer-employee relationships by the creation of the Central Working Party between the major industries represented by the industrialist Hugo Stinnes and the Social Democrat Carl Legien who represented the employees. This working party for a short time in effect removed not only the problem of nationalization but a whole sector of social legislation from the government into its own hands. An essential problem of a new pluralist power structure, the re-ordering of the distribution of social and economic power, was left in the hands of the respective interest groups. A third compromise of a later phase (26 February 1919) meant that the provisional government abandoned attempts at a more unitary restructuring of the Reich, making allowances for Germany's historical traditions. The first compromise, by the cooperation of the parties which had represented the Reichstag majority since the peace resolution of 1917, sanctioned a large element of continuity by combating revolutionary attempts and ultimately stabilized the state by means of the Weimar Coalition, the result of the elections to the National Assembly.

Continuity was preserved in the administration of the Reich: the civil servants who had loyally served the Kaiser largely served the Weimar Republic with equal loyalty, as they were to serve the Third Reich. Thorough reforms were carried out only at Land level, notably in Prussia, where the Social Democrats under Otto Braun overhauled the entire administrative and executive apparatus. The central administrative and executive offices of the Empire were retained; secretaries of state now became ministers, and parliamentary under-secretaries were introduced.

The first major decision of the provisional government had been to agree to an armistice. This looked rather different from its projected form on the basis of Wilson's fourteen points. But the disarray at home did not allow any resistance it was accepted upon the advice of the army and it amounted to unconditional surrender. To carry it out on the allied side there was the International Permanent Armistice Commission, on the German side the German Armistice Commission. The armistice was a limited one and was renewed periodically until the peace treaty was signed. In view of the internal unrest there was little reaction to the severe armistice conditions imposed by the allies. The German public only woke up when the conditions of peace were made known in May 1919. Another immediate problem at home concerned the army, in which the soldiers' councils had advocated radical changes. The OHL had accepted the introduction of councils in the field army, where they proved an asset in facilitating speedy and disciplined withdrawal. This was not the case at home since they advocated measures similar to those introduced in the Red Army in Russia. The so-called 'Hamburg Points' included the removal of officers' epaulettes. Ebert was in a dilemma, formally endorsing the demands but informally obstructing them until the time came when soldiers' councils would be obsolete. The majority of soldiers' councils in the field army opposed government by councils and at Bad Ems on 1 December 1918 unanimously supported Ebert, and the election of a National Assembly.

COUNCILS OR PARLIAMENT?

The months of November 1918 to January 1919 were dominated by the call for 'All Power to the Councils' on the one side and by the demand for elections for a National Assembly on the other. The Executive Committee called for a General Councils' Congress, while the provisional Reich government called for a Reich conference of all German Lands for 25 November. Delegates from twenty-three out of the twenty-five Lands attended, to be addressed by Ebert who pleaded for the call for elections to a Constituent National Assembly. He gained the support of the conference but at the expense of a unitary solution for the structure of the Reich. Secretary of State Solf submitted a report about the external situation and insisted upon strong executive powers for the provisional government. This demand was misunderstood and Solf found himself compelled to affirm his loyalty to the Republic publicly. But the controversy was not over and a few weeks later he had to resign. However, Solf's call for the quick election of a National Assembly was accepted. Scheidemann warned the conference of the consequences of establishing a Councils' Republic: it would mean allied intervention in Germany. Against that background the USPD's protests were rejected. But in calling the elections two problems had to be solved first. German Austria had declared itself a constituent part of the German Republic, and provision was made for its deputies in the National Assembly. However, the allies vetoed this measure. Alsace-Lorraine was included as the thirty-eighth constituency, with the reservation that Germany did not wish to preempt the decisions of the peace treaty. In fact the French prohibited elections in Alsace-Lorraine, nor did they allow its former Reichstag members to attend the National Assembly.

The active franchise was given to all men *and women* of 20 years of age and over, the passive franchise to all those who had been German citizens for at least a year. While this problem was being solved, that of military reform came to the fore again. Social Democrats and USPD called for a Republican army, but the project ultimately failed because there were not enough republicans willing to bear arms, a legacy of the pre-war 'anti-militarist' propaganda of SPD's left wing, the Spartacus groups and the pacifist societies. Therefore they had to make do with the soldiers there were. Moreover, such 'Republican' forces as came into existence proved to be a nest of unrest and unreliability, which posed more of a threat to the provisional government than a safeguard. The return of the frontline troops into Berlin seemed to promise stabilization. Ebert greeted them with 'Im Felde unbesiegt' – unvanquished on the battlefield – which tallied with the view of those returning. But, as already mentioned, once home from the front they wanted to return to their families and this in turn led to the formation of the *Freikorps*.

Lastly there was the problems of the Reichstag. Should it continue or had its role ended? The Reichstag President, the Centre deputy Konstantin Fehrenbach, pointed out the dangers, particularly in the context of imminent peace negotiations, of a Reichstag not being in session, plus the danger that the absence of a representative assembly posed for the unity of the Reich. Elections ought to be held as soon as possible. The provisional government decided in favour of this. At the same time Secretary of State Solf had been forced to resign. On 5 December 1918 he had broken off diplomatic relations with Russia when German police discovered masses of propaganda material which the Soviet embassy in Berlin intended to hand over to the USPD and the Spartacus League. The USPD therefore demanded his resignation as he was an obstacle to good Russo-German relations. However, the former Soviet ambassador, Joffe, publicly confirmed the delivery of propaganda material plus arms and weapons purchased (he supplied details of number and types of weapons, and the quantity of ammunition). He added that the quantity of weapons bought and handed over to the USPD member Barth was far in excess of what he had bought for export to Russia. Moreover Barth had been supplied with several hundred thousand marks from Soviet funds. Barth tried to talk himself out of it but finally made an implicit admission. Solf was nevertheless replaced by the former German envoy in Copenhagen, Count Ulrich von Brockdorff-Rantzau. War Minister Scheüch also resigned because of the continuous propaganda of the radicals against the army and the alleged failure of the government to prevent it. He was replaced by Colonel, later General, Walther Reinhardt, a Württemberger like Groener.

The General Congress of Soldiers' and Workers' Councils in Berlin produced a good deal of revolutionary rhetoric, but no practical results, despite its crucial majority vote in favour of electing a Constituent National Assembly. One quick-witted Berlin delegate labelled the radical propagators of a 'council system' as 'the Pan-Germans of the German revolution'. As the election date was settled for the 19 January 1919, the provisional government could be satisfied, but not the revolutionary elements, particularly in Berlin. Here they tried to reverse the decision by force of arms. After initial successes, particularly in Berlin, volunteer formations re-established order there in the course of which Karl Liebknecht and Rosa Luxemburg were callously murdered. To escape the chaos of Berlin the provisional government decided to hold the first session of the National Assembly at Weimar. Simultaneously it used decrees to make great strides in social legislation, in the realm of wage negotiations, workers' representatation in factories, and arbitration procedures in cases of labour conflict, in cooperation with the Stinnes-Legien Committee. Church and State were formally separated, and in place of the Prince or King as Supreme Head of the Church, the administrative functions of this task were transfered to state offices. The influence of the churches in the educational system was curbed, though in Prussia signs of misuse for the political purposes by the SPD soon became evident. These measures, though general in character, varied in application from Land to Land.

The first confrontation between the revolutionary forces, notably the People's Naval Division, and the government, when regular troops were used unsuccessfully, had led to the break-up of the coalition between the SPD and the USPD. Barth, Dittmann and Haase left the government and were replaced by the Majority Socialists, Gustav Noske, Rudolf Wissell and Paul Löbe. Noske's inclusion was the most important. He had made his reputation in Kiel and was now entrusted with military affairs and thus became associated and deeply involved not only with the *Freikorps* but with the rebuilding of the German army as a whole. In Reinhardt as Minister of War he had a willing and dedicated cooperator. Both successfully prevented the execution of the 'Hamburg Points' which, among other things, aimed at the transfer of power of command from the army to the soldiers' councils at local level and the abolition of military insignia of rank.

THE PARTIES OF THE REPUBLIC

It would take a separate volume to detail the re-establishment of governmental authority throughout Germany. Therefore, before discussing the Weimar Constitution, we shall have to turn to the reorganization of the party-political spectrum in Germany. Here, except for a few changes and the emergence of the Communist Party, on the whole there was continuity with the Empire. Essentially the five-party system as it had emerged prior to 1848 was maintained. The National Conservative Right, essentially agragrian orientated, was joined by numerous other right-wing bodies and became the DNVP, the German National People's Party; there was the Catholic Centre, with its Bavarian off-spin the Bavarian People's Party, the BVP; the National Liberal Centre backed by industry became the DVP, the German People's Party; the Democratic-Liberal Left, many of them former Progressives, became the DDP, the German Democratic Party; and finally there were the Social Democrats, including the USPD. The DNVP had initially lost much of its actual and potential membership as a result of the defeat. In the Empire the Conservatives had never acted as a permanent government party. Depending on the issues at stake they opposed every Chancellor from Bismarck to Bethmann Hollweg and to Max von Baden; their criticism had extended to the Kaiser himself. Its members came from the Junker landowners and higher civil servants of the Prussian bureaucracy. In the war they had advocated a fight to the finish and were thus branded with the label of imperialists, annexationists and militarists. Obviously they had to brush up their image and on 16–19 December 1918 they announced their first party political programme as the DNVP. They appealed to the national and liberal middle classes to 'regenerate national pride, Germany's position in the world, private enterprise, social progress, Christian education and freedom of conscience'. The party encompassed German Conservatives, Free Conservatives, Christian Socialists, German Socialists and the German Reform Party. The former Prussian State Minister Oskar Hergt was elected as their first chairman. They realized that they had little chance of winning sufficient votes in the immediate post-war elections to participate in government. Instead they tried jointly with the other middle-class parties to prevent a socialist majority and to exert their influence in the drafting of the new constitution.

Basically the Centre Party was also a conservative party. Originally Bismarck's *Reichsfeinde*, after 1879 they had quickly integrated into the Empire. Their one liability was Matthias Erzberger who had proved so flexible and unprincipled. Nevertheless he was the man who on 13 and 14 November 1918 had begun to create a new central party apparatus of the kind which the Centre had never had before. There were rivalries between the group in Berlin and that in Cologne in which the Mayor of Cologne, Konrad Adenauer, played no small role, but they were over minor issues which were soon settled. Its strategy was one of adaptation and resistance. It maintained its position with great tactical flexibility, and in Bavaria, under the soviet regime, it was one of its most hard-headed opponents. By the end of December 1918 its first chairman Adolf Gröber conducted a session of the Reich Committee (also a creation of Erzberger) which included women deputies for the first time. It demanded the unity of Germany and the maintenance of its federal structure. It conceded to the Reich Executive decision over matters of military and foreign policy, while it held that it would be up to the federal states to regulate church, state and educational questions. 'Greater Germany' was still their ideal, as well as the demand for colonies. While insisting on the sanctity of private property it also held that it should be subordinated to the common weal. Furthermore it sponsored a land resettlement policy on property formerly part of state domains, and uneconomic large landholdings. High income groups were to be taxed heavily, especially war profiteers. In place of revolution it wanted evolution. Its Bavarian branch, the BVP, agitated with the slogan 'Bavaria for the Bavarians', protesting against the vast migration of labour from central Germany into Bavaria, a by-product of Bavaria's growing pre-war industrialization. Its federalism was closer to particularism and there was also a strong monarchist streak in it, concentrated on Crown Prince Rupprecht of Bavaria.

The Liberals had a more difficult position, coming as they did from left wing supporters and the National Liberals. To the founders of the Liberal Party a National Liberal like Stresemann was not liberal enough and he was therefore excluded. Nor did they have a precise programme on hand. Among signatories to a call for a new Liberal Party were National Liberals like Johannes Junck, left-wing liberals like Heinrich Dove, and a number of others who had hitherto stood outside politics like Albert Einstein, the publisher Rudolf Mosse, the brilliant journalist Theodor Wolff, who edited one of Mosse's papers, the *Berliner Tageblatt*, the financial expert banker Hjalmar Schacht, Otto Nuschke (later to become Foreign Minister of the DDR) and others. On 20 November they founded the DDP but could not agree, generalities apart, on a common programme. The lack of a clear programme, of unanimity and inner unity was far more the cause of their decline, than was the general decline of liberalism in Germany.

The German People's Party was founded by the former National Liberals, Gustav Stresemann, Robert Friedberg and Paul Vogel, all men who had made their name during the Empire. They endeavoured to continue National Liberal policies under changed circumstances, supported Austria's *Anschluss*, as well as the League of Nations, and demanded colonies. They tended towards laissez-faire individualism in economic affairs, and on the whole enjoyed the support of the industrialists. The DVP did not welcome the revolution but accepted it as a fact.

The central issue for the Socialists was revolution or reform, an issue over which, as we have already seen, they were divided. The Majority Socialists, the SPD were in full agreement with Prince Max von Baden's reform programme: they saw no need for reorientation and reconstruction. After the revolution they affirmed their belief in 'democratic socialism' and a 'democratic republic', but even they did not want to leave the word 'Reich' out of the constitution. They opposed the dictatorial tendencies of the extreme Left.

Among the Independents, the USPD, the differences over which way the party should move were extremely pronounced. The Radicals leaned heavily on the Spartacus group of Liebknecht and Rosa Luxemburg and wanted nothing more or less than to emulate Lenin's revolutionary proletarian dictatorship, while the Right leaned more towards the SPD. USPD moderates and radicals were equally represented within the party committee. Both groups were at one in their aim to conquer the power of the state for the proletariat.

The extreme left, embodied in the Spartacus League, had fought at first within the ranks of ths USPD, but then it reconstituted itself into a separate group which produced the Communist Party, the KPD, on 1 January 1919. There is ample evidence to show that they were financed and armed by the Russians, and they soon moved into direct opposition to the Majority Socialists. They aimed at creating a soviet republic, restricting the franchise to the working population, without any clear definition of how this was to be done. Among the early members, apart from Rosa Luxemburg and Karl Liebknecht, were Wilhelm Pieck (who when arrested with Liebknecht and Luxemburg probably saved his own life by providing extensive information to his interrogator Captain Papst and was later to be the first President of the German Democratic Republic (DDR), Leo Jogiches, Paul Levi, Otto Rüble and Paul Fröhlich.

THE ELECTIONS OF JANUARY 1919

In the election of 19 January 1919 the main question was whether the socialist parties could obtain an overall majority (the KPD as a revolutionary party refused to take part). A record poll of 83 per cent produced a disappointing result. The Socialists won only 185 seats, out of 421, 22 of which were for the USPD. The only party openly in favour of a restoration of the monarchy, the DNVP, won only 44 seats; the DVP won 21, the Centre, including the BVP, 90, and the DDP 75, a figure the Liberals never reached again. In other words, in spite of the 'revolution', the bourgeois parties had gained the majority; the party political system of the Empire had been restored. That women voted for the first time had no significant effect on the outcome. The Majority Socialists accepted the verdict but they failed in their attempt to form a coalition with the USPD. The National Assembly met at Weimar on 6 Febrary 1919, and on the 13th of the same month a coalition cabinet comprising SPD, Centre and DDP was formed with Scheidemann as Chancellor. Other SPD members included Noske and Landsberg, while the Centre was represented by three members including Erzberger, and the DDP by Hugo Preuss and three other members. Brockdoff-Rantzau, who had no party affiliation, kept his office as Foreign Minister.

During this period until the middle of May all militant revolutionary activity was put down throughout Germany. At the same time the individual German states framed their own new constitutions, which were so similar to one another that they do not require discussion.

Within the newly elected German National Assembly the DNVP had 44 deputies. Compared with the elections of 1912 when there had been three conservative parties, they had lost about 30 per cent of their previous vote, while the DVP, the successor to the National Liberals, led by Stresemann, which now had 21 seats, had lost about 50 per cent. The Centre with 72 and the BVP with 18 seats had together almost the same number of seats as in the previous Reichstag. Until early 1920 the Centre and the BVP acted as one parliamentary party. On the surface continuity had been preserved within the Centre but the real focus of power in the party had shifted from the Right to the Left. Among the deputies returned were the former Centre leader Trimborn, Konstantin Fehrenbach and Wilhelm Marx. Gröber, the leader of the parliamentary party, tended towards the Left, as did Erzberger, the trade union leaders Heinrich Imbusch, Joseph Joos and Adam Stegerwald, as well as Ludwig Kaas, a Catholic priest. The DDP, with its impressive gains, was in a position of strength unprecedented for the Liberals since 1890. Among its members were the former Progressive, Vice-Chancellor von Payer, and the former National Socialist Liberal Friedrich Naumann. Former National Liberals included the Secretary of State Eugen Schiffer and the Chairman of the German Farmers' League, Wachhorst de Wente. At the same time members of the women's movement like Marie Baum, a social worker, and Gertrud Bäumer, schoolteacher and editor, were represented within its ranks, as was the German pacifist movement with Ludwig Quidde and Walther Schücking, an expert on international law. The leader of the parliamentary party until May 1920 was Payer, except for a short time when Schiffer took his place.

The Majority Socialists, who had 85 seats in the old Reichstag, returned to the National Assembly with double their strength. They were headed by Friedrich Ebert, who resigned this post and his parliamentary seat after his election as provisional Reich's President on 11 February 1919. Among the SPD members returned there were old and proven parliamentarians who had been in the Reichstag since 1890, among them Herman Molkenbuhr, Carl Legien, Scheidemann, Noske, Carl Severing, Otto Wels, Hermann Müller and many others. The USPD with its 22 seats had actually lost 2 seats. The parliamentary party leader Haase, the deputies Oskar Cohn, women such as Lore Agnes, a housewife, and Luise Zietz, a leader of the pre-war women's movement, were among the deputies. However, a number of prominent Independents, among them Eduard Bernstein, Dittmann, Hilferding, Kautsky, Ledebour and others were not even represented in the National Assembly.

The question of whether there was to be rule by the workers' and soldiers' councils or by the National Assembly had now been formally resolved. In practice, however, it was not resolved until the Ruhr rising of 1920, or for that matter not even until 1923. The Central Council of the German Socialist Republic handed over its powers to the National Assembly together with a number of suggestions for the future constitution, such as organizing Germany into a strong unitary state. The USPD and the extra-parliamentary Communists immediately accused them of treason against the workers' and soldiers' councils, a charge which the Central Council rejected.

The chairman of the Council of the People's Deputies, Friedrich Ebert, formally opened the first session of the National Assembly on 6 February 1919, handing over to it, as he described it, 'the mandate of the revolution'. He demanded self-determination for the German people and claimed this meant the unity of the Reich with German Austria, and that the National Assembly should draft a constitution which would provide Germany with a strong democracy permeated by a social spirit and socialist action. On the following day the National Assembly elected as presidial members, headed by the Majority Socialist Eduard David, Vice-President Konstantin Fehrenbach (Centre), Conrad Haussmann (DDP), and Hermann Dietrich (DNVP). A day later the Secretary of State of the Interior, Hugo Preuss, submitted a draft of a law for the provisional powers of the Reich which was passed two days later with the USPD opposing. Then the National Assembly unanimously agreed that the Council of the Peoples' Deputies should provisionally continue in office.

This law amounted to a provisional constitution and put an end to the period in which executive and legislative functions were united. It also, to a considerable degree, ignored the demands for a strong unitary state. The old and virtually extinct Budesrat was replaced by a Committee of States which was given access to the constitution-making process. The term 'Socialist Republic' was abolished as an official designation. The law of 10 February even avoided the word 'republic', though other official communications referred to the 'German Republic'. Constitutional power resided in the hands of the National Assembly; neither the Committee of States nor any of the individual German states had a vote, though they could make their influence felt during the deliberations. One fatal flaw, which was to have consequences until 1924, was that Bavaria, partly due to the state of confusion there, took no part in these deliberations. This was one reason why subsequent Bavarian governments until 1924 claimed they were not bound by the Constitution or its provisions. Legislative power lay solely within the hands of the National Assembly by virtue of the elections of 19 January. If the Committes of States had any objections it could submit them to the National Assembly. However, the former could veto any legislation passed and this veto could then be overridden by a plebiscite called by the Reich President. In fact this provision had no consequences and in time this power of veto was almost completely eroded. The rights and privileges of the deputies were very much the same as they had been under the old constitution, including the right to *Diäten*, i.e. to be paid for attendance. The 'business of the Reich' was transferred into the hands of the Reich President who was to be elected provisionally by an absolute majority of the National Assembly. His term of office was limited to the period yet to be stipulated in the future constitution. His powers included representing the Reich internationally, negotiating treaties and accrediting envoys, but the right to declare war as well as to make peace was put into the hands of the National Assembly and the Committee of States. A further transitional law of 4 March 1919 also endowed him with most of the powers which had previously been enjoyed by the Kaiser.

The law of 10 February appointed a Reich Ministry to conduct the business of the Reich. Its members were appointed by the Reich President but they had to have the confidence of the National Assembly to be able to carry out their duties. In that way the pre-parliamentarian procedure was fused with the parliamentary system. Nothing was said about who was to head the Reich Ministry, although provisionally the term Reich Minister President was introduced. Subject to this ministry were not only all Reich offices but also the OHL. The actions of the latter required the counter-signature of a minister and this again corresponded to the constitutional norms as established by the law of 28 October 1918. The power of supreme command over the armed forces was transferred to the Reich President.

The Reich President was to be elected on 11 February. The SPD felt strong enough to claim this office, though there was brief rivalry between Ebert and Scheidemann, which ended in Ebert's favour. Of 379 votes in the Assembly 277 members of the SPD, the Centre and the DDP voted for Ebert. As Reich President Ebert had to give up party politics, but he acquired powers rather wider than the first constitutional draft of Hugo Preuss had envisaged. Eduard David, the President of the National Assembly, greeted Ebert's election with the words, 'That the German revolution has not followed the Russian one, that bloody chaos and dissolution of law and order has not come about in Germany as in Russia . . . is to a great extent due to the efforts of the man whom you have elected to the head of the Reich.' Though there was no provision for it, Ebert swore an oath upon the constitution of the German Republic.

Negotiations about forming a government had already begun early in February between the SPD, the Centre and the DDP. The Centre was at first reluctant to participate because of the overwhelming majority of the SPD, but Erzberger overcame that reluctance. To appease its left wing as well as to exert pressure on the middle-class parties the SPD also entered negotiations for a coalition with the USPD, but the latter turned them down because the SPD provided no guarantee to secure the 'achievements' of the revolution against the bourgeoisie and military 'autocracy'. After Ebert's election the negotiations for a SPD, DDP and Centre coalition came to a speedy and successful conclusion. Secretaries of State now became Ministers and their offices Ministries with the exception of the *Auswärtige Amt*, the Foreign Office, which retained its traditional title. Of 15 ministers, 7 belonged to the SPD, 3 to the DDP, 3 to the Centre and 2 without party affiliation included the Foreign Minister, Count Brockdorff-Rantzau. Only four previous Secretaries of State lost their posts; on the whole continuity seemed to have prevailed.

A first budget, on a provisional basis as a supplementary budget to that of 1918, was passed; the new cabinet was given a vote of confidence by the National Assembly and a transitional law was enacted, as was the law concerning the provisional *Reichswehr*, for the period of constitutional deliberations. The transitional law gave legal *expost facto* sanction to the dictatorial decrees of the revolutionary period, while at the same time depriving the President of the right to dissolve the National Assembly. The law concerning the provisional *Reichswehr* was framed in ignorance of the peace conditions stipulated at Versailles. Since it was formulated and passed while the *Freikorps* were still establishing law and order in Germany, the government could be sure of middle-class support. *Reichswehr* Minister Noske defended the law with great eloquence. He only met opposition from the USPD whose deputy Oskar Cohn during the debate admitted having received money from the Soviet ambassador, Joffe, for party and revolutionary purposes early in November 1918. The law was accepted by a great majority and provided the basis for the future *Reichswehr*. Although the War Emergency Law of 1914 had been abolished, certain of its provisions were still maintained in view of the present state of Germany, such as the law to secure 'the feeding of the public'. Three Enabling Laws were passed, one concerning Alsace-Lorraine which was to provide aid to Germans and German Alsace-Lorrainers expelled by the French; the second concerning the execution of the armistice demands which gave the government far-reaching powers of intervention to carry out the armistice conditions. The third endeavoured to simplify the economic legislation necessary for the transition from a war to a peacetime economy. A number of old laws of the Empire remained in force for the time being, notably the law proclaiming the local state of siege as well as the regulation of 19 March 1914 concerning the use of arms by the army in case of internal upheaval. These laws were applied during the suppression of revolutionary attempts by the *Freikorps* and the provisional *Reichswehr*. Noske's *Schiesserlass* (shooting order) of 20 January 1919 was based on that regulation, but he handed the order over to the Chief of Staff of the *Gardekavalleriekorps*, Captain Papst, who rephrased it drastically and also ambivalently, thus causing up to the end of May 1919 a number of serious excesses by government troops. But Noske's order had the backing of the National Assembly and in fact remained on the statute-book until 1936.

THE WEIMAR CONSTITUTION

Initial discussion about the new constitution had already begun in December 1918 when the then Secretary of State of the Interior submitted his first constitutional draft to the Council of the People's Executive, which was formally completed by 3 January 1919. Its provisions aimed at a strong unitary state on a decentralized basis. It included Austria in its provisions and divided the Reich into sixteen provinces. The Reichstag was to have two chambers, a popular Diet as such and a *Staatenhaus* for the provinces. The President was to be popularly elected for a ten-year period of office. The Reich Cabinet was to be headed by a Chancellor responsible for laying down guidelines of overall policy. He was to have the power of appointment and dismissal of government and a temporary veto against legislation as well as to be entrusted with emergency powers. There were only three enumerated basic civil rights, equality before the law, liberty of faith and conscience, and protection of national minorities. Constitutional differences were to be settled ultimately by an independent State

Court, before which members of the government could be arraigned. This first draft was countered by a second which was also in favour of a strong unitary state, but the sixteen provinces were scrapped and Prussia was to be dissolved. The SPD, though in favour of a unitary state, opposed the dissolution of Prussia because its power base was there, and it feared that a redrawing of the constitutional boundaries would operate against the bases of its support. Although the participation of the German states in framing the constitution had not been envisaged, the government soon realized that it was essential to consult them, so as to achieve as broad a consensus as possible. Under Ebert's chairmanship twenty-five delegates of the Reich and its states assembled and set up a commission to discuss detailed questions. The consultation of the Committee of the States was not only a concession to but also a victory for the federal principle. Only Bavaria's delegate was hampered in the execution of his duty by the confusion in southern Germany and lack of any directives. However, he still spoke in favour of federalism and was backed by Prussia. Under the influence of the Committee of States a third draft evolved which made greater allowances for the federal principle. While the Reich could conduct foreign affairs, the individual German states maintained the right to conclude foreign treaties in cases which related to their own Land, such as a Concordat with the Holy See. While the Reich President was to have supreme command of the army, this was to be recruited within each German state from the German citizens residing there, the Reich only having supervisory powers. Bavaria, Saxony and Württemberg insisted on the restoration and expansion of the reserved powers which they had enjoyed during the Empire. Postal, railway and water communications were also to come within their competence. As far as territorial reforms were concerned, these should only affect the remaining minor enclaves which should be joined to existing larger states. In case of conflict over this issue the Reich was to arbitrate or even introduce legislation changing the constitution. The Bundesrat was now to be replaced by the Reichsrat, composed not of elected members but of members appointed by the states. If there was a conflict over legislation between Reichstag and Reichsrat, the former could introduce legislation changing the constitution or in the last resort call for a plebiscite.

Crucial in this third draft was the introduction of the new Reich's colours of black, red and gold, the colours of 1848. This automatically transformed the imperial colours of black, white and red into the colours of the right-wing opposition. Ultimately a compromise was reached over this issue. While the flag was to be black, red and gold internally, on the high seas it was to be black, white and red, with a small black, red and gold area in the upper corner of the flag. A number of other minor changes were made before the final draft was submitted to the Reichstag on 21 February 1919 by Hugo Preuss. He defended the maintenance of the term 'Reich' in place of 'republic', though in Paragraph 1 of the Constitution he had to concede the formula 'The German Reich is a Republic'. The SPD opposed the term Reich at first; also some of its members complained of the excessive concessions to the federal principle and above all the guarantee of private property which meant that the former princely and royal houses had to be paid compensation for any expropriation. They demanded new initiatives for the nationalization of key industries and economic enterprises. Although lack of central intervention in the realm of education was criticized, the Centre Party on the whole was satisfied with the draft. In the main the Centre only demanded further extension of religious rights and the recognition of religious communities as corporate bodies before the law. It affirmed the maintenance of the Reich, which would act as a brake on the new state after the demise of the monarchies. The DDP was of much the same opinion, but demanded greater emphasis on basic rights while at the same time underlining the necessity of driving home to the citizens not only their *rights* but also their *duties*.

The DNVP in opposing the constitution maintained that this document was not a foundation of German unity but a means for its gradual dissolution. The provisions for altering the constitution would have to be made easier since constitutions are living organisms necessary and subject to change. The DNVP also demanded the inclusion of unified principles concerning the relationship between church and schools, in which they were supported by the Centre and other minor political bodies. But the main issue was the new colours of the Reich. In spite of its opposition role the DNVP had made suggestions which after the first reading of the constitution were included when it was referred to the committee stage. Draft V was submitted to a second reading which led to conflict among the parties of the government coalition, especially over education issues, but a breach was avoided and on 29 July the final Draft VI was submitted to a third reading. A compromise over Reich and Republic mentioned above was reached, and over the colours of the Reich. The President was to be popularly elected for a period of seven years. If in the presidential elections none of the candidates managed to achieve an absolute majority, a second election would follow between the three candidates with the most votes. In this second election a simple majority would suffice for a candidate to win. Initially members of royal or princely houses were to be excluded from the presidency, but this clause was dropped because it would demonstrate a lack of self-confidence by the new democracy. The government would be conducted by a Reich Chancellor and his cabinet; within the cabinet majority decisions were binding. The Reichstag was to be elected on the basis of proportional representation for four years.

Three main questions may be asked in judging an electoral system. Is it numerically equitable? Does it produce close contact between constituencies and representatives? Does it jeopardize governmental stability? In the case of the Weimar Constitution only the first question can be answered in the affirmative: the other two merit a firm 'No'. A population of 65,000,000 was divided into 37 constituencies (compared with Great Britain where 47,000,000 inhabitants at the time had 610 constituencies). The average size of a German constituency was 1,700,000 inhabitants or 1,150,000 voters, hardly a size to foster contact between electorate and representative. These constituencies were then regrouped into sixteen conjoint constituencies (*Wahlverbände*); the average number of seats per constituency was fifteen. The parties put up a list of candidates; parties were named on the list since the voter was unlikely to know the party political affiliations by the name of the candidate alone. Each party was designated on the ballot paper by a number, which in turn was determined by the strength of the party in the last Reichstag. Thus at the beginning of the Weimar Republic No. 1 on the list was the SPD, from July 1932 the NSDAP. Electors had one vote each, which they had to enter on the ballot paper. A party was entitled to one member for each 60,000 votes. Surplus votes (say 20,000 in the case of 260,000 votes) were collected and aggregated within each of the sixteen conjoint constituencies, and again there was one seat for the party concerned for each 60,000. Surpluses of the conjoint constituencies were put together and ascribed to the *Reichslist*, i.e. the list of candidates each party put up for the whole of the Reich, and 60,000 again secured one mandate. If there was still a surplus left, 30,000 plus secured one mandate. Since there was no provision for by-elections each party drew up a list of substitutes who were to fill vacancies during a parliamentary session. Thus constituencies were large, the lists were lengthy, and there were no by-elections.

Prussia lost its dominance in the Reichsrat as it only had two fifths of the votes. Its elected delgates, like those of the previous Bundesrat, were subject to instruction by their respective governments, only Prussia allowing its delegates to make their own decisions.

There was a problem about the legislation for the Reich since southern Germany feared that its extension would interfere in their own legislative process. Again a compromise formula was found, which allowed legislation to be submitted to a national plebiscite. The President was granted the right to use exceptional powers in exceptional circumstances, such as the Reich Executive Action and temporary assumption of governmental powers based on the emergency powers clause of the constitution, Articles 48 and 49. If Article 49 were invoked seven basic rights could be suspended. But in its final version Articles 48 and 49 were fused into Article 48. This was to be further refined by executive laws which, however for reasons which we shall never know, were not drafted, let alone submitted to the Reichstag. Nor was a demand for them ever raised. The constitution also accepted the possibility of constitutional change, or the enactment of laws altering parts of it. Provisions for this were made in Article 76 which stipulated that a bill changing the constitution can only become law 'if two thirds of the legally required members [of the Reichstag] are present and at least two thirds of them vote in favour of it'. This provision was to have consequences in March 1933 which none of the members of the Constituent National Assembly could foresee in 1919. But, so it seems, two generations of historians and experts on constitutional law have never taken the trouble to read the Weimar Constitution thoroughly and hence have failed to realize the implications of this provision and the role it played in the context of Hitler's Enabling Law of 23 March 1933. Reams of paper have been spent on anaylsing the reasons why the Centre Party voted for it, volumes of monographs have been published on this subject, all of them as we shall see just so much waste paper because the fixation on Hitler's 'conspiracy' took precedence over reading what the Weimar Constitution actually stipulated.

The constitution contained no provisions which anchored the political parties within the constitutional framework – that was taken for granted – nor did it contain provisions directed against individuals or groups attempting to subvert constitutional life. Those wanting a unitary Reich scored a victory on military matters in Article 79: 'The defence of the Reich is a matter for the Reich', which put an end to the reserved military rights of certain states.

Military jurisdiction was to be abolished. Some SPD members wanted it firmly stated that it had already been abolished, but Noske, because of operations still going on inside Germany, insisted that 'was to be abolished' was correct. The SPD's bid to end capital punishment was defeated.

Constitutional differences were to be settled by a Reichs Court, the *Reichsgericht*, which was also to settle disputes between states. But as time showed it was to become a highly political and politicized instrument. The territorial restructuring was considered a necessity, which was affirmed, but the constitution left open the question of how it should be done. This issue of *Reichsreform* remained on the agenda throughout the entire history of the Weimar Republic.

Basic rights alone comprised fifty-six articles to which the DNVP and DVP in particular were the main contributors. The *Sozialer Volksstaat* had its spokeman in Friedrich Naumann, but he failed to formulate this idea in legally and constitutionally acceptable language. His influence resulted mainly in numerous social reservations limiting basic rights, which included equality before the law; the liberty of person and property, opinion, association and assembly; liberty of contract and of commerce. But no provisions were made binding the legislators actually to enforce these rights. Basic rights were considered as guidelines and limits in legislation, administration and justice. Ironically it was the conservative elements who indicted the all-embracing powers of parliament. In addition to the basic rights institutional guarantees were given to religious associations, to education and science as well as the right to communal self-administration. The demands by the Centre Party concerning church and school were also resolved by compromise with the SPD, by which schools were established attended by both Catholics and Protestants; parallel to the *Simultanschule*, the interdenominational school, were to be purely Catholic schools and choice of school was left to parents. Details were to be regulated by Reich as well as individual state laws. In the economic and social sector there were guarantees of private property, and anyone affected by nationalization or by expropriation was to receive financial compensation. There was to be land reform, social insurance and the protection of the *Mittelstand*[1]. How the latter was to be protected against such establishments as chain-stores and the like was left open. Initially attempts were made to retain the existing Councils in industries, but after much controversy, these were superseded by a *Betriebsrat*, an advisory council to be established in large enterprises, which was to settle any differences between shopfloor and management. Nationalization of the Reich's minerals were rejected; instead the government was to exercise a supervisory function. Before the constitution was ratified the SPD member Löbe expressed his concern about the emergence of a bloc of 'bourgeois parties' in the voting over the nationalization of minerals and mines, over the function of the Councils and the exclusion of former princes or royalty from presidential office, adding that he could only hope that the organic development would ultimately be stronger than the paper obstacles.

The final vote was taken on 31 July 1919. Of the 420 deputies 338 participated, with 82 deputies absent. The Weimar Constitution was passed by 262 votes to 75; one deputy abstained. It was approved by the SPD, the Centre, the DDP and such small party groupings as the German Hanoverians and the German Democrats. The DNVP rejected it in spite of the considerable contribution it had made in its formulation, as did the DVP, the Bavarian Farmers' League, one member of the Centre, a Bavarian, and the USPD. Slightly more than half of the deputies, 62 per cent, had voted for it, hardly a very auspicious sign for the young republic. The constitution did not require the assent of the Land governments or parliaments nor that of the Committee of States. In contrast to the constitutions of 1866–67 and 1870–71, this time not only the institutions of the Reich but those of most of the states and parliaments had actively participated. With the exception of Bavaria between 1919 and 1924, none of the German states ever seriously questioned its validity. On 11 August 1919 the Reich President submitted the constitutional document to the cabinet for counter-signature. It came into force legally on 14 August 1919.

THE IMPACT OF VERSAILLES

The suppression of revolutionary ferment inside Germany and the problems on her eastern frontier apart, the most important issue which overshadowed the making of the Weimar Constitution was that of peace. Germany was filled with hopes for a classic peace which would allow the vanquished nation to enter the international community of nations as an equal partner. But Wilson's notes had already shown strong signs of interference in its constitutional life. The Germans had parted with the monarchic system very largely in the expectation of getting a favourable peace. When in the first instance, contrary to the internationally accepted practice and for the first time in modern history, the defeated state, which was preoccupied with stamping out the attempts at emulating the example of Soviet Russia on German soil, was excluded from the actual negotiations in Versailles, German disillusionment began to appear. And when in May 1919 the actual peace conditions were submitted to the Germans the disgust about the act of betrayal committed by Wilson cut across parties. Long-term occupation of the right bank of the Rhine; permanent demilitarization of the Rhineland and, psychologically even more important, the 'war guilt clause' and the demand for the handing over of 'war criminals'; the separation of East Prussia from the Reich; severe limitations on armaments; the imposition of a man-power limit on the army of 100,000 the handing over of the German High Seas Fleet (which the commander Admiral Ludwig von Reuter prevented by scuttling it in Scapa Flow and thus at least delivering the British from the horns of a silent dilemma); the reduction of her mercantile fleet to insignificance; all these conditions in many respects intruded upon Germany's consti-tutional sovereignty. It was a peace of truly Carthaginian dimensions and Lloyd George correctly forecast its ultimate outcome – but not before he had achieved Great Britain's war aims. In spite of the harsh conditions Marshal Foch claimed to speak on behalf of France when he protested against the temporary occupation of the Rhineland: he demanded its permanent subjugation under the military admini-stration of the allies – and between 1919 and 1924 France and Belgium tried hard enough to achieve just that.

The German peace delegation travelled to Versailles, expecting to negotiate, but was simply called in to receive the peace conditions. Clemenceau made it clear that any oral discussion was superfluous. Brockdorff-Rantzau's appeal to reason evaporated, as any such demand that was not backed by effective power would have. Germany could have got no worse peace with the Kaiser and the constitutional reforms of September 1918. It is true that some minor changes in the territorial provisions by way of plebiscite were made, but they were insignificant compared with the enormity of the peace conditions.

Scheidemann's protest to 'world opinion' shared the fate of that of his Foreign Minister: the revolution had robbed the German government of the effective military power which, though it could never have won the war, could have compelled genuine negotiations. It was the Württemberger Minister of War Reinhardt who, together with other German generals, opposed acceptance at the risk of dividing Germany to save its Prussian substance and continue to fight, having as its hinterland the Baltic states in which German forces had successfully pushed out the Bolsheviks. Within that plan lay, as we shall see, the genesis of the Kapp *putsch* little more than nine months later. However, the realism of that other Württemberger, General Groener, prevailed; military resistance was hopeless in a divided nation. There was nothing that could be done but sign the infamous document, but not before Scheidemann resigned in order not to sign this peace himself. Within the cabinet it was Erzberger who argued busily for an unqualified acceptance of the peace conditions. Noske, who at first had shared Reinhardt's sentiments, came to accept Groener's point of view. Scheidemann, Brockdorff-Rantzau, Landsberg and Robert Schmidt as well as the Democrats Bernhard Dernburg, Georg Gothein and Preuss opted for rejection; the SPD members David, Noske, Bauer, and Wissell, Erzberger, Johannes Bell and Johann Giesberts from the Centre, opted for acceptance. Ebert, too, was in favour of rejection, as was the military leadership under Reinhardt and the naval chief Admiral Adolf von Trotha. Noske called for a meeting of the commanding generals, and won over the majority in favour of acceptance. Rejection would have meant invasion by the allied forces which Germany could not have countered. But the generals commanding the forces in the east forecast problems, as they expected their formations to disobey the order to evacuate the territories they held.

Brockdorff-Rantzau and Erzberger developed their opposing points of view before the Committee of States. Bavaria evaded a clear decision, while the Prime Ministers of Württemberg, Saxony, Baden and Hesse spoke in favour of acceptance because only this step would save the unity of the Reich. The Hanseatic cities of Hamburg, Bremen and Lübeck as well as Lippe opted for rejection. Prussia opted for acceptance. Since it was the largest German state this proved decisive, but there were also divided counsels in Prussia. Along with the generals the Social Democrat Reich Commissioner and Plenipotentiary in East Prussia and the Baltic, August Winnig, argued that in case of rejection the population itself would defend the eastern territories. The Reich Commissioner for Silesia Otto Hörsing opposed this notion. The Centre Party and the Majority Socialists dismissed any idea of national resistance.

In the Reichstag even the pacifist Schücking advocated rejection. Erzberger, forever seeking compromise, suggested the formula of 'conditional acceptance' by eliminating the war guilt and the war criminals paragraph. When Scheidemann insisted that if these two conditions were not to be accepted the whole treaty should be rejected, the majority of his own party did not have the courage to accept his argument. Thereupon Scheidemann, Brockdorff-Rantzau and Landsberg decided to resign. The cabinet was clearly divided. The allies rejected the attempt at 'conditional acceptance'. After the resignations a new government had to be formed. Gustav Bauer (SPD) became Chancellor. During the new government's first phase it consisted of 8 Socialists and 4 Centre Party members, with 3 DDP members joining in November 1919. Hermann Müller (SPD) became Foreign Secretary.

The new government made one vain attempt at 'conditional acceptance' but they were turned down. The OHL, that is to say Hindenburg, advised rejection. The Chief of Military District III (Berlin), General von Walther von Lüttwitz, declared that his forces would oppose the government if it did not reject the peace conditions. Thereupon *Reichswehrminister* Noske handed in his resignation to Ebert since he could no longer expect the support of the officer corps. Groener again saved the situation, declaring at noon on 23 June that except for local successes, resistance would be hopeless, but if the treaty were accepted unconditionally then *Reichswehrminister* Noske would have to take over the leadership of the people and the responsibility for the conclusion of peace. That would make sure the army stood behind the government and prevent a potential *coup d'état* inside Germany. It appears that Hindenburg sanctioned Groener's demands. Only Groener's firm attitude convinced Ebert that he should support the Bauer government in their unconditional acceptance of the peace treaty. He rejected Noske's resignation, but he ignored Groener's demand to put Noske at the head of government.

On the afternoon of 23 June Chancellor Bauer addressed the Reichstag, speaking in favour of unconditional acceptance of the peace treaty. The Reichstag accepted with the DNVP, the DVP, parts of the Centre and the DDP opposing. In the afternoon the German envoy, Edgar von Haniel, handed the chairman of the Peace Conference a note declaring Germany's readiness to sign in the face of 'overpowering force'. The formal signature took place on 28 June 1919, the signatories being the German Foreign Minister Hermann Müller and the Reich Colonial Minister Johannes Bell. They also signed the agreement concerning the occupation of the Rhineland by allied forces. Both required the assent of the National Assembly. Ratification was carried out with 208 votes in favour and 115 against. The one important issue left open in the peace treaty was the question of the scale of reparations. Wilson's note of 5 November 1918 on the basis of his fourteen points had rejected any reparations but only demanded that Germany make financial recompense to the civilian population of the Entente and their property damaged by the war. Articles 231–44 of the peace treaty, however, included all the war pensions of the allies. A commission was established which was yet to settle the final sum of reparations demanded.

On 23 June, while the debate raged in the National Assembly, the German Army publicly burnt the battle colours of the French army seized in 1870–71 and deposited their own in the Berlin *Zeughaus* (Arsenal). That, and the scuttling of the German High Seas Fleet in Scapa Flow, were the only military gestures of defiance against the Versailles Treaty.

THE FEDERAL STATES

The upheaval in Germany during 1918–19 demonstrated on the individual Land level the same divisions as during the revolution of 1848. On the one hand there was a strong German unitary current, on the other a strongly particularist one. This emerged clearly in the Constituent assemblies which had gathered more or less simultaneously in the individual German Lands. The particularist forces gained their first success in opposing the 'dictatorship' which had been assumed by the Berlin Executive Council. Nevertheless the main force for further constitutional development lay with the central institutions of the Reich rather than with its constituent Lands. The German National Assembly had been strong enough to devise the new German Constitution on its own without decisive influence from the states. It had managed to extend its competence far beyond the range which the Bismarckian Constitution had possessed, so much so that the individual Lands found the concept of state more or less meaningless, and it had also introduced measures in the German Constitution which were binding for the constitutions of the Lands.

On the whole the constitutions of the various Lands were identical with one another. At that level the same general, equal, direct and secret franchise existed for all Germans without difference in race, religion or sex. Almost all Lands introduced the one-chamber system, the *Landtag*, the Diet or Land parliament, because support was lacking for a second chamber based on the nobility or the upper strata of society. The one exception was Prussia which created a State Council, the *Preussisches Herrenhaus*, whose function within Prussia corresponded with that of the Reichsrat of the German Republic. It represented the individual Prussian provinces and it cooperated in the introduction of legislation: the executive could veto legislation passed by the *Landtag* but a two-thirds majority within the *Landtag* or devices of direct democracy such as the plebiscite could overrule any veto by the *Herrenhaus*. It did have an unconditional veto against expenditure voted by the *Landtag* which exceeded the actual submissions made by the Prussian government. Dr Konrad Adenauer, the first Chancellor of the German Federal Republic and since 1919 Mayor of the City of Cologne, was one of its members because of that position. Very much towards the end of his life he was asked in what parliament or representative assembly in which he had participated during his long political life had the level of discussion and debate been the highest, and he answered without hesitation: 'In the Prussian *Herrenhaus*'.

Unlike the Reich, a supreme executive elected by popular franchise did not exist in its Lands. The Diet elected the executive, that is to say in most cases it elected a Prime Minister, in some Lands also called State President, who formed his cabinet; in others it elected the entire ministry. The executive was fully dependent on the Diet and had to resign in the face of a vote of 'no confidence'. No Land government was entitled to dissolve the *Landtag*. This could only happen in Prussia but it required the common assent of the Prussian Prime Minister, the President of the *Landtag* and that of the State Council. In other Lands a general referendum in favour of the dissolution of the *Landtag* had the same effect. Thus in the Reich as in its constituent parts the population was called upon to participate directly in government. In practice, however, the Diets remained virtually unimpeded in the exercise of their power.

The constitutional reality in the Lands, however, corresponded very much to what existed at Reich level; the latter aspect will be discussed below. The multiplicity of parties in the Diets corresponded very much with that of the Reichstag and led ultimately to the failure of the parliamentary system. This applied to the difficult task of reforming the administration (Prussia, ruled by the Social Democrats, was probably most successful in this respect), which as a result of the disastrous financial position of all the German Lands required drastic rationalization, affecting local administrations which in the course of time had come to represent many of the local interests. It also applied to the formation of governments. When the Weimar Republic was on its death-bed the largest Lands such as Prussia, Bavaria, Saxony and Württemberg no longer had a parliamentarian but a provisional government.

The immediate practical consequences of this, however, were not particularly serious because through the extension of the legislative powers of the Reich as well as its administration, particularly in the realm of finance, the function of the Land governments had been reduced in the main to administrative agencies where power was wielded by the local civil service. But precisely the excessive party political pluralism and its instability, which affected the civil service as well as the electorate at large, appeared anachronistic to many. It seemed to represent one of the main arguments, virtually from the beginning of the Weimar Republic, in favour of a thoroughgoing Reich reform to limit further or even abolish Land parliaments. Naturally the danger of the Lands being reduced to provinces of the Reich also provoked a counter-movement, carried on by the local civil service which feared its posts would be jeopardized, and also especially in southern Germany by large parts of the population with their emotional reaction against any centralizing tendencies from Berlin. The reaction was particularly strong when on 20 July 1932 (see below) the state of Prussia had a Reich Commissioner appointed over it by the emergency decree of the Reich President. It was Bavaria and Baden which raised the most serious protest and called upon the *Reichsstaatsgerichtshof*,[2] the German Supreme Court, to rule against the invocation of Article 48 of the Weimar Constitution, which in cases of emergency transferred the legislative power from the Reichstag to the Reich President: they feared that the example of Prussia could serve as a precedent which might soon be applied to them as well. The Court responded to those appeals, but because of the advent of the National Socialist government, no practical steps could be taken to implement its decision.

NOTES

1. *Mittelstand* is a difficult term to translate. It does not specifically mean middle class, but connotes the middle-class economic interests of artisans, shop-keepers, small manufacturers, white-collar employees and similar groups.
2. Established in 1921 in accordance with Article 19 of the Constitution, the *Reichsstaatsgerichtshof* had the ultimate power to settle differences between Reich and states, and between several states. It also had the power to settle differences over their constitutions, though *not* the Reich constitution.

Chapter 8

THE CONSTITUTIONAL REALITY OF THE WEIMAR REPUBLIC

In examining the constitutional reality of the Weimar Republic it is first of all necessary to isolate the critical points in its history whose interaction contributed to its ultimate disintegration. We find them in the area of foreign policy and in the constitution itself, in the excessive party political pluralism, to a greater or lesser degree in its executive institutions, in the social and economic problems of the time, in generally anti-parliamentarian trends and last but not least in cultural factors.

It is impossible to discuss each of these points within the framework of a Constitutional History in which the Weimar Republic occupies only one chapter. Hence only those will be discussed which are directly relevant and not necessarily in the order in which they have been listed above.

ARMY AND REPUBLIC

It is undisputed that the Weimar Republic and its constitution were the progeny of defeat. Equally it is beyond dispute that at first the parliamentarization introduced into the Bismarckian Constitution, the break with that constitution and the devising of a new one, were to a large part carried out with the hope that under the influence of 'Wilsonian international morality' a mild and just peace would emerge. That Germany's military impotence in the vital months between November 1918 and June 1919 left the victors able to do very much as they pleased was the result of the attempts at revolution and the almost complete disintegration of Germany's armed might once the troops returned home. Such effective combat units as could still be raised, namely the *Freikorps*, were the product of two factors, firstly the Ebert–Groener alliance which put down the revolution at home, and secondly Article XII of the armistice which compelled Germany to keep her forces in their positions in the east until such time as the allies saw fit to recall them. They were meant to be part of the allies' intervention against the 'Bolshevik menace' and as far as the history of that intervention is concerned were the only forces who were successful: Latvia and Lithuania were cleared of Bolsheviks. But these very forces felt a sense of betrayal when the country for which they believed they had fought accepted the Versailles peace treaty, and whose government virtually disowned them after their return to Germany. From then on rumours of an impending *putsch* would not stop. For them as for the German public at large the Versailles Treaty was the great betrayal, or as Ernst Nolte put it, the disappointed hopes of Versailles were as much the grave-digger of the Republic as the stab-in-the-back legend.

The Weimar Constitution had been founded on the principle of national self-determination. That principle was seriously violated as far as the Germans were concerned. Though plebiscites were held in Eupen-Malmédy, in Northern Schleswig, in West and East Prussia and in Upper Silesia, in the case of Eupen-Malmédy it was a travesty of a plebiscite, and in Upper Silesia the industrial regions which voted overwhelmingly in favour of Germany were handed over to the Poles. German Austria, whose National Assembly had proclaimed itself part of the German Republic on 12 November 1918, had its decision annulled both by the Treaty of Versailles and that of St Germain. French attempts to establish separate buffer states on both the left and right bank of the Rhine failed abysmally even when supported by the full might of France's and Belgium's armed forces after the Ruhr occupation of 1923. Their leaders had to run for their lives chased out by the Rhenish and Palatinate population supported by national activists from Germany, Courland, Styria and Upper Austria.

In spite of the occupation of Germany's western territories, at least the unity of the Reich was maintained. To do justice to the Weimar Constitution one has not only to look at its origins, the impact of a lost war, the revolutionary experience, but also at the continued pressure exercised upon Germany after the peace treaty by the Entente Powers. A direct result of the provisions of the Versailles Treaty was the Kapp-Lüttwitz *putsch*. Up to March 1920 three currents can be discerned within the German army. Firstly, the monarchist current shot its bolt in March 1920. No doubt Lüttwitz was a dyed-in-the-wool monarchist, something that can also be said of Kapp who even expressed his monarchist sentiments personally to Ebert, but as one contemporary characterized him, 'technically he is a Bonaparte, psychologically a Captain of Köpenick'. Yet the small body of forces that supported him, namely Naval Brigade II under Captain Hermann Ehrhardt, was anything but monarchist: Ehrhardt himself had never forgiven the Kaiser for seeking exile in Holland. Nor did their published programme call for the abolition of the Republic. What they did call for was a government of experts who would be capable of mastering the crisis and above all they called for elections. These had been outstanding since the election to the constituent National Assembly, and Bauer's cabinet hoped to postpone them until the end of 1920 when the harvest would be in, food supplies more ample, and thus the election result would be favourable to the Social Democrats and their coalition partners. As it happened the Kapp-Lüttwitz *putsch* evaporated like a puff of smoke. The bulk of the *Reichswehr* refrained from supporting it and some units opposed it openly. Among Germany's Left it is a deeply cherished myth that it was the general strike announced by the trade unions which put an end to the *putsch*. Since it happened on a Saturday – and Kapp had already virtually given up by Sunday evening – the strike could not have come fully into effect until Monday by which time the *putsch* had come to an end. More serious were its consequences, because under the guise of the general strike USPD and Communists attempted to salvage their soviet system, seeing it as their last chance. In the Ruhr and central Germany large-scale and well prepared risings of the extreme Left with their own Red Army took place which could only be put down with great diffi-culty, and in part by using the same troops which had participated in the Kapp-Lüttwitz *putsch*. However, the net result was the end of Noske-Reinhardt era as well as the end of the monarchist current in the the *Reichswehr*. The Social Democrats had once and for all lost their influence in the army, an army they had helped to re-establish, because in 1918–19 volunteers for a republican army were not forthcoming. A new era was to begin.

The second current was the national revolutionary one, coming mainly from the *Freikorps*, and disintegrating and dispersing mainly to the extreme Right and Left as well as in party-political terms to the 'homeless' Right and Left, a current which because of its fragmented character and the relatively quick consolidation of the Republic had no political significance.

The third current was that represented by General Hans von Seeckt: an étatism, which supported the state and accepted the Republic as the lesser of a number of evils. Above all the army's service was pledged to the abstract state, whose historical continuity and national virtue the *Reichswehr* believed it represented. Seeckt's policy, and the role of the army within the Weimar Republic, was not dissimilar to that of the French army between 1871 and 1898: no internal politics, formal respect for outside authorities, dedication to the pursuit, as far as Versailles allowed, of the task in hand.

There were also of course evasions of the treaty, particularly with the Red Army with which the *Reichswehr* had already taken up tentative contacts late in 1919, which came to full bloom during the

1920s. More unsavoury aspects arose in connection with the Upper Silesian problem between 1919 and 1921, the active resistance in the Ruhr in 1923, the build-up of an intelligence network and the Black *Reichswehr*. In spite of the Polish insurrections in Upper Silesia in 1919, 1920 and 1921 the *Reichswehr* was forbidden to intervene directly. Thus it supported illegal German self-defence groups which both Poles and French countered by trying to infiltrate them, sometimes with success. Since there was no possibility of recourse to ordinary civil or military courts, infiltrators were liquidated. This was the beginning of the *Feme* murders, crimes which were often the result of decisions made by Kangaroo Courts, sometimes not even that. The same applied to the active resistance in the Ruhr which was backed both by the *Reichswehr* and Transport Ministry which, however, failed to inform the Prussian Ministry of the Interior. Thus Albert Leo Schlageter, one of the prominent leaders of the resistance there, when caught had at the same time a warrant out for him in unoccupied Germany because he was suspected as a member of an extreme right-wing organization. The leader of a commando unit about to liberate Schlageter contacted the local German police authorities and together with his comrades was promptly arrested. Only after Schlageter's execution did the muddle emerge and Carl Severing, then Minister for the Interior, made a note to the effect that because of this confusion it was little wonder that the activists felt themselves betrayed by their own government. The provisions of the Versailles Treaty forbade the *Reichswehr* to set up an intelligence department. Ehrhardt, by that time in Bavaria, where he found shelter from legal prosecution after the abortive Kapp-Lüttwitz *putsch*, was approached by the *Reichswehr* because naval personnel were believed to have world-wide experience and hence to be most suitable for the task. However, the *Reichswehr* acted according to the German motto: 'Wash my fur but don't make me wet' – in other words while supplying funds for Ehrhardt's *Organisation Consul*, OC for short, would promptly disown any agent or an operation if discovered. Infiltration by necessity led to further *Feme* murders. Much the same applied to the Black *Reichswehr*, a reserve force set up by Seeckt in case of complications on Germany's western or eastern frontiers. Communists and agents of the Inter-allied Commission supervising German disarmament infiltrated it and again, as there was no possibility of recourse to the ordinary course of justice, the Black *Reichswehr* had to take justice into its own hands. Only in late 1923 when the Black *Reichswehr* tried to pursue its own political course, culminating in the Küstrin *putsch* under Major Bruno Buchrucker, did Seeckt drop the Black *Reichswehr* and dissolve it. When in the mid 1920s news of the *Feme* murders became public knowledge and their perpetrators were prosecuted by the judiciary, the *Reichswehr*, notably General Kurt von Schleicher, did their best to delay the trials to help the accused to escape.

THE PROBLEM OF THE JUDICIARY – UNITARY TRENDS OF THE CONSTITUTION

Much blame for this has been placed on the German judiciary, as one of the bastions of reaction. Yet when the judiciary did get hold of political assassins the sentences handed down were very stiff, for example in the case of the associates of the murderers of Rathenau. The discrepancy in legal judgments against right and left-wing extremists emerges clearly if we look at the following table:

Right-wing putsch *attempts*

March 1920	Kapp-Lüttwitz
October/	Küstrin
November 1923	Hitler

Left-wing putsch *attempts*

November/ December 1918	Independents and Spartacists
January 1919	Independents and Spartacists
March 1919	Independents and Spartacists
April 1919	Soviet Republic in Bavaria
March 1920	Independents and Communists
July 1921	Communist rising in Central Germany
October 1922	Local Communist risings
October 1923	Communist risings in Hamburg and central Germany

Conservative estimates put the victims of left-wing uprisings at between 3,000 and 4,000, those of the Right at 41. In its early phase the Weimar Republic was far more endangered by the forces of the extreme Left than by those of the extreme Right. Consequently the sentences of the judiciary against the left-wing extremists were bound to be far more numerous than those against the Right. In this context one may also consider the court action which President Friedrich Ebert initiated; he had been called a traitor by a local paper because of his participation in the January 1918 munitions strike. The jury at the Magdeburg trial on 23 December 1924 came to the conclusion that he had committed treason because of his participation in the strike, although according to his own testimony he had done so to calm things down. But one can only expect formal judicial judgments from a judiciary, since it is not competent to do anything else. The short-coming lies in the circumstance that a political role is too often imposed on the judiciary and that the role is then exploited by the media. A judiciary operating on the basis of a codified law (in contrast to the Anglo-Saxon common law) can do no more than stick to the letter of the law.

In general it can be said that the development of the Weimar Constitution was heavily influenced by the liabilities coming from the pressures exerted upon Germany from without, especially in its early years. The assassination of such an opaque political personality as Erzberger in 1921, the Kapp-Lüttwitz *putsch* of the previous year, the assassination by German nationalists of the potentially most able politician next to Stresemann, Walther Rathenau, in 1922, and the Hitler *putsch* in 1923 which resulted from the breaking off of the Ruhr struggle, were direct consequences of events in the field of foreign policy. The London Conference of 1924, the Locarno Treaty in 1925, and Germany's entry into the League of Nations in 1926 brought a certain easing of the internal situation which only lasted a short while until the depression caused a new and longer crisis not only in Germany's economic sphere but also on the domestic scene. Then the Republic could no longer master the problem of unemployment. Hence throughout the Weimar Republic one cannot speak of the constitution functioning under normal circumstances, yet despite that fact certain lines of constitutional development are discernible.

Basically, like the Bismarckian Constitution, that of Weimar moved in a unitary direction. The most important instruments facilitating this were the massive body of legislation passed to implement it. Virtually immediately after it had been enacted the entire Bavarian and Württemberg railways as well as their postal services were taken over by the Reich, and as a result of the modified obligations arising out of the Dawes Plan the railways were formed into an independent *Reichsbahngesellschaft*. Germany's waterways were also taken over by the Reich, while the financial independence of the Lands, a feature dominant in the Bismarckian Constitution, was eroded by the establishment of a Reich Finance Administration. While the individual Lands had collected the Reich taxes until 1919, this was now done by the Reich. The Reich also assumed the full burden of paying pensions to war invalids and to those families deprived of their breadwinner by the war. It now collected all income and property taxes in contrast to the material contributions paid by the German Lands before 1919. In the economic sphere, economic activity became dependent on the Reich by the mere fact that it administered and distributed coal and potash. It gained even greater influence through the depression. All banking institutions came under its control as did much of heavy industry through the payment of subventions. The reverse side of the coin on the economic side, however, was the increasing influence of economic pressure groups. These as well as the political parties made their weight felt in the politics of Weimar Germany, to such an extent that all these factors threatened the state through the organized pluralist social, political and economic forces.

Unemployment insurance, introduced in 1927, with funds for a maximum one million unemployed, was the product of Reich legislation and like all the other branches of social insurance was transferred into the hands of autonomous self-administering bodies. Even the individual Lands played no role in them. But the whole problem reverted to the German state once unemployment figures exceeded the one million mark and it once again became the task of the Reich to find the necessary monies to fund the vast unemployment benefits.

Even internal domestic crisis operated in favour of unitary tendencies. This had already been the case during 1919 when the forces of the Reich had to suppress attempts at revolution in many parts of the country. The situation continued after the murder of Erzberger when the Ministry of the Interior issued a decree allowing the temporary suspension of newspapers and journals and the prohibition of rallies and assemblies suspected of agitating against the constitution. After the murder of Rathenau this decree was renewed in the form of the Law for the Protection of the Republic which came into force on 21 July 1922. It not only established a State Court whose competencies extended to violations of law by Land governments, but it also empowered the Minister of the Interior to request the authorities of the Land governments to carry out specific police measures such as the prohibition of public assemblies and the confiscation of publications. Its provision also allowed the judiciary to bring to book associates of the Rathenau murder. *But* it was retroactive legislation; to protect the Republic from extremism the legislators broke the hallowed principle of German legal theory and practice of *nullu poena sine lege* – no punishment without an already existing law. This action was further complicated by the one-sided application of the *Republikschutzgesetz*, the Law for the Protection of the Republic, which when it was introduced into the Reichstag was made clear by the Social Democrat Minister of Justice, Dr Gustav Radbruch, who stated 'that the concern of the workers, that this decree directed against radicalism from the Right could afterwards be applied to the Left is completely unfounded'. Again there is a direct continuity between the Law for the Protection of the Republic of 1922 and the *lex van der Lubbe* of 1933. A precedent had been created of which Htiler was to make good use.

The Reich Criminal Police Law went even further. Enacted on the same day it made even greater inroads into the administrative sphere of the German Lands. A Reich Criminal Police Office was established to centralize the battle against crime, both political and non-political. It was to ensure uniformity in and coordination of the effort of all Criminal Offices of the Lands and also had the right to issue orders to them. If several Lands were involved in the investigation of a particular crime it could detach its own executive officers to the Lands to investigate.

BAVARIA AND THE REICH

However, until 1933 this law never came into operation because this degree of centralization could still not surmount the opposition of the forces of German particularism. Bavaria only very reluctantly gave up the reserved rights it had enjoyed during the Empire to the Weimar Constitution. As 'one of the oldest European states and the oldest German state' it was not prepared to take one step further in the direction of centralization than had already been taken. Branded by the experience of the 'Eisner regime' and the 'Soviet Republic' Bavaria had become a hotbed of right-wing sedition and a refuge for nationalist activists from all over the Reich. The Social Democrats had lost their control of government there after 1920 and were replaced by the Bavarian People's Party (BVP). It had already raised serious objections to the 1921 decree, especially against the extended competencies of the Reich Ministry of the Interior. The Berlin government found itself compelled to alter important parts of the decree in favour of Bavarian self-administration. This only increased Bavaria's opposition against 'the Marxist-ridden' government in Berlin. To speak of this as the opposition of Bavarian particularism would be to oversimplify matters. Of course there were Bavarian particularists: there were Bavarian monarchists aiming at the restoration of an independent Bavaria under the crown of the House of Wittelsbach, and there were also monarchists who aimed at a restoration of the Empire but under the Wittelsbachs (in comparison to whom the Hohenzollerns were mere upstarts), and there were German national revolutionaries dedicated to driving out the 'Reds' from their seat of power in Berlin. Increasingly the name was mentioned of a man stepping out of the shadows of obscurity, and, more importantly, making his own voice heard: Adolf Hitler. His party, the German Workers' Party, to be renamed in 1921 the National Socialist Workers' Party (NSDAP), made considerable inroads, although not at polls because it refused initially to participate in elections, conceiving itself as a revolutionary movement. By 1920 Hitler's power of oratory exercised such magnetism on the masses that his party could do what no other dared to do: charge an admission fee to Hitler's speeches. His assemblies were full to capacity with thousands still outside clamouring for entry.

This was the state of affairs in Bavaria. And Bavaria firmly opposed the implementation of the Law for the Protection of the Republic. Instead the government enacted its own legislation which only corresponded partially to the law enacted by the Reichstag. The government in Berlin could have had recourse to the Reich Executive to force acceptance of the law, but wisely it refrained from doing so. Instead it negotiated with Bavaria and the Law for the Protection of the Republic was finally accepted on 24 August 1924. This was at the expense of the Reich Criminal Police Law which was quietly dropped.

Relationships between Bavaria and the Reich became more serious during 1923 when Social Democrat/Communist coalition governments in Saxony and Thuringia established themselves. In Bavaria the nationalists began to mobilize, including Hitler and the Bavarian *Reichswehr* Division, on the initiative of its commander General Otto von Lossow, ostensibly to unseat the governments across their northern frontier where the Communists were slowly gaining the upper hand, but aiming to march on Berlin to establish a new nationalist government there. Their model was the 'Angora solution' of Kemal Ataturk who had moved from the provinces and seized power in Turkey to reform it, and Mussolini's 'March on Rome' of the previous year. However, the Berlin government pre-empted the move by sending *Reichswehr* contingents into Saxony and Thuringia and re-established bourgeois governments there. At a time when the Reich was facing extreme danger because of the Ruhr occupation by the French and Belgians, Bavaria, instead of closing ranks with Berlin, considered the opportunity favourable to resume a policy of independence. On 26 September 1923 it proclaimed a 'state of emergency' and transferred executive power to Gustav Ritter von Kahr, a strong supporter of the anti-Berlin course. The Reich, so as to act uniformly throughout Germany, proclaimed a state of national emergency and transferred executive power first to Noske's successor Otto Gessler and finally to General von Seeckt, the chief of the army. Conflict ensued between Gessler and Kahr when the former ordered him to enforce the suspension of Hitler's paper, the *Völkischer Beobachter*, which had published an attack on Seeckt. Kahr refused and Gessler ordered Lossow to execute the order. He too refused, whereupon he was relieved of his command. But the Bavarian government re-appointed Lossow as Commander and made the Bavarian division swear an oath to Bavaria. It tried to justify this step with the argument that only Bavaria represented the true interests of the Reich, against the Marxists in Berlin, although the Social Democrats no longer headed the German government.

This development culminated in the Hitler *putsch* of 8–9 November 1923 by which time neither Kahr nor Lossow were prepared to follow Hitler's course to destroy the whole framework of government in Germany by a national revolution. Hitler, on his own, was easily defeated and paid for it by more than a year's imprisonment, including custody before the trial. In view of the complicity of the Bavarian government in the *putsch* plans of 1923 it was easy for Hitler at his trial in April 1924 to attack not only the Bavarian government but the whole Weimar Republic. Sentenced to four years' fortress detention he was only kept in prison until December 1924 when he was released. He was only saved from deportation as a stateless person – he had given up his Austrian citizenship and not yet acquired German – by his war record and by highly-placed officials in Munich.

Article 48 of the constitution had been invoked first in 1921 after the murder of Erzberger, then in 1923 because of the events in Saxony, Thuringia and Bavaria. On 9 November 1923 full executive power was placed in the hands of Seeckt and the *Reichswehr*, which he handed back in March 1924. That does not mean that Seeckt did not have his own political plans, but he was not prepared to carry them out without the support of President Ebert and against the letter of the constitution. Article 48 was also invoked and an Enabling Bill enacted to carry out the urgent currency reform and to end raging inflation, the achievement of five men: Gustav Stresemann (DVP), Karl Helfferich (DNVP), Hans Luther, a man then without party affiliation, and Hjalmar Schacht, one of the founders of the DDP, first Reich Currency Commissar and then President of the *Reichbank*, and Rudolf Hilferding (SPD).

THE EMERGENCE OF THE NSDAP – FROM EBERT TO HINDENBURG

With the end of inflation political extremism seemed for the time being, and on the surface at least, to have come to an end. But this is a deceptive picture. In spite of economic stabilization and in spite of the 'golden twenties', unemployment figures between 1924 and 1929 were rarely under the one million mark. The KPD, the Communist Party founded in 1919 from the Spartacus League and members of the USPD – which dissolved itself, the majority becoming Communists, the remainder going back into the fold of the SPD – made very slow but steady progress. So did Hitler's NSDAP, refounded in 1925 after Hitler had decided to obtain power by legal and not by revolutionary means. Its organizational structure and functioning was less the work of Hitler himself than of Hermann Esser, Franz Xavier Schwarz and Rudolf Hess, to whom after 1925 must be added the immense organizational talent of Gregor Strasser in northern Germany. In the elections of 1924 the National Socialist Liberal Movement gained 32 seats, 10 of the deputies being direct supporters of Hitler. This is often contrasted with the poor showing of the NSDAP in the Reichstag elections of May 1928 when it only won 12 seats. The elections occurred at a time when Gregor Strasser was reorganizing the electoral strategy of the NSDAP, which soon began to pay handsome dividends in Land and local elections between 1928 and 1930. Consequently the election result of 1930 when 107 NSDAP deputies were returned is not such a surprise as it has seemed to many historians since then. Nor is it by any means certain that the Depression was the cause of the NSDAP land-slide. Its serious effects were only felt in Germany towards the end of the year and the party's electoral support came mainly from areas in which 'cottage industries' were dominant and rural areas, especially those of northern Germany, heavily affected by excessive tax burdens.

In the meantime, on 28 February 1925, the Republic's first president, Friedrich Ebert,had died. On 29 March 1925 the first presidential elections took place. Chief among the candidates were the Duisburg Lord Mayor, Karl Jarres (DVP), the Social Democratic Prime Minister of Prussia, Otto Braun, and the candidate of the National Socialists, General Erich Ludendorff. While Jarres gained 10.8 million votes, Ludendorff only gained 211,000. Jarres had missed an absolute majority, so that a second election was necessary. The Centre, DDP and SPD put forward the former Chancellor Wilhelm Marx. The right wing, essentially DVP and DNVP, put forward the Emperor's former Field Marshal, Paul von Hindenburg, at that time already 78 years of age. Hindenburg refused at first; he felt himself unsuited to be the President of a democratic republic. Only after lengthy persuasion by his former comrade Admiral von Tirpitz, and an appeal to his patriotic duty, did he finally accept. He was supported by the voters of the DVP, DNVP and also by the BVP and NSDAP. The Communists nominated their leader Ernst Thälmann. At the elections held on 26 April 1925 Hindenburg won 14.66 million votes, Marx 13.75 and Thälmann 1.93 million.

There were initial fears that the forces of reaction had triumphed, but they were unfounded. Hindenburg remained more loyal to the Republic than could have been expected of him. In his first term of office he was more republican than many other republicans. If one looks at the politicians of Weimar it is difficult to find one who defended German democracy and the Republic when they were in their final agony more successfully and tenaciously against Hitler than this stubborn royalist. Hindenburg's election did not by any means dig the grave of the Republic. It is true that he was an *Ersatzkaiser*, a fact that reflects less unfavourably on him than on those who elected him. But because of his loyalty to the Republic and to the Constitution Hindenburg under normal circumstances could have been the bridge between black, white and red and black, red and gold. But times were anything but normal and the Weimar parliamentarians contributed a good deal to this state of affairs.

PARTIES AND THE AGE OF MASS POLITICS

The five parties at the birth of the Weimar Republic had taken the political culture of the Empire into the Republic, not realizing that the great central problem of the structural changes in democratic practice was the change from the system of liberal representation to the multi-party state based on the masses. Most Weimar deputies conceived themselves as being responsible to their own conscience rather than to the electoral base which had given them their mandate. They failed to realize that the preconditions no longer existed which had inspired Burke's letter to his constituents at Bristol. The very existence of the belief in free responsibility, of a free mandate of parliamentarians and government in the age of mass politics carried within it an explosive centre. Or, to put it differently, there was the old tradition which believed in the existence of the *state above the parties*, and those who believed in a parliamentarian party state democracy. It is this dichotomy which represents one of the major factors on which Weimar ultimately failed, even before Hitler became a serious contender for power. In addition most parties were dominated by ideology, something they had been able to afford in the days of the Empire when they were never called to assume governmental responsibility, but which they could no longer afford after 1919, yet indulged in all the same. The very fact that in the early years of the Republic cabinets of 'experts' without party affiliation existed did not augur well for its future. After 1920 the old coalitions were necessary. The formation of the governments of 1925, 1926 and 1927 came about only with the greatest difficulties. The Centre Party, whose ideological premise lay outside the field of day-to-day politics as long as confessional schools were allowed, was the only party with sufficient flexibility to join all sides. Therefore it was the great coalition maker and was always the basis of all coalitions. But given the ideological inflexibility of the parties these coalitions were very fragile. Of the sixteen cabinets before that of Heinrich Brüning in 1930 only two were defeated on a vote of no confidence, the rest fell because the coalitions dissolved.[1]

After the elections of May 1928 the only possibility of forming a majority government was that of a great coalition which could be formed only after weeks of hard bargaining. Little wonder that the German electorate became tired of what appeared to them as parliamentary horse-trading. But the leading ministers Hermann Müller (SPD), Carl Severing (SPD), Rudolf Wissell (SPD), Gustav Stresemann (DVP) and Julius Curtius (DVP) soon found themselves in conflict. A joint policy necessary in the interests of the state was at odds with the demands from their respective parties. It was not only tension but conflict between constitutional law and constitutional reality. The pressures from below both in the SPD and DVP led to the abysmal failure in March 1930 when the SPD Chancellor Müller and his SPD colleagues voted against the legislation their own government had put forward. While the pressure in the SPD from below was exerted by the party's left wing led by Rudolf Breitscheid and the trade unions, in the DVP pressure was exerted by the employers' pressure groups. Moreover most of the old parties had an over-aged and fossilized leadership, with functionaries dating back to Imperial days. Within the SPD there was an argument over whether it should in fact be a 'party upholding the state' or the 'party of the class struggle.' At the Magdeburg SPD rally of 1929 the younger elements were fervent advocates of class struggle, supported by the former members of the USPD. The deputy Hans Wendt declared, to great applause, that 'I consider this standing above parties by the government a throwback to bourgeois-liberal mentality', while Breitscheid envisaged the break-up of the Great Coalition. He said that a dissolution of the Reichstag would hardly change anything because the formation of a majority government without the SPD would be impossible. He then asked the rhetorical question of what would happen:

> Then we will face a real crisis of parliamentarism, and the exploitation of certain paragraphs of the constitution which do not correspond with the spirit of democracy, but which exist in the constitution all the same, their exploitation by certain desperadoes which amongst other things could give the Reich President rights which fundamentally are not in accord with democracy. Then we could get a kind of cabinet of civil servants, which in itself would already be a veiled dictatorship.

All the same, Breitscheid went on, the SPD should not make every sacrifice to save the parliamentary system because the moment could come when the forces of Germany's Social Democracy would have to have recourse to the 'means of power, which the organized workers possess outside parliament, to save parliamentarism and democracy without appealing to the Communists'.

A year later Social Democracy and German democracy as a whole faced precisely this situation. Müller considered maintaining the government by invoking Article 48. But Hindenburg refused, not because of aversion to the Great Coalition, but because of aversion to applying Article 48 in the first place. Müller as a freely acting and responsible Chancellor had failed and there remained nothing else for him but to resign. The party base had won. His Finance Minister and party colleague Rudolf Hilferding analysed the situation correctly when he said the failure of parliament 'extends the power of the Reich President at the expense and through the guilt of parliament, and the Reich President must exercise functions which the Reichstag denied to itself'. There were very few voices like that of the DVP deputy who exclaimed: 'Another government than the present one is not possible under the prevailing circumstances . . . I take the standpoint that we should sacrifice the party if we can save the fatherland!' The age of mass politics had come: only the Communists and the NSDAP were aware of the practical consequences of this change and acted accordingly.

Thus the linchpin of all Weimar coalitions, the Centre Party, found itself on its own in the position of a minority government. What Hindenburg had refused to Müller, the invocation of Article 48, he had to cede with great reluctance and hesitation (in the end it was only the argument that Ebert had used it before him which made him give way) to his successor Heinrich Brüning. Controversy arose about the interpretation of Article 48 because an executive order concerning it had never been issued. Neither was it beyond dispute whether the phrase 'disturbance or danger to public security and order' could be extended to a constitutional crisis or later to an economic emergency. In favour of such an interpretation was the circumstances that the wording of Article 48 did not distinguish between legislative emergency in case of disturbances of the normal legislative process, in case of war or internal unrest.

THE BUREAUCRACY

Hindenburg was the first to admit that he understood nothing about politics, and he did not possess the political judgement and foresight to see the full implications of the use of Article 48. He had recourse to it with great hesitation in the hope that sooner rather than later a majority government, preferably of a Centre to Right vintage would be re-established. He hardly foresaw that he and his government would have to live and govern with it for almost three years. He expected that a presidential cabinet, in true Prussian tradition, would stand above the parties. Inevitably the more the Reichstag ceased to fulfil its function as legislator and integrator of the national will the more influence was gained by extra-parliamentary bodies and individuals such as the bureaucracy, notably his Secretary of State Otto Meissner and the *Reichswehr* in the person of the then Colonel, later General, Kurt von Schleicher. Yet, as in the case of the judiciary, it is no more than part of various conspiracy theories which believes that the failure to 'democratize' the civil service was one of the root causes of the failure of the Weimar Republic. The civil service did its duty, under the Emperor and under the Weimar Republic, and it was to continue to do it under Hitler as well as under Konrad Adenauer. Meissner is an excellent example. He loyally served Ebert, Hindenburg and Hitler. Dr Hans Globke, author of the legal commentary on the racialist Nuremberg laws of 1935, is another example.

Nor at this stage was the German public prepared to look to extremes, which had been demonstrated already during the days of the Great Coalition when the campaign against the Young Plan to modify reparation payments was mounted by the forces of the Right and Extreme Right. They managed to raise enough votes for a referendum, but when the referendum was carried out on 22 December 1929, instead of the 21 million votes required for the rejection of the Young Plan they gained only 5.8 million, no more than the DNVP, the NSDAP and other extreme right-wing groupings could muster. Versailles, disillusion with the party state, authoritarian desire, racial, anti-semitic or other traditions and emotions, the whole perfidious nationalist vocabulary, could not seriously endanger the Republic, as the Young referendum shows. It only formed the basis for what was coming, when economic hardship and complete hopelessness gripped the throat of the masses. Without the war Hitler would probably never have become a politician, without Versailles he would have hardly remained one for any length of time, and without the sense of injury of his fellow Germans his successes would have remained within their proper limitations – he had to thank the economic crisis alone for victory. Any other factor which may have contributed to it could conceivably be ignored, but not this one. What the Anti-Young Plan agitation did achieve was the breakthrough of the NSDAP from its hitherto regional to the national level.

THE CRISIS OF PARLIAMENTARISM

Under Hindenburg problems such as *Reichsreform*, (the reorganization of internal boundaries) continued, although they were minor compared with what was looming on the horizon. Slow progress was made: a few minor enclaves were absorbed by Prussia and while the number of German Lands in 1919 was still 25, by 1933 they had shrunk to 17. That was all that was achieved in this sphere. The institutions countervailing the Reichstag, such as the Reichsrat and the Reich Economic Council, gained relatively little significance, since the use of direct democracy at Land and state level could nullify any potential veto. Hence the parliamentary crisis of the Reichstag was all the more serious. Germany was by no means an isolated case. Of all the new states created by the application of the principle of national self-determination in the Paris peace treaties only one democracy remained: multi-national Czechoslovakia. But in the words of the Czech historian Boris Czelovsky, while there was plenty of debate in the parliament in Prague, the Czechs made sure that they had the last word. Italy had become fascist, Spain experienced the dictatorship of Primo de Rivera, Salazar rose in Portugal, Pilsudiski in Poland, not to mention the Balkan states. Even the motherland of democracy, Great Britain, was affected by this crisis of parliamentarism and the question has often been asked why there the Great Depression did not produce the ultimately disastrous results which it did in Germany. For one thing democracy and democratic attitudes cannot be decreed; they are the product of centuries of organic growth. However democratic their constitution, Germans, electorate, parliamentarians and politicians, could not be democratic in a matter of months or a few years. Given a relatively stable and quiet development, free from excessive pressures from without and within, democracy might have struck firm roots. The real situation did not allow this and led on the one hand to excesses of democracy and on the other to the demand for more authoritarianism, both further destablizing the democratic process. For another the Depression affected Great Britain in a different way. After a quick but short economic recovery, economic problems and the associated one of unemployment set in in Great Britain from about 1922 onwards and continued right through the 1920s and 1930s. In other words Britain did not experience the extremes of Inflation and the Great Depression, separated by only a short period of relative prosperity, as did Germany. Britain were used to the consequences of economic crises and unemployment figures were never as high as in Germany. In Great Britain this all took place against the background of victory, in Germany against that of defeat and a peace settlement which was too soft for the harshnesses it contained – a factor important because of its psychological effects.

Reparations and an easy-going, often irresponsible, economic policy, not only by the industrial manufacturing sector, but also by the state and the Lands down to the municipalities, wasted much of the legacy of economic stability that had once existed. It uprooted wide sections of the *Mittelstand* which had hitherto been the pillars of the state and which with the onset of a new economic catastrophe opposed the state and became an easy prey to National Socialism. Another question often asked is why did the proletarized *Mittelstand* fail to unite with the Social Democrats or Communists to prevent an authoritarian dictatorship. Firstly, the NSDAP did not propagate the idea of an authoritarian dictatorship but the principle of the national community, the *Volksgemeinschaft* with equality of opportunity for all

293

Germans, a concept that had its roots in the nineteenth century. Sociological surveys among the NSDAP's 'old fighters' made during the time of the National Socialist regime in Germany by American social scientists have shown that the main reason for joining the NSDAP was the concept of the *Volksgemeinschaft*; anti-semitism as a motivating factor ranked fairly near the bottom of the scale, if at all. Secondly, although proletarized by inflation, the *Mittelstand* did not conceive of itself as a proletariat, and to join the forces of the Left would have been an admission that it had voluntarily moved down to the bottom of the social status ladder. Quite apart from this, they were the product from childhood of an education which stressed patriotic virtues and the importance of the nation compared with the utopian internationalism of the left wing of the SPD and the Communists. Nor did the constitutional parliamentary parties help; instead of educating their electorate to assume their democratic duties they found it easier to give in to their demands, as the break-up of the last Great Coalition has demonstrated.

BRÜNING'S ECONOMIC POLICY

The weight of power and its exercise now shifted to the presidency. With the Reichstag impotent the President sought and found advice outside it, although of course the appointment of Brüning as Chancellor was accompanied by the hope that he would be able to rally a Reichstag majority behind him.

To cure the depression Brüning set out on a deflationary, or what we now would call a monetarist policy. He pursued the line of honouring the payment of reparations, as had Rathenau, with the same objective as the latter, namely to demonstrate that with the best will in the world reparations could not be paid and would ultimately have to be cancelled. 'All measures of economic policy, particularly measures of customs policy, will have to be viewed from the point of view of reparations', as he put it. And of course all measures would have to be avoided that could lead to inflation. In practice it meant the raising of tariffs, the maximization of Germany's agricultural output to reach self-sufficiency and be independent of imports in basic foodstuffs. That in turn meant first of all the financial consolidation of German agriculture, particularly the indebted estates east of the Elbe, the origins of the so-called *Osthilfe* programme. Financial support was given to the estate owners to put them in a position to increase their output and to make a profit. Reparations were paid, and though they were listed in the budget as expenditure their effect was one of capital withdrawal with deflationary effects. German industry was equally called upon to maximize its output and achieve exports with a reduced work-force whose income either remained static or declined, to keep exports as cheap as possible. Wages and civil service salaries were cut. By 1931 Brüning had achieved a balanced budget but at the expense of rising unemployment and of legislation which could only be carried out by invoking Article 48 of the constitution. A Reichstag majority could not be obtained. Strikes were endemic but when arbitration was called in, as in the Berlin strike of metal workers in November 1930, the result was that their wages were cut by 8 per cent. Arbitration was made compulsory by emergency legislation; the miners of the Ruhr, too, had their wages cut by 8 per cent, while civil service salaries and state pensions were cut to the level of 1927, a reduction of 10 – 15 per cent. Rents and interest rates were forced down in order to make the reduction of income acceptable. But these policies in turn discouraged any individual economic initiative. However, Germany's trade balance improved rapidly. While between 1924–1929 it had been in the red to the tune of 8,000 million marks, the deficit was turned into a profit reaching 1,624 million marks, in 1930, 2,872 in 1931 and, in spite of retaliatory foreign tariffs, 1,073 in 1932, and this despite the reparation payments as regulated by the Young Plan and massive capital withdrawals from Germany from late 1930 onwards. Obviously Brüning's economic and fiscal policy was as unpopular at home as it was abroad, but in order to pay reparations Germany, up to Brüning's chancellorship had to raise loans from abroad which were soon no longer available or force the level of exports up to raise the funds for these payments. The French Communists clearly realized this when they blamed German reparations payments for the rising unemployment in France: 'Exportations massives des produits allemands, réduction des importations françaises en Allemagne ont déjà fait sentir leurs conséquences pour le prolétariat français.'

Brüning's economic success was considerable; the export surplus of 1931 would have been sufficient to pay the interest rates on debt contracted abroad plus the full reparation payments – the latter without recourse to foreign loans – if the massive withdrawal of foreign capital had not occurred. The committee appointed on the recommendation of the London Conference of 1931 summed up Brüning's policy as follows: 'It will accentuate the world depression by reducing sales from other countries to Germany, and by creating intense competition from her exports in other markets. If, as is to be feared, this results in other countries taking counter-measures to protect their markets, the level of trade will be further depressed. We consider it is highly undesirable that Germany should be compelled to adopt so drastic a solution', by which it meant the continuation of a deflationary policy to obtain an export surplus. Brüning's answer to this was to maintain his course or obtain the cancellation of reparation payments. Ultimately he achieved the latter, though at a time when he was no longer the political beneficiary of his policy. The cost of the policy at home was high: during the winter of 1930–31 there were almost five million unemployed, falling in the summer of 1931 to four million and then in February 1932 reaching 6,128,000.[2] Little wonder therefore that any hopes, including those of Hindenburg, of a return to a parliamentary government receded even further. Presidential cabinet government based on Article 48 of the constitution continued. Obviously there were plenty of suggestions for a change of course, for reforms, but they all contained an inflationary element, and the fear of inflation, deep-seated in Brüning after recent experience of it, made him reject them all. When the landslide of the 1930 elections – which Brüning called two years prematurely without there being a real need for it – brought the National Socialists 107 seats in the Reichstag, opinions were first voiced on the Right to draw the NSDAP into the government to provide it with the mass support in the country and the votes in the Reichstag which it lacked. But Hitler would not hear of it. In the first instance he would never consider serving under anyone, but would have to be Chancellor himself; in the second the NSDAP did not want to be tainted with a policy which produced so much hardship at home, though it also caused an influx into its ranks. The greater the domestic crisis the greater the benefits for the NSDAP – and for the Communists as well. While Brüning kept his nerve, the nation lost it.

HITLER'S 'CONSTITUTIONALISM'

As already mentioned, in this atmosphere of crisis General von Schleicher as well as the bureaucracy moved more into the political foreground. Seeckt had been compelled to resign in 1926 over an essentially minor affair. It did not affect the officer corps, since it felt equally close ties with its Commander-in-Chief, Hindenburg. Seeckt's successors, Helmuth Heye (1926–29) and Kurt von Hammerstein (1929–33), did not play a political role. Even when Otto Gessler was replaced by Groener – the former successor to Ludendorff – as *Reichswehrminister*, he proved completely loyal to the Republic.

But his political adviser General von Schleicher proved to be a political activist. Hence it is more correct to state that Schleicher rather than the *Reichswehr* moved to the fore. The judgement of historians has been harsh on him. He was not simply an ambitious intriguer who exploited the confidence of Groener and his own friendship with Hindenburg's son Oskar, with whom he had served in the Third Guards Regiment, for his own benefit, finally to open the gate of power to Hitler. The impotence of the Reichstag had created a power vacuum which challenged him to intervene on the political scene. The governmental crisis of spring 1930 provided him with his first opportunity. Due to his influence Brüning was made chancellor without the customary preliminary 'horse-trading'. Like most men of the conservative Right, Schleicher considered Hitler an upstart, and the formations of the NSDAP, notably the storm-troopers, the SA, a rabble. But it was a rabble or mob with a difference. It was imbued with nationalism: its programme contained socialist aspects to benefit the whole *Volksgemeinschaft*; it could also provide potentially a reservoir of manpower for the *Reichswehr*. In Schleicher's eyes and in those of many others there was nothing in the SA which a few weeks' solid square-bashing would not cure. Furthermore when three young lieutenants of the Ulm garrison were accused of spreading National Socialist propaganda among their comrades and arraigned before the Reich Court in Leipzig in September 1930 Hitler was called as a witness. In his evidence, Hitler rejected any notion of a conspiracy between the NSDAP and the SA on the one side and members of the *Reichswehr* on the other, adding, however, that once he came to power he would try to infuse the National Socialist spirit into the army. The presiding judge asked a number of further questions, for instance concerning a remark attributed to Hitler that if the National Socialists should come to power 'heads will roll in the sand'. Hitler replied: 'May I assure you, when our movement in the course of a legal struggle comes to power then a German State Court will come and November of 1918 will find its revenge and heads will roll.' A little later the presiding judge asked him: 'How do you imagine the establishment of the Third Reich?', to which Hitler replied: 'The National Socialist Movement will endeavour to attain its aims by constitutional means. The Constitution prescribes for us the methods but not the aims. In a unconstitutional manner we shall obtain the decisive majorities in the legislative bodies in order that from the very moment when we are successful we may cast the state in the form which corresponds with our ideas.' The judge once again asked Hitler; 'You mean by constitutional means?' to which Hitler simply replied: '*Jawohl!*'

Hitler had never made any bones about his anti-parliamentarian sentiments, as in 1930 when he publicly stated 'We National Socialists have never asserted to be representatives of a democratic point of view, but we have openly declared that we only use democratic means in order to gain power, and that after our seizure of power we shall deny to our enemies ruthlessly all those means granted to us while in opposition.' And again in the same year: 'For us parliament is not a means in itself, but a means to an end. We are in principle not a parliamentary party because that would be in contradiction to our entire conception. We are a parliamentary force by necessity, and what compels us to use such means is the Constitution.' Even in the election campaign for the March elections of 1933 Hitler declared that it was his life's task to sweep the political parties out of Germany.

Hence there could be no doubt about Hitler's ultimate intentions once in power. One of the weaknesses of the Weimar Constitution was that it contained no provisions against political parties or movements intent on changing or even overthrowing it, provided this was done constitutionally, as defined by Article 76. No one in 1933 could say he did not know what Hitler intended.

FROM BRÜNING TO PAPEN

In the meantime Hindenburg's first term of office was about to expire. Brüning tried to avoid the excitement of an election by extending the presidential term by parliamentary means. This would have required a law to change the constitution which would need, to be passed, a two-thirds majority, but the Right opposed it. Hindenburg, after much persuasion, agreed to enter the presidential election again. The Right was divided: the NSDAP put up Hitler as their presidential candidate, the DNVP and the DVP put up the leader of the veterans' organization, Theodor Duesterberg, the Communists Ernst Thälmann, and the Centre to moderate Left, Hindenburg. However, the only serious contenders were Hindenburg and Hitler. The first elections were on 13 March. Hindenburg gained 18.65 million votes, Hitler 11.34, Thälman almost 5 million, Duesterberg only 2.5 million. On 10 April 1932 the second elections were held, this time only between Hindenburg and Hitler. Hindenburg gained 19.35 million, Hitler 13.4 million. Of Germany's electorate 37 per cent were now on Hitler's side. Hindenburg, the candidate of the Right in 1925, had become the candidate victor of the Centre and Left in 1932, which made the old man rather uncomfortable. By that time the state of open civil war which had marked the beginning of the Republic, but continued below the surface, had broken into the open again. SA, Red Front, and the Republican *Reichsbanner* fought one another openly in the streets. Groener, who quite wrongly identified Hitler's SA as the sole cause and was by that time Minister of the Interior as well as *Reichswehrminister*, had Hindenburg sign a decree proscribing the SA and SS (Schutzstaffel, initially Hitler's personal bodyguard) on 13 April 1932.

However, presidential victory or not, in April 1932 Brüning was no nearer to establishing a parliamentary majority than he had been in 1930. Schleicher was convinced he could harness the extreme Right to his side and at the same time believed that another government was necessary, one that would explicitly listen to his advice. Hence Brüning had to go. Constitutionally the President was quite within his rights to dismiss him. In his place stepped a man hitherto totally unkown to the German public at large, Franz von Papen, while

Schleicher took over the *Reichswehr* Ministry from Groener. Papen was to be the figurehead behind which Schleicher hoped to govern.[3] Whether Papen was as stupid as he is often portrayed to be may be doubted. His later performance under Hitler as ambassador to Turkey seems to contradict this assumption as do his job-creating programmes while he was Chancellor. Rather like Schleicher he overestimated his own freedom of action and his own capacity. At first he also hoped to win over Hitler and the NSDAP, but Hitler's demands proved too exorbitant. Still, he hoped to win him round by dropping the pro-scription of the SA and SS – which Hitler correctly interpreted as a sign of weakness. When this did not work he tried to pursue politics on his own much to the surprise of his mentor, Schleicher.

Papen proceeded from the correct premise that one of the ills of the Weimar Constitution lay in its allowing excessive party political pluralism. As many as twelve parties or party-political groupings were represented in the Reichstag. At elections well over thirty parties, or bodies, laying claim to be such, appealed to the voters. Thus at each election millions of votes went down the drain. Papen therefore con-sidered constitutional changes which would reduce the number of parties. Ideally he would have liked the Westminster system but he kept an open mind on the precise number of parties to be represented in the Reichstag. At the same time, however, since the extreme Right could not be tamed, it would have to be dealt with by the government and suppressed, and the same went for the extreme Left, the Communists. Since it was unlikely that they would dissolve by govern-ment decree it was the job of both the police and the *Reichswehr* to ensure such a suppression. And once the political life of parliament had stabilized itself again, a monarchical restoration under a con-stitutional monarch of the House of Hohenzollern would be an additional bonus.

While thinking of his constitutional schemes, a constitutional crisis developed in Prussia where the obstructionist policies of the NSDAP and the Communists had made it increasingly difficult for the govern-ment headed by the Social Democratic Prime Minister, Otto Braun, to govern. His government resigned on 19 May 1932, but since the parties in the Prussian Diet were at odds with one another no coalition could be formed, which resulted in Braun's government staying provi-sionally in office. On 17 July 1932, in Altona, now a suburb of Hamburg, then still a Prussian governmental district, a column of NS storm-troopers was met with rifle and machine-gun fire in this tradi-tionally Communist stronghold. Fifteen men were killed and a great many more wounded. For Papen this was evidence enough that the Prussian government was no longer in a position to maintain law and order and since his constitutional plans also envisaged a greater trend towards unitary government in Germany, Prussia seemed the obvious choice as the first Land in which these ideas could be tried out. On 20

July 1932 Papen had the provisional Prussian government dismissed and appointed himself as Reich Commissar. The Braun government appealed to the State Court with the result that Papen and his team were allowed to continue in their functions, but they were not to be represented in the Reichsrat, the Reichstag, or *vis-à-vis* any other German Land. That remained the prerogative of the Braun provisional government. As already indicated, Bavaria and Baden, which had supported Braun, received Papen's personal assurance that his action in Prussia would not be a precedent applied to them or any other German Land. Papen's position was strengthened by the suspension of 105 civil servants, and he now had the Prussian administrative apparatus and the police in his hands. This *coup d'état* was carried out without any opposition: not even the Social Democrats or the Communists took to the streets.

THE JULY AND NOVEMBER ELECTIONS, 1932

But if Papen was to succeed at the Reich level and gain a parliamentary majority (and this is what he wanted), he had either to go to the polls or carry out his constitutional reform. First he tried his hand at national elections on 31 July 1932, at a time when there were 5.4 million unemployed. The fact that he reaped the fruits of Brüning's labours, namely the cancellation of reparation payments at the Lausanne Conference, made little impact upon the electorate. The NSDAP fielded 13.7 million voters, 300,000 more than at the presidential elections, and by the increase in seats from 110 to 230 became the strongest single party in the Reichstag, which allowed it to appoint the Reichstag's president, a position occupied by the man next to Hitler Hermann Göring, the last commander of the 'Richthofen Circus'. The Communists also gained, increasing their 78 seats to 89. The Social Democrats lost 3 seats, the Centre gained 6 and the BVP 3. The DNVP lost 5 seats and was reduced from 42 to 37. The big losers were the DVP, the Liberals and the other minor parties. But the total of the so-called 'national opposition' amounted to 46.5 per cent of the Reichstag's deputies and therefore could not form a majority government even when allied together. NSDAP and KPD together totalled 54 per cent and the two together now completely blocked any positive role the Reichstag could play – since September 1930 they had already possessed a 'blocking minority'.

For Papen the election result was all the more reason to try his hand at constitutional reform. This, however, required the cooperation of the *Reichswehr*. Schleicher, in his capacity as *Reichswehrminister*, had a war game carried out at the *Truppenamt*, – the name under the guise of which the forbidden General Staff operated – which concluded that the *Reichswehr* and its 100,000 men were in no position to face a potential civil war against the extremes of Right and Left which clearly formed the majority, while at the same time protecting Germany's frontiers, especially the eastern one where Poland was expected to take advantage of any serious internal disturbance in Germany. Papen, lacking the support of the *Reichswehr*, had to suffer a vote of no confidence in the Reichstag by 512 votes against 42 on 6 November 1932.

That he had used an emergency decree on 4 September to put into motion an economic programme that, firmly rejecting the policy followed by Brüning, was to provide one and threequarter million people with work, was not honoured at the polls when new elections were called for on 6 November. The electoral turn-out was 3.4 per cent lower than in July: the parties as well as the electorate were tired. The NSDAP lost 43 seats but still remained the strongest single party, while the DNVP and the DVP made some gains, as did the Communists who now obtained 100 seats and thus were only a little smaller than the SPD with 121 seats. The real sensation was the loss of 2 million votes by the NSDAP, but the July elections had been its zenith and its decline was now expected.[4] The only positive achievement of this Reichstag was a constitutional change requiring a two-thirds majority for Article 51 of the constitution about the appointment of the deputy for the Reich President in case of the latter's incapacity, be it because of illness or other reasons. According to the original version, in case of the president's incapacity his power went at first to the Chancellor, and in case of longer incapacitation a ruling was to be made by a special law. This article was now altered to the effect that under all circumstances in case of incapacity presidential power should go to the President of the Reichs Court. Why this was not raised in June/July 1934, when Hindeburg was obviously incapacitated, is a question which has yet to be answered.

SCHLEICHER'S FAILURE

Papen was now quickly made impotent. Unable to produce a government backed by a parliamentary majority, unable to carry out his constitutional reforms which he now had modified towards a 'New State' without parties and trade unions but with an authoritarian apex, a two-chamber system and plurality franchise as in the Anglo-Saxon countries, left in the lurch by his own ministers, he had against Hindenburg's inclination to make way for General von Schleicher.

Schleicher himself was not particularly enthusiastic about moving into the limelight. He had preferred to work behind the scenes. However, initially Schleicher did not incur so much hostility in the *Reichstag* as Papen had. It seemed as though it shied away from a new dissolution. With the votes of the NSDAP it prorogued itself. Schleicher tried two options, one with the Left, the other with the Right. He hoped to split Hitler's party. Gregor Strasser pleaded for the NSDAP to tolerate the Schleicher government: in the latter's scheme Strasser was to become Vice-Chancellor. Objectively it looked as though conditions were favourable for splitting the NSDAP. For thirteen years they had fought for power; they had made their breakthrough in 1930; they had become the largest single party and yet were as far from power as ten years before. There was some unrest within the party, especially within the SA, but Hitler quickly asserted his position, playing an all-or-nothing game, and Strasser resigned his party offices on 8 December 1932. The opening to the Right was closed to Schleicher. The opening to the Left seemed more promising, especially in view of the favourable attitude of the trade unions, but in the end SPD's suspicion of Schleicher in particular and anything military in general predominated and nothing came of that either. The 'armistice' which prevailed during the Christmas weeks of 1932 allowed him to extend Papen's job-creation programme, to introduce 'Winter Aid', and voluntary labour service, and as the western powers had on 10 December conceded Germany's equality in armaments in principle he could also introduce a militia year, plus a settlement policy in the east, first initiated by Brüning. The state was to buy up all hopelessly indebted estates and divide them up among unemployed urban workers, to draw the pressure away from the cities towards greater land cultivation, a scheme which encountered the immediate opposition of the agrarian interest group, the *Reichslandbund*, which was already dominated by the NSDAP.

HITLER *ANTE PORTAS*

Hitler's accession to power cannot be described in detail, but we must simply ask the question, did he come to power legally and constitutionally or merely by a back-stage intrigue? Schleicher's options were now all closed, except for Hitler. He believed he could afford to wait for Hitler to come to him, but Hitler did not come. Any toleration by the NSDAP in the Reichstag over the long term was unlikely: whenever the Reichstag might reconvene the parliamentary stalemate was bound to recur. Schleicher could not deliver the goods Hindenburg desired: the return to normal parliamentary government and the end of government by emergency decree. The formation of a new government lay in the air. This, or a military dictatorship under Schleicher, were the only options, though Hindenburg would not sanction the latter. Where Schleicher had failed, Papen tried anew, namely to renew contact with Hitler, procedures quite normal within the framework of the democratic process. Papen at first envisaged the chancellorship for himself, but Hitler was adamant that he would have to be Chancellor, while on the other hand he showed himself extremely moderate in his demands for ministerial posts compared with those he had demanded in the summer and autumn of 1932. Only two other National Socialists were to be included in the cabinet. Papen in the end acquiesced, being content with the post of Vice-Chancellor, believing that together with his conservative colleagues he would control politics using Hitler as a figurehead and having the mass support which they so sadly lacked behind them. The one obstacle in the way was Hindenburg who throughout January opposed appointing Hitler as Chancellor. As late as 26 January he declared to an enquiry by General von Hammerstein, the commander of the *Reichswehr*, that he did not intend making the Bohemian corporal Chancellor. But gradually it dawned on him too that there were few alternatives. Schleicher could not deliver the goods, nor could Papen without Hitler, therefore it had to be Hitler with Papen.[5] The Weimar Republic had burnt up politicians like a blast furnace: there was no other option except a coalition between SPD and KPD, but that coalition would not have produced a majority either, apart from being quite unthinkable for a man of Hindenburg's cast. Moreover, the Communists were now more engaged in fighting the SPD, the 'Social Fascists' as they were called, than the NSDAP. For the KPD the coming to power of Hitler was 'a historic necessity', he too would be burnt out in a few weeks or months and then the moment would come for the take-over by the proletariat.

In the end the decisive factor for Hindenburg was who would be *Reichswehrminister*. It came as a relief to him to hear that Hitler did not lay claim to this office for his party. He had had enough of Schleicher, and his son knew a truly conservative General who could be entrusted with the office, Werner von Blomberg, Commander of Defence District I (East Prussia) and at the time attached to the Commission in Geneva discussing disarmament. What neither Hindenburg nor his son knew was that Blomberg had become susceptible to the ideas of the NSDAP. He had come into touch with them via his Chief of Staff, Colonel Walther von Reichenau, who in turn had been infected by a divisional chaplain, Ludwig Müller, later to become 'Reichsbishop' and head of the abortive creation of the NSDAP, the 'German Christians'. Keeping the army out of Hitler's hands was Hindenburg's major concern; once that problem had been solved he had no more objections. But Hitler still needed a coalition ally, and he found this in the DNVP under Alfred Hugenberg, the press and film magnate. Hugenberg did not want to see a dissolution of the Reichstag; Hitler prevaricated, but actually wanted new elections believing that once at the head of government the public would be won over and the NSDAP gain an absolute majority.

Blomberg was recalled from Switzerland and in the early morning hours of 30 January 1933 was taken directly from the station to the presidential palace where he was sworn in as *Reichswehrminister*. Only a few hours later at about 11 o'clock Hitler and his cabinet were sworn in. Shortly before the ceremony an argument flared up between Hitler and Hugenberg about the proposed elections. Hugenberg was about to withdraw his cooperation when the overpowering figure of Meissner appeared in the doorway reminding the gentlemen that they had kept the President waiting for almost a quarter of an hour. It was like a rap on the knuckles and they all entered Hindenburg's study and went through the procedure. Hitler had brought with him two other National Socialists, Hermann Göring and Wilhelm Frick. If anything in all this violated the constitution, then it was the formal and prior appointment of Blomberg as *Reichswehrminister*. After all, according to Article 53, it was the task of the Chancellor to select his cabinet and submit it to presidential approval and to that of the Reichstag. But this is cancelled out by the fact that Hitler had been told about Blomberg's proposed appointment and found it perfectly acceptable. Nor would he have raised any objections to Schleicher being reappointed to that post as the cabinet papers, yet to be published, show. But as far as Hindenburg was concerned Schleicher was too dangerous. Throughout his chancellorship rumours of a military *coup d'état* never ceased, though as we now know they were quite unfounded. Both the NSDAP and the DNVP each put up three ministers; the other five were taken over from the Schleicher cabinet – they had also served under Papen. But Hitler at long last achieved what he had set out to achieve fourteen years before.

Why then did the Weimar Republic come to such an abysmal end, why did it fail? This is a question to which there can be no answer that could claim exactitude and precision. The most important reasons lie in the pressures exerted on the Republic from without and the mental attitudes held within. One cannot say on the basis of empirical verification that a majority of the population was not prepared to accept the political system and its constitutional fabric over the long term. At best a large portion of the German population maintained an ambivalent attitude to it, outright radical opposition being confined to the extraparliamentary intelligentsia of Left and Right. The ambivalence of a large part of the electorate turned into outright opposition only from the moment when the teeth of the Great Depression began to bite deeply in Germany, from late 1930 onwards. The traditions and attitudes present in the spectrum of the traditional German political parties outlined above were transposed upon the Weimar constitutional system, weak from the very beginning, suffering from the burden of their origin. The Weimar Republic was never allowed to forget that it was a progeny of defeat, neither by Germany's former enemies, nor by its enemies within. In conjunction with this the purely functional brand of proportional representation as laid down in the constitution exercised a centrifugal effect: instead of uniting the nation's political will, it led to its fragmentation and precluded the establishment of a basic consensus among the electorate. Anti-republican tendencies within the bureaucracy, the judiciary and the army existed within limits, and their potentially destructive force did not come to the fore until after Hitler had come to power. Even then, during Hitler's first years precisely these institutions exercised a re-straining influence until they had been fully brought under the control of the National Socialist polycracy.

In short, population, political parties and pressure groups allowed Weimar to fail because, as we can see with the benefit of hindsight, they made the wrong decisions. This is admittedly a banal conclusion, but then banality was one of the hallmarks of the Weimar Republic.

NOTES

1. Stresemann's second cabinet, 6 Oct. – 23 Nov. 1923, and Luther's second cabinet, 21 Jan. – 12 May 1926.
2. It is often said by historians such as K.D. Bracher that by late 1932 Germany had overcome the worst of the depression and was on the way to a recovery from which Hitler was to benefit. This is an untenable argument, not backed by any empirical data. On the contrary, as the experience of Great Britain shows, as well as that of the USA, despite the 'New Deal' the depression was far from over, and sustained economic recovery in these countries did not set in until the outbreak of the Second World War.
3. Schleicher, in order to secure the NSDAP, had already, prior to Papen's official appointment and without his knowledge, assured Hitler that the new government would revoke the ban on the uniformed formations of the NSDAP.
4. Again, the argument that from then on the decline of the NSDAP would have been inevitable is purely speculative. It would have been just as possible for it to retain its high number of supporters, as did the SPD and the Centre. Nevertheless the setback was not lost on Hitler.
5. Hindenburg has been severely criticised for conceding to Hitler what he denied to Schleicher: continued presidential government by the use of Article 48. This criticism overlooks the fact that there was no chance for Schleicher ever to attain a parliamentary majority, in contrast to Hitler whose appointment would, so it was believed, lead back to constitutional government.

Chapter 9

THE 'FÜHRER' STATE

THE SIGNIFICANCE OF ARTICLE 48

Article 55 of the Prussian Constitution of 30 November 1920 runs as follows:

> When the maintenance of public security or the removal of an unusual emergency requires it urgently, and the Diet is not assembled, the state ministry can, in agreement with the permanent committee provided for by Article 26, issue decrees with the force of law as long as they are not contrary to the constitution. When the Diet reassembles these decrees are to be submitted to it for its approval. If this approval is refused then it is repealed by publication.

Article 48 of the Weimar Constitution, however, did not contain any such constraints. On the contrary, the Reich President could expressly suspend the seven most important basic rights, if he considered it necessary, namely liberty of the individual (Art. 114), inviolability of one's home (Art. 115), secrecy of one's mail (Art. 117), freedom of opinion (Art. 118), freedom of assembly (Art. 123), freedom of association (Art. 124) and the right to property (Art. 153). Moreover the Reich President had the exclusive right to decide when a disturbance of public order and security had taken place. It was also his function to introduce those measures necessary for the restoration of normal conditions, i.e. of public security and order. Instead of detailed and precise emergency legislation the President was endowed with thinly-veiled dictatorial powers. These extraordinary powers were expanded further by Article 25 which allowed him to dissolve the Reichstag and hold new elections.

However, the controlling function of parliament was not completely eliminated by Article 48. According to its third paragraph the President, upon the request of the Reichstag, had to withdraw all his measures. The Reichstag could request the suspension or abolition of any emergency legislation, but it could not by itself revoke it: it had to request the President to do so. If there was the slightest danger that the Reichstag would reject emergency legislation the President could take the pre-emptive step of dissolving the Reichstag first, as was the practice of 1931–32. Thus the dictatorial powers of the President were fairly extensive but not unlimited. The Reichstag was not all-powerful but neither was it impotent. Insofar as the Reichstag decided to have emergency legislation withdrawn, the President had to follow this demand or dissolve parliament. However, between 1919 and the end of 1932, 233 pieces of emergency legislation were enacted.

Hitler was appointed Chancellor on the basis that the Reichstag would be dissolved, that new elections would be carried out and that an Enabling Bill would be introduced. Everyone knew that Hitler's appointment was likely to involve profound changes. After all, the NSDAP party programme, like that of the KPD, profoundly differed from those of any of the other parties. Unlike the Basic Law of the Federal Republic of Germany, there was nothing in the Weimar Constitution declaring it illegal to try to overturn the constitution provided it was done constitutionally. The Weimar Constitution did have instruments of direct democracy like the referendum and the plebiscite and the possibility of unlimited constitutional changes by way of legislation according to Article 76. Hence Hitler's appointment was in conformity with the constitution and was rather more constitutional than all the governments since the break-up of the Great Coalition. His appointment, according to the letter of the constitution, returned government to its normal parliamentary channels, as outlined in Articles 54 and 32, which stated that the Chancellor and Ministers required the confidence of the Reichstag to carry out their offices. The Reichstag only needed a simple majority to show its confidence. Up to that point everything was normal; the abnormal situation only arose in March 1933 when Hitler introduced the Enabling Act.

THE REICHSTAG FIRE AND THE MARCH 1933 ELECTION

In the meantime, however, new elections were to be held; the Reichstag was dissolved on 1 February 1933. Given the civil war atmosphere in which the last two Reichstag elections had been carried out, it was not unnatural that emergency legislation should be introduced to curb the excesses. After Göring, as Deputy Commissar for Prussia, had issued on 30 January and 2 February decrees relating to Prussia prohibiting Communist demonstrations, national emergency legislation followed on 4 February based on Article 48 of the constitution. This subjected all public assemblies to prior police approval and prohibited all political assemblies in the open which could threaten public order and security. Press freedom was also limited and publications prohibited which might 'endanger public security and order'. The fact is that, as Hans Mommsen has shown in his study on the consequences of the Reichstag fire, there is ample evidence that the National Socialists did expect a Communist uprising. They did not suppose that they would obtain and consolidate their own power without having to fight for it on the streets. Göring in Prussia absorbed the SA and SS into the police as an auxiliary force, and in the process of their 'executive duties' they inevitably settled old scores. The high point was reached when the Dutchman Marinus van der Lubbe set fire to the Reichstag building, destroying the entire interior. As Mommsen demonstrates, the subsequent emergency legislation, also based on Article 48 of the Weimar Constitution, was not the product of a long-term plan but was an *ad hoc* improvisation, in the belief that a Communist rising was imminent. It suspended all the basic rights (see above) guaranteed by the constitution and was supplemented on 21 March 1933 by a law against treacherous attacks on the government of the 'National Revolution' (supplemented more than a year later by a law against treacherous attacks on party and state and for the protection of party uniforms). Although the Communist rising never materialized this legislation remained in force until the end of the Third Reich.

For the emergency legislation enacted in early February there were ample precedents. For years Hitler had been forbidden to speak in various Lands in Germany as had been his paramilitary formations. At a national level they had been proscribed as recently as April 1932 by Groener. Of greater importance was the precedent established in 1922 which had enacted retroactive legislation. The *lex van der Lubbe*, which retroactively imposed the death sentence on the Dutchman who had set fire to the Reichstag, invoked the precedent of 1922.

In spite of this legislation the Communist Party was not yet outlawed, although such a course was advocated in cabinet, but opposed by Hitler. Though numerous Communists were arrested, they were still allowed to participate in the election but deputies elected were not allowed to take their seats. Nevertheless the elections held on 5 March 1933 were a disappointment for the NSDAP. It did not gain the absolute majority it desired but only 43.9 per cent of votes cast and it was only thanks to its DNVP allies that it could claim that 56 per cent of the German population had voted for the government of the 'National Revolution'. Hitler used this position at the first meeting of the Reichstag to introduce his Enabling Bill which was to give him power to enact laws deviating from the constitution (Article 2) for a period of four years for the 'recovery of Germany'. Hitler's aim was to gain unlimited power. He had said so often enough.

THE ENABLING LAW

Hitler was aware that over the long term Article 48 of the constitution would be entirely inadequate; what he needed was a blank cheque. This he could only achieve by means of Article 76, according to which the constitution could only be changed or done away with altogether by way of legislation, and any change required a two-thirds majority. Hitler got more than his two-thirds majority: he got four-fifths of the Reichstag vote, 444 votes in favour 94 against. Only the Social Democrats voted against. Even had the Communists been present, which they were not because they were prohibited from exercising their mandate, Hitler would still have had the required majority.

All non-NSDAP Reichstag members who voted in favour knew Hitler would break with the parliamentary system. They also knew what was meant by ths six articles of the `Law for the Recovery of the People and the Reich from Suffering`, which was released the following day. Article 1 stated bluntly: `Apart from the procedure laid down in the Reich Constitution laws can also be passed by the Reich government.` The principle of the separation of power was ignored, as were the people's representatives, and those who were ignored sanctioned this action. Article 2 stated that the laws enacted could also deviate from the constitution. In this way the executive gained full legislative powers – and all by constitutional means.

Much has been said and written about the pressure exercised on the Reichstag deputies and about the alleged atmosphere of terror and intimidation – most of it, of course, after 1945. But even if true the question remains: why did the SPD *en bloc* vote against the Enabling Act while 82 per cent of Germany's full-time politicians allegedly endowed Hitler with powers the purpose of use of which were beyond doubt? Hitler was quite forthright and honest in his speech advocating the acceptance of the bill. He stated that;

> The spirit of the national revolution and its purpose would be contradicted if the government had to request the agreement of the Reichstag for all its measures. The government does not intend to abolish the Reichstag as such. On the contrary it reserves for itself the right to inform the Reichstag from time to time about its measures. . . . Since the government as such has an actual clear majority, the number of cases which will need to have recourse to this law is itself a limited one. All the more therefore the government of the National Revolution must insist on the passing of this law. In any case it prefers a clear decision. It offers the parties the possibility of a quiet German development and from that a way towards understanding in the future, but it is just as determined and ready to accept rejection and thus the proclamation of resistance. May you now, *meine Herren Abgeordneten* (Deputies), make your own decision over peace or war.

This was clear enough and the Social Democratic deputy Otto Wels in a speech defending the attitude of the SPD pointed to all the implications, after which no deputy could maintain that his eyes had not been opened. He stated that the government had certainly obtained a clear majority in the elections, but with the Enabling Act the National Socialists intended nothing other than to take the last step in the direction of the dissolution of parliamentary democracy. His party and the parliamentary party could not be used for this purpose.

In other words the parties of the Weimar Republic were not deceitfully removed by the National Socialists, or even smashed; they removed themselves. Hjalmar Schacht remarks that the democratic parties gave up, without needing to, any parliamentary influence, 'an act of political self-emasculation unknown in the history of modern democracy'. The parties are said to have put out of action both themselves and those parts of the constitution decisive for a democratic structure, without being forced to do so. They thus voluntarily had pleaded for their own dissolution. The Republic had not been destroyed, as in an act of war, fighting to the last. It had no unconditional defenders, but always reliable enemies. Its trenchant left-wing critics, such as the writer Kurt Tucholsky who admitted this himself shortly afterwards, lacked any sense of the boundaries between change and destruction. It was carried out by parties whose democratic loyalty exhausted itself in loyalty to their own party programme, and on occasions not even that. Weimar did not die because of its enemies, but because it possessed no genuine friends, not even among the Left, as the example of Breitscheid's pronouncements at the Magdeburg party rally of 1929 has already shown. It did not have parties that supported the state, only pallbearers that carried the coffin. What the acceptance of the Enabling Act proves is that the parties of the Weimar Republic were at one in their opinion that the liberal system on whose existence their own existence depended no longer had any viability for future political life. The last act had ended, the curtain had come down.

Yet most of what has just been said is really beside the point. However welcome the agreement of the Centre, the Liberals and other groupings was for the purpose of window-dressing, Hitler did not need it. His alleged deception of the Centre Party is completely irrelevant, for there was no need for it. To demonstrate this we have to recall the wording of Article 76 of the Weimar Constitution and then look at the results of the March election. A bill changing the constitution can only become law 'if two thirds of the legally required members are present and at least two thirds of them vote in favour of it'. Because of the extraordinarily high turn-out at the election of 5 March 1933 (88.1 per cent as against 79 per cent in the previous November) 647 deputies were elected as against 593 in November 1932. Therefore the presence of 432 deputies was required to represent a quorum to debate the Enabling Bill. Although the NSDAP had failed to obtain an absolute majority, it had increased its number of seats to 288, and these 288 votes represent precisely two thirds of the required presence of 432 deputies. Actually present in the Reichstag were a total of 538 deputies. The combined total of Centre Party and SPD deputies present was 166, too few to form a blocking minority against the combined vote of NSDAP and DNVP which increased the vote of the government of the 'National Revolution' to a total of 341 votes. If Hitler had wanted to make absolutely sure to have his Enabling Bill passed he could have reduced the attendance figure to 511 by taking into 'protective custody' another 27 deputies which, however, he did not do because he was certain of his victory. The Centre Party under Prelate Kaas was unlikely to join the SPD which had torpedoed the Great Coalition in 1930 and whose increasing drift to the radical Left since then could not be ignored. The Communists, who had won 81 seats, had been forbidden to take their seats because of the Reichstag fire, but even they, together with the SPD, would not have amounted to a blocking minority. Only the certainty of victory could have caused Hitler to challenge the deputies to choose between 'peace or war'.

Hitler in his own fashion did keep his promise: he did not abolish the Reichstag, but merely changed its composition to that of an assembly acclamatory of the NSDAP which was occasionally called together and informed about 'the measures of the government'. He even had the Enabling Act renewed on three occasions: in 1937, in 1939 and during the Second World War in 1943. And he kept his promise that 'heads would roll'. In 1934 the National Socialist People's Court was installed, endowed solely with the task of prosecuting and sentencing perpetrators of acts of treason.

Even before the passing of the Enabling Act the process of *Gleichschaltung* was happening all over Germany: Lands were coordinated into the Reich, each under a *Reichsstatthalter*, though Hitler still expressed himself in favour of some degree of decentralization. For this reason he allowed his Gauleiters considerable liberties, one of the many examples which demonstrate that the Third Reich, rather than being a firm monolith, was very much a polycratic structure in which, however, Hitler had the last say. By July 1933 all political parties other than the NSDAP had disappeared. All this was possible because, besides the self-emasculation of the Reichstag, the *Reichswehr* did not intervene. After Hitler had become Chancellor Blomberg agreed with Hitler's domestic 'revolution' provided that the army retained the monopoly of armed force. *Reichswehr* and NSDAP were the twin pillars of the state and in order to establish the armed forces' relationship firmly on the side of Hitler the army took measures, such as the application of the Aryan paragraph, the wearing of the NS insignia on its uniforms, and finally, on Hindenburg's death, the swearing in of the army to Hitler personally, which were welcome to Hitler but not requested or ordered by him in the first instance. Hitler in turn reaffirmed that the *Reichswehr* was the sole bearer of arms and in the

June purge of 1934 had,among others, his former mentor, supporter and friend Ernst Röhm executed.[2] As a consequence of Hindenburg's death he fused the offices of Chancellor and President. Henceforth there was only the 'Führer and Reich Chancellor' in one person. Hitler's position had been consolidated. However, although in one of his first speeches after coming to power he had spoken of a National Socialist Constitution being devised and ultimately put to the people, this never materialized. Nor was there ever an official body which concerned itself with it. Thus in purely legal terms the Weimar Constitution remained in force, albeit with vital sections suspended, until the end of the Second World War. But from August 1934 onwards one can no longer speak of any constitutional development: this was replaced by the *Führerbefehl*, itself a product of the National Socialist leadership principle.

THE NATIONAL SOCIALIST LEADERSHIP PRINCIPLE

One major aspect, however, requires discussion since upon it rested National Socialist rule in all aspects of German life: the National Socialist *Führerprinzip*. Already in *Mein Kampf* Hitler had emphasized the role of the *Führer* and his unlimited power from the family unit to the *Führer* of the State. The leadership principle may not be a specifically National Socialist invention but rather the characteristic of hierarchic structures, but its establishment in Germany after 1933 proceeded almost unnoticed, because even before the days of the Weimar Republic the idea of an authoritarian leadership had gained pretty wide currency in Germany. If anything, the Weimar Republic had furthered the popularization of this process through its very actions, or rather lack of them. Ironically, Hitler, always intent on having a legal or pseudo-legal basis for his actions, never anchored the leadership principle institutionally or legally. It is not contained in the party programme of 1920 nor in any piece of legislation after 1933. Instead it could build upon the mental militarization of the German people, which ranged from the Conservatives to the Communists, from non-party Youth Leagues to the Hitler Youth. By making reference to the leadership principle the Nationalist Socialists struck a chord already in existence. They immediately adapted its external trappings, the ritual of the leader and followers as exemplified in National Socialists public ceremonies, to which they added pseudo-religious and liturgical forms. After all, the leader was not to provide a solution but salvation, or as one jurist of the period put it in an official journal: 'The German people are united in the opinion that because of its disunity it requires a *Führer*.'

The leadership principle had no basis in law or in the party programme, it was vague, ambivalent, unlimited and therefore extremely flexible – the power of the *Führer* was devoid of any legal constraint. It became an undefined absolute, from which followed that not only did *Führerbefehle* become orders which had to be unconditionally obeyed but also that the will of the *Führer* became the guideline, the yardstick for all actions. Hitler mobilized energies in the German people which were without precedent; his appeal to the irrational led to this breakthrough. Some National Socialists tried to derive the leadership principle from traditional historical sources, the development of political ideas since the French Revolution of 1789, but this apparently rational justification was soon swept away by slogans such as the feeling of the *Volk*, intuition and so forth. Existing German constitutional law was replaced by slogans, postulates and general clauses. The *Führer*'s powers could be understood only 'intuitively', legal limitations were swept away because they contradicted the 'depth and width' of the leadership principle. Liberal abstract systems of thought were dismissed, and into their place stepped the 'concrete' values of the community. What precisely these values were remained undefined. The NSDAP spoke of a *völkische Gesamtordnung*, but what this meant in terms of law remained an open question. It also spoke of a *völkische Verfassung*, a constitution, but that constitution never materialized, perhaps because however it might have been formulated it would inevitably have contained rights and duties, thus erecting constraints to the exercise of power, and it was precisely in order to be free from such constraints that Hitler needed the Enabling Act.

In its most absolute form the leadership principle was to be carried out within the judiciary. Thus in the early years of the Third Reich the principle of the independence of judges was not formally thrown overboard: it was merely to be 'reshaped' in the National Socialist spirit. As early as 1933 the legal scholar Carl Schmitt published an article in which he stated that the independence of the judges rested on their bond with the law, and the law of the state. Without that bond their actions would be arbitrary. It was an attempt to reconcile the independence of judges with the leadership principle, which found quick oppositional response from National Socialist judges themselves who insisted on the continuance of the judges' independence, while on the other hand linking it also with the will of the *Führer*, 'the *Führer* is the highest German judge, he is *the* German judge'.

Paragraph 1 of the Law for Securing the Unity of Party and State of 1 December 1933 reads: 'After the victory of the National Socialist Revolution the National Socialist German Workers' Party is the bearer of the idea of the German State and thus indissolubly united with the State'. Hence the rule of Hitler and the NSDAP claimed virtual infallibility in all their actions in all spheres of life in Germany. Institutionally therefore political, administrative and judicial leadership were inextricably intertwined, at the top the *Führer und Reichskanzler*, at the lower level the personal union of the offices of *Landrat* and *Kreisleiter*. From the top the *Führerbefehl* became the most decisive instrument and Hitler normally entrusted one of his 'old fighters' with the task of seeing that it was carried out. They could demand that the existing bureaucracy assist them, but they could also act over their heads. Organizationally the predominance of the NSDAP over the state was established through a whole host of offices which duplicated existing state institutions. The NSDAP clearly stated that the German State took only second position to it and the National Socialist ideology, a demand reflected for instance in the German Civil Service Law of 1937, in which the civil servant is defined as the executor of the will of the state embodied in the NSDAP. The civil servant owed loyalty to the *Führer* unto death. His entire behaviour had to be guided by the fact that the NSDAP, indissolubly tied to the *Volk*, is the bearer of the idea of the German State. As for the judiciary, Germany's highest court, the *Reichsgericht*, in 1939 pronounced that not the state but the *Volk* was the decisive criterion. Thus the NSDAP became the primary element of all *völkisch* life and the example for the state yet to be created, while the existing state in its present form was considered to be only of a temporary nature. Appointments within the bureaucracy and judiciary and promotions were all subject to the agreement of the NSDAP.

National Socialism understood itself to be the ultimate form of the expression of the *Volksgemeinschaft* which it claimed to lead. This was a blanket rejection of the liberal legal system embodying personal liberties and rights contained in the Weimar Constitution. What was subject to endless argument until the outbreak of war was whether the Weimar Constitution ceased to be in force after 30 January 1933 or whether it was put out of operation section by section through National Socialist legislation that was tantamount to constitutional change. Such legislation for instance was the suspension of basic rights in the wake of the Reichstag fire. The National Socialists left no doubt about it: 'The present legislation has only for the sake of order and quiet . . . used the formal procedures laid down in the Weimar Constitution, but it does not derive its justification from it'. The constitution and the legal principles based on it had been overruled by the *Volksgemeinschaft* and the National Socialist *Weltanschauung*. Thus in 1935 in a trial of Jehovah's Witnesses in Hamburg the continuation of the Weimar Constitution was negated and declared irreconcilable with the National Socialist concept of the state. Changes to the constitution by the judiciary were declared admissible: some judges went as far as to consider the NSDAP party programme as the legal basis of their arguments, something which even Hitler was personally rather reluctant to do. And Carl Schmitt noted in 1934 that 'it is quite evident that any discussion concerning the constitutional structure must begin with the simple sentence: "The Weimar Reich Constitution is no longer valid" '. This view was in fact correct. The law concerning the establishment of the People's Court was already outside the framework of the constitution and so of course was the legislation which *post factum* justified the Röhm purge, as was subsequent legislation which forbade German lawyers to represent 'Non-Aryans' before German courts and which also applied to gypsies. Once the war against Poland had begun and Poland was occupied, this prohibition was not formally applied to Poles but lawyers were advised 'to consider the interests of the national community and to impose upon themselves great self-restraint'. The National Socialist leadership principle superseded and replaced any legal constraints and if the Third Reich had lasted longer than it did, would ultimately have produced chaos in all spheres of the law, unless a new constitutional framework had been created.

LEGAL IMPLICATIONS OF GERMANY'S SURRENDER

In terms of international law the end of the Third Reich is interesting since, should a general European settlement ever come about such as a peace treaty with Germany, it would not be without constitutional implications. The allies in 1945 had two alternatives, one to destroy military resistance to such a degree that no state authority would function any more, the other to enter into a contractual arrangement with the existing German government, then the government under Grand Admiral Karl Dönitz, to bring hostilities to a close. The former alternative would have brought about a state known in international law as *debellatio* in which the allies would have had Germany fully at their mercy, though not without regard for the principles of natural law. However, by entering into negotiations with the Dönitz government they entered into a contractual relationship which *de facto* recognized it. With its assistance the war in Europe was terminated. These considerations had indeed played a role in allied thinking. On 25 July 1944 a document for 'political unconditional surrender' had been drawn up containing fourteen points, Point 12 of which stipulated that the supreme governing power in Germany would be exercised by the USA, the United Kingdom, and the USSR, which would take all measures necessary to ensure peace and security including the complete disarmament and demilitarization of Germany. At the Yalta Conference this point was amended to include the 'dismemberment of Germany'. Such a document was available in General Eisenhower's headquarters. All that needed to be inserted was place, date and signature. When, early in May 1945, Admiral Hans von Friedeburg and General Alfred Jodl arrived at Eisenhower's headquarters in Rheims, Eisenhower's staff very much feared that Dönitz would not sign such a blank cheque and therefore, rather hurriedly, a rather shorter non-political text for purely military capitulation was drafted. Those who drafted this document believed it would save lives and end German military resistance through a German military order. But this ignored, as one member of the European Advisory Commission put it, two significant political points. By allowing the German Supreme Command to sign a purely military capitulation in the field, the allies forfeited the opportunity to obtain the German recognition of a political surrender. This shortcoming put a question mark over the highest authority which the allies intended to exercise in Germany. A purely military capitulation kept in force for an indefinite period the provisions of the Geneva and Hague Conventions and would, from a judicial point of view, prevent the allies prosecuting war criminals, and cause them to maintain the institutions in Germany as they existed. Hence a clause was added in the shorter document of military surrender to the effect that this document would not prejudice its replacement by a general instrument of surrender which would be imposed upon Germany and its forces in the name of the United Nations. Such a document was never imposed and the German government in Flensburg, unaware of the existence of a rather more detailed political as well as military instrument of surrender, could only conclude from the actual document it signed not only the recognition of the government but the political acceptance of Germany as a State.

Eisenhower's main concern was to bring the war in Europe to a speedy end, which, as Lord Strang put it, he could only achieve 'if the military conditions of the surrender were not too drastic'. It is doubtful whether Dönitz would ever have signed such a document as was left in Eisenhower's desk drawer, in which he would have been asked to accept the dismemberment of Germany. But such a signature was neither demanded nor given, and whatever has happened on German soil on the initiative of the victorious allies is, in terms of international law, for the Germans only *res inter alios acta* – the Latin expression in international law for a procedure in which alien powers deal with a third power which has not offered its agreement, and therefore is not compelled to accept what has happened, however long ago. The allies of course tried to cut the Gordian knot they themselves had tied by arresting and dispersing the German government once the military surrender had been completed, though this amounted to a gross violation of what they had fought the war to defend: the inviolability of international law.[3]

The implications of these events will inevitably play a role if a general German settlement is ever concluded and will then inevitably reverberate within the constitutional framework of the provisional German successor states.

NOTES

1. The Enabling Law did contain some restraints. According to Article 2, legislation was not to affect the *Institution* of the Reichstag or the *Reichsrat*, nor was it to affect the rights of the Reich President. It would cease once 'the present government was replaced by another one'. In actual practice the *Institution* of the Reichstag was maintained though its composition was changed by the establishment of a one-party state, an objective which Hitler even before the 1933 March elections had publicly proclaimed. The provisions concerning the *Reichsrat* were already irrelevant by the time the Enabling Bill was debated, when in the process of *Gleichschaltung* most German states were headed by a *Reichstatthalter* under whom the land governments, staffed with NS personell, continued to operate but in a purely administrative capacity and subject to the Reich Ministry of the Interior. The *Reichsrat* dissolved itself, and the rights of the Reich President were not tampered with in Hindenburg's lifetime. But on 1 August 1934, one day before his death, the cabinet unanimously passed a law fusing the offices of Chancellor and President, which came into force the day after Hitler subjected this law to a referendum and the majority voted in favour, though it did come as a disappointment that the majority was three million down on the vote cast the previous November in the referendum endorsing Germany leaving the League of Nations. The 'present government' continued, though there were changes of individual ministers, the first being Hindenburg in 1933 because of his performance at the World Economic Conference in London, where he aggressively raised demands which, as yet, Hitler had not made and which in Hitler's view were bound to alienate his potential ally, Great Britain.
2. Hitler had these executions legally sanctioned by the 'Law concerning Measures of Self-Defence for the State in an Emergency' of 3 July 1934. In his speech to the Reichstag, justifying his actions, he claimed on this occasion to have acted as 'Germany's Supreme Lord of the Law'. This was the first public step by Hitler, usurping the judicial power in the Reich, which culminated in his Reichstag speech of 26 April 1942 in which he claimed for himself the title not only of 'Supreme Possessor of all Executive Power' but also of 'Supreme Lord of the Law' – not, as Göring put it, 'bound by the existing law'. Thus all judicial power emanated from Hitler. He could impose any sentence, change any judgment, and appoint and dismiss any member of the judiciary.
3. However, Hitler in 1944 had already created a precedent. The military members of the 20 July 1944 conspiracy would have been subject to trial by the highest court of the German armed forces. In order to be able to try them by the People's Court, Hitler created a 'Court of Honour' of the *Wehrmacht*, which expelled those concerned from the armed forces and then handed them over to the People's Court. The Allies in 1945 first deprived of their prisoner-of-war status those it wished to prosecute for war crimes, which put them outside the Geneva Convention. Since at the Nuremberg trials not only individuals but also entire governments were tried and found guilty, many Germans – members of the *Waffen*-SS for instance – changed overnight from prisoners of war into criminals.

Chapter 10

THE TWO GERMANIES

At the Potsdam Conference held between 17 July and 2 August 1945, the USA, the United Kingdom and the USSR decided to set up a 'Council of Foreign Ministers' where these three powers, as well as France and China, would be represented and whose task would be to draft and conclude peace treaties with Germany's former allies. An Allied Control Council was set up for Germany representing the four occupying powers (including France) with its seat in Berlin. Its decisions were to be unanimous; in other words any decision could be vetoed by any one of the four powers. The Council of Foreign Ministers was also to prepare a document for a peace settlement with Germany, which a new German government could accept once it had been formed. This meant that the Potsdam Conference proceeded from the assumption that Germany after her political capitulation (which in fact had not occurred), and a period of occupation would once again have a government and thus continue to exist as a state. But for the time being there was to be no central German government, only administrative offices under Secretaries of State for Finance, Industry, External Trade, Transport and Traffic under the supervision of the Allied Control Council. Germany was defined as existing within the boundaries of 1937, although the German territories east of the Oder-Neisse line had already been put under Polish and Soviet administration. The fate of these territories was to be finally settled at a German peace conference. The industrial territory of the Ruhr was put under international control: the Russian demand to participate was rejected by the western powers. However, the western allies sanctioned the expulsion by Poland, Czechoslovakia and Russia of their German population. Although Stalin claimed that these Germans had already fled, in fact over 5.6 million were still east of the Oder-Neisse line apart from those still living in the Sudeten regions – about half the number of Germans who had lived there for centuries.

THE ALLIES AND THE GERMAN PROBLEM, 1945–47

The first conference of the Council of Foreign Ministers took place in ,London from 11 September to 2 October 1945. Because of the number of issues discussed there, no time was left to consider the German problem, at a period when the working of the Allied Control Council had begun to stagnate because of the French attitude. The provisional French government under General de Gaulle had not been invited to the Potsdam Conference and the French therefore did not accept its conclusions. Instead it advocated a separation of the Rhineland and the Ruhr from any future German government control to satisfy France's requirements for security. Events in East Asia and Iran sharpened the tensions between the USSR and the United States to such an extent that Secretary of State Byrnes in a speech of 18 February 1946 stated that the west might have to face the possibility of an armed conflict. America then still had a monopoly of the atomic bomb.

With the work of the Allied Control Council virtually blocked, the military governor of each of the four zones of occupation acted as he thought best. Only the Russians, as will be seen, had a clear concept of what they wanted in Germany. In May 1946 General Clay, then still deputy to General Eisenhower as military governor of the American zone, wrote a memorandum in which he stated that the de-industrialization of Germany as envisaged in the Morgenthau Plan presupposed its treatment as a unified economic territory. But if the zones of occupation were being cut off from one another, as the Soviet and French zones were, the industrial production in the American and British zone would have to be raised to keep the German population there alive. He advocated the setting up of a German central administration as determined at the Potsdam Conference as well as a Council of Minister Presidents of the German Lands from all four zones which was to draft a new German Constitution for a state of between nine and fifteen German Lands. It was to be approved by the Allied Control Council. The new Germany was to be a federal state; a parliament was to be elected in which at least two parties were represented. Furthermore he advocated the continued expulsion of Germans in territories east of the Oder-Neisse line and their acceptance by the western allies. While supporting the French claim for an economic union between the Saarland and France, he rejected French claims to the Ruhr and the Rhineland.

The second meeting of the Council of Foreign Ministers took place in Paris on 25 April 1946. It was prorogued and resumed from 15 June to 12 July. As the Foreign Ministers were unable to compromise on non-German issues, invitations for a General Peace Conference to be held on 29 July 1946 in Paris were issued. France now proved flexible. Foreign Minister Bidault was prepared to accept a loose German federation subject to previous agreement on Germany's frontiers. The French realized that the division of Germany was an accomplished fact; any unification would inevitably bring western Germany into the Soviet orbit. Molotov opposed the French demands for frontier rectifications in the west and the federalization of Germany. He demanded German unity and Russian participation in the control of the Ruhr without, however, offering the western allies participation in the economic control of the Soviet zone. Byrnes opposed the Russian demands since he saw them as nothing but a means to destroy the Ruhr industries which were an essential component of a healthy European economy. The Morgenthau Plan was dead and buried. As a result of the diverging positions no peace treaty for Germany could be drafted and the peace conference dissolved.

On 6 September 1946 Secretary of State Byrnes gave a speech in Stuttgart before members of the military government and a select circle of German politicians. In it he proposed a reversal of western policy in Germany, the formation of a German government and the fusion of the occupation zones. If Russians and French would not participate then the USA and Great Britian would go it alone in their zones. The west could not afford to let Germany become the poor-house of Europe; the German and European economies were dependent upon one another. He implicitly acknowledged the Oder-Neisse line, but also made it subject to a general peace settlement with Germany. As far as Germany's western frontiers were concerned he expressed his support for the French demand for the economic union of the Saarland with France, but opposed their demands for the Rhineland and the Ruhr. Russia's response was favourable as far as Byrnes's comments went on the fate of the German territories east of the Oder-Neisse line. After all, he asked, 'Who could think that the resettlement of the Germans was only a temporary experiment?' That this policy of 'resettlement' had been carried out in a way which cost the lives of further millions of Germans was not mentioned by either East or West. When one of the few supra-regional German newspapers, the *Süddeutsche Zeitung*, in a commentary drew attention to this aspect the American military government suspended its publication for a fortnight.

Three days after Byrnes's speech, on 19 September Winston Churchill, gave a speech in Zürich which he proclaimed a United States of Europe, based on the friendly relationship between France and Germany, as the eventual aim. This was immediately opposed by the Soviet Union, since Lenin had been against this idea and in 1930 the Soviet Union had in no small measure contributed to the failure of just such a scheme, worked out between Briand and Stresemann.

The third session of the Council of Foreign Ministers met between 4 November and 11 December 1946 in New York. It worked out the peace settlements with Germany's former allies, which were signed on 11 February 1947 in Paris. But the German problem remained as open as it had been before. In the meantime tensions between East and West increased further and because of Great Britain's economic weakness the USA assumed her responsibilities in the eastern Mediterranean in the form of the 'Truman Doctrine.'

The exclusion of France from the Potsdam Conference had led to her adopting a very obstructionist attitude over the German question. Only when France and Great Britain on 4 March 1947 signed the Treaty of Dunkirk, a defensive alliance directed against Germany, did France feel some measure of security and gradually adopted a more positive attitude to the Anglo-American policy in western Germany. The Treaty of Dunkirk a year later was to include Belgium, Holland and Luxemburg which in the form of the Western European Union was joined by Italy and the Federal Republic of Germany in 1955 – a development that could not be foreseen in 1947.

The Council of Foreign Ministers in its fourth session in Moscow from 10 March to 24 April dealt intensively with the German question. General George Marshall, US Secretary of State since January 1947, had previously been on a mission in China to bring about a compromise solution between Chiang Kai-shek and Mao Tse-tung and put an end to the civil war. His failure there led him to adopt a firm attitude towards the Soviet Union in particular and Communism in general. At the Moscow Conference he supported the cession of only south-east Prussia and the Upper Silesian industrial area to Poland. In this he had the support of the British Foreign Minister, Ernest Bevin. France adopted the attitude that this question was only of formal legal importance. In return Molotov supported France over the Saar. But the central issue was German unity. The western and eastern conceptions excluded one another. Britain and the USA supported a single plurality franchise or a mixed franchise as already practised in the British and American zones; Russia was in favour of proportional representation as in the Weimar Republic. Molotov also rejected the federal structure and advocated a unitary solution: in drafting the constitution mass organizations as well as parties should be represented as in all 'people's democracies.' Bevin submitted a plan for a temporary constitution to be drawn up by an elected body, which the Control Council would have to approve, to be based on the Weimar model. No unanimity could be achieved over this, any more than over the question of establishing a German central administration. The only conclusion this conference could come to was the dissolution of the State of Prussia, which was already dead and buried in any case. Nor could agreement be reached over economic issues.

The western powers from then on acted on their own, and the USA,

321

contrary to her intentions at the time of the capitulation of the German armed forces, now decided to keep her forces in Germany as long as any other power did the same. Economically the USA committed herself to the creation of a stable and productive Germany. The American diplomat and historian, George F. Kennan, then adviser to the State Department, coined the phrase 'containment', which was adopted by Marshall and combined with his European Recovery Programme (ERP), the Marshall Plan, which aimed at making western and central Europe economically prosperous again and thus less vulnerable to Communist propaganda. He announced his plan on 5 June 1947 in a speech at Harvard University. This volume is not the place to discuss the Marshall Plan in outline, let alone in detail, except to state that it represents one of the pegs on which the division of Germany rests and that it marked the final break-up of the east–west alliance of the former allies of the Second World War.

GERMAN POLITICAL DEVELOPMENT AFTER 1945

Germany's political and constitutional development took place within this context. A month before the Potsdam Conference the central committee of the KPD in Berlin, consisting mainly of KPD members who had found refuge in Moscow during the Third Reich, issued a proclamation reconstituting itself. Originally this had not been intended by the Russians, but because of the lack of resistance by the Germans, the Russians considered it opportune to give the KPD its chance, and Berlin, still entirely in Russian hands, seemed a suitable base. On the same day Marshal Zhukov also issued a proclamation which allowed the organization of democratic parties generally. Wilhelm Pieck, since 1935 chairman of the KPD in exile, brought a proclamation with him, drafted in Moscow, which contained none of the traditional Communist demands of the Weimar period. It explicitly stated that it would be considered wrong to impose the Soviet system upon Germany, because this did not correspond with Germany's present political development. Instead it advocated the establishment of an anti-Fascist democratic regime, a parliamentarian democratic republic, with all democratic rights and liberties for the people. Concepts like the proletarian revolution and class struggle were not mentioned at all. But Walter Ulbricht, who together with the Soviet Military Administration (SMAD) was the actual moving spirit, was quick to fill the key posts of the five Land governments established immediately with reliable Communists, especially in the police, personnel and cultural sectors.

Since the KPD at the height of its success in the Weimar Republic had not achieved more than 16.9 per cent of the poll it required a mass base. Because of this the demand arose for the fusion of the KPD and the SPD. This demand was also put forward by a faction within the SPD which included Otto Grotewohl, a former USPD and later SPD member, and member of the Reichstag. He had stayed in Germany throughout the Third Reich. The SPD in its proclamation of 15 June 1945 demanded the unity of the German working class.

However, there was a second group, the SPD leadership in exile in London under Erich Ollenhauer. Ollenhauer during his exile actively participated in allied propaganda work against the Third Reich until the Casablanca Declaration demanding Germany's unconditional surrender. From then onwards he withdrew from the allied effort in protest, unlike Willy Brandt, who did not decide on which nationality he should have and whether or not to discard allied military uniform until 1948. Ollenhauer in contrast made up his mind at once and looked at the idea of fusion between KPD and SPD with scepticism and reserve.

The third group of Social Democrats under Kurt Schumacher, an army volunteer in 1914, who had lost his right arm, was the decisive one. In 1918 he had joined the SPD and spent the years of the Third Reich in its concentration camps. Several years before his death in 1952 he also lost a leg. This cripple was nevertheless possessed by energy and an indomitable spirit and, above all, an unassailable integrity. He believed Germany's Social Democracy was free from guilt for the wrongs of the past and therefore destined to lead her. He endeavoured to activate the party organization throughout Germany and, once that had been done, a German SPD rally was to be called which would establish a legitimate government by democratic means. He opposed Communist dictatorship as fanatically as he had opposed the National Socialist one. Therefore, in agreement with the London group he opposed amalgamation with the Communists.

THE SOVIET ZONE

The KPD, aware that it could not count on a majority, adamantly pursued the course of amalgamation, backed by SMAD. It was further strengthened in its resolve to achieve this when the Austrian Communist Party (KPÖ) suffered a crippling defeat in the election of 25 November 1945. Schumacher advised Grotewohl, in case of obstruction by SMAD, publicly to dissolve the SPD in the Soviet zone, but Grotewohl rejected the idea of moving into a futile opposition and instead tried to gain as much ground as possible within the existing framework. By February 1946 the Central Committees of the SPD and KPD decided to hold parallel party rallies in Berlin and then in a joint rally to amalgamate under the name *Sozialistische Einheitspartei*, Socialist Unity Party (SED).

In order to test whether this accorded with the wishes of the rank and file the Berlin SPD put it to the vote of its members. However, SMAD prohibited such a poll in the Soviet sector and it was therefore restricted to the western sectors. In West Berlin 73 per cent of the SPD members took part in the poll and 82 per cent opposed the amalgamation, while two thirds pleaded for cooperation with the KPD. Only 12.4 per cent voted in favour of amalgamation. But irrespective of this outcome Ulbricht, Pieck and Grotewohl went ahead and on 21 and 22 April 1946 the amalgamation was carried out and Wilhelm Pieck and Otto Grotewohl elected as joint chairmen. In October 1946 the communal elections in the Soviet zone were carried out, in which the SED competed with the Christian Democratic Union (CDU) and the Liberal Democratic Party (LDP). The SED exploited Soviet backing to the utmost. In some areas the other two parties had not been established and were prevented from doing so until after the elections, with the result that there was only the SED candidate to vote for. The election result reflected this manipulation: SED 57 per cent, LDP 21.1, CDU 18.8 per cent, other mass organizations such as trade unions 3 per cent. In the elections for the Land Diets the SED vote was reduced to 47.8 per cent, while the other parties polled: 22.7, CDU 26.5, mass organizations 3 per cent. The result in the election of the City Council of Greater Berlin was quite different. Here manipulation could not be carried out as extensively as in the Soviet zone and the SPD was allowed whereas it had been prohibited in the Soviet zone after the foundation of the SED. The results were: SPD 48.7, SED 19.8, LDP 9.3, CDU 22.2 per cent. It was a serious defeat for the SED, demonstrating that it was really a minority movement. It forced them and SMAD to reverse the course proclaimed on 10 June 1945: the SED was organized on the lines of the Communist Party of Russia and became a Bolshevik party.

THE WESTERN ZONES

The preconditions for the Communists in the western zones were rather different. First of all political parties were only allowed gradually and rather late. Not before September to December 1945 did the western allies allow the official formation of parties. The Communists also tried to amalgamate the KPD and SPD, but apart from being forbidden to do so by the occupying powers, Kurt

Schumacher's opposition nullified any such hopes. Hence the KPD in the west became an offshoot of the SED of the Soviet zone and its leaders, such as Max Reimann, for a time belonged to the praesidium of the SED. The KPD, until its prohibition in 1956, worked under instructions from the SED, much as the DKP, its successor, does at present. At first they had some successes. They managed to gain a total of 113 seats in the parliaments of the western zones in 1946–47. By 1949–51 they had declined to 29, in only five of the Land parliaments.

The core of the SPD was the circle around Kurt Schumacher in Hanover. What Schumacher, however, failed to do was to give it a new face to correspond to what was then needed. He adhered to the old Weimar and pre-Weimar programmes, which placed the party in permanent opposition until 1969 when it achieved its breakthrough to power but even then only in coalition with the Free Democrats (FDP). Only in 1959, seven years after Schumacher's death, and then under the chairmanship of Erich Ollenhauer and the guidance of the former Communist, Herbert Wehner, was the Bad Godesberg programme formulated. This no longer emphasized evolution or revolution, but a process of permanent reform based on liberal principles combined with social justice. It transformed the SPD from a class party into a people's party with a membership of 800,000. In the realm of foreign policy, an area hotly contested previously between Adenauer and Schumacher, it also moved towards a bilateral policy with the CDU/CSU.

The CDU the Christian Democratic Union, is a completely new party which emerged from the debris of the Third Reich. It was not created by a joint plan but emerged from a number of groups whose common aim was to establish a socially equitable society within a Christian context. It expressed solidarity between Protestants and Catholics. These groups believed that an important cause for the failure of the Weimar Republic was that it had not bridged the gap between the different social groups. The name Christian Democratic Union was coined in Berlin by a group who had belonged to the active resistance to Hitler, men like Jakob Kaiser, Andreas Hermes, Hans Lukascheck and Ernst Lemmer, a trade unionist. It was backed by leaders of the Protestant Church like Bishop Otto Dibelius, and men of international renown such as the surgeon Professor Ferdinand Sauerbruch. The Soviet authorities licensed this party on 26 June 1945. The Cologne Circle, comprising members of the former Centre Party and the Christian trade unions, was independent of it. Another group formed itself in Schleswig-Holstein under Hans Schlange-Schöningen who had held office under Brüning, essentially Christian Conservatives, former Liberals and members of the former German People's Party. Another group emerged in Frankfurt led by former members of the Catholic youth movement; in Bavaria Adam Stegerwald, the former chairman of the Christian trade unions, rallied to his side the lawyer Josef Müller, once a member of the German *Abwehr* under Canaris and who had belonged to the military opposition to Hitler, had been caught by the Gestapo, sent to a concentration camp, and eventually liberated by the allies.

The first supra-regional conference of the various groups took place in Bad Godesberg in December 1945 where the CDU was formally formed, while the Bavarians retained their separate party, the Christian Social Union (CSU). For the time being only the British occupation authorities allowed the CDU to organize on a supra-Land basis. The man who rapidly emerged to lead it, though not at the very beginning, was Konrad Adenauer, from 1917 to 1933 Lord Mayor of Cologne, a post he occupied again after the 1945 until he was dismissed by the British. He did the necessary preliminary work on a party programme and on 1 March 1946 was elected party chairman in the British zone. But the CDU did not become what could be called a national party, until more than a year after the creation of the Federal Republic, except in Bavaria where the CSU maintained its role.

On 3 February 1947 the CDU proclaimed at Ahlen the so-called 'Ahlen Programme' in which it renounced a purely capitalist economy as not being equitable to the interests of the German people. State capitalism was similarly denounced, as were monopolies and cartels. The latter would have to be dissolved, and where this could not be done, they would have to be nationalized. Employees were to be fully involved with employers in all fundamental questions of economic and social planning, but planning and management were not to become ends in themselves. The CSU drew up its own programme which differed only in relation to the economic structures in Bavaria, then still largely agrarian compared with the highly industrialized area of the British zone. Both the CDU and the CSU expressed a deep distrust toward an uncontrolled capitalist economy, sharing these views with the SPD. The difference lies in the sources for their basic ideas and in the different social groups they represented. Wide divergences between the two parties soon appeared in their attitudes towards foreign policy, a contrast embodied by Adenauer on the one hand and by Kurt Schumacher on the other. Adenauer saw Germany's future differently, differing even with his party colleague Jakob Kaiser who planned to make Berlin the centre of the CDU, a plan torpedoed by Adenauer. As early as 1945 Adenauer was convinced that the splitting of Germany into western and eastern zones of occupation would lead eventually to its permanent division. It was therefore of paramount importance to shift the point of gravity away from Berlin to western Germany and pursue the integration of at least one part of Germany into the western community. European integration had a clear priority over national integration in Adenauer's mind. Schumacher placed as his priority a unified Germany.

Although the CDU membership hovered only around the 300,000

mark, in the polls it outmatched the SPD and to this day has remained, together with the CSU, the strongest single party in western Germany. Its electoral support originally came from former Centre Party voters but over the decades the electoral support for both CDU/CSU and SPD has tended to cut across class and religious lines.

The third new party, but with far less support than the CDU/CSU and SPD, is the Free Democrats (FDP), with traditions deriving from the former Liberals, the DVP, the National Liberals and the Progressives. The various liberal groupings in the western zones only formed the FDP on 12 November 1948 under the chairmanship of Theordor Heuss, a former associate of Friedrich Naumann and the National Social Association, and a Liberal during the Weimar Republic. Until well into the 1960s the FDP stood to the right of the CDU, even absorbing into its ranks former functionaries of the NSDAP. Early in 1953 this led the then British High Commissioner for Germany Sir Brian Robertson, to carry out a number of arrests because of suspected National Socialist infiltration of the FDP in North Rhine-Westphalia. It was an ill-judged step: all those arrested were promptly released and no charges were brought against them. The programme of the FDP, which was heavily influenced by Friedrich August von Hayek, then teaching at the London School of Economics, tried to ensure a maximum of individual liberty within a modern industrial society with its monopolistic power concentration of industry or trade unions and thus prevent social collectivization. In the first elections of the Federal Republic the FDP managed to win 43 seats out of 410. Yet its influence has become much stronger than its actual voting support would suggest. It was the key party in most of Adenauer's coalition until 1969 when the CDU/CSU failed to get an absolute majority and it opted for coalition with the SPD, a position maintained until the end of September 1982 when the FDP terminated this arrangement and formed a new coalition government with the CDU/CSU under Chancellor Helmut Kohl.

A number of smaller parties emerged, such as the Deutsche Partei (DP), essentially conservative and sharing views similar to the CDU and FDP, but finally absorbed by the CDU in the early 1960s. Bavarian separatism was represented in the *Bavernpartei* (BP), founded in 1946 by the former CSU member and Bavarian Minister of Economics, Josef Baumgartner, to guarantee Bavaria's independence within the framework of the German and European community of states. It was represented in the first federal parliament by seventeen deputies (the same as for the DP), but as a result of a number of serious financial scandals it declined and though it still exists, its electoral support has moved over to the CSU.

A party with far greater chances of success at first was the *Block der Heimatvertriebenen und Entrechteten* (BHE) (Bloc of Refugees and the Disowned), founded in 1950, which in the year of its foundation in

Schleswig-Holstein managed to win 23.4 per cent of the votes. It appealed to the refugees of Germany's eastern territories as well as to those discriminated against because of former active NSDAP membership. But as soon as the refugees were integrated into West German society and former NSDAP membership faded as a political, social and economic stigma, the BHE lost its attraction and was largely absorbed by the CDU and FDP. On the extreme right was the Socialist Reich Party (SRP), founded in 1949, which initially managed to score successes at local elections, and because of its National Socialist tendencies was outlawed by the Federal Constitutional Supreme Court in 1952. It had various successors, which failed to gain a significant foothold, until the period of 1966–69 when the National Democratic Party under Adolf von Thadden (half brother of Elisabeth von Thadden, a member of the resistance to Hitler and executed for it in 1944) seemed a new threat on the democratic horizon. After a number of spectacular local successes it just failed to clear the 5 per cent hurdle (see below) in the 1969 elections and from then on declined and in the elections of 1980 polled less than one per cent, a result repeated in 1982.

OCCUPATION POLICIES AND POLITICAL PARTIES

In describing and analysing the political parties in Germany we have jumped, so to speak, the chronological fence, and must now return to its political and constitutional development since 1945. After the SED realized that little could be achieved with free democratic elections, under the protection of SMAD it gradually took over the reins of political life in the Soviet zone. As Walter Ulbricht put it: 'It must look democratic, but we must have everything in our hands.' Even this could not be put into practice. Already on 14 July 1945 the political parties licensed by the Russians were formed into an anti-fascist Bloc in which 'the workers take over the determining role in the democratic development'. On the initiative of SMAD two new parties were founded. The first was the National Democratic Party of Germany (NPD) which was to appeal to former NSDAP members who had not incriminated themselves, though in fact its members included former *Wehrmacht* generals and others who had acted as lay judges in the notorious People's Court. The second was the Democratic Peasants' Party of Germany (DBP) which was to free the peasants from bourgeois influence. Both parties – their leaders had been KPD members during the Weimar Republic – immediately subordinated themselves to the SED. Those who did not, for instance the CDU under Andreas Hermes, Jakob Haiser and Ernst Lemmer, had to make way for more pliant instruments – they subsequently left for the western zone. Mass organizations like the trade unions, *Freier Deutscher Gewerkschaftsbund* (FDGB), the Free German Youth (FDJ) and others, could have their members elected and were under the direct control of the SED. The same applied to the press. The Russification of political life in the eastern zone led many leading party functionaries, including SED members, to seek refuge in the west.

The eastern zone originally consisted of five Lands: Mecklenburg, Saxony, Thuringia, Brandenburg and Saxony-Anhalt. These were reduced by 1952 to provincial status and their State Diets dissolved: what remained was a centralized zone directed from East Berlin.

When on 20 October 1946 the Diets of the Lands were elected by proportional representation, the results were disappointing for the SED. In Saxony the SED vote increased from 48.4 to 49.1 per cent; that of the CDU and LDP from 39.9 to 48.1 per cent; in Saxony-Anhalt the SED declined from 49.5 to 45.8 per cent; while the CDU/LDP rose from 31.1 to 51.8 per cent. The SED lost a total of 430,000 votes while the CDU/LDP gained 750,000. In the communal elections in Brandenburg and Saxony-Anhalt the SED lost its majority. Saxony-Anhalt then got a new LDP Prime Minister, all other Prime Ministers being SED members. Moreover the SED insisted on occupying the Ministry of Culture in all Lands. With the exception of Brandenburg, all Ministers of the Interior were SED and former KPD members. SMAD and the SED by and by established central institutions which subordinated the Land governments particularly in economic matters and trade, in education and justice. SED members in leading positions who had been former Social Democrats were weeded out and replaced by Communists. The pretext for this was the eradication of 'Fascism' but this soon became a term which embraced all those who opposed the SED. While former prominent NSDAP members continued to be employed as long as they were specialists in a particular field, they were thoroughly purged, together with any remaining bourgeois elements, from the judiciary. Eighty-five per cent of the judges were dismissed and SED lay judges replaced them. The police was under direct Soviet control, officered by former *Wehrmacht* officers who in Russian captivity had been members of the National Committee for a Free Germany and the Leage of German Officers (NKFD and BDO respectively). From 1945 until 1950 the concentration camps of Buchenwald, Oranienburg and Bautzen continued to function under Russian supervision and housed undesirable elements from all political tendencies as well as former NSDAP members. The prison population of these three camps amounted to an estimated 130,000: 50,000 died in them while a further 30 – 50,000 died while in investigative detention or were deported to the Soviet Union.

On 14 June 1947 SMAD ordered the formation of a German

Economic Commission with directive powers over the Land governments. Its main job was to organize reparations for Russia. Russia's policy of relentless extraction and exploitation of economic resources was the cause for smouldering disquiet among the German population to an extent that made the Soviet zone a liability to the USSR rather than an asset. After Stalin's death, it appeared that Russia under Malenkov, in return for the guarantee of the Oder-Neisse line and other compensations, would have been glad to rid itself of its central German possession. But at exactly this point of time unrest in the Soviet zone reached its climax and on 17 June 1953 the first rebellion among Russia's satellites against Soviet and SED over-lordship took place throughout central Germany. Irrespective of their original wishes Russian forces had to intervene to prop up the faltering regime of Pieck, Grotewohl and Ulbricht. From then onwards Russia's demands became more reasonable and the economy slowly recovered.

In western Germany politics seemed at first to be influenced by separatist issues, many Germans wanting to be included in Denmark, hoping to escape the hardships which the aftermath of war had brought. But the Danish government wisely declined, considering it, correctly, to be only a temporary phenomenon. A separatist strand was also discernible in Bavaria, the only German territory which had a historical tradition dating back to the early Middle Ages. But this current was also quickly absorbed and made harmless by the CSU. In the Saar on the other hand France tried to force events by announcing in February 1946 that it intended to remove this territory from the competency of the Allied Control Council. In December 1946 the Saarland was separated from the rest of Germany by a customs frontier. Of the Saar parties only the Communists opposed separation from Germany. Johannes Hoffman, who had already agitated before 1935 for the separation of the Saar, was installed as Prime Minister. His government operated under the direction of the French High Commissioner, the Gaullist Gilbert Grandval. The Customs Union between France and the Saar was introduced on 30 March 1948. (No one could foresee then that the population of the Saar would be given the opportunity eight years later to vote for or against return to Germany. A majority vote opted for Germany and the Saarland became part of the Federal Republic on 1 January 1957.) Substantial territorial changes took place within the three western zones. The Lands of Lower Saxony, Schleswig-Holstein and North Rhine-Westphalia were formed in 1952 and Hamburg and Bremen became city states again. Bavaria remained essentially in its traditional form in the American zone. Since the demarcation frontier between the American and French zones of occupation divided Württemberg and Baden, in 1952 the French and American parts were fused into the Land Baden-Württemberg, and a third state, Hesse, was established in addition to Bremen, where Bremerhaven was an American enclave in the British zone.

The French zone contained Württemberg-Hohenzollern, Baden and Rhineland-Palatinate. The latter was created in 1946 out of the former Bavarian Palatinate, the part of Hesse-Darmstadt on the left bank of the Rhine, and parts of former Prussian possessions.

During the early phase of occupation each western power went its own way. France placed great emphasis on preventing German re-unification, obtaining a maximum of reparations, increasing its cultural influence and not allowing political parties at Land level till March 1946. But it also encouraged cultural life, as for instance in the founding of a new university, the University of Mainz, in the new Land of Rhineland-Palatinate. The French refused to accept any refugees from Germany's eastern territories, though this zone was the least affected by the war. However, France's administrative apparatus was excessively inflated. For every 10,000 German inhabitants there were 18 French compared with 10 British and 3 American officials.

In the British zone the military government was influenced by the Labour Party. Bevin displayed a marked reserve towards the German problem but whatever part the issue of nationalization of industries played in Great Britain, as far as the British zone was concerned he acted pragmatically and in cooperation with the United States, which blocked any nationalization tendencies in the western zones. The strongest influence on German political parties came from the British zone, the initial field of operations of both Adenauer and Schumacher. The same applies to the formation of trade unions. These developed speedily under British guidance and British trade unionists produced a model which their comrades at home prevented them from applying in Britain. Instead of a multiplicity of unions a few strong trade unions, such as had already existed under the Weimar Republic, were formed. In spite of its division into Lands the British military government treated the zone as a unified whole, in contrast to the French.

The competencies of the Lands were therefore more limited. Central zonal officers were established, the most important being the Central Economic Council in Minden. On 15 February 1946 the British also created a German zonal advisory council in Hamburg, which a year later was parliamentarized, that is to say its members were nominated by the various Land parliaments, though it did not possess any legislative or executive powers. The constitutional order of the British zone rested upon the statutes proclaimed by the British, with the result that the Lands in this zone were empowered to draft and pass their own constitutions later than in any other zones of Germany, the last being that of Hamburg in 1952.

The strongest and most determining supra-zonal political influences on the future of western Germany came from the American military government. This applied to the process of de-Nazification by which the Germans established their own de-Nazification courts which, however, with the onset of the Cold War, were allowed to wither away. Above all, this influence applied to economic and political co-operation. The Joint Chiefs of Staff Directive 1067, largely framed against the background of the Morgenthau Plan, was soon abandoned. From the time of the Byrnes speech in Stuttgart US policy moved in the direction of integrating western Germany into the then still infant anti-Soviet bloc and using the German economy for the consolidation of the western European economy as a whole. Next to the Russians the Americans were the first to delegate legislative and executive functions to German-administered governments. The American zone was the first of the three western zones to carry out communal and Land elections. In May 1945 the Americans had already established a Bavarian government headed by Fritz Schäffer (later Adenauer's Minister of Finance) who, however, was dismissed for publicly opposing the thesis of 'collective guilt'. The Commander of the American forces in Bavaria, General Patten, was also dismissed from his post because he expressed doubt in public about the value of the process of de-Nazification and because he kept cadres of German forces in being and under arms in the belief that war against Russia would be inevitable.

The Social Democrat, Wilhelm Hoegner, who between 1933 and 1945 had lived in exile in Switzerland, was appointed Schäffer's successor. In September 1945 the Liberal Reinhold Maier was appointed Prime Minister for Baden-Württemberg, in October Karl Geiler for Hesse and the Social Democrat Wilhelm Kaisen of Bremen as Burgermaster and President of the Senate, an office he held until 1965. In the early phase these governments included members of most major parties, including Communists. By the end of 1945 the Americans had created advisory Land Councils made up of the representatives of the political parties. The democratic legitimacy of these bodies from the commune to the Land was established by elections during the first six months of 1946. On 30 June 1946 elections were held for constituent assemblies at Land level. In Bavaria they produced an absolute majority for the CSU, in Württemberg-Baden a relative majority for the CDU, while in Hesse and in Bremen the SPD was victorious. The Americans on the whole refrained from intervening in constitutional discussions, except in Bavaria where they insisted on the wording that Bavaria would join a German 'federal state', rather than a 'league' as the Bavarian assembly had originally expressed it. In Hesse the demand for nationalization of coal, iron and railways was made subject to a referendum, under American pressure. On 24 November 1946 the Baden-Württemberg Constitution was ratified by two thirds of the popular vote, Bavaria and Hesse following on 1 December. Elections to the Land parliaments were held simultaneously and these brought little or no change. In Hesse, however, 62.7 per cent voted in favour of nationalization, a vote which the Americans ignored, simply prohibiting this step, arguing that the issue would have to be reserved for a future German government. Bremen was the last Land to ratify its constitution on 12 October 1947.

As a result of the November – December 1946 elections the first parliamentary legitimized governments were formed. In Bavaria Hoegner was out. Hans Ehard, a lawyer and in 1924 prosecutor in the trial of Hitler and his associates, became Prime Minister, forming a coalition cabinet including the SPD. Coalitions followed in Hesse, and an all-party government in Baden-Württemberg. The competencies of the government were widened and from the moment France blocked the formation of German central administrative agencies they worked in the direction of supra-zonal cooperation in economic matters. A Land Council (*Länderrat*) was to assist the Americans in this. A directory of the *Länderrat* emerged in June 1946 from this institution. In contrast to the British, the Americans put federalism in their zone on its feet, by means of the federal legitimacy endorsed by free elections, and the Germans were given greater responsibility. But the idea soon gained ground among General Clay and his advisers that the *Länderrat* could provide the organizational pattern for supra-regional and even supra-zonal coordination, an opinion strongly shared by German federalists. As things stood supra-zonal cooperation could only be carried out at first between the British and American zones of occupation. By September 1946 the British and Americans agreed to establish five bi-zonal offices, for food and agriculture, traffic, the economy, finance, and posts and communications. Each of these administrative councils comprised members of both zones. They were controlled by an Anglo-American Bipartite Board. The Bi-zone was finally created in December 1946 and came into operation from 1 January 1947. Bi-zonal cooperation began to develop its own dynamics. The bi-zonal offices were subjected to German parliamentary control and on 10 June 1947 the United Economic Territory with its office in Frankfurt was founded. It comprised fifty-two members from the individual Land parliaments and represented an indirect organ of the people's representation. Its competency was widened and given legislative powers. This development clearly pointed in the direction of the formation of a separate German state.

CONSTITUTIONAL DEVELOPMENTS

When discussing the constitution of the German Lands one can omit those of the Soviet zone since, as already indicated, these were reduced to the status of administrative districts in 1952.

The Lands of the American and French zones as well as Greater Berlin received their constitutions between September 1946 and May 1947, while those of the British zone received them later, after the founding of the Federal Republic – in the interim they worked according to organizational statutes issued by the British military government. However, those Lands which did have a constitution by mid 1947 were still not fully-fledged states with their own sovereignty, but operated under the supervision of their respective military governments. As the latter began to loosen their reins they slowly moved towards becoming federal states. Their constitutions – the basic rights of the individual they contained and the social, economic and political order they established – were the guidelines of the Parliamentary Council in 1948–49 in drafting the Basic Law, i.e. the provisional Constitution for the Federal Republic.

As in the Weimar Constitution basic rights guaranteed the classic liberal liberties of the person, faith, conscience and the freedom of opinion. They also included the right to strike and the right to education. These basic rights are expressly formulated and put at the head of the constitutions of Rhineland-Palatinate, Baden, Baden-Württemberg and Hesse. In those of the other Lands of western Germany they are included in the form of what amounts to self-denying ordinances by the state. The constitutions of Hesse and Bremen explicitly state the individual's right of resistance to any violation of the constitution by the state. On the other hand the state's right to protect itself against the excess and misuse of personal rights led to provisions which allowed the state to act against any unconstitutional activity – the ultimate decision lying with courts.

The separation of powers is the basis of the constitutions. The separation of the legislative power was particularly advocated by the CDU/CSU in southern Germany, where a two-chamber system was demanded. However, this failed to get the necessary support but the idea left traces in the Bavarian Constitution which established a Senate as well as a parliament, though with very limited functions. Bavaria was also the only Land which described itself in the constitution from the outset as a state, the *Freistaat* Bayern, a term coined by the revolutionary Eisner government in 1918–19. A further peculiarity of the Bavarian Constitution is that it contains no provision for the recall of the government by parliament but stipulates a full four-year period of office, with the limitation that the Prime Minister has to resign if he loses the confidence of parliament. The standing of each Land as a state is emphasized in all constitutions of this period in various ways, as also in some cases its ultimate integration within a republic, federal republic or federal league. The Constitution of Baden, however, only refers to a community of German Lands, while that of Rhineland-Palatinate declared it to be a member state of Germany, leaving the question open about Germany's future as a federal state or a league of states. The Bavarian Constitution expressly referred to a league of states. These differences already show centralizing, federal or even particularist currents at work. That the power of the state was not consolidated but separated the very basis of a liberal parliamentary democracy, is shown by the provisions for an opposition in parliament in the form of political parties. Neither the Bismarckian nor the Weimar constitutions had contained any provisions for them. The Constitution of Baden was the first to regulate the public legal position of political parties. It expressly refers to opposition parties and their responsibility for guiding the state.

As far as social and economic aspects are concerned West German constitutions contain identical features: the rejection of economic power concentrations by monopolies and cartels, the recognition of the freedom of coalition, i.e. the right of employees to organize themselves in trade unions, collective bargaining, the right to strike and arbitration, the support of workers' co-determination, and the recognition of the need for a limited degree of planning in the economy to guide production in order to satisfy a limited degree of planning in the economy to guide production in order to satisfy the essential requirements of each citizen. Except in Hesse private property is one of the basic rights: the Constitution of Rhineland-Palatinate goes as far as to consider it a natural law. Employees are to participate in the profits, and many constitutions also envisaged nationalization of key industries should the common interest demand it. Employers and employees enjoy equal rights within chambers of commerce and industry in order to assist in guiding the economy. The Bavarian Constitution declares that all natural resources such as minerals etc., energy and railways are public property. Bremen's Constitution envisaged the nationalization of important major industries and enterprises, while Hesse unequivocally demanded the nationalization of mining, the iron industry and the railways. The Hesse Constitution, while recognizing the right to strike, prohibits lock-outs.

To sum up, it can be said that the constitutions of the west German Lands all display a clear and determined will to achieve social reform, and that at a time when large parts of Germany's industry such as mining, heavy industry and chemicals were in allied hands.

THE EMERGENCE OF TWO GERMANIES

The constitution-making process was well under way when the Marshall Plan, and with it the western policy of 'containment' of the Soviet Union, was initiated. To maximize the effects of the aid given by the Marshall Plan the Organisation for European Economic Co-operation (OEEC) was founded. Its members lowered tariffs and created customs unions, for instance the Benelux countries. In 1947 this had been preceded on a world-wide level by the General Agreement on Tariffs and Trade (GATT), concluded in Geneva on 30 October 1947 between twenty-four nations. All member states were to enjoy between themselves most-favoured-nation status in imports and exports. The Federal Republic has participated in GATT since 1950, becoming a full member in 1951.

Although the Soviet Union was invited to join the Marshall Plan it rejected the invitation on the grounds that the Plan threatened the sovereignty of the member states. Poland and Czechoslovakia, which were inclined to join were held back by the Soviet Union. In opposition to the Marshall Plan the Council for Mutual Economic Assistance (Comecon) came into being in 1949 in Eastern Europe.

On the very day George Marshall proposed his plan at Harvard on 5 June 1947 the prime ministers of all four zones of occupation met in Munich, the first and only meeting of heads of the German Lands. The original initiative had come from the President of the Bremen Senate Wilhelm Kaisen who intended it to take place in Bremen in October 1946, but the French occupation authorities prohibited the participation of the prime ministers of their zone. Only the Thuringian Prime Minister Rudolf Paul came from the eastern zone. Nevertheless that October conference drafted a resolution to form a Land Council consisting of the prime ministers of all four zones under the parliamentary control of the delegates from the various Land parliaments. In the Soviet zone the driving force was Jakob Kaiser, the Chairman of the CDU, and Eugen Schiffer, chairman of the LDP. In the western zone the idea found particular support in the CDU/CSU, which on 15 March 1947 wrote to the SPD, SED and LDP calling for a meeting to prepare the first stage of a united German representative assembly of the people, which was to represent it until German re-unification could be realized. The SED and LDP accepted. The FDP did not yet exist as a party. But the invitation was met with outright rejection by Kurt Schumacher and the SPD on the grounds that the latter was prohibited in the Soviet zone, and not until this prohibition was revoked would he be prepared to sit with the SED at one table. Konrad Adenauer was sceptical since he did not share Jakob Kaiser's optimism about a synthesis of socialism and liberty and his belief that it was Germany's historic mission to build a bridge between east and west. Adenauer neither supported nor obstructed the plan. The attempt failed firstly because of Schumacher's opposition, and secondly because of lack of civic courage on the part of some of the west German prime ministers to disobey the explicit instructions of the French military governor.

The Bavarian Prime Minister, Ehard, had invited his colleagues to

Munich for 6 and 7 June. The purpose of the meeting was 'to prevent the further decline of the German people into a hopeless economic and political chaos'. Schumacher instructed the Social Democratic prime ministers of western Germany to obstruct the creation of any institution ranking higher than the existing Lands. The agenda was to deal with only three points: the shortage of foodstuffs, the economic emergency, and the refugee problem. The French military government gave their prime ministers explicit instructions that the topic of German unity must not be debated under any circumstances. When the prime ministers of the Soviet zone arrived in Munich they demanded first of all the discussion of the creation of a German central administration by agreement with the democratic parties and the trade unions for the creation of a German unitary state. This was found to be unacceptable by the west German prime ministers who insisted on their three-point agenda. The Thuringian Prime Minister, Paul, was prepared to make concessions and declared himself ready to agree that the representatives of each zone should air their views on the issue of future German unity instead of participating in a formal discussion of the formation of centralized German administration. The west German prime ministers were not to be drawn, even after a second appeal by Paul. Then the prime ministers of the Soviet zone withdrew for further debate to consult among themselves, and when they had done so declared that they had to break off their participation in the conference. Ehard then declared that this would mean the division of Germany.

The final result of the conference was a memorandum by the west German prime ministers which called for a currency reform and the lowering of taxation, coupled with an appeal to the victorious powers to release those German prisoners of war still in their hands. Added to it were demands to create German economic unity, credits for imports of foodstuffs, raw materials and other industrial goods. However, because the Allied Control Council was so divided among itself, the memorandum could not be submitted.

By that time the western powers had decided to go it alone and to include their zone of occupation in the European Recovery Programme. They allowed a marked increase of the German production quotas to the level of 1936. A last meeting of the Council of Foreign Ministers in London from 25 November to 15 December failed, because the west was not prepared to recognize the Russian demands for reparations and participation in the control of the Ruhr industry. In the eastern zone Jakob Kaiser and Ernst Lemmer were forced out of their position by SMAD, and the CDU and LDP were separated from their west German counterparts. In the western zones the Economic Council was revised and its membership increased from 52 to 104. The CDU/CSU and SPD each had 40 seats, followed by delegates from the remaining parties. The *Länderrat* began its activities, each Land

represented by two deputies. The directors of the individul administrative agencies were united into an Administrative Council which
had the position of a quasi-parliamentary government with direct
legislative powers. The appointment of Ludwig Erhard as Economic
Director was important for the future.

Between 23 February and 6 March 1948 the USA, Great Britain,
France and the Benelux states decided that the Bi-zone and the French
zone were to participate in the programme for economic recovery and
to be represented in the permanent organization for this purpose. The
Soviets replied by leaving the Allied Control Commission in Berlin. In
the west the Treaty of Dunkirk, then still directed against any potential
German aggression, was expanded to include the Benelux states. On 6
March the London conference published a communiqué which outlined the stages in which a separate western German state was to be
created. The powers of the prime minister were to be expanded; they
would have to call a constituent assembly consisting of deputies from
the Land parliaments to draft a constitution on the basis of a federal
structure with the guarantee of individual rights, to be approved by the
military governors and then ratified by the population. France had
totally reversed her attitude since in view of her present military
guarantees she could drop demands for the separation of the German
territories on the left bank of the Rhine and give up the political
isolation of the French zone of occupation.

The currency reform in western Germany's three zones, announced
on 18 June 1948 and to come into force on 21 June, and the decision of
the Economic Council in favour of a free social market economy were
the bedrock of West Germany's economic recovery. Russia responded
by the Berlin Blockade, which firmly divided the city but in the end as
far as western Berlin and west Germany were concerned transformed
former enemies into potential allies.

THE FOUNDING OF THE GERMAN FEDERAL REPUBLIC

On 1 July 1948 the military governors in Frankfurt handed over to the
prime ministers the so-called Frankfurt Documents. In the first of the
three documents the prime ministers were empowered to go ahead
with the creation of a new German state by calling a constituent
assembly by 1 September 1948 at the latest, whose deputies were to
come from the Land parliaments. The constitution was to be a federal
and democratic one. After approval by the military governors it was to
be ratified by plebiscite by the population of west Germany and would
then come into force. The second document asked the prime ministers
to examine the boundaries of their Lands and if necessary suggest

alterations. The third contained guidelines for a 'Statute of Occupation.' The occupying powers still reserved to themselves the control of west Germany's foreign affairs, the creation of an organization controlling the Ruhr, as well as all aspects of reparations, decentralization and demilitarization. They were and remained the executors of supreme power.

The prime ministers met between 8 and 10 July 1948 in Koblenz and accepted the documents, stating, however, that everything would have to be done to prevent giving the new creation the character of a state. What they were to create was to be only provisional, because of the territorial limitation upon West Germany as well as because of the limitation of their competencies through the reserved powers of the western allies. For this reason they also dispensed with the plebiscite. Furthermore a reorganization of the Lands could only take place once the democratic parliamentary institutions had been created. Finally the Ruhr question was to be settled outside the framework of the constitution. The final consultations between military governors and the prime ministers occurred on 26 July 1948 and the former accepted the German Constitution, to be called a Basic Law, because a constitution could only be drafted once Germany was reunited. They also abandoned their demand for a constitutional plebiscite. Ultimately the demand about the Land boundaries was also dropped. Nor was a Constituent Assembly to be called, but a Parliamentary Council which during its deliberations was to be kept informed about the development of the Statute of Occupation which was in the process of being framed.

The conference of prime ministers then called a committee of experts in constitutional matters. This met on the island of *Herrenchiemsee* in Lake Chiemsee in Bavaria between 10 and 23 August 1948. It provided the first draft for the Basic Law for the Parliamentary Council, and the final Basic Law closely corresponded to the original draft.

The Parliamentary Council met at Bonn on 1 September 1948. The Lands could elect one deputy per 750,000 of the population, a total of 65. The deputies of West Berlin, in view of its Four-Power Status, only had an advisory capacity but no vote. The composition was as follows. CDU/CSU 27 plus 1 from West Berlin, SPD 27 plus 3 from West Berlin, FDP 5 plus 1 from West Berlin, DP 2, Centre 2, KPD 2. Konrad Adenauer was elected President, while the chairman of the main committee, with a number of sub-committees below it, was Carlo Schmid of the SPD.

The initial question was: whence did the Council derive its power. The majority opinion was in favour of the German people as a whole, while a minority opted in favour of the Lands. Berlin was a problem which could only be solved by denying the vote to the Berlin deputies, but the Basic Law included Berlin as one of the Lands of the Federal

Republic. Nor was Berlin to be governed by the Federal Republic. This called for special legislation which only came into force in 1951, according to which federal laws were to be enacted in West Berlin within a month of having been passed by the Federal Parliament. Another question of major debate concerned the role and representation of Lands in the Federal Republic. Were they to be represented by delegates instructed by the Land governments or by elected deputies, similar to the US Senate? The majority opted for a Bundesrat consisting of the prime ministers of the Lands or their deputies. The relationship between the central power and the Lands was not only hotly debated within the Parliamentary Council but also by the occupying powers. Both Adenauer and Schumacher often conducted heated debates with them because all parties were agreed that they were democratically legitimized and not solely the executors of the will of the occupying powers. Adenauer, with his calm decisiveness, had rather more impact than did Schumacher's fanaticism. The CDU/CSU were in favour of a Bundesrat, though the CSU demanded more powers for it, but failed to carry the majority. As a result the Bundesrat was not furnished with equal legislative powers with the Bundestag, the parliament. The Bundesrat is restricted in its functions to seeing proposed legislation before it is submitted to the Bundestag. It can voice its opinion and for that matter pass a delaying veto, which will bring into action the *Vermittlungsausschuss*, an arbitration committee. If no compromise can be reached on a bill, it will be submitted again to the Bundestag and can be passed by a simple majority. The legislative functions of the Bundesrat are restricted to taxation, questions determining the amounts of money derived from income and corporation taxes to be distributed between Bund and States. Its agreement is also necessary if federal executive action has to be carried out against a Land for not complying with federal laws, a case, in contrast to the Weimar Republic, which so far has not arisen.

The legislative competencies of the Federal Government and parliament in the Basic Law amount to a relatively short list, comprising foreign policy, to which in 1955 was added defence, currency, finance and citizenship. There is a rather longer list of matters in which the competencies of the Lands might conflict, but the rule is that federal laws supersedes the Land law. The entire spectrum of economic and social legislation is encompassed, only education and communal affairs having remained the exclusive domain of the Lands. The Bundesrat also participate in *legislative emergencies*. This is the case when the Bundestag refuses to pass a vote of no confidence while the Federal President refuses to use his power to dissolve parliament, and when legislation considered necessary by the government does not receive the assent of the Bundestag. In such a case the vote of the Bundesrat in favour of this legislation allows it to be passed. Such a legislative emergency is limited to six months and would occur if there existed only a negative majority in the Bundestag which rejects the Chancellor in office but is unable to muster the necessary majority for a vote of no confidence.

The Weimar experience is very much reflected in the Basic Law's treatment of exceptional circumstances and emergencies, as in the article concerning defence against dangers threatening the existence of the Federal Republic. The individual Lands, if confronted by a danger threatening the democratic order, are empowered to demand the assistance of police forces from other Lands, while the Federal Government has the temporary power to put police forces of the Lands under its own direction. This makes the Basic Law rather different from the Weimar Constitution which under Article 48 had granted extensive emergency powers to the President. Furthermore from 1948 until 1955 the western powers by the Statute of Occupation had reserved these emergency powers to themselves. To ensure that parties opposing the government but agreed on nothing else do not abuse a vote of no confidence, this can only be passed if the parties moving it are also able to nominate a successor to the Chancellor. They can then topple the Chancellor and must request the Federal President to appoint their nominee, and the President has to accede to this request.

The Parliamentary Council was also of the opinion that the political parties, as in the Baden Constitution, would have to be mentioned in the Basic Law to give them constitutional status, and at the same time allow the government, in the case of parties threatening the constitution, to prohibit them if necessary, through action by the Federal Constitutional Court. The Basic Law puts the parties under constitutional control but the actual law originally envisaged was not enacted until 1967. Only on two occasions, as we have seen, has the Constitutional Court prohibited parties, the right-wing radical SRP in 1952 and the KPD in 1956.

The Basic Law contains no provisions about the electoral franchise. The question of whether this matter was to be regulated by the Lands or by Parliamentary Council was left open. The latter claimed it had competency for it. The CDU/CSU tended towards a relative majority, the SPD and the other parties who had the majority, pushed through their demand for a modified proportional system. Half of the Bundestag deputies are elected directly, the other half by party lists. No maximum percentage of the vote was considered necessary to be elected into the Bundestag, since the Parliamentary Council was of the opinion that the excessive party pluralism of the Weimar Republic had not been the cause of its demise, but rather the existence of two radical extremes on Right and Left. At this point the military governors intervened declaring the Lands competent as regards legislation concerning the franchise. Adenauer shared this opinion. However, the prime ministers were agreed in favour of a unified procedure valid for the whole Federal Republic. An electoral law was passed against the votes of the CDU/CSU and the prime ministers managed to add a further modification. The relationship of direct and list mandates was changed from 50:50 to 60:40, and a 5 per cent minimum of votes was added before a party could send a deputy to the Bundestag. Parties polling less than 5 per cent of the popular vote are not represented. The electoral law of 1 June was enacted on that basis.

So as to avoid the excessive number of elections which had marked the final phase of the Weimar Republic, the President is not elected by popular vote but by the Federal Assembly, comprising the members of the Bundestag, and an equal number of deputies selected from the different Land parliaments by these parliaments. His tenure is for five years, while the Bundestag sits for four years before new elections have to be held. The Federal Constitutional Court was established to ensure the safety and security of the constitution and to safeguard it from attacks from without as well as from unconstitutional legislation. Its members are elected by votes from the Bundestag and the Bundesrat in equal proportions. Through a change made on 29 January 1969 individuals or communes can now raise constitutional complaints, based on a belief that basic rights or rights of self-administration have been infringed by an act of public power.

Basic rights are formulated precisely, in contrast to the Weimar Constitution. They head the Basic Law and are inalienable: they cannot even be affected by constitutional changes. The relationship between church and state is very much the same as in the Weimar Constitution: the churches remain public corporations with certain historically-based rights *vis-à-vis* the state.

In contrast to many Land constitutions the Basic Law is rather vague about the social and economic order. It confines itself to stating that compensation should be paid for any necessary expropriation, and leaves open the possibility of transferring ground, natural resources and means of production into public ownership in return for due compensation. This reserve of the Basic Law was mainly due to the influence of the SPD which thoroughly misjudged West Germany's economic development.

One other issue which troubled the Parliamentary Council was what name to give the child it had produced. Jakob Kaiser, for instance, demanded that the name of the Reich should be included so as to deprive any potential right-wing movement of an easy handle. But he spoke for a minority. Most were convinced that a new start should be made and this should be signified in the choice of name, so that Theodor Heuss's arguments in favour of 'Federal Republic of Germany' won the day. Heuss also, a little later, argued in favour of a new national anthem, which was composed and first played on New Years' Eve 1950/51. But it was so unpopular that the Federal Republic retained the *Deutschland Lied*, and its third verse is sung on public occasions.

From the point of view of a unified German state the Basic Law was and still is a fragment, but since reunification has receded into the indeterminate distance it is a constitution which has proved its value. The occupying powers did not insist on all their demands and when the three western foreign ministers in April 1949, after the creation of the North Atlantic Treaty Alliance, deliberated about the Basic Law, they gave it their blessing. In West Germany it was put to the vote of the Parliamentary Council and was accepted on 8 May 1949 with 53 votes in favour from the CDU, SPD and FDP, and 2 from the CSU, while 6 CSU members together with the DP, Centre and KPD voted against it. The Statute of Occupation had already been in force from 10 April but a review was promised after a year. The military governors were replaced by High Commissioners John McCloy for the USA, Sir Brian Robertson for Great Britain, and André François-Poncet for France. The High Commission was still entrusted to exercise supreme allied power in the Federal Republic and its Lands. But its function was separated from the High Command of the respective forces of occupation. At the same time an international Control Commission for the Ruhr was created, its members comprising the USA, Great Britain, France and the Benelux states as well as the Federal Republic.

On 12 May the Basic Law was subjected to ratification by the Land parliaments. All ratified it except Bavaria, but the necessary two-thirds majority had been achieved and it was formally enacted on 23 May 1949. Bonn was also chosen by a narrow majority as the provisional centre of government. On 14 August 1949 the first federal elections were held. Electoral participation amounted to 78.5 per cent, and confronted by the alternative of a free social market economy or socialism the electorate gave the CDU/CSU 139 seats plus 2 for Berlin, the SPD 131 plus 5 for Berlin, the FDP 52 plus 1 for Berlin, the *Bayernpartei* 17, DP 17, KPD 15, WAV (Economic Recovery Party, which soon declined into insignificance) 12, Centre 10, DRP (German Reichs Party) 5, candidates without party affiliation 3 and the South Schleswig Electoral Association 1. The CDU/CSU, FDP and DP formed a coalition and thus had the majority. On 12 September, after preliminary negotiations between the parties, Theodor Heuss was elected Federal President and on 15 September with a majority of one – his own vote – Konrad Adenauer as Chancellor. Convinced of the necessity of integrating Germany with the west, and burying the centuries of enmity between France and Germany, Adenauer steered a course which soon won him the confidence of the allies. Originally opposed to the Ruhr Statute with the Federal Republic's representation in its organization, he aimed at a union of the iron, steel and coal industries of Western Europe. He was therefore ready to have the Federal Republic join the European Council together with the Saar. In April 1949 the North Atlantic Treaty Organization (NATO) had been formed and by the Brussels Pact the Western European Union

(WEU). Adenauer's readiness to cooperate, exemplified in joining the Security Office which was to supervise the demilitarization of western Germany, accepting of the Ruhr Statute, and participating in the European Council alongside the Saar, caused the western allies gradually to lift restrictions, such as the limitation on ship-building, the establishment of West German consulates and thus the beginnings of a West German foreign policy. On 22 November 1949 the Petersburg Agreement was settled, the first freely negotiated agreement between the occupying powers and the Federal Republic. By the end of 1949 the Federal Republic sent its delegates to the OEEC; on 8 July 1950 it became an associated and in 1951 a full member of the European Council. Adenauer in respect of the Ruhr was first opposed to the 'Ruhr Statute' which would put the Ruhr industries under international control. But he changed his position, realizing that by the Federal Republic's participation the first foundations for a united western Europe could be laid. He found a like-minded spirit in the French Foreign Minister, Maurice Schumann. His plan to unify the Franco-German coal and steel production under joint supervision coincided with Adenauer's own ideas. Other nations were invited to join and on 18 April 1951 the Federal Republic, France, Italy and the Benelux countries signed the Treaty for the foundation of *Montan-Union*, the European Iron and Steel Community, which came into force on 23 June 1952 – the germinal cell of the European Economic Community.

Demands for West German rearmament were first heard publicly on the floor of the US Senate in the summer of 1948 at the height of the Berlin crisis. Since then the issue has never died, though it was highly unpopular in western Germany. The outbreak of war in Korea made the issue a live one, since what was happening there was considered a dress rehearsal for Europe. Adenauer on his own initiative submitted to the American High Commissioner the offer of German forces within an integrated European army. The plan for such an army was actually first publicly submitted by M. Pleven of France in the form of the European Defence Community (EDC). The debate over Germany's defence contribution raged for over four years until August 1954. Then the French Government under Pierre Mendès-France submitted the necessary treaties, which the Federal Republic had already signed in 1952, to the French chamber where they were promptly defeated. This defeat was premeditated. Earlier in the year France had required Russian mediation to allow France to extricate itself from its disastrous predicament in Indo-China. With Russian help a settlement was reached there. The Russian demand was that France scuttle the EDC. Mendès-France was only too willing to oblige: Thanks to the British initiative, notably by the British Foreign Secretary, Sir Anthony Eden, a substitute solution was found within a few months which now meant the creation of a West German national army integrated within NATO. The core of this solution were the Paris treaties of 1954 by which the Federal Republic regained its former sovereignty while the Statute of Occupation was cancelled. On 8 May 1955 the Federal Republic of Germany became a sovereign state; in the same year its first Minister of Defence, Herbert Blank, was appointed and a year later the first formations of the *Bundeswehr* were created, to become the strongest conventional force in western Europe within twenty-five years.

THE GERMAN DEMOCRATIC REPUBLIC

The Soviet Zone already possessed a nucleus of military forces of all three services by 1949. Its constitutional development had also proceeded since 1948, but in the hands of Walter Ulbricht, the Secretary of the Central Committee of the SED, there was no separation of powers, all powers being placed in the hands of a parliament, the *Volkskammer*, which like Hitler's Reichstag only contains delegates which toe the SED line. On 14 November 1946 the term *Deutsche Demokratische Republik* (DDR) was coined, and the first steps towards creating a separate German state within the Soviet orbit go back to 1947. A German People's Council of 400 members was formed which accepted a draft constitution submitted by the SED on 22 October 1948, based on a draft of 14 November 1946. The draft was finally approved on 19 March 1949 and then submitted to the People's Congress which met on 25 May 1949. This had emerged from elections in which the number of seats for the deputies of each party had already been determined according to an agreed key. The voter could only say 'yes' or 'no' in an open ballot. The SED had 25 per cent of the seats, the CDU and LDP 15 per cent each, the NDPD and Peasants' Party 7.5 per cent each. The remaining votes went to the mass organizations such as trade unions and the FDJ. On 30 May 1949 the People's Congress affirmed the new constitution of the DDR and at the same time elected a new People's Council of 400 members. This Council put the constitution into force on 7 October 1949 and then declared itself the provisional *Volkskammer*. On 11 October 1949 the provisional People's Chamber and Land Chamber elected Wilhelm Pieck as President of the DDR, with Otto Grotewohl as Prime Minister. Formal elections for the people's chamber were only held a year later on the same basis as the previous elections. On 11 November 1949 SMAD transferred its administrative functions to the DDR and turned itself into the Soviet High Commission. Article 1 of the constitution stated that 'Germany is an indivisible democratic Republic'; by 1968 this was changed to read that the 'German Democratic Republic is a

Socialist State of the German Nation'; on 27 September 1974 this article was changed again, all reference to German unity omitted and instead stating that the 'German Democratic Republic is a Socialist State of Workers and Peasants'. Initially the flag of the DDR, like that of the Federal Republic, was black, red and gold. It was only in 1959 that the hammer and compass surrounded by corn sheafs was added. As in the Weimar Constitution, 'all power derives from the people'. The DDR Constitution lists no inalienable individual human rights but the rights of citizens which are also limited in the sense that it prohibits propagation of hatred against religious faith, race and peoples, as well as propaganda for war – provisions sufficiently flexible and wide to allow the SED to take steps against any opponents. The DDR Constitution does not exclude the pluralist parliamentarian principle, but the constitutional reality institutionalized the hegemonic claims of the SED. For the rest the traditional basic rights of the inviolability of one's dwelling, freedom of the press, secrecy of mail and the right to emigrate are included, but it is added that this right can be limited by a Law of the Republic. Freedom of choice of profession is guaranteed but not the free choice of one's place of work. While the constitution guarantees the co-determination of the workers, in practice shop stewards had already been removed in 1948. In contrast to the Basic Law, nationalization is specified and the economy is a planned economy 'controlled by the people.' The sections concerning family and motherhood correspond with the Basic Law. Freedom of art, research and teaching are guaranteed provided they do not contradict the spirit of the constitution. Provisions for education are more extensive than in the Basic Law, and lay down alternative routes and opportunities to gain access to institutions of higher learning, i.e. the universities. Freedom for the exercise of religion, of conscience, and culture are guaranteed, again as long as they do not contradict 'the spirit of the constitution'. In practice these liberties are so restrained that they are limited to the private, personal sector. The final part of the constitution deals with the structure of the powers of the state. 'The People's Chamber is the supreme authority of the people.' Electoral procedures are laid down in great detail and contain no provisions for a secret ballot. The competencies of the People's Chamber include legislative initiative and the supervision of all state activities, by 23 May 1952 the essential controlling functions had been transferred to the government of the DDR. The People's Chamber can also examine the legislation and its constitutionality. A constitutional court therefore does not exist. Originally provisions were also made for the Lands but since these were dissolved on 23 July 1952 and divided into fourteen administrative districts they have become irrelevant: the Lands had become obstacles to a centrally-directed planned economy.

Article 92 of the constitution is of major importance. It confers the office of Prime Minister on the strongest party and thus ensures that the SED will be in control permanently. As in the Basic Law the office of President has been removed from the sphere of popular elections and put in the hands of the People's Chamber.

'The administration of justice shall be independent and subject to the law.' In practice the extensive use of SED lay judges 'appointed on the proposal of democratic parties and organizations' ensured a politized judiciary, while the establishment of a supreme court and state prosecution allows legal decisions made in the courts to be suspended on the demand of the state prosecutor if such a decision violates the law or contradicts the principles of justice, a provision so flexible as to bring into question the impartiality of the entire judiciary.

The Soviet High Commission at first exercised considerable pressure upon the DDR, since its government was a mere recipient of Soviet orders, particularly in the economic field. Only when the pressure ultimately erupted in the 1953 rising did the USSR relent and since then the DDR has developed slowly but steadily into the strongest economic power in the eastern bloc next to the Soviet Union. The population has shared in this to some extent. That this was far from adequate was shown by the simple fact that as long as the population of the DDR had the opportunity, millions voted against it – with their feet – by fleeing to the west. To contain and throttle this development the DDR leadership found itself compelled on 13 August 1961 to erect the Berlin wall and to seal off their territory hermetically from the west by inhuman means and devices.

OSTPOLITIK

Only the policy of *détente*, already envisaged by Adenauer in the early 1960s but slowly inaugurated during the Great Coalition of 1965 – 69 in the Federal Republic when Willy Brandt became Foreign Minister, and carried on by leaps and bounds since the SPD/FDP coalition of 1969 – some would argue excessively so and their verdict may yet be vindicated – culminated in the treaties between Bonn and Moscow in 1970, followed by a treaty with Warsaw and finally by the *Grundlagenvertrag*, the Basic Treaty between the Federal Republic and the DDR in 1972. That Policy at last relaxed some of the restrictions imposed by the DDR upon its population, and widened access to it. It is essentially a one-way road, with limited access for the west, while the exit from the DDR is restricted to old-age pensioners. Even here in 1981 the DDR found it necessary to tighten the screws again. How far the DDR has moved from its original aim of German re-unification has already been demonstrated by the changes in Article 1 of the constitution. Furthermore, while the DDR until 1974, two years after the Basic Treaty had been signed, still considered it the constitution's duty to overcome 'the division imposed upon the German nation', it now 'forever and irrevocably is united with the Union of Socialist Soviet Republics.'

What actually has been gained by the treaty between Bonn and Moscow is the subject of controversy. Certainly Willy Brandt and the brains behind the *Ostpolitik*, his adviser Egon Bahr, were under pressure of success; within a few shorts months Bahr and the Soviet Foreign Minister Gromyko came to agree on a wide range of issues. Whether by a more patient process of negotiation the Federal Republic could not have gained greater Soviet concessions must remain a matter of speculation. The Federal Republic's recognition of the Oder-Neisse Line is irrelevant for two reasons: firstly, the Federal Republic has no common frontier with Poland; secondly, this recognition has by no means meant the abandoning of the Potsdam Agreements of 1945, whose validity the Soviet Union insists to this very day, which also stipulate that the settlement of Germany's frontiers should be regulated by a final peace conference between Germany and the former allies. That the Brandt/Bahr *Ostpolitik* brought the Federal Republic material benefits in terms of Russo-German trade is contradicted by the pattern of trade between the Federal Republic and the USSR which was strongly developing before 1970 and has continued on the same lines ever since. In constitutional terms nothing at all has been gained.

After the conclusion of the treaty the Federal Republic handed a letter to the Soviet Foreign Ministry in which it insisted on Germany's ultimate aim of reunification. In other words neither Bahr, nor the Federal German Foreign Minister Walter Scheel, who did no more than sign what Bahr and Gromyko had agreed upon, managed to get into the text of the agreement any clause concerning this. The Soviets acknowledged the receipt of the letter but refrained from replying or commenting on it.

The Basic Treaty between Bonn and the DDR contained nothing about reunification either, a reason why the Bavarian government asked for submission of the treaty to the Federal German Constitutional Supreme Court to examine whether it corresponded with the preamble of the Basic Law which made the issue of reunification binding on all Federal German Governments. The Court accepted the treaty but in its judgment complained that it had not been called on to examine its constitutionality before it was signed. It also emphasized that the Basic Law proceeded from the premise that the German Reich continued after the collapse of 1945 and that with the establishment of the Federal Republic a new west German state had not been created, but that instead the Federal Republic 'is identical with the German Reich'. The preamble of the constitution has not only political significance but also a legal content. German reunification 'is a constitutional order', an order obligatory for any Federal German government. In other words the judgment of 31 July 1973 continues to insist on the legal position as it had existed for the Founding Fathers of the Basic Law in 1949. The constitutional maxim is still 'Germany one and indivisible'.

DOMESTIC CONSTITUTIONAL PROBLEMS, 1972–83

Constitutional issues were not raised by the Federal German *Ostpolitik*, When in 1969 the FDP for the first time since 1949 shifted their weight towards the Social Democrats, the two parties together commanded a majority over the CDU/CSU. From the elections of that year emerged the SPD/FDP coalition which was to last until 1982; first, until 1974, with Willy Brandt as Chancellor, and followed after Brandt's resignation by Helmut Schmidt. Brandt had conducted the 1969 election campaign with the slogans of 'more democracy' and 'greater transparency of government'. Yet within little more than two years after becoming Chancellor, jointly with the prime ministers of the individual Lands of the Federal Republic he issued the *Radikalenerlass*, a decree against employment of 'radicals' in the public service of the federal or Land governments. Civil servants at federal or Land level have to swear an oath on the Basic Law upon appointment and to promise to uphold liberty and the democratic basic order. Appointment as a civil servant means tenure of office for life, but civil servants in Germany are not merely the upper echelons employed in ministries, but virtually everyone employed by the federal or Land governments. Thus the locomotive driver employed by the state railways, the postman, the primary and grammar-school teacher and the university professor, to mention but a few of many examples, are all civil servants. The Federal Government in its early phase, in order to counter potential threats from the extremes of both Left and Right, had appealed to the *Bundesverfassungsgericht*, the Federal Constitutional Supreme Court, to outlaw and prohibit the extreme right-wing *Sozialistische Reichspartei* (SRP). The court did so in 1952, declaring the SRP as a successor party of the NSDAP. In 1956 the KPD had been equally outlawed as a party with aims that contradicted the values and aims of the Basic Law. But ten years later new successor parties had emerged, all of them professing strict adherence to the Basic Law. On the Left this was first the German Peace Union (DFU) which was heavily infiltrated by Communists, until the Communists reconstituted themselves into the DKP, the German Communist Party. On the right emerged in the 1960s the *Nationaldemokratische*

Partei Deutschlands (NPD). Neither party has been proscribed as no evidence could be produced proving that they aimed at the overthrow of the democratic basic order. However, since 1967, outside the party political framework, within the context of the students' protest movement, developed the Extra-parliamentary Opposition (APO), some groups of which agitated on behalf of radical aims and from which terrorist groups such as the Baader-Meinhof group, the Red Army Faction and their successors emerged. Against this background Brandt had issued the decree against 'radicals' that is to say, against their employment in the public sector of the federal and Land administration. It is directed against members of the DKP and NPD and other known radical factions. With this decree a constitutional abnormalty has been introduced. While it is theoretically perfectly constitutional for a DKP or NPD member to become a member of parliament, to obtain a ministerial post, in fact have access to the highest elected office in the country, such a person and other radicals can be stopped from becoming civil servants. That is what has now become known as the *Berufsverbot*, the prohibition to become a civil servant. Though each case is examined individually, extreme applications of the *Radikalenerlass* have been numerous. To mention but one example, one female applicant for the post of librarian in a state library has been turned down simply because as a sixth-former she had once distributed radical leaflets in her school. Since then she had no longer been politically active and had successfully completed her university education at undergraduate and post-graduate level. Here obviously lies a constitutional problem unresolved to this day. Absurdities do not end here. A Hamburg judge, author of a highly polemical book throwing doubt on the extent of the 'Holocaust', had his doctor's title withdrawn in 1982 by the University of Göttingen, which had originally awarded it, on the basis of a law enacted by Hitler in July 1939.

These domestic issues are still very much in the background. To the fore of the public debate stands the NATO decision to deploy Pershing II and Cruise missiles, a decision which in conjunction with the deteriorating economic climate and the rise of unemployment lies at the root of the break-up of the SPD/FDP coalition. Over the last five years the Social Democrats have been heavily losing ground at Land level, primarily because of their internal divisions. At a federal level Helmut Schmidt had had to fight against three fronts at once: against the growing number of dissenters within his own party, against the FDP within his own cabinet, and against the CDU/CSU opposition in parliament. The FDP, which since 1969, has never won more than 8 per cent of the votes cast in federal elections, nevertheless is the weight which tilts the scale one way or the other. Only once has a party gained an absolute majority: the CDU/CSU in 1957. Since 1961 the FDP has been crucial in the formation of a coalition government. When in the autumn of 1982 the SPD/FDP coalition split, the FDP backed the

CDU/CSU and thus, for the first time since 1969, made it possible for another CDU/CSU politician, Helmut Kohl, to become Chancellor. Kohl had a majority in parliament, and the legislative term still had another two years to run, but he decided to hold elections in March 1983. In order to bring about a dissolution of parliament he needed a vote of 'no confidence' on a minor issue. Defeated by artificial means, parliament was dissolved and new elections called. The constitutionality of these proceedings was challenged but the Federal Constitutional Supreme Court upheld the decision, though not without issuing warnings and reservations in order to stop this procedure from becoming a precedent.

CENTRAL EUROPEAN NEUTRALISM?

The CDU/CSU-FDP coalition emerged victorious and strengthened from these elections, but the problems which had led to the break-up of the SPD/FDP coalition still exist and divide German public opinion, especially outside the parliamentary scene. Germany as the battlefield for a nuclear exchange between the two superpowers haunts Germans on both sides of the Iron Curtain. Equally noticeable are sounds of nationalistic rumblings. The DDR has slowly but steadily begun refurbishing images of German national continuity which had once been denounced. The *Wehrmacht*-style uniforms of the National People's Army were an early sign. But what was once banned and banished in the cultural sphere has been returned to its traditional place, such as the equestrian statue of Frederick the Great in *Unter den Linden* in Berlin, a monarch now largely rehabilitated in East Germany's historiography. A first revision of the Bismarck image, especially his foreign policy, has begun in 1982. And the present chairman of the State Council, Erich Honecker, himself a Saarlander, allowed himself to mention what had become taboo in the official language of the DDR when in January 1981 he stated that once the Federal Republic became a Socialist state the question of reunification would be raised again and then 'We need not expand on what our response would be'.

For a new generation of Germans the experiences of their fathers and grandfathers becomes increasingly irrelevant. The *Pax Americana* is visibly weakening, the *Pax Sovietica* certainly is under challenge not only among its satellites but also from sections of its subject nationalities, notably in the Baltic provinces. In the Federal Republic the consensus established by its founding fathers is in the process of erosion. In the 1983 election campaign the SPD, for the first time since 1949, expressly fought the election under the slogan 'in the German national interest'. That they failed to gain a majority does not contradict the fact that the process of erosion is at work. The question of 'the German nation' is put anew, combined as it is with the clamour and search for security in Central Europe. The answers given to the German problem between 1949 and 1955 are no longer uncritically accepted – they are no longer the only answers that are thinkable. An important point is that the 'German question' is not raised to the level of public debate by the fringe of the extreme right, but by respectable and renowned historians, sociologists and political scientists, National Liberals and Socialists alike, persons like Peter Brandt, the son of the former Chancellor. A new generation has become suddenly acutely aware that their country is divided and that even the exchange of tactical nuclear weapons on German soil would not only put an end to German reunification, but to Germany as such. Both German states still represent stable parts of a world that has become increasingly unstable but, the representatives of a 'Central European Gaullism', ask how long will it be before the two German sections are dragged into the maelstrom of destruction? History is catching up with Germany. No one knows what the future holds but, even ignoring the new stirrings in the two Germanies, there is unanimity at the apex of both that Germany as whole must never again become the source of another conflagration which would be lethal in the most literate sense of the term. A generation is emerging which is no longer beholden to the superpowers for its status, nor prepared to accept the 'burden of guilt' of its forefathers – a generation which raises issues over which there exists a degree of unanimity in Germany.

NOTE

1. In both German states the armed forces are fully integrated in their respective pact systems. The *Bundeswehr* is under strict civilian, parliamentary control, and the DDR's *Volksarmee* is under the control of the SED. The continuance of the Potsdam Agreements means that neither state is fully sovereign. In both Germanies, the 'Allies' still possess a considerable number of reserved powers, especially in the 'security' and 'defence' areas, which further impinge upon sovereignty.

BIBLIOGRAPHY

To assist readers with no knowledge of German to select English language publications the titles are signalled with ★

Chapter 1: The dissolution of the Holy Roman Empire

Good introductions are provided by the classic work of James Bryce, ★ *The Holy Roman Empire*, republished in 1961, especially chapters XIV, XIX XXII. Published a little later in 1967 is Agatha Ramm's ★*Germany 1789–1919*, though rather weak on constitutional aspects and the rise of consti-tutionalism in the German states. These shortcomings are also shared by two standard German texts on German constitutional history – F. Hartung, *Deutsche Verfassungsgeschichte vom 15. Jahrhundert bis zur Gegenwart* (1969); E. Forsthoff's *Deutsche Verfassungsgeschichte der Neuzeit* (1961). The great exception is E. R. Huber's *Deutsche Verfassungsgeschichte seit 1789*. (1960/1980) – to which the present work is heavily indebted – and of which so far six massive volumes have been published. As yet the work is far from complete; at least two further volumes can be expected. A useful survey of the current state of research is provided by E. Fehrenbach's *Vom Ancien Régime zum Wiener Kongress* (1981). *Die Entstehung der politischen Strömungen in Deutschland 1770–1815*, by Fritz Valjavec is fundamental to any discussion of the emergence of political currents in Germany, and is a work – though he has not acknowledged it – from which the late Klaus Epstein has heavily borrowed in his work ★*The Genesis of German Conservatism* (1966). John Weiss's slim volume, ★*Conservatism in Europe 1770–1945* (1977) is rather superficial and sweeping in its generalizations. Of greater substance is R. Aris's ★ *History of Political Thought in Germany from 1789 to 1815* (1936). Still very worthwhile reading (in spite of its often extreme partisanship and harsh judgements) is

H. v. Treitschke's *German History in the Nineteenth Century*, especially volumes 2–5, which discusses in great detail the constitutional ideas up to the eve of 1848 and also manages, within the context of a political history, to integrate a great deal of German cultural history, something which is missing in most recent studies. A south German corrective to Treitschke is provided by Franz Schnabel's *Deutsche Geschichte im neunzehnten Jahrhundert* (4 vols, 1929/1950) which unfortunately is not available in English. Nationalism and its development is well discussed in H. Kohn, ★*The Idea of Nationalism* (1950) and his *Prelude to Nation-States: The French and German Experience 1789–1815* (1967) as well as by C. J. H. Hayes, ★*The Historical Evolution of Modern Nationalism* (1831). One of the best analyses of this phenomenon is E. Lemberg's *Nationalismus: Psychologie und Geschichte* (1964). To this must also be added M. Boucher's *Le Sentiment national en Allemagne* (1947) and also J. Breuilly's recent study ★*Nationalism and the State* which, however, suffers from the attempt to try to do too much within the scope of one volume. Constitutional aspects of individual German states as well as those within the Confederation of the Rhine find mention in J. C. Sauzey, *Les Allemands sous les aigles françaises. Essai sur les troupes de la Confederation du Rhin 1806–13* (1902–09); E. Driault, *Napoleon et l'Europe. Le Grand Empire* (1924); M. Dunan, *Napoléon et l'Allemagne, le système continental et les débuts du Royaume de Bavière 1806–1810* (1942). However, on the whole English readers are badly served with histories and institutions of individual German states. F. L. Carstens provides a useful background in his ★*Princes and Parliaments in Germany: From the fifteenth to the eighteenth century* (1959). Most of the historiography in English concentrates upon Prussia such as H. W. Koch,★ *A History of Prussia* (1978); a wealth of primary sources on constitutional aspects in Prussia is contained in J. R. Seeley's ★*Life and Times of Stein or Germany and Prussia in the Napoleonic Age* (Cambridge 1878). Later studies concentrate on individual aspects of the Prussian Reform Movement like P. Paret's recent works ★*Yorck and the Era of Prussian Reform 1807–1815* (1966), and ★*Clausewitz and the State* (1976). W. M. Simon offers a sound study in ★*The Failure of the Prussian Reform Movement* (1971). A rather older but nevertheless still highly valuable study is that by H. A. L. Fisher, ★*Studies in Napoleonic Statesmanship: Germany* (1903) to whose conclusions, statistical data apart, the recent collection of essays in the volume edited by H. Berding and H. P. Ullmann, *Deutschland zwischen Revolution und Restauration* (1981), have nothing new to add.

There is nothing in English on the development of south German constitutionalism. Bavaria, Baden, Württemberg, Hesse are blanks for readers who only read English. The same applies to the problem of state and church during the period, except, of course Treitschke's somewhat polemical discussion.

Chapter 2: The German Confederation

See Treitschke, Ramm, Aris, Valjavec and Epstein op. cit, (Ch. 1 Biblio.) and as far as sources are concerned G.F. v. Martens, *Recueil des principaux traitès depuis 1761* (1791/1801) with supplement (1802/08) and continuation under the title *Nouveau recueil des traitès* (1817). Also, Ph. A.G. v. Meyer, *Corpus Juris Confederationis Germanicae, 1858–69* and Seeley op. cit. (Ch. 1). For secondary literature see Kohn *Prelude* op.cit. (Ch. 1) as well as his article ★'Arndt and the character of German Nationalism' in *American Historical Review*, 1949 and his study ★*The Mind of Germany: The education of a nation* (1961). Important also are also W. Mommsen, *Die deutsche Einheitsbewegung* (1930); A. Berney, 'Reichstradition und Nationalstaatsgedanke 1789–1815' in *Historische Zeitschrift* (1929); and E. Zechlin, *Die deutsche Einheitsbewegung* (1967). A very perceptive study is offered by R. H. Thomas, ★ *Liberalism, Nationalism and the German Intellectuals 1822–1847* (1952); Heinrich Ritter v. Srbik, *Metternich*, 2 vols (1978 reprint); G. Ritter, *Stein*, 2 vols (1931); J. Hanoteau (ed.) *Lettrés du Prince Metternich à lu Comtesse de Lieven* (1909); C. van Duerm (ed.) *Correspondance du Cardinal Consalvi avec le Prince de Metternich 1815–23* (1899); K. O. Frhr. v. Aretin, 'Metternichs Verfassungspläne 1817li' in *Historiches Jahrbuch* (1955); H. Rössler, *Österreichs Kampf um Deutschlands Befreiung*, 2 vols (1940); Th. Hamerow, ★*Restoration, Revolution, Reaction: Economics and Politics in Germany 1815–1871* (1958); F. Mehring, *Zur deutschen Geschichte von der französischen Revolution bis zum Vormärz 1789–1847* (1965); Heinrich Ritter v. Srbik, *Deutsche Einheit*, vol. 1 (1935); J. L. Klüber (ed.) *Acten des Wiener Kongresses*, 9 vols (1815/35); A. Alison, ★*Lives of Lord Castlereagh and Sir Charles Stewart* (1861); J. G. Lockhart, ★*The Peacemakers 1814–15* (1932); J. Marriot, ★*Castlereagh* (1936); H. Nicolson, ★ *The Vienna Congress, 1912–22* (1944); Ch. K. Webster, ★*England and the Polish-Saxon Problem at the Congress of Vienna* (1913) and by the same author, ★*British Diplomacy 1813–15. Select Documents Dealing with the Reconstruction of Europe* (1921); W. Conze (ed.) *Staat und Gesellschaft im deutschen Vormäi. 1815–1848* (1962); H. Hanmann (ed.) *Vom Hotzenwald bis Wyl: Demokratische Tradition in Baden* (1977); W. Herzberg, *Das Hambacher Fest: Geschichte der revolutionären Bestrebungen in Rheinbayern um das Jahr 1832* (1908, reprint 1982). Social and economic aspects of this period are well covered in: J. H. Clapham, ★*The Economic Development of France and Germany 1815–1915* (1951); W. O. Henderson, ★*The Zollverein* (1939); J. Kuczynski, *Geschichte des Alltags des deutschen Volkes*, vol. 3, *1870–1870.* (1982); H.-U. Wehler (ed.) *Moderne deutsche Sozialgeschichte* (1968); K. Wessel, *Das Wartburgfest der deutschen Burschenschaft am 18. Oktober 1817* (1954); W. Treue, *Wirtschaftszustände und Wirtschaftspolitik in Preussen 1815–25* (1937); A. H. Price, ★ *The Evolution of the Zollverein* (1949); F. Lenz, *Friedrich List, der Mann und das Werk* (1936); *Friedrich List, Schriften, Reden, Briefe* (1936): On the impact on the constitutional life of some of the German states see R. Kosselek, *Preussen zwischen Reform und Revolution* (1967); M. Doeberl, *Entwicklungsgeschichte Bayerns*, vol. 3 (1931); C. V. Fricker-Th. v. Gessler, *Geschichte der Verfassungs Württembergs* (1869); W. Grube, *Der Stuttgarter Landtag 1457–1957* (1957); A. Allgaier, *Die Stände Badens mit besonderer*

Berücksichtigung der zweiten badischen Kammer (1896); W. Hesse, *Rheinhessen in seiner Entwicklung von 1798–1834* (1835); M. Eckel, *Die politische Presse Hessens von 1830–50* (1938); R. Kolb, *Herzog Wilhelm von Nassau* (1892); O. v. Heinemann, *Geschichte von Braunschweig und Hannover*, 4 vols (1884/92); Ph. Losch, *Geschichte des Kurfürstentums Hessen 1803–66 (1922); G. Schmidt, Die Staatsform in Sachsen in der ersten Hälfte des 19. Jahrhunderts* (1966); J. F. Herbart, 'Erinnerungen an die Göttingsche Katastrophe in Jahre 1837' in *Sämmtliche Werke*, vol. 12 (1852); E. R. Huber, *F. C. Dahlmann und die deutsche Verfassungsbewegung* (1937); K. Morg, *Das Echo des hannoverschen Verfassungsstreites 1837–40 in Bayern* (1930); G. M. Willis, *Ernestus Augustus, Duke of Cumberland and King of Hanover* (1954); P. Weber, *Histoire du Grand-Duché de Luxembourg* (1949); T. M. C. Assere, *Le Duché de Limbourg et la Confédération germanique* (1863).

Chapter 3: Eighteen Forty Eight

E. M. Butler, ★*The Saint Simonian Religion in Germany. A Study of the Young German Movement* (1926); F. G. Eyck, ★'English and French influences on German Liberalism before 1848' in *Journal of the History of Ideas* (1957); *idem*, ★Mazzini's Young Europe' in *Journal of Central European Affairs* (1957/58); G. Ras, *Börne und Heine als politische Schriftsteller* (1927); L. Männer, *K. Gutzkow und der demokratische Gedanke* (1921); G. Freytag, *Karl Mathy* (1870); K. Baumann (ed.) *Das Hambacher Fest* (1957); E. Franz, *Die bayerischen Verfassungskämpfe* (1926); E. Bauer, *Geschichte der constitionellen und revolutionären Bewegungen im südlichen Deutschland 1831–34 (1845): F.L. Ilse, Geschichte der politischen Untersuchungen, welche durch die neben der Bundesversammlug errichteten Kommissionen geführt sind* (1860); K. Marx, *Revolution und Konterrevolution in Deutschland* (1896)–English translation in F. Engels,★ *The German Revolutions* (L. Krieger, ed.) (1968); K. Marx and F. Engels, ★*The German Ideology*,(1967); Th. Eschenburg, *Staat und Gesellschaft in Deutschland* (1956). On the development of political parties see Th. Nipperdey, *Gesellschaft, Kultur. Theorie* (1976), especially 'Grundprobleme der deutschen Parteigeschichte im 19. Jahrhundert' and 'Kritik oder Objektivität? Zur Beurteilung der Revolution von 1848'; A. Wahl, *Beiträge der deutschen Parteigeschichte im 19. Jahrhundert* (1910); C. J. Friedrich, *Der Verfassungsstaat der Neuzeit* (1953); G. E. Levau, *Les Partis politiques et réalités sociales* (1953); Th. Schieder, 'Die Theorie der Partei im älteren deutschen Liberalismus' in *Festschrift für Ludwig Bergsträsser* (1954). For specific party-political currents see literature cited in Chapters 1 and 2 bibliographies as well as for Conservatism; A. Müller, *Elemente der Staatskunst* (1809); K. L. v. Haller, *Restauration der Staatswissenschaften* (1840).

For the emergence of socialist currents see: K. Marx and Engels cited above; K. Rodbertus, *Die Forderungen der arbeitenden Klassen* (1837); W. Weitling,

Die Menschheit wie sie ist und wie sie sein sollte (1838); K. Marx und F. Engels, *Werke* (1957); D. Caute, ★*The Left in Europe since 1789* (1966); E. Nolte, *Deutschland und der kalte Krieg* (1974); especially part I; W. Conze/D. Groh, *Die Arbeiterbewegung in der nationalen Bewegung* (1966); H. Grebing, *Geschichte der deutschen Arbeiterbewegung*, (1966); J. H. Jackson, ★*Marx, Proudhon and European Socialism* (1957); F. Kool/W. Krause, *Die frühen Sozialisten* (1972); F. Mehring, *Geschichte der deutschen Sozialdemokratie. 1. Teil 1830 bis zum preussischen Verfassungsstreit 1863* (Berlin 1960); H. Mommsen, *Arbeiterbewegung und nationale Frage* (1979); Sh. Na'aman, *Lassalle* (1970); F.J. Radatz, *Karl Marx: Der Mensch und seine Lehre* (1973); R. W. Reichard, ★*Crippled from Birth: German Social Democracy 1844–1870* (1969); W. Treue (ed.) *Quellen zur Geschichte der Industriellen Revolution* (1966); F. v.d. Ven, *Sozialgeschichte der Arbeit*, vol. 3 (1972); G. D. H. Cole, ★*A History of Socialist Thought. The Forerunners 1789–1850* (1953); C. Jantke, *Der vierte Stand. Die gestaltenden Kräfte der deutschen Arbeiterbewegung im 19. Jahrhundert* (1955); W. G. Oschilewski, *Grosse Sozialisten in Berlin: Born, Marx, Engels, Lassalle* (1956).

The eve of the outbreak of the Revolution of 1848 in Germany is best dealt in L. Kulenkampf, *Der erste Vereinigte Preussische Landtag 1847 und die öffemtliche Meinung Südwestdeutschlands* (1912/13); L. v. Gerlach, *Denkwürdigkeiten* (1892); H. Rothfels, *Theodor v. Schön, Friedrich Wilhelm IV. und die Revolution von 1848* (1937); H. Boberach, *Wahlrechtsfragen im Vormärz* (1959); H. Rothfels, ★'1848 – one hundred years after' in *Journal of Modern History* (1948). By far the best treatment of the 1848 Revolution both from social and constitutional perspective comes from V. Valentin, *Geschichte der deutschen Revolution 1848–49*, 2 vols (1970 reprint), which in a truncated version has been translated into English in one volume, ★*1848: Chapters of German History*, which does the German original less than justice. For general treatments see: F. Fejtö (ed.) *The Opening of an Era: 1848, W.d.. L. B. Namier, ★*1848: The Revolution of the Intellectuals* (1946); P. Robertson, ★*Revolutions of 1848: A Social History* (1952); O. Vossler, *Die Revolution von 1848 in Deutschland* (1967); J. Droz, *Les révolutions Allemandes* (1957); Th. S. Hamerow ★'History of the German Revolution of 1848' in *American Historical Review* (1954). Of interest on the general level is K. Obermann (ed.) *Flugblätter der Revolution 1848/49* (1973).

For the March revolution in southern Germany refer to literature cited above as well as to: J. M. Söltz, *Max der Zweite, König von Bayern* (1867); K. Th. v. Heigel, *Ludwig I. König von Bayern* (1872); F. Kurz, *Der Anteil der Münchner Studentenschaft and den Unruhen 1847–48* (1893); F. Frhr. v, Pölnitz, *Die deutsche Einheits- und Freiheitsbewegung in der Munchner Studentenschaft 1826–1850* (1930); K. Bachmann, *Die Volksbewegung 1848/49 im Allgäu* (1954); and H. Rall 'König Max II, von Bayern und die katholische Kirche' in *Historisches Jahrbuch* (1965).

For Württemberg and Baden see W. Schöttler, *Württemberg in den Jahren 1848/49* (1851); A. L. Reyscher, *Erinnerungen aus alter und neuer Zeit* (1884); E. Schneider, *Ausgewählte Urkunden zur württembergischen Geschichte*

(1911); F. Hecker, *Die Erhebung des Volkes in Baden für die deutsche Republik im Frühjahr 1848* (1848); C. Moral, *Der badische Aufstand in seinem inneren Zusammenhange mit der Reformbewegung Deutschlands* (1848); G. v. Struve, *Geschichte der drei Volkserhebungen in Baden* (1849); F. Lipp, *G. Herweghs viertägige Irr- und Wanderfahrt mit der Pariser deutsch-demokratischen Legion in Deutschland und deren Ende durch die Württemberger bei Dossenbach* (1850); H. Roeckel, *Baden im Kampt um die Freiheit* (1949); H. Derwein, *Heidelberg im Vormärz und in der Revolution 1848/49* (1958).

For the Hesses, Nassau and Frankfurt see D. Schäfer, *Prinz Emil von Hessen-Darmstadt in der deutschen Revolution 1848–50* (1954); Ph. Losch, *Geschichte des Kurfürstentums Hessen 1803–66* (1922); V. Valentin, *Frankfurt a. M. und die Revolution 1848/49* (1908). For Saxony, Thuringia and Central Germany: C. Geyer, *Politische Parteien und Verfassungskämpfe in Sachsen 1848–49* (1914); H.G. Holldack, *Untersuchungen zur Geschichte dec Reaktion in Sachsen 1849–55* (1921); P. Wentzke, 'Thüringische Einheitsfragen in der deutschen Revolution 1848' in *Historische Zeitschrift* (1917): For northern Germany see H. Bodemeyer, *Die Hannoverschen Verfassungskämpfe seit 1848* (1861); A. F. Ventker, *Stüve und die hannoversche Bauernbefreiung* (1935); E. Pleitner, *Oldenburg im 19. Jahrhundert* (1900); J. Wiggers, *Die Mecklenburgische Konstituierende Versaamlung und die voraufgegangene Reformbewegung* (1850); J. G. Gallois, *Hamburgische Chronik*: vol. 5. *1843–60* (1870); P. E. Schramm, *Neun Generationen. Schicksale einer Hamburger Bürgerfamilie* (1964); H. Entholt, *Die bremische Revolution 1848* (1951).

For Prussia see literature already cited above and E. Bleich, *Die Verhandlungen des zum 2. April zusammengerufenen Vereinigten Landtags* (1848); idem, *Die Verhandlungen der Versammlung zur Vereinbarung der preussischen Staatsverfassung* (1848/49); M. Lenz, *Bismarcks Plan einer Gegenrevolution im März 1848* (1930); A. Streckfuss, *Berliner März 1848* (1948); D. Hansemann, *Das Preussische und Deutsche Verfassungswerk* (1850); F. J. Stahl, *Die Philosophie des Rechts* (1837); idem, *Das monarchische Prinzip* (1845); idem, *Die Revolution und die konstitutionelle Monarchie* (1848); E. Jordan, *Die Enstehung der konservativen Partei und die preussischen Agrarverhältnisse von 1848* (1914); W. O. Shanahan, ★*German Protestants Face the Social Question* (1954); W. Mommsen, *Stein, Ranke, Bismarck* (1954); E. R. Huber, 'Lorenz von Stein und die Grundlegung der Idee des Sozialstaates' in *Nationalstaat und Verfassungsstaat* (1965).

For political catholicism see L. Bergsträsser, *Studien zur Vorgeschichte der Zentrumspartei* (1910); idem, *Geschichte der politischen Parteien in Deutschland* (1955); G. Goyau, L'Allemagne religieuse: part 1, 'Le Catholicisme 1800–1870' (1908); Cl. Bauer, 'Wandlungen der sozialpolitischen Ideenwelt im deutschen politischen Kotholizismus des 19. Jahrhunderts' in *Die soziale Frage und der Katholizismus* (1931); A. Wegener, *Die vorparlamentarische Zeit Peter Reichenspergers* (1930).

For the various brands of liberalism see: G. de Ruggiero, ★*The History of European Liberalism* (1927); F. Meinecke, *Weltbürgertum und Nationalstaat* (1928); A. L. v. Rochau, *Grundsätze der Realpolitik, angewendet auf die staatlichen Zustände Deutschlands* (1853); J. Droz, *Le Libéralisme rhénan 1815–48* (1945); A. E. Zucker, ★*The Forty-Eighters: Politcal Refugees of the German Revolution of 1848* (1950); R.H. Thomas, ★*Liberalism, Nationalism and the German Intellectuals, 1822–47* (1952); F. C. Sell, ★*The Tragedy of German Liberalism* (1950); H. Rössler, 'Hans Christian von Gagern und die Politik seiner Söhne 1848–52' in *Festschrift für O. Becker* (1954); P. Wentzke/ W. Klötzer (eds) *Deutscher Liberalismus im Vormärz. Heinrich v. Gagerns Briefe und Reden 1815–1848* (1959); H. Rosenberg, 'Theologischer Rationalismus und vormärzlicher Vulgärliberalismus' in *Historische Zeitschrift* (1930); W. Hock, *Liberales Denken im Zeitalter der Paulskirche* (1956); W. Bussmann, 'Zur Geschichte des deutschen Liberalismus im 19. Jahrhundert' in *Historische Zeitschrift* (1958).

For German radicalism see: B. Bauer, *Vollständige Geschichte der Parteikämpfe in Deutschland während der Juhre 1842–1846* 2 vols (1847); G. Mayer, 'Die Anfänge des politischen Radikalismus im vormärzlichen Preussen' in *Zeitschrift für Politik* (1913); idem. 'Die Junghegelianer und der preussische Staat' in *Historische Zeitschrift* (1920); W. Mommsen, 'Julius Fröbel: Wirrnis und Weitsicht' in *Historische Zeitschrift* (1956); H. C. Bock (ed.) *Unter dem Regenbogen: Historische Portraits zum frühbürgerlichen Regenbogen* (1982); W. Grab/U. Friesel (eds) *Noch ist Deutschland nicht verloren: Historisch-politische Analayse unterdrückter Lyrik von der französischen Revolution bis zur Reichsgründung* (1973); P. Reichensperger, *Erlebnisse eines alten Parlamentariers im Revolutionsjahr 1848* (1882); F. Thimme, *König Friedrich Wilhelm IV. General von Prittwitz und der 1811–19. Märzrevolution* (1903); W. Andreas, *Die russische Diplomatie und die Politik Friedrich Wilhelms von Preussen* (1927); E. Marcks, *Bismarck und die deutsche Revolution 1848– 51* (1939).

The Frankfurt Assembly is discussed with great discernment and insight by F. Eyck, ★*The Frankfurt Parliament* (1968). Important primary sources are the *Aktenstücke zur neuesten Geschichte Deutschlands Offizieller Bericht uber die Verhandlungen zur Gründung einer deutschen Parlaments* (1848). See also; L. Bergsträsser, Die parteipolitische Lage beim Zusammentritt des Vorparlaments' in *Zeitschrift für Politik* (1913); F. Wigard (ed.), *Stenographischer Bericht über die Verhandlungen des Deutschen Konstituierenden Nationalversammlung zu Frankfurt a. M.* (1848/49); J. G. Droysen (ed.), *Die Verhandlungen des Verfassungsauschusses der Deutschen Nationalversammlung* (1849); V. Valentin, *Die erste Deutsche Nationalversammlung* (1919); F. Schnabel, *Der Zusammenschluss des politischen Katholizismus in Deutschland 1848* (1910); St King-Hall/R. K. Ullmann, *German Parliaments. A Study of the Development of Representative Institutions in Germany* (1954); W. Hock, *Liberales Denken im Zeitalter der Paulskirche* (1957); H. Precht, *Englands Stellung zur deutschen Einheit* (1848–50); F. Eyck, *The Prince Consort.* (1959); R Pascal, ★'The Francfort Parliament and the Drang nach Osten' in *Journal of Modern History* (1946); H. C. Mayer, ★*Mitteleuropa in German Thought and Action* (1956); H. Böhme, *Deutschlands Weg zur Grossmacht. Studien zum Verhältnis von Wirtschaft und Staat 1848–1881*

(1966); H. R. Fischer-Aue, *Die Deutschlandpolitik des Prinzgemahls Albert von England 1848–52* (1953); G. Ritter, ★*The Sword and the Sceptre*, vol. I (1970/71) represents the current state of research and debate on the problem of the relationship between armed forces and German society while G. A. Craigs, ★*The Politics of the Prussian Army 1648–1945* was already out of date when published in 1955. The naval question is covered by K. Haenchen, *Die deutsche Flotte 1848* (1925) and M. Bär, *Die deutsche Flotte 1848–52* (1898). The problem of Schleswig-Holstein is well discussed in English by W. Carr, ★*Schleswig-Holstein, 1815–64,* while in A. J. P. Taylor's volume, ★*The Struggle for Mastery in Europe* (1954), preconceived notions which are already implied in the title mar the discussion of this topic. See also A. O. Meyer, *Deutschland und Schleswig-Holstein vor der Erhebung* (1918); idem, *Das Erwachen des deutschen Nationalbewusstseins in Schleswig-Holstein* (1928).

For the second phase of the revolution see K. Obermann, *Die deutschen Arbeiter in der Revolution 1848* (1953); G. Mayer, 'Die Anfänge des politischen Radikalismus im vormärzlichen Preussen' in *Zeitschrift für Politik* (1913) as well as the literature on radicalism and early socialism cited above. The renewed struggle for a constitution in Prussia is discussed by Eyck, Valentin and others (already cited) as well as by P. Goldschmidt, 'Die oktroyierte preussische Verfassung' in *Preussische Jahrbücher* (1906) and by H. Wegge, *Die Stellung der Öffentlichkeit zur oktroyiertern Verfassung und die preussische Parteibildung 1848/49* (1932).

The constitution devised in the meantime in Frankfurt was published by D. Hansemann, *Die Deutsche Verfassung vom 28. März 1849* (1849); see also L. Bergstässer, *Die Verfassung des deutschen Reiches vom Jahre 1849* (1913); H. v. Sybel, *Über das Reichsgrundgesetz der Siebzehn Vertrauensmänner* (1848); E. Eckhardt, *Die Grundrechte vom Wiener Kongress bis zur Gegenwart* (1913); G. Oestreich, *Die Idee der Menschenrechte in ihrer geschichtlichen Entwicklung* (1951); W. Schneider, *Wirtschafts- und Sozialpolitik im Frankfurter Parlament 1848/49* (1923). The literature on the problem of little or greater Germany appears to exceed in terms of quantity virtually all other topics of the revolution; hence one should turn back to the summaries contained in the standard texts already cited and add: M. Doeberl, *Bayern und die deutsche Frage in der Epoche des Frankfurter Parlaments* (1922); W. Fenske, *J. G. Droysen und das deutsche Nationalstaatsproblem* (1930); H. v. Möller, *Grossdeutsch und kleindeutsch, Die Entstehung der Worte 1848–49* (1937); W. Mommsen, *Föderalismus und Unitarismus* (1954); L. Freundt, *Der deutsche Kaiser* (1848); F. Engels, *Die deutsche Reichsverfassungskampagne* (Marx-Engels *Werke*, vol. 7, 1960); A. Brass, *Der Freiheitskampf in Baden und in der Pfalz 1849* (1849), is one of several accounts of the abortive May revolution of 1849. B. Bauer, *Der Untergang des Frankfurter Parlaments* (1849) is one of several accounts of the final failure of 1848/49, an incisive analysis of which has been carried out by Th. Nipperdey cited above, and more recently by the brilliant essay of the British historian David Blackbourn but unfortunately in German, 'Wie es eigentlich nicht gewesen' in D. Groh (ed.) *Sozialgeschichtliche Bibiothek* (1980).

Chapter 4: The era of reaction

The Erfurt Union and the road to Olmütz is discussed in the standard texts already mentioned to which should be added G. Mann, ★*German History Since 1789* (1968) and W. Carr, ★*German History 1815–1945* (1945). The latter work is, to the best knowledge of this author, the only work in English which is fully aware of the constitutional intricacies and implications of German constitutional history in the nineteenth century. The constitutional conflict in Prussia over the army reform is discussed by H. W. Koch in ★*History of Prussia* cited above, also in greater detail by G. Ritter, *op. cit.*, vol. I. Again only the most accessible and important biographies of Bismarck can be mentioned here. E. Eyck's ★*Bismarck and the German Empire* (1950) is again a truncated English translation of a two-volume German original. His interpretation is that of a 'Gladstonian liberal' though he adopts this stance at its face value. A. J. P. Taylor's ★*Bismarck: The Man and Statesman* (1955) is still readable today but like Eyck's work overtaken by the current state of research. The most recent addition to Bismarck's biographies is E. Crankshaw's ★*Bismarck* (1981), which adds nothing we do not know already and treads steadily along the well-trodden path of clichés familiar over more than half a century. An outstanding biography, *Bismarck, der weisse Revolutionär*, has been written by the German historian Lothar Gall and was published in 1981. It virtually supersedes all previous biographies but its sheer volume is likely to deter publishers from having it translated. In all these biographies the Prussian constitutional conflict from 1859 to 1866 occupies naturally a prominent place. Supplementary to the biographies are also other studies, especially F. Stern's ★*Gold and Iron* (1977), a biography of Bismarck's personal banker and 'court Jew', Gerson Bleichröder, who played a crucial role in helping Bismarck and the Prussian state to ride the waves of the constitutional conflict successfully, at least in financial terms. G.A. Rein's *Die Revolution in der Politik Bismarcks* (1957), provides an excellent insight into the extent of use by Bismarck of revolutionary means for conservative ends and also into what extent the fear of revolution determined Bismarck's thought and political action throughout his political life. M Stürmer's *Das ruhelose Reich, Deutschland 1866–1918* (1983) draws heavily on and benefits from recent research in this field. G. A. Craig's ★*Germany 1866–1945* (1978) displays a wonderful grasp of German cultural history but little else. It seems that the work of international scholarship of the past 30 years has passed him by. Otto Pflanze's ★*Bismarck* (1965) has remained an incompleted torso and reads like the indictment of the Nuremberg major war criminals. For the war of 1864, the clamour for the reform of the German Confederation, the Austro-Prussian War and the end of the German Confederation all the volumes just cited are highly relevant. So too are: L. Bergsträsser, *Geschichte der Politischen Parteien,* vol. 2, *1848–1945* (1965); L. v. Stein, *Die Lehre von der vollziehenden Gewalt* (1866); K. Reich-Erkelenz, *Das Verordnungsrecht des Monarchen im deutschen konstitutionellen Staat* (1966); R. Schwemer, *Die Reaktion und die neue Ära* (1921), E. Zechlin, *Bismarck und die Grundlegung der deutschen Grossmacht* (1930).

Chapter 5: The Bismarckian Empire

See the literature cited in previous chapter on Bismarck. Also W. Richter, ★*Bismarck* (1954), a German Bismarck biography in English. H. Böhme (ed.) ★*The Foundations of the German Empire* (1971) places great emphasis on the economic aspects, as do G. Seeber/H. Wolter (eds), *Die Preusisch-Deutsche Reichsgründung* (1981). Important details on the North German Confederation are contained in O. Pflanze's ★Bismarck and German Nationalism' in *American Historical Review* (1954/55) and in his ★*Bismarck and the Development of Germany* (1963). The relationship between the North German Confederation and the south German states is examined in W. Schüssler, *Bismarcks Kampf um Süddeutschland and 1867* (1929) and O. Becker, *Bismarcks Ringen um Deutschlands Gestaltung* (1958). Interesting and critical light is also offered in the correspondence by the Prussian Princess with her mother Queen Victoria in Sir F. Posonby (ed.) ★*The Letters of Empress Frederick* (1928). See also K. A. v. Müller *Bayern 1866 und die Berufung des Fürsten Hohenlohe* (1909); Th. Schieder, *Die Kleindeutsche Partei in Bayern in den Kämpfen um die nationale Einheit 1863–71* (1936); R. Vierhaus, *Das Tagebuch der Baronin Spitzemberg* (1960); E. Vogt, *Die hessische Politik in der Zeit der Reichsgründung 1863–71* (1914); L. Gall, *Der Liberalismus als regierende Partei. Das Grossherzogtum Baden zwischen Restauration und Reichsgründung* (1968); J. Garsou, *Le Grand-Duché de Luxembourg entre la Belgique, la France et la Prusse 1867–71* (1936); H. Böhme (ed.) *Probleme der Reichsgründszeit* (1968); E. Engelberg/R. Weber (eds) *Im Widerstreit um die Reichsgründung: Eine Quellensammlung* (1970); H. Fenske (ed.), *Der Weg zur Reichsgründung* (1977); W. A. Fletcher, ★*The Mission of Vincent Benedetti to Berlin 1864–1870* (1965); *Historische Zeitschrift, Beiheft:* 'Europa und die Reichsgründung' (1980); Th. Schieder/E. Deuerlein (eds), *Reichsgründung: Tatsachen, Kontroversen, Interpretationen* (1970); H. J. Schoeps, *Der Weg ins Deutsche Kaiserreich* (1970); P. Wiegler, ★*William the First: His Life and Times* (1929); E. Zechlin, *Die Reichsgründung* (1981); and V. Valentin, *Bismarcks Reichsgründung im Urteil englischer Dimplomaten* (1937). For the background to the Franco-German conflict 1870/71 in so far as it is not already dealt with in the works cited above, see the bibliography in H. W. Koch, ★*A History of Prussia* (1978). Still very readable are M. Busch, ★*Our Chancellor: Sketches for a Historical Picture*, 2 vols (1884) and idem ★*Bismarck; Some Secret Pages of his History*, 2 vols (1898). Economic aspects of the empire are also dealt with by K.D. Barkin, *The Controversy over German Industrialisation* (1970); W. O. Henderson, ★*The Rise of German Industrial Power 1834–1914* (1975); J. Kuczynski, *Geschichte des Alltags des deutschen Volkes*, vol. IV (1982); G. A. Ritter/J. Kocka (eds), *Deutsche Sozialgeschichte*, vol. II; *1870–1914* (1977); D. G. Rohr, ★*The Origins of Social Liberalism in Germany* (1963); W. W. Rostow, ★*Stages of Economic Growth* (1963); G. Stolper, ★*The German Economy: 1870 to the Present* (1967): Th. Veblen, ★*Imperial Germany and the Industrial Revolution* (1915, reprint 1967); H. -U. Wehler (ed.) *Moderne Deutsche Sozialgeschichte* (1968). On German political parties see Th. Nipperday 'Die Organisation der deutschen Parteien vor 1918' in *Historische Zeitschrift* (1961); idem, 'Interessenverbände und Parteien in Deutschland vor dem Ersten Weltkrieg' in *Politische Viertel-*

jahrs-Schriften (1961); H. Grebing, *Geschichte deutschen der politischen Parteien* (1962). For the *Kulturkamp* see the literature on Bismarck cited above. Also W. M. Simon, ★*Germany in the Age of Bismarck* (1968); G. Goyau, *Bismarck et l'église. Le Culturkampf 1870–78* (1924); M. Becker, *Das 1. Vatikanische Konzil im Spiegel der bayerischen Politik* (1970); C. de Germiny, *La politique de Leon XIII* (1902); R. Beazley, ★ Bismarck and the Papacy under Leo XIII'. *Quarterly Review* (1950). On the anti-socialist struggle see: H. Heidegger, *Die deutsche Sozialdemokratie und der nationale Staat 1870–1920* (1956); H. Grebing, *Geschichte der deutschen Arbeiterbewegung* (1966); G. Hildebrand, *Die Erschütterung der Industriewirtschaft des Industriesozialismus* (1910); F. Kool/E. Oberländer (eds) *Arbeiterdemokratie oder Parteidiktatur*, 2 vols (1972); H. Mommsen, *Arbeiterbewegung und nationale Frage* (1979); C. E. Schorske, ★*German Social Democracy 1905–1917. The Development of the Great Schism* (1965); R. Tilly, *Kapital, Staat und sozialer Protest in der deutschen Industrialisierung* (1980); H.-U. Wehler, *Sozialdemokratie und Nationalstaat* (1971); idem, *Krisenherde des Kaiserreiches* (1973); P. Gay, ★*The Dilemma of Democratic Socialism 1850–1918* (1962); L. Stern, *Der Kampf der deutschen Sozialdemokratie in der Zeit des Sozialistengesetzes 1878–90* (1956); G. Erdmann, *Die Entwicklung der deutschen Sozialgesetzgebung* (1956) For Alsace-Lorraine see: D. P. Silverman, ★*Reluctant Union: Alsace-Lorraine and Imperial Germany 1871–1918* (1972); H. -U. Wehler, *Krisenherde des Kaiserreiches* (1973) which is also relevant for Germany's eastern provinces as is H. v. Gerlach, *Der Zusammenbruch der deutschen Polenpolitik* (1919). On Germany's colonial policy and its constitutional repercussions see: A. J. P. Taylor, ★*Germany's First Bid for Colonies 1884/85* (1938); W. Aydelotte, ★*Bismarck and British Colonial Policy. The Problem of South-West Africa 1883–83* (1937); W. O. Henderson, ★*Studies in German Colonial Policy* (1962); J. D. Hargreaves, ★*Prelude to the Partition of West Africa* (1963); P. Gifford/W. Roger Louis (eds) ★*Britain and Germany and Africa* (1976); P. R. Anderson, ★*The Background to Anti-English Feeling in Germany 1890–1902* (1939); W. L. Langer, ★*European Alliances and Alignments* (1900) idem, ★*The Diplomacy of Imperialism* (1955); O. J. Hale, ★*Publicity and Diplomacy* (1939); M. Erzberger, *Die Wahrheit über die deutschen Kolonien* (1909); K. Epstein ★'Erzberger and the German colonial scandals 1905–10' in *English Historical Review* (1959); H. Bley, *Kolonialherrschaft und Sozialstruktur in Deutsch-Südwestafrika 1894–1914* (1968); G. Sudholt, *Die deutsche Eingeborenenpolitik in Südwestafrika* (1975); G. Graudenz/H. M. Schindler, *Die deutschen Kolonien* (1982); W. J. Mommsen, *Das Zeitalter des Imperialismus* (1969); idem, *Der europäische Imperialismus* (1979); G.H. Nadel/P. Curtis, ★*Imperialism and Colonialism* (1964); C. Peters, *Gesammelte Schriften*, 3 vols (1943); N. -Ch. Schröder *Soziallismus und Imperialismus* (1968); H. -U. Wehler (ed.), *Imperialismus* (1970).

Chapter 6: The German Empire under Wilhelm II

The best biography of Wilhelm II is M. Balfour's ★*The Kaiser and his Times* (1964). See also: V. Cowles, ★*The Kaiser* (1963); J.v.Kürenberg, ★*The Kaiser*

(1954); W. Schüssler, *Kaiser Wilhelm II.* (1962); E. Eyck, *Das persönliche Regiment Wilhelms II.* (1948); I. V. Hull, ★*The Entourage of Kaiser Wilhelm II 1888–1918* (1982); W. Görlitz (ed.) *Der Kaiser . . . Aufzeichnungen des Chefs des Marinekabinetts Admiral Alexander v. Müller* (1965); *idem, Regierte der Kaiser? Aufzeichnungen Admirals v. Müllers 1914–1918* (Göttingen 1959). For the Caprivi and Hohenlohe chancellorships see J. C. G. Röhl, ★*Germany Without Bismarck* (1967); for Bülow see P. Winzen, *Bülows Weltmachtkonzept. Untersuchungen zur Frühphase seiner Aussenpolitik 1897–1901* (Boppard 1977). On the army see: G. Ritter, ★*The Sword and the Sceptre*, vols 2–4 (1971–74); K. Demeter, ★*The German Officer Corps* (1968); W. Görlitz, *Kleine Geschichte des deutschen Generalstabs* (1967); H. H. Hoffmann (ed.) *Das deutsche Offizierskorps 1860–1960* (1980); M. Kitchen, ★*The German Officer Corps 1890–1914* (1968); Militärgeschichtliches Forschungs amt Freiburg, *Handbuch der deutschen Militärgeschichte*, vols 2–3 (1979); H. Rosinski, ★*The German Army* (1966); B.-F. Schulte, *Die deutsche Armee 1900–1914: Zwischen Beharrung und Veränderung* (1977). For the German Navy see A. v. Tirpitz, ★*Memoirs*, 2 vols (1922); a satisfactory account of the rise of German naval power is still outstanding. The most balanced studies so far are the three works by W. Hubatsch, *Kaiserliche Marine. Aufgaben und Leistungen* (1975); *idem, Die Ära Tirptiz. Studien zur deutschen zur deutschen Marinepolitik 1890–1918* (1955); *idem, Der Admiralstab und die oberstan Marinebehörden in Deutschland 1848–1945* (1958). H. Herwig's study, ★*The German Naval Officer Corps. A Social and Political History* (1973), is full of conflicting evidence while his book ★*The Luxury Fleet* (1980), is more of a *tour de horizon* than a scholarly analysis. V. R. Berghahn, *Der Tirpitz-Plan* (1900), sees the German navy under the aspect of the primacy of domestic politics, an interesting but untenable position. W. Deist 'Die Politik der Seekriegsleitung und die Rebellion der Flotte Ende Oktober 1918' in *Vierteljahrshefte für Zeitgeschichte* (1966) places great emphasis on rumours and loose talking but virtually ignores the plan of operations and its implications. See also H. Schottenlius/W. Deist (eds) *Marine und Marinepolitik im kaiserlichen Deutschland 1871–1914* (1979). Perhaps the best account in English is J. Steinberg's ★*Yesterday's Deterrent: Tirpitz and the Birth of the German Navy* (1965). For German naval planning in October 1918 see Ch. Vidil, *Les Mutineries de la marine Allemande 1917/18* (1931). For general accounts of the German Empire W. H. Dawson's ★*The Evolution of Modern Germany* (1908) and ★*The German Empire 1867–1914*. 2 vols (1919), still offer a wealth of social and economic material as well as balanced judgement. For new party political developments see D. Düding, *Der Nationalsoziale Verein 1896–1903* (1972), and G. Eley, ★*The Reshaping of the German Right* (1980). For the constitutional implications of the 'Daily Telegraph Affair' see W. Schüssler, *Die Daily Telegraph Affaire* (1952). For recent biographies of Bethmann Hollweg see K. H. Jarausch, ★*The Enigmatic Chancellor: Bethmann Hollweg and the Hubris of Imperial Germany* (1973); E. v. Vietsch, *Bethmann Hollweg. Staatsmann zwischen Macht und Ethos* (1969); W. Gutsche, *Aufstieg und Fall eines kaiserlichen Reichskanzlers: Bethmann Hollweg 1856–1921* (1973) and H. -G. Zmarzlick, *Bethmann Hollweg als Reichskanzler 1909–1914* (1957). Also K. D. Erdmann (ed.) *Kurt Riezler – Tagebücher. Aufsätze, Dokumente* (1972). The literature on the July Crisis is too voluminous to be included here; readers are referred to H. W.

Koch (ed.), ★ *The Origins of the First World War: German War Aims and Great Power Rivalries*, completely revised and new edition, (1984) and the bibliography contained in this volume. For the interaction between German peace feelers and the Reichstag see W. Steglich, *Bündnissicherung oder Verständigunsfriede. Untersuchengen zu dem Friedensangebot der Mittelmächte am 12. Dezember 1916*, (1958); idem, *Die Friedenspolitik der Mittelmächte 1917–18* (1964) and F. Fischer, ★ *Germany's War Aims in the First World War* (1965). For Erzberger's role see K. Epstein, ★ *Matthias Erzberger and the Dilemma of German Democracy* (1959), though the German translation, published in 1962, is to be preferred – as Epstein, in the light of recent research, had to revise substantially his judgement on Erzberger, the revisions being contained only in the German translation. Aspects of domestic reform are treated exhaustively in D. Grosser, *Die Verfassungspolitik der deutschen Parteien im letzten Jahrzehnt des Kaiserreiches* (1970). For Germany's Social Democracy and the Socialists in general see literature cited above, as well as: E. Matthias/E. Pikart (eds), *Die Reichstagsfraktion der deutschen Sozialdemokratie 1898–1918*, 2 vols (1966); A.J. Berlau, ★ *The German Social Democratic Party 1914–1921* (1949); J. Joll, ★ *The Second International 1889–1914* (1956); G. Haupt, ★ *Socialism and the Great War. The Collapse of the Second International* (1972); P. Gay, ★ *Eduard Bernstein* (1972); U. Bermbach, *Vorformen parlamentarischer Kabinettsbildung in Deutschland. Der interfraktionelle Ausschuss 1917–18 und die Parlamentarisierung der Reichsregierung* (1967). Economic and social aspects in Germany during the First World War are covered by R. B. Armeson, ★ *Total Warfare and Compulsory Labor. A Study of the Military-Industrial Complex in Germany 1914–18* (1964) and G. D. Felman, ★ *Army, Industry and Labor in Germany 1914–18* (1966).

Chapters 7 and 8: From Parliamentary government to revolution and republic/The constitutional reality of the Weimar Republic.

A. Rosenberg, *Entstehung der Weimarer Republik; Geschichte der Weimarer Republik* (1961); E. Eyck, ★ *The History of the Weimar Republic*, 2 vols (1962). A comprehensive up-to-date history of the Weimar Republic in English is still a desideratum. See also: W. Laqueur, ★ *Germany and Russia* (1964); Z. A. B. Zeman (ed.), ★ *Germany and the Revolution in Russia 1915–18. Documents from the Archives of the German Foreign Ministry* (1958); J. V. Bredt, *Der deutsche Reichstag im Weltkrieg* (1926); E. Matthias/R. Morsey, *Die Regierung des Prinzen Max von Baden* (1962); H. R. Rudin, ★ *Armistice 1918* (1944); K. Schwabe, *Deutsche Revolution und Wilson-Frieden* (1971); A Dorpalen, ★ Empress Auguste Victoria and the fall of the German monarchy' in *American Historical Review* (1952); H. W. Koch, *Der Deutsche Bürgerkrieg* (1978); A. J. Ryder, ★ *The German Revolution of 1918* (1967); Ch. B. Burdick/R. H. Lutz (eds) ★ *The Political Institutions of the German Revolution 1918–1919* (1966); H. J. Gordon, ★ *The Reichswehr and the German Republic 1919–1926* (1957); D. W. Morgan, ★ *The Socialist Left and the German*

Revolution (1975); A. Mitchell, ★*Revolution in Bavaria 1918/19* (1965); U. Kluge, *Soldatenräte und Revolution* (1975); E. Kolb (ed.), *Vom Kaiserreich zur Weimarer Republik* (1972); W. Becker, *Demokratie des sozialen Staates* (1971); J. Berlin (ed.), *Die deutsche Revolution 1918/19* (1979); F. L. Carsten, ★*Revolution in Central Europe 1918–19* (1972); H. H. Herwig, ★'The first German congress of workers' and soldiers' councils and the problem of military reforms' in *Central European History* (1968); J. P. Nettl, ★*Rosa Luxemburg*, 2 vols (1966). On early party formations see L. Hertzmann, ★'The founding of the German National People's Party' in *Journal of Modern History* (1958); idem, ★*DNVP. Right-Wing Opposition in the Weimar Republic 1918–24* (1963); R. Morsey, *Die Deutsche Zentrumspartei 1917–23* (1966); M. Eksteins, *Theodor Heuss und die Weimarer Republik* (1969); D.W. Morgan, ★*The Socialist Left and the German Revolution: USPD 1917–1922* (1975); G. Jasper, *Der Schutz der Republik* (1963); E. Matthias/R. Morsey (eds) *Das Ende der Parteien* (1960); K. D. Bracher, *Die Auflösung der Weimarer Republik* (Villingen 1955); W. Becker, *Demokratie des sozialen Staates: Politische Haltung der Frankfurter Zeitung, der Vossischen Zeitung und des Berliner Tageblattes 1918–1924* (1971); W. Benz (ed.), *Politik in Bayern 1919–1933: Berichte des württembergischen Gesandten Moser v. Filseck* (1971); W. Besson, *Friedrich Ebert* (1963); H. Brüning, *Memoiren 1918–1934* (1970); K. Buchheim, *Die Weimarer Republik: Grundlagen und . politische Entwicklung* (1966); J. G. Williamson, ★*Karl Helferich 1872–1924. Economist Financier. Politician* (1971); F. Deppe/W. Rossmann, *Wirtschaftskrise und Faschismus: Gewerkschaften 1929–1933 (1981); J. A. Moses, ★German Trade Unionism from Bismarck to Hitler*, 2 vols (1981); J. Fleming/C. D. Krohn/D. Stemann/ P. Chr. Witt (eds) *Republik von Weimar: Das Politische System*; idem, *Das soziookonomische System* (1979); V. Hentschel, *Weimars letzte Monate* (1978); H. Muth, 'Carl Schmitt in der deutschen Innenpolitik des Sommers 1932'in *Historische Zeitschrift*, Supplement 1, *Beiträge zur Geschichte der Weimarer Republik* (1971); H. Holborn, (ed.), ★*Republic to Reich* (1972); G. Jasper, (ed), *Von Weimar zu Hitler 1930–1933* (1972); D. Junker, (ed.), *Deutsche Parlamentsdebatten 1919–1933* (1971); H. Lutz, *Demokratie im Zwielicht: Der Weg der deutschen Katholiken aus dem Kaiserreich in die Republik 1914–1925* (1963); H. Mommsen/D. Petzina/B. Weisbrod (eds) *Industrielles System und Entwicklung in der Weimarer Republik*, 2 vols (1977); G. Niedhart (ed.), *Die ungeliebte Republik* (1980); F. v. Papen, ★*Memoirs* (1952); H. J. Schoeps, (ed.) *Zeitgeist im Wandel: Zeitgeist der Weimarer Republik* (1968); H. Schulze, *Otto Braun oder Preussens demokratische Sendung* (1977); idem, *Weimar: Deutschland 1917–1933* (1981); K. D. Erdmann/H. Schulze (eds), *Weimar Selbstpreisgabe einer Demokratie* (1980); K. Sontheimer, *Anti-demokratisches Denken in der Weimarer Republik* (1962); A. Thimme, *Flucht in den Mythos: Die Deutschnationale Volkspartei und die Niederlage von 1918* (1969); H. Ashby Turner, ★*Stresemann and the Politics of the Weimar Republic* (1965); idem, ★*Emil Kirdorf and the Nazi Party*' in *Central European History* (1968); idem, ★'Big Business and the rise of Hitler' in *American Historical Review* (1969); idem ★'The Ruhrlade' in *Central European History* (1970); idem, 'Grossunternehmertum und Nationalsozialismus' in *Historische Zeitschrift* (1973); idem, 'Fritz Thyssen und das Buch "I paid Hitler"fi' in *Vierteljahrshefte für Zeitgeschichte* (1971); H. A. Winkler, *Mittelstand, Demokratie und*

Nationalsozialismus (1972); R. F. Hamilton, ★*Who Voted for Hitler?* (1982); For para-military units see: V. R. Berghahn, *Der Stahlhelm: Bund der Frontsoldaten* (1966); K. Rohe, *Das Reichbanner Schwarz-Rot-Gold* (1966); A. Werner, *SA und NSDAP 1920–1933* (1964). For the rise of the NSDAP see W. S. Allen, ★*The Nazi Seizure of Power* (1965); H. Bennecke, *Hitler und die SA* (1962); E. Deuerlein (ed.), *Der Hitler-Putsch* (1962); idem, *Der Aufstieg der NSDAP in Augenzeugenberichten* (1968); G. Franz-Willing, *Die Hitler-Bewegung 1919–22* (1962); idem, *Putsch und Verbotszeit der Hitlerbewegung 1923–25* (1977); idem, *Krisenjahr der Hitlerbewegung* (1975); H.J. Gordon, Jr, ★*Hitler and the Beer Hall Putsch* (1972); H. H. Hofmann, *Der Hitlerputsch* (1961); W. Horn, *Der Marsch zur Machtergreifung: Die NSDAP bis 1933* (1972); idem, *Führeideologie und Parteiorganisation in der NSDAP* (1972); M. H. Kele, ★*Nazis and Workers: NS Appeals to German Labor 1919–1933* (1972); H. W. Koch, ★*The Hitler Youth: Origins and Development 1922–1945* (1975); H. Höhne, ★*The Order of the Death's Head* (1979); A. Krebs, *Tendenzen und Gestalten der NSDAP* (1959); W. Maser, *Die Frühgeschichte der NSDAP: Hitlers Weg bis 1924* (1965); D. Orlow, ★*The History of the Nazi Party*, 2 vols (1969 & 1971); G. Pridham, ★*Hitler's Rise to Power: The NS Movement in Bavaria 1923–33* (1973); Th. Schnabel, *Die Machtergreifung in Südwestdeutschland 1928–1933* (1982); Th. Vogelsang, *Reichswehr, Staat und NSDAP 1930–1932* (1900); F.L. Carsten, ★*The Reichswehr and Politics 1918–1933* (1966). See also: A. Dorpalen, ★*Hindenburg and the Weimar Republic* (1964); Th. Eschenburg *et al.*, ★*The Road to Dictatorship* (1970); R. Fischer, ★*Stalin and German Communism* (1948); R. P. Gratwohl, ★*Stresemann and the DNVP* (1980); L. Hertzmann, ★*The DNVP* (1963); R. N. Hunt, ★*German Social Democracy 1918–1933* (1900); A.J. Nicholls/E. Matthias (ed.), ★*German Democracy and the Triumph of Hitler* (1971); D. Abraham, ★*The Collapse of the Weimar Republic* (1981); H. A. Winkler, ★'From social protectionism to national socialism' in *Journal of Modern History* (1976); P. H. Merkl, ★*Political Violence Under the Swastika* (1975); J. Noakes, ★ *The Nazi Party in Lower Saxony* (1971); F. W. Bennet, ★*Germany and the Diplomacy of the Financial Crisis* (1962); D. Petzina, ★'Germany and the Great Depression' in *Journal of Contemporary History* (1969); H. W. Winkler, ★'German society, Hitler and the illusion of restoration' in *Journal of Contemporary History* (1976); H. Bennecke, *Wirtschaftliche Depression und politischer Radikalismus* (1970); H. Lebovics, ★*Social Conservatism and the Middle Classes in Germany 1914–1933* (1969); F. Stern, ★*The Politics of Cultural Despair* (1961); A. Mohler, *Die Konservative Revolution in Deutschland 1918–1932* (1975); K.v. Klemperer, ★*Germany's New Conservatism* (1968); J. Petzold, *Webgereiter des des deutschen Fashismus: Die Jungkonservativen in der Weimarer Republik* (1978); E. O. Schüddekopf, *Linke Leute von Rechts* (1961); E. v. Salomon, ★*The Answers of E. v. Salomon* (1945); W. J. Helbich, *Die Reparationen in der Ara Brüning. Zur Bedeutung des Young Plans für die deutsche Politik 1930–1932* (1962); E. Matthias, 'Hindenburg zwischen den Fronten. Zur Vorgeschichte der Reichspräsidentenwahlen 1932' In *Vierteljahrshefte für Zeitgeschichte* (1960).
The Akten der Reichskanzlei since 1919 have been published over more than a decade and a half. Beginning with the Cabinet Scheidemann, they have now reached the Brüning cabinet until February 1931. This edition is carried out

under the auspices of the Historische Kommission bei der Bayerischen Akademie der Wissenschaften under K. D. Erdmann and the President of the Bundesarchiv, H. Booms.

Chapter 9: The Führer State

Much of the literature cited in the previous section is of relevance, though there is preciously little on constitutional aspects. See K. D. Bracher, ★*The German Dictatorship* (1971); K. D. Bracher/W. Sauer/G. Schulz, *Die national sozialistische Machtergreifung* (1960). For a discussion of the NS-leadership principle see H. W. Koch, *Im Namen des deutschen Volkes: Roland Freisler und der NS-Volksgerichtshof 1934–1945* (1984), and the sources cited for Chapter 2 bibliography. See also M. Broszat, ★*Hitler's State* (1981). Of constitutional relevance is also Fritz Tobias's painstaking investigation of the Reichstag fire and the documents, especially the minutes of cabinet sessions reprinted in it: *Der Reichtagsbrand* (1961). See also H. Mommsen, ★'The political consequences of the Reichstags fire' in H. Holborn, (ed.) *From Republic to Reich* (1973). Unfortunately the English translation of Tobias's work has been so heavily truncated as to make it useless for the purposes of scholarship. Of importance within the context of this volume is still F. Neumann, *Behemoth* (1942); W. Runge, *Politik und Beamtentum im Parteistaat* (1965); H. Mommsen, *Beamtentum im Dritten Reich* (1966); J. Becker 'Zentrum und Ermächtigungsgesetz' in *Vierteljahrhefte für Zeitgeschichte* (1961); P. Diehl-Thiele, *Partei und Staat im Dritten Reich. Untersuchungen zum Verhältnis von NSDAP und allgemeiner Staatsverwaltung 1933–1945* (1969); E. Fränkel, ★*The Dual State* (1941); P. Hüttenberger, 'Nationalsozialistische Polykratie' in *Geschichte und Gesellschaft* (1978); H. Herrfahrdt, *Die Verfassungsgesetze des National sozialistisschen Staates dem Text der Weimarer Republik gegenügestellt* (Marburg 1935); O. Koellreuter, *Der Führestaat* (1934); idem, *Deutsches Verfassungsrecht* (1936); H. Nicolai, *Grundlagen der kommenden Verfassung* (1933); E. N. Peterson, ★*The Limits of Hitler's Power* (1969); C. Schmitt, *Legalität und Legitimität* (1932); idem, *Staat, Bewegung, Volk* (1934).

Chapter 10: The two Germanies

K. Dönitz, *Zehn Jahre und zwanzig Tage* (1958); W. Lüdde-Neurath, *Regierung Dönitz. Die letzten Tage des Dritten Reiches* (1964); K. D. Erdmann, 'Die Regierung Dönitz' in *Geschichte, Wissenschaft und Unterricht* (1963); R. Hansen, *Das Ende des Dritten Reiches Die deutsche Kapitulation 1945* (1966); M. G. Steinert, *Die 23 Tage der Regierung Dönitz* (1967); P. E. Schramm (ed.), *Das Kriegstagebuch des Oberkommandos der Wehrmacht 1944–1945*, vol. IV (1961). For the revised text of the document of capitulation Ph. E. Moseley in *Foreign Affairs* (April 1950); W. Bedell-Smith, *Moscow Mission* (1950); J. F. Byrnes, ★*Speaking Frankly* (1947); H. Feis, ★*Churchill-*

Bibliography

Roosevelt-Stalin. *The War They Waged and the Peace They Sought* (1957); ★*Foreign Relations of the United States. Diplomatic Papers: The Conferences at Malta and Yalta 1945* (1955); ibid. ★*The Conference of Berlin (The Potsdam Conference) 1945*, 2 vols (1960); W. Strang, ★*Home and Abroad* (1956); S. Welles, ★*Seven Decisions That Shaped History* (1951); E. Deuerlein, *Die Einheit Deutschlands* vol. I (1961);W. A. Williams, ★*The Tragedy of American Foreign Policy* (1962); H. Feis, ★*From Trust to Terror. The Onset of the Cold War 1945–1950* (1970); B. J. Bernstein (ed.), ★*Politics and Policies of the Truman Administration* (1970); E. Nolte, *Deutschland und der Kalte Krieg* (1974); M. Balfour, ★*Four-Power Control in Germany and Austria* (1956); N. Balakins, ★*Germany Under Direct Controls* (1964); ★*The Basic Law of the Federal Republic of Germany* (1974); L. D. Clay, ★*Decision in Germany* (1950); L. J. Edinger, ★*Kurt Schumacher* (1965); E. Deuerlein, ★*Potsdam 1945* (1963); M. Dönhoff, *Die Bundesrepublik in der Ära Adenauer* (1963); C. FitzGibbon, ★*Denazification* (1969); B. Freudenfeld, *Deutsche Existenz* (1964); P. Frisch, *Extremistenbeschluss* (1976); G. Grass, ★*Speak Out!* (1968); K. Adenauer, ★*Memoirs* (1966); M. Balfour, ★*West Germany* (1968); L. Eheard, ★*Prosperity Through Competition* (1958); W. D. Graf, ★*The German Left Since 1945* (1976); A. Grosser, ★*The Federal Republic of Germany* (1964); J. Gimbel, ★*The American Occupation of Germany* (1968); W.G. Grewe, *Rückblende* (1978); A. Heidenheimer, ★*Adenauer and the CDU* (1960); H. -A. Jacobsen/O. Stenzl, *Deutschland und die Welt: Zur Aussenpolitik der Bundesrepublik 1949–1963* (1964); K. Knorr (ed.), ★*Nato and U.S. Security*, (1959); W. F. Griffith, ★*The Ostpolitik of the Federal Republic of Germany* (1978); E. Jaeckel (ed.), *Deutsche Parlamentsdebatten:* vol. 3, *1949–1970* (1971); M. Jenke, *Verschwörung von Rechts?* (1961); G. Bartsch, *Revolution von Rechts? Ideologie und Organisation der Neuen Rechten* (1975); H. H. Knutter, *Ideologien des Rechtsradikalismus im Nachkriegsdeutschland* (1961); P. Brandt/H. Ammon (eds), *Die Linke und die nationale Frage* (1981); G. -K. Kaltenbrunner (ed.), *Die Herausforderung der Konservativen* (1974); A. Mohler, *Was die Deutschen fürchten* (1965); C. v. Schrenk-Notzing/A. Mohler (eds), *Deutsche Identität* (1982); W. Venohr (ed.), *Die deutsche Einheit kommt bestimmt* (1982); B. Willms, *Die Deutsche Nation* (1982); R. Löwenthal/H. P. Schwarz (eds), *Die Zweite Republik: 25 Jahre Bundesrepublik Deutschland* (1974); J. Mander, ★*Berlin: Hostage of the West* (1962); W. D. Narr/D. Thränhardt (eds), *Die Bundesrepublik Deutschland: Entstehung. Entwicklung, Struktur* (1979); C. v. Schrenk-Notzing: *Charakterwäsche: Die amerikanische Besatzung und ihre Folgen* (1965); idem, *Zukunftsmacher: Die neue Linke in Deutschland und ihre Herkunft* (1971); H. -P. Schwarz, *Handbuch der deutschen Aussenpolitik* (1975); R. Thilenius, *Die Teilung Deutschlands* (1957); A. Baring, *Aussenpolitik in Adenauers Kanzlerdemokratie* (1969); idem, *Machtwechsel: Die Ära Brandt-Scheel* (1982). For eastern Germany see: J. P. Nettl, ★*The Eastern Zone and Soviet Policy in Germany 1945–1950* (1951); W. Leonhard, ★*Child of the Revolution* (London 1956); D. Childs, ★*East Germany* (1969); A. Baring, ★*Uprising in East Germany* (1972); C. Stern, ★*Ulbricht* (1965); R. Bahro, ★*The Alternative in Eastern Europe* (1978); E. Deuerlein (ed.), *DDR: Geschichte und Bestandaufnahme 1945–1970* (1971); W. Hangen, *DDR: Der unbequeme Nachbar* (1966); idem, ★*The Muted Revolution* (1966); R. Havemann, *Fragen-Antworten-Fragen: aus der Biographie eines deutschen Marxisten* (1970); P. C. Ludz, ★*The Changing Party Elite in East Germany*

(1973); idem, *Die DDR zwischen Ost unf West 1961–1976* (1977); E. Honecker, ★*From My Life* (1981); E. Richert, *Die DDR-Elite – oder unsere Partner von Morgen?* (1968); K. Sontheimer/W. Bleek, *Die DDR: Politik, Gesellschaft, Wirtschaft* (1973); Th. Vogelsang, *Das geteilte Deutschland* (1966); J. Steele, ★*Socialism With a German Face* (1977); R. Dahrèndorf ★*Democracy and Society in Germany* (1969).

MAPS AND TABLES

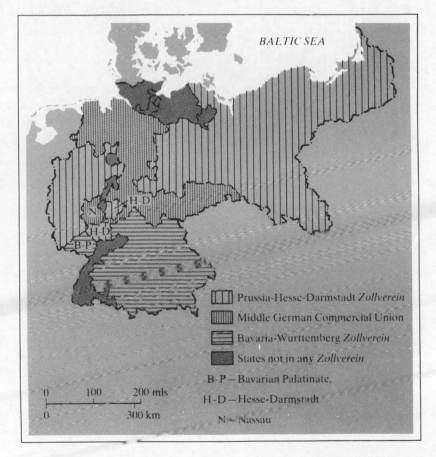

BALTIC SEA

|||| Prussia-Hesse-Darmstadt *Zollverein*

||||| Middle German Commercial Union

Bavaria-Wurttemberg *Zollverein*

States not in any *Zollverein*

B-P — Bavarian Palatinate,

H-D — Hesse-Darmstadt

N — Nassau

0   100   200 mls

0   300 km

Map 1(a)   The Customs Unions of 1828

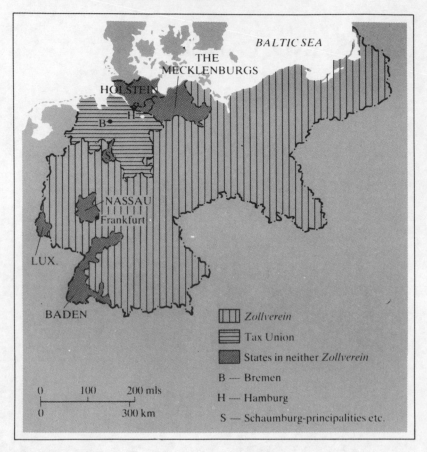

Map 1(b)   The *Zollverein* and the Tax Union, 1834

Map 1(c)   The new *Zollverein*, 1867

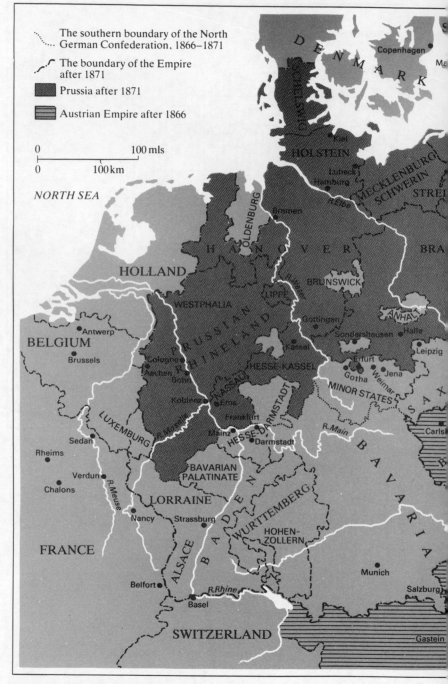

Map 2   The unification of Germany

Map 3   Germany divided
376

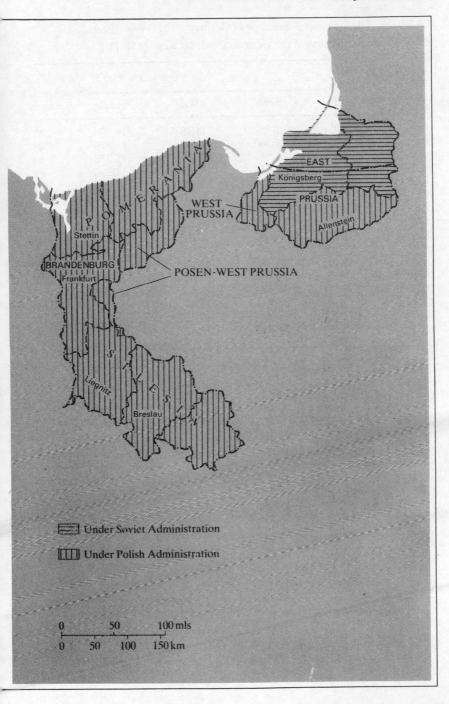

TABLE 1. The area and population of Germany, 1817–1980

(a) Area and population of the German Confederation 1817–71

Year	Area (000 km²)	Population (000's)			Inhabitants per km²
		Total	Male	Female	
1817	533.1	23,759	11,781	11,978	45
1822	533.1	25,560	12,684	12,876	48
1825	533.1	26,533	13,176	13,357	50
1831	533.1	28,216	14,006	14,210	53
1837	533.1	29,974	14,966	15,008	56
1841	533.1	31,477	15,705	15,772	59
1843	533.1	32,229	16,084	16,145	60
1846	533.1	33,197	16,579	16,618	62
1849	533.1	34,562	17,275	17,287	65
1852	533.1	34,366	17,145	17,221	64
1855	533.1	34,581	17,243	17,338	65
1858	533.1	35,441	17,654	17,787	66
1861	533.1	36,604	18,033	18,571	69
1864	533.1	36,814	18,111	18,703	69
1867	533.1	38,594	19,112	19,482	72
1871	533.1	39,478	19,453	20,025	74

(b) Area and population of the Reich territory of the German Empire 1871–1910

Year	Area (000 km²)	Population (000's)			Inhabitants per km²
		Total	Male	Female	
1871*	540.6	41,058.8	20,152.1	20,907.6	76
1875	539.8	42,727.4	20,986.7	21,740.7	79
1880	540.5	45,234.1	22,185.4	23,048.6	84
1885	540.6	46,855.7	22,933.7	23,922.0	87
1890	540.5	49,428.5	24,230.8	25,197.6	91
1895	540.7	52,279.9	25,661.3	26,618.7	97
1900	540.7	56,367.2	27,737.2	28,629.9	104
1905	540.8	60,641.5	29,884.9	30,756.6	112
1910	540.9	64,926.0	32,040.2	32,885.8	120

* figures include Alsace Lorraine as well as results of new territorial surveys

(c) Area and population of Germany 1910–39

Year	Area (000 km²)	Population (000's)			Inhabitants per km²
		Total	Male	Female	
1910	540.9	64,926.0	32,040.2	32,885.8	120
1925	468.7	62,410.6	30,196.8	32,213.8	133
1933	468.8	65,218.5	31,685.6	33,532.9	139
1939*	583.4	79,375.3	38,761.6	40,613.6	136

* Germany including Austria and the Sudetenland

(d) Area and population of Germany 1945–80

Year	Area (000 km²)	Population (000's)	Inhabitants per km²
(i) Areas of Western zones of occupation including West Berlin and Saarland (From 1949 Federal Republic of Germany):			
1945			
1946	248.9	46,648.7	187
1950	248.9	50,798.7	204
1955	248.9	53,468.7	215
1970	248.9	60,650.6	244
1980	248.9	61,561.3*	247
(ii) Eastern zone including East Berlin (from 1949 German Democratic Republic):			
1945	107.2		
1946	107.2	18,350.0	171
1950	107.2	18,390.0	172
1955	107.2	17,830.0	166
1970	107.2	17,040.0	159
1980	107.2	17,028.0*	159

* approximate figures

TABLE 2. The area and population of the German Confederation according to Federal states and administrative provinces in 1841

States and provinces	Area (km²)	Population
(a) Kingdoms		
Prussia	281,261.4	15,171,044
East Prussia	38,893.2	1,401,191
West Prussia	25,972.7	929,247
Posen	29,541.9	1,253,614
Pomerania	31,755.9	1,070,864
Berlin	69.9	332,213
Brandenburg	40,354.0	1,544,600
Silesia	40,824.4	2,904,651
Saxony	25,363.7	1,656,046
Westphalia	20,273.6	1,398,388
Rhineland	27,064.0	2,618,730
Hohenzollern	1,148.1	61,500
Bavaria	76,399.9	4,392,600
Right of Rhine	70,441.5	3,810,000
Left of Rhine	5,958.4	582,600
Hanover	38,470.3	1,745,053
Württemberg	19,508.3	1,653,000
Saxony	14,972.2	1,716,300
(b) Grand Duchies and Duchies		
Baden	15,330.1	1,294,800
Kur-Hesse	9,153.7	734,500
Grand Duchy of Hesse	8,408.1	816,000
Holstein-Lauenburg	9,602.4	859,900
Brunswick	3,729.4	265,000
Mecklenburg-Schwerin	13,261.4	498,246
Mecklenburg-Strelitz	2,725.1	90,500
Nassau	4,707.9	401,198
Saxe-Weimar	3,632.0	249,400
Saxe-Coburg-Gotha	2,009.2	141,900
Saxe-Meiningen	2,549.4	153,500
Saxe-Altenburg	1,277.5	123,200
Oldenburg	6,264.0	268,701
Anhalt	2,383.1	149,600
(c) Principalities		
Schwarzburg-Sondershausen	966.9	57,400
Schwarzburg-Rudolstadt	958.1	67,300
Waldeck	1,155.2	58,400
Reuss (senior line)	345.8	33,200
Reuss (junior line)	834.2	74,100
Schaumburg-Lippe	352.4	27,700
Lippe-Detmold	1,139.8	102,531

States and provinces	Area (km²)	Population
(d) Free Cities		
Lübeck	364.5	41,400
Frankfurt	100.8	66,200
Bremen	252.2	71,968
Hamburg	351.9	189,476
Total	522,467.2	31,514,117

TABLE 3(a). Number entitled to vote and actual participation in elections to the Prussian Diet, 1849–67*

Election Year	Inhabitants (000's) (1858,62 and 63 not available)	Entitled to vote						Election participation			
		Total (000's)	% Ist class	IInd class	IIIrd class	Total (%)	Total (000's)	Votes cast (%) Ist class	IInd class	IIIrd class	(%)
1849	15,472	3,256	4.72	12.59	82.69	21.0	1,038	55.4	44.7	28.6	31.9
1855	17,203	2,908	5.02	13.89	81.09	16.9	467	39.6	27.2	12.8	16.1
1858		3,119	4.80	13.42	81.78	18.1	703	50.2	37.1	18.5	22.6
1861	18,491	3,363	4.73	13.49	81.77	18.2	916	55.8	42.4	23.0	27.2
1862		3,451	4.65	13.36	81.98	18.7	1,183	61.0	48.0	30.5	34.3
1863		3,549	4.46	12.78	82.76	19.2	1,097	57.0	44.0	27.3	30.9
1866	19,255	3,637	4.20	12.34	83.45	18.9	1,145	60.4	47.5	27.6	30.4
1867	24,048	4,672	4.28	12.18	83.45	19.4	822	41.2	28.3	14.8	17.6

* Figures for 1852 and 1870 not available

TABLE 3(b) Elections and distribution of seats in the Prussian Diet, 1849–1918

Legislative period		Conservatives	Free conservatives	Catholic faction (Centre)	Old Liberals (Right Centre)	National liberals	Left Liberals (Left Centre)	Radicals (Progressive Party)	Poles	Social Democrats	Without party affiliation
No	Year										
1	1849–	53	–	–	121	–	99	59	15	–	3
2	1849–52	114	–	–	154	–	–	–	15	–	69
3	1852–55	128	33	53	58	–	–	–	11	–	69
4	1855–58	181	–	51	48	–	–	–	6	–	66
5	1859–61	47	44	57	151	–	–	–	18	–	35
6	1862–	14	–	54	91	–	48	104	23	–	18
7	1862–63	11	–	28	19	–	96	133	22	–	43
8	1863–66	35	–	26	–	–	106	141	26	–	18
9	1866–67	119	7	15	24	34	53	61	21	–	8
10	1867–70	125	4	–	15	99	35	48	17	–	45
11	1870–73	114	41	58	11	123	–	49	19	–	17
12	1873–76	30	35	88	3	174	–	68	18	–	16
13	1877–79	41	35	89	–	169	–	63	15	–	21
14	1879–82	110	51	97	–	85	–	57	19	–	14
15	1882–85	122	57	99	–	66	–	53	18	–	18
16	1886–88	133	62	98	–	72	–	40	15	–	13
17	1889–93	129	64	98	–	86	–	29	15	–	12
18	1894–98	144	65	95	–	84	–	18	17	–	8
19	1899–1903	144	58	100	–	75	–	36	13	–	7
20	1904–8	144	64	96	–	76	–	33	13	–	7
21	1908–13	152	60	104	–	65	–	36	15	7	4
22	1913–18	147	53	103	–	73	–	37	12	10	8

TABLE 4. Reichstag elections, 1871–1912

	1. Reichstag 1871, Elect. participation 51.0%		2. Reichstag 1874, Elect. Participation 61.2%		3. Reichstag 1877, Elect. participation 60.6%		4. Reichstag 1878, Elect. participation 63.4%		5. Reichstag 1881, Elect. participation 56.3%	
	Votes (%)	Seats	Votes (%)	Seats	Votes (%)	Seats	Votes (%)	Seats	Votes (%)	Seats
Conservatives	14.1	57	6.9	22	9.7	40	13.0	59	16.3	50
Reich Party (Free Cons)	8.9	37	7.2	33	7.9	38	13.6	57	7.4	28
National Liberals	30.1	125	29.7	155	27.2	128	23.1	99	14.7	47
Liberals	7.2	30	1.0	3	2.5	13	2.7	10	—	—
Liberal Association	—	—	—	—	—	—	—	—	8.4	46 }
Progressive Party	8.8	46	8.6	49	7.7	35	6.7	26	12.7	60
German People's Party	0.5	1	0.4	1	0.8	4	1.1	3	2.0	9
Centre	18.6	63	27.9	91	24.8	93	23.1	94	23.2	100
Guelphs	1.6	7	1.8	4	1.6	4	1.7	10	1.7	10
Social Democrats	3.2	2	6.8	9	9.1	12	7.6	9	6.1	12
Poles	4.5	13	3.8	14	4.0	14	3.6	14	3.8	18
Danes	0.5	1	0.4	1	0.3	1	0.3	1	0.3	2
Alsace-Lorraine	—	—	4.5	15	3.7	15	3.1	15	3.0	15
Antisemite Economic Ass.	—	—	—	—	—	—	—	—	—	—
Others	2.0	—	0.9	—	0.5	—	0.3	—	0.3	—
Total	—	382	—	397	—	397	—	397	—	397

6. Reichstag 1884, Elect. participation 60.6%		7. Reichstag 1887, Elect. participation 77.5%		8. Reichstag 1890, Elect. participation 71.6%		9. Reichstag 1893, Elect. participation 72.5%		10. Reichstag 1898, Elect. participation 68.1%		11. Reichstag 1903, Elect. participation 76.1%		12. Reichstag 1907, Elect. participation 84.6%		13. Reichstag 1912, Elect. participation 84.9%	
Votes (%)	Seats	Votes (%)	Seats	Votes (%)	Seats	Votes (%)	Seats	Votes (%)	Seats	Votes (%)	Seats	Votes (%)	Seats	Votes (%)	Seats
15.2	78	15.2	80	12.4	73	13.5	72	11.1	56	10.0	54	9.4	60	9.2	43
6.9	28	9.8	41	6.7	20	5.7	28	4.4	23	3.5	21	4.2	24	3.0	14
17.6	51	22.3	99	16.3	42	13.0	53	12.5	46	13.9	51	14.5	54	13.6	45
—		—		—		—		—		—		—		—	
17.6	67	12.9	32	16.0	66	3.9	13	2.5	12	2.6	9	3.2	14	12.3	42
						8.7	24	7.2	29	5.7	21	6.5	28		
1.7	7	1.2	—	2.0	10	2.2	11	1.4	8	1.0	6	1.2	7		
22.6	99	20.1	98	18.6	106	19.1	96	18.8	102	19.8	100	19.4	105	16.4	91
1.7	11	1.5	4	1.6	11	1.3	7	1.4	9	1.0	6	0.7	1	0.7	5
9.7	24	10.1	11	19.8	35	23.3	44	27.2	56	31.7	81	28.9	43	34.8	110
3.6	16	2.8	13	3.4	16	3.0	19	3.1	14	3.7	16	4.0	20	3.6	18
0.3	1	0.2	1	0.2	1	0.2	1	0.2	1	0.2	1	0.1	1	0.1	1
2.9	15	3.1	15	1.4	10	1.5	8	1.4	10	1.1	9	1.0	7	1.3	9
—	—	0.2	1	0.7	—	3.5	16	3.3	13	2.6	11	3.9	16	2.9	13
0.2	—	0.6	2	1.0	7	1.7	5	4.5	18	3.5	11	3.0	17	2.0	6
—	397	—	397	—	397	—	397	—	397	—	397	—	397	—	397

TABLE 5(a) Reichstag elections 1919–33 (% of valid votes)

Parties	January 1919	June 1920	May 1924	December 1924	May 1928	September 1930	July 1932	November 1932	March 1933
NSDAP			6.5	3.0	2.6	18.3	37.3	33.1	43.9
DNVP	10.3	15.1	19.5	20.5	14.2	7.0	5.9	8.3	8.0
Christians Socialist Volk Service						2.5	1.0	1.2	1.0
Agrarian League			2.0	1.6	0.6	0.6	0.3	0.3	0.2
Agrarian Volk Party					1.9	3.2	0.2	0.1	
DVP	4.4	13.9	9.2	10.1	8.7	4.5	1.2	1.9	1.1
Economic Party	0.9	0.8	2.4	3.3	4.5	3.9	0.4	0.3	
BVP		4.4	3.2	3.7	3.1	3.0	3.2	3.1	2.7
Centre Party	19.7	13.6	13.4	13.6	12.1	11.8	12.5	11.9	11.2
DDP	18.5	8.3	5.7	6.3	4.9	3.8	1.0	1.0	0.9
SPD	37.9	21.7	20.5	26.0	29.8	24.5	21.6	20.4	18.3
USPD	7.6	17.9	0.8	0.3	0.1				
KPD		2.1	12.6	9.0	10.6	13.1	14.5	16.9	12.3
Others	0.7	2.2	4.2	2.6	6.9	3.8	0.9	1.5	0.4
Total	100	100	100	100	100	100	100	100	100

TABLE 5(b) Results of the 1928 and 1933 elections according to constituencies (% of valid votes)

Constituencies	NSDAP 1928	NSDAP 1933	DNVP 1928	DNVP 1933	Centre/BVP 1928	Centre/BVP 1933	SPD 1928	SPD 1933	KPD 1928	KPD 1933
East Prussia	0.8	56.5	31.4	11.3	7.4	6.5	26.8	14.6	9.5	8.7
Berlin	1.4	31.3	15.7	9.1	3.3	4.7	34.0	22.5	29.6	30.1
Potsdam	1.7	41.4	22.1	12.8	2.6	4.0	32.6	20.7	17.3	17.9
Frankfurt/Oder	1.0	55.2	29.6	11.1	6.0	6.0	33.1	18.6	6.0	7.4
Pomerania	1.5	56.3	41.6	17.0	1.0	1.1	30.2	16.2	6.1	7.6
Breslau	0.9	50.2	23.0	7.1	15.8	13.3	37.8	19.3	4.5	8.2
Liegnitz	1.2	54.0	24.5	9.1	7.9	6.4	37.8	21.4	4.2	6.7
Oppeln	1.0	43.2	17.1	7.5	40.0	32.3	12.6	6.9	12.7	9.3
Magdeburg	4.7	47.3	16.2	10.7	1.6	1.8	43.0	27.6	7.2	10.5
Merseburg	1.7	46.4	21.4	11.9	1.4	1.5	23.9	16.4	24.4	21.5
Thuringia	3.7	47.2	8.2	11.5	4.1	4.1	33.3	19.2	12.4	15.2
Schleswig-Holstein	5.0	53.2	23.0	10.1	1.1	1.0	35.3	22.2	7.9	10.7
Weser-Ems	3.5	41.4	8.4	10.6	17.1	16.1	29.3	19.6	5.1	7.9
Hanover	1.2	50.6	9.6	8.9	3.5	3.5	41.4	25.1	4.2	7.5
Westphalia	3.6	34.3	8.9	6.7	27.4	25.5	27.0	16.1	10.4	13.8
Hesse-Nassau	1.6	49.4	10.0	4.9	14.8	13.9	32.2	18.7	8.0	9.0
Rhine Province	5.3	34.1	9.5	6.5	35.1	29.8	17.3	12.5	14.3	15.3
Bavaria	8.1	40.4	5.4	3.6	36.1	31.7	20.3	19.4	3.6	6.4
Franconia	5.6	45.7	18.8	5.4	25.7	22.4	28.5	16.8	3.0	5.0
Palatinate	1.8	46.5	2.8	2.5	26.4	22.7	29.0	28.4	7.1	9.0
Dresden-Bautzen	1.9	43.6	11.5	7.7	1.4	1.9	39.1	30.1	10.3	13.4
Leipzig	4.4	40.0	5.6	6.5	0.6	1.0	37.0	21.3	16.1	17.4
Chemnitz-Zwickau	1.9	50.0	9.1	5.4	0.5	0.6	33.5	14.7	16.2	19.0
Württemberg	2.9	42.0	6.2	5.1	20.4	17.7	23.6	11.9	7.2	9.2
Baden	1.9	45.4	8.1	3.6	32.8	25.4	22.5	21.7	7.3	9.8
Hesse-Darmstadt	2.6	47.4	3.4	2.9	16.0	13.6	32.3	26.9	8.7	10.9
Hamburg	2.6	28.9	12.8	8.0	1.6	1.9	36.8	26.5	16.8	17.6
Mecklenburg	2.0	48.0	16.3	14.9	0.7	0.8	41.7	—	5.6	7.4
Total	2.6	43.9	14.3	8.0	15.1	14.0	29.8	18.3	10.6	12.3

TABLE 6. Federal German elections, 1949–83

1. Period of legislation: 1949–53
Date of election: 14 August 1949
Elect. participation. 78.5%

	%	No. of seats
CDU/CSU	31.0	139
SPD	29.2	131
FDP	11.9	52
KPD	5.7	15
BP	4.2	17
DP	4.0	17
Centre Party	3.1	10
WAV	2.9	12
DRP	1.8	5
RSF	0.9	
SSW	0.3	1
EVD	0.1	
RWVP	0.1	
Independents	4.8	3
		402

3. Period of legislation: 1957–61
Date of election: 15 September 1957
Elect. participation: 87.8%

	%	No. of seats
CDU/CSU	50.2	270
SPD	31.8	169
FDP	7.7	41
GB/BHE	4.6	
DP	3.4	17
DRP	1.0	
FU	0.8	
BdD	0.2	
UDM	0.1	
SSW	0.1	
DG	0.05	
		497

2. Period of legislation: 1953–57
Date of election: 6 September 1953
Elect. participation. 85.8%

	%	No. of seats
CDU/CSU	45.2	243
SPD	28.8	151
FDP	9.5	48
BHE	5.9	27
DP	3.2	15
KPD	2.2	
BP	1.7	
GVP	1.2	
DRP	1.1	
Zentrum	0.8	3
DNS	0.3	
SSW	0.2	
		487

4. Period of Legislation: 1961–65
Date of election: 17 September 1961
Elect. participation: 87.7%

	%	No. of seats
CDU/CSU	45.3	242
SPD	36.2	190
FDP	12.8	67
GDP	2.8	
DFU	1.9	
DRP	0.8	
DG	0.1	
SSW	0.1	
		499

5. Period of legislation: 1965–69
Date of election: 19 September 1965
Elect. participation: 86.8%

	%	No. of seats
CDU/CSU	47.6	245
SPD	39.3	202
FDP	9.5	49
NPD	2.0	
DFU	1.3	
AUD	0.2	
CVP	0.1	
		496

6. Period of legislation: 1969–72
Date of election: 28 September 1969
Elect. participation: 86.7%

	%	No. of seats
CDU/CSU	46.1	242
SPD	42.7	224
FDP	5.8	30
NPD	4.3	
ADF	0.6	
BP	0.6	
EP	0.2	
GDP	0.1	
		496

7. Period of legislation: 1972–76
Date of election: 9 November 1972
Elect. participation: 91.1%

	%	No. of seats
SPD	45.8	230
CDU/CSU	44.9	225
FDP	8.4	41
NPD	0.6	
DKP	0.3	
		496

8. Period of legislation: 1976–80
Date of election: 3 October 1976
Elect. participation: 90.7%

	%	No. of seats
CDU/CSU	48.6	243
SPD	42.6	214
FDP	7.9	39
AUD	0.1	
DKP	0.3	
KPD	0.1	
KBW	0.1	
NPD	0.3	
		496

9. Period of legislation: 1980–84
Date of election: 5 October 1980*
Elect. participation: 90.8%

	%	No. of seats
CDU/CSU	45.5	226
SPD	43.7	218
FDP	10.6	53
		497

10. Period of legislation: 1983–87
Date of election: 6 March 1983*
Elect. participation: 89.1%

	%	No. of seats
CDU/CSU	49.0	244
SPD	38.8	193
FDP	6.8	34
GREENS	5.4	27
		498

*in both elections (1980 and 1983) Communist and extreme right wing NPD gained less than ½% of the poll.

389

INDEX